RURAL MARKETING

RURAL MARKETING

Bir Singh

ANMOL PUBLICATIONS PVT. LTD.
NEW DELHI - 110 002 (INDIA)

ANMOL PUBLICATIONS PVT. LTD.
H.O.: 4374/4B, Ansari Road, Darya Ganj,
New Delhi-110 002 (India)
Ph.: 23278000, 23261597
B.O.: No. 1015, Ist Main Road, BSK IIIrd Stage
IIIrd Phase, IIIrd Block,
Bangalore - 560 085 (India)
Visit us at: www.anmolpublications.com

Rural Marketing

First Published, 2006

PRINTED IN INDIA

Printed at Mehra Offset Press, Delhi.

Contents

Preface

"Rural Marketing" as a paper is being taught at M.Com., M.B.A. and Other Management Courses at various universities and institutions. This book is designed as an introductory text to the above paper, encompassing vital information on all pertinent aspects. Thus the material presented here would be of interest as well as of great use to the students, teachers and professionals of Management Courses. This book will provide complete knowledge of the nature and characteristics of rural marketing, rural development and marketing of consumer durables, retail trading, distribution channels of rural marketing, marketing of agricultural inputs, selling in rural markets, rural trade and challenges, agriculture marketing in india, classification of agricultural products, nature and scope of co-operative marketing, role of agricultrual price structure, etc. to the students.

The major topics dealt in this book are—Nature and Characteristics of Rural Marketing; Rural Development and Marketing of Consumer Durables; Attitude and Behaviour of Rural Marketing; Retail Trading; Distribution Channels of Rural Marketing; Marketing Structure and Performance; Marketing of Agricultural Inputs; Selling in Rural Markets; Customer—Retailer Relationship; Rural Trade and Challenges; Development of Agriculture in Economy; Agriculture Marketing in India; Classification of Agricultural Products; Institutions and Organisations in Agriculture Marketing; Nature and Scope of Co-operative Marketing; Fertilizers, Seeds and Plant Protection; Role of Agricultrual Price Structure; Defects of Agricultural Marketing etc.

It is hoped that all those will benefit from the contents of this book for whom it is meant. The author will feel amply rewarded, if motive is achieved.

Editor

1

Nature and Characteristics of Rural Marketing

Indian market for the consumer products is made up of two distinct parts, one is urban and other is rural market. It has been a matter of great enquiry both for the marketing academics and practitioners whether there is a need for developing separate strategy for rural markets. By and large, Indian market scenario shows that marketers have rarely come out with separate marketing strategy for rural markets overtly, however, marketers did develop separate marketing mix for rural markets covertly. Whenever it is rural marketing for their brands, marketer tended to price their products low, keeping the products quality at an average level, cutting costs on the extra frills added to the product. The essence of the present thesis lies in opening up a debate as to the need for a separate marketing strategy in the context of unique features of the rural market compared to urban market. In what follows, we present a frame or an outline of marketing strategy for rural marketing.

The vastness of the rural market poses both a challenge and an opportunity to the marketers. The desire to improve the living standards is felt as keenly in the rural areas as in the urban areas. Rural incomes are rising and the poverty ratio is falling. The marketing strategy to tap this vast market potential must take into account the special characteristics of the rural areas, attitudes and socio-psychological characteristics of the rural population. In fact, improving the marketing channels and distribution outlets and communication facilities can themselves being about a transformation of the rural areas.

The design and development of a marketing strategy essentially has to flow from a thorough understanding of the consumer, in this context it is the rural consumer. Therefore at the first instance, the rural consumer has to be understood and next the differences between the rural and urban consumer.

The rural consumer in majority of the cases is illiterate, a low income consumer, more price sensitive, more of social interaction within his group, psychologically emotional, guided by opinion leaders, having lower aspirational levels, and having imitational characteristics. This fact matrix leads a greater challenge to deal with the rural consumer. The marketer in rural area has to investigate:

(a) Market segmentation by market potentials which would help the assessment of the markets by consumer demand and purchasing ability.

(b) Consumer behaviour and the rural consumer's priorities and preferences in consumer expenditure, sources of buying, quantum of each purchase, and time and conditions of purchase.

(c) How best to win over the rural consumer, and make effective use of media.

(d) Who are the catalytic agents of change and what role can they perform *vis-a-vis* ones products?

Against this background of the rural consumer, the marketing strategy has to be evolved. Further, there are constraints associated with rural market, the inaccessibility, scattered villages, unprofessional retailers.

We now present certain aspects of marketing strategies for rural markets.

Product Management

In marketing strategy, product strategy occupies a pivotal place. A marketer has to decide whether he should modify a product slightly to suit the rural consumer needs and perceptions or market a totally separate product or brand for rural market. Marketing a totally separate product or brand for the rural market may not be possible in some cases. Whereas in some cases it may very well be possible to develop entirely different brands to suit rural market. For example consumer non-durables or convenience products can be developed exclusively for rural markets. It may be difficult to carry out the same exercise for consumer durable products. Where different branding strategy is not possible marketers may try on products aspects such as packaging and quality. For instance there may be a greater preference for smaller packs due to the lower income levels and therefore, in product design it would be appropriate to go for smaller packs for rural markets. On the quality front, a rural consumer may not be given great promises, maintaining a consistent and assured quality.

In planning products for villages, irrespective of the country, it is important to ensure that the packaging is sturdy and robust. Products meant for rural markets have to travel longer distances and the external packaging should withstand frequent handling. Moreover, considering the poor purchasing power of the weakest rural consumers, small pack sizes containing enough product for a day or a week are essential.

It would be of great relevance to discuss the role of branding in rural marketing as a part of product strategy. It has been mentioned earlier that majority of the rural consumers are illiterate or less literate. Against this background the importance of brand, logo and even the pack would be highest. A rural consumer may not be able to read the name of a brand but having heard the brand name and having seen he would be able to recognise the brand easily. Therefore, a firm, while deciding upon its branding strategy, should carefully underscore the preferences of rural consumers. This leaves an immense scope to marketers to develop brand loyalty in the rural market. Therefore, distinct colours, logos, and pack facilitating an easy identification of the brand is a must in rural marketing.

Price Management

Pricing is crucial element in the rural marketing mix. The price of a product should be reasonable and should be in tune with the afford ability of rural consumer. If the product is over-priced, it may necessiate the marketer to modify the price or to withdraw the product. The price of the product is thus a critical determinant of the fate of a product in the rural market. The market share and volumes of the company are influenced significantly by the price of the product.

Price revolves around two elements—utility and value. Utility is the generic property of the product to satisfy a need or want of the consumer. Value is the quantitative worth the consumer attaches to the product for which he is willing to part with a certain quantum of money. In rural market both the elements of pricing, *i.e.* the utility factor and the value factor are equally important due to the limited disposable incomes with the rural consumer. The villager seeks products which not only meets his need but also gives a fair exchange for the money that is parted with.

The task of selling products in the villages is rather onerous and demands attention to a number of other variables like distribution, propaganda, demonstrations, publicity etc. It is, therefore, pragmatic for a company to simplify its pricing policies by maintaining the same price, throughout the country. It can introduce variations in the price through other mechanisms like promotions and discounts.

The pricing objectives pursued by a company in the villages depend on a number of factors, *viz.,* the marketing goals of the company, the life cycle stage of the product and the financial objectives of the company. As a regards price management, it is proved that, by and large, the rural markets are price conscious. If rural market for a product is to be tapped a sound and relevant price strategy is required, undoubtedly, penetration pricing will score an edge over the skimming strategy in rural market. The rationale for penetration strategy in rural market is due to income level and structure of the market. Not only economic factor but also psychologically, a rural consumer compared to urban consumer would aim to save more and more in his purchase decisions.

The rural purchaser mostly does haggling over each purchase. This is because of want of price uniformity and Impopularity of Agmarking and ISI marking. As a consequence, personal inspection also becomes a habit. Perhaps, these factors made, Westfall and Boyd conclude that, "Indians are great bargainers" and majority of the Indian consumers are rural consumers.

In spite of the advent of green revolution, the discretionary buying power is not likely to be much with most of the villagers. Hence, necessities of life as well as other products must be low-priced. The village customer will prefer dust tea as against leaf tea, tooth-powder as against toothpaste and Bharat blades as against Topaz on account of cheaperness. It is the cheap, single band, medium wave, battery operated, portable transistor which meets the needs of a village family. The chairman of Hindustan Lever Ltd. says that, "we will also need to take another look at our product and market strategy." Some clear pref rence—low unit price for example —already distinguish the rural from urban consumers.

Therefore it may recognised that price is a key element in the marketing strategies for rural market.

Promotion Management

Promotion Management involves developing communications and sales promotion strategies residing upon the media mix. Developing communication is a tricky exercise. There is a need to talk of not only rural language that even dialect specific in rural messaging. The marketers need to indulge in a thorough research prior to the communication decision. The use of a model, the tone, in print or out door advertising, the colours used, projection of logo will all make a severe impact. All these have to be developed keeping the rural consumer personality in view. The marketing communications must match the rural consumer aspirations and culture. The communications strategy of a marketer therefore has to be in tune with the rural consumer psychology.

As the rural consumer are price sensitive, the impact of sales promotion may be highly significant. Innovative sales promotion measures would surely induce a rural consumer to try a brand. A constraint one may face would be in terms of retailer cooperation. The retailer has to be properly motivated, monitored and persuaded to effect sales promotion measures announced by a company.

As regards media, thanks to satellite televisions, the rural consumer is actively competing with his urban counter-part in terms of product and brand awareness. The penetration of TV into the rural market has been of a high order leading to informational boom in the country. However compared to urban consumer a rural consumer is likely to stick on to the main two or three TV channels. A focussed media research would enable marketer to facilitate his media mix decisions.

Promotions in villages consist of participation in local rural activities like fairs, festivals, carnivals, religious functions and sports events. Rural promotions should ideally be conducted in the post-harvest period when the farmers are flush with money from the sales proceeds of their crops. Promotions should be avoided during the sowing period when the farmer is investing heavily in agricultural inputs and is spending time in the field?

In promotion management a marketer may have to go beyond the conventional media and try to reach rural consumer.

Media Mix in the Rural Context

I. Formal/organised media

Press and other print media.

Direct mail.

Radio.

Cinema.

TV.

PoPs.

Outdoors.

II. Non formal/rural specific media

Audio-visual vans or publicly vans.

Demonstrations.

Puppet shows, dance-dramas, rural art forms like Harikatha and Villupattu performed at village melas and temple festivals.

Study classes.

Mike announcements, processions.

Carrying advertisement panels, decorated bullock carts carrying ad panels.

Music records.

House-to-house campaigns by special promotion squads. Information centres giving free advice on company's product/services

Channel Management

There are at least three problems pertaining to channel management *viz.*, transportation, warehousing and communication. The transportation facilities still continues to be poor in rural India, which makes the delivery of the product extremely difficult proposition, and same is the case with warehousing. The rural consumers should have access to products at their doorsteps. For this, retail outlets become necessary in the rural areas. But, marketing is not an important activity in rural India. In fact, there is some evidence that urban markets, dose to the centres of production, are increasingly favoured over rural markets because high transport costs are involved in moving goods to the villages.

The cities and towns can readily absorb whatever is produced. This is a pity because greater attention needs to be given to the requirements of rural areas, where newly affluent farmers have disposable cash in respect of both product development and distribution.

While the rural retailer have meager communication facilities, the problem is to some extent solved in the recent years. In the light of this it becomes mandatory to marketers to design his own transportation system and warehousing.

It is extremely relevant and necessary to train and organise rural retailer to make him fall in line with the philosophy of the company. A retailer in rural markets is less or unprofessional in his approach to consumers. Owing to illiteracy and ignorance and also due to credit needs of rural consumers, rural retailer may develop the tendency of consumer exploitation. A two pronged approach is therefore necessary in rural markets, one is to bring about behavioural change in retailer, developing a professional outlook, and the second is to awaken the rural consumer continuously by mass educational campaigns to make him exercise his choice in his own way. It was identified in a study that there is a need to get deeper into the distribution mode—communication to arrive at the right media/ messaging mix. It is found that as much as 81 per cent of visitors to haats are on regular basis, and as much as 85 per cent attribute that buying at haats leads to the better pricing. So a haat is a better opportunity for promotion than for brand building. Bargain-hunters are more likely to remember the product, brand for price-off; than for image or positioning. A large captive audience at haats is.also ideal for product demonstrations and even sampling.

Consumer product companies need to learn a great deal about selling in rural markets. The trouble with most rural marketing campaigns is that they centre on retail outlets, a very urban phenomenon: Although most villages have small shops, they are used infrequently. Villagers usually prefer to make all their purchases at weekly haats or at melas. And yet, few companies participate in such bazaars or fairs. Instead of trying to change the shopping habits of the rural consumer, companies should tune their distribution and merchandising to rural habits.

Mobile traders serve the needs of remote villages having low density of demand and are to be found in most districts of the country. This channel of sale continues to be popular despite the development of rural areas and offers excellent possibility for relationship marketing. But it has been completely ignored by the corporate sector. These mobile traders who may not cost much can be employed by companies to market their brands. It may be direct marketing, for a cluster of villages one trader may be appointed with a given schedule. In this a credit policy also may be designed by companies to attract rural consumers.

The logistics of feeding two million outlets spread over 6,30,000 villages is a daunting task indeed. But, perhaps, this is not necessary if we realise that the average monthly sale per village shop is a mere Rs. 5,000 which is a low sale volume and restricts the variety and range of products stocked. Moreover, since a significant portion of the sale is on credit, it puts most village shops in a self limiting sales cycle. Companies need to, therefore, focus on the 2,000+ population villages only, totalling 60,000 for their distribution efforts.

About 47,000 haats and 25,000 melas are held in rural India. In spite of the development of permanent shops, haats play a vital role in the village economy. Most haats are held once a week, the average number of stalls is 300 and the sale exceeds Rs. 2 lakh per haat day. Each haat caters to the needs of about 4000 people from minimum 10 to a maximum 50 villages. Larger haats are generally held in larger villages because of better road and transport connections and higher purchasing power available in these villages. Of the total 47,000 haats, 4,300 are held in the 5,000 + population villages and another 10,300 in the 2,000-4,999 population villages. On an average people come from 20 villages to a haat, by targeting just 14,600 distribution points, a consumer company can hope to reach almost 50 per cent of the rural population.

Only commercial melas are of interest to corporate India. The average number of stalls per mela is 854, the average sale per mela per day (this offers a better idea of a mela's commercial importance than the total sale, since the duration of a mela varies form one to 45 days) ranges from a low of Rs. 0.6 lakh in Assam to Rs. 88 lakh in Haryana, the average number of visitors is 7.61akh per mela. Unlike haats which cater primarily to the essential needs of the local people, melas cater to a much larger population, both rural and urban, not only for their basic needs but also for the purchase of the more sophisticated factory-made products. In fact, almost half the outlets at melas sell manufactured goods. Companies should pick the melas closest to the largest villages, where people are relatively more urbanised and therefore already exposed to brands. The list of the longer duration, regional and national level commercial melas is unlikely to exceed 500 all over India. By using these melas as mileage building events, a company can hope to reach almost half the population of rural India, a fraction of the cost when compared with TV, video vans or other equally expensive media options.

Nature of Rural Marketing

The rural market is quite different from urban markets. Agriculture is the chief economic activity in rural areas, the entire village population is associated directly or indirectly to agriculture. In the process of development of civilisation agriculture and pastoral life along river banks are the first form of settled life. In the bronze age, major civilisation evolved. Archaeological evidence reveals that bronze industry supplied tools and implements to agriculture. Textiles, paper, iron and furniture making developed to lid man in his economic activities.

Agriculture supplies inputs for fabrication into manufactures cotton, oil seeds spices etc. All food items had a mral origin. Villages were selfcontained units, which traded their produce for gold, arm and precious stones. The rural society has high status persons and the poor ones. The distribution of land was made by state, which belonged to the state: The British rule for more than three centuries was the worst blow to the rural society. The worst blow was to cottage and small scale industries, cultivation of indigo, tea and jute, development of timber trade and denudation of forests. The terms of trade were not favourable to Indian farmers. In these circumstances farmers were forced to live in deprivation and poverty. British India was with the princely states under the administration of Rajas and Nawabs; the big states had all the powers except defence and foreign affairs.

Agriculture and industries based on raw-materials and local skills are identified for the development of the rural economy. An integrated approach was evolved to take care of projects ranging from milk and milk-products to horticultural products like fruits, vegetables, flowers, herbs, etc. The processing of these is not widespread in rural areas. Modern technology is to accessible to enterprises there. It is beyond the financial capacity of an average entrepreneur. The low cost and labour based technologies have been the common mode of village inqustry. As a result, the rural products do not enjoy competitiveness in a wider market. Most of the products are consumed locally.

Organisation and Working of Rural Market

However, a few produc of rural industry have a fair share of the market through co-operative dairies, mandis (rural markets) under the control of co-operative marketing societies, and co-operative warehousing societies, to cite a few. By looking at mandis in different states, some salient features of the rural market can be deduced from their organisation and working.

In the first instance, co-operative marketing societies are formed with membership drawn from among the farming class. The membership fees meet the cost of organisation and administration. The office-bearers are elected representatives. Policies are formulated by the general body, and the executive powers are vested in the management committees.

The day-to-day working of mandis is entrusted to the management committee. It exercises its power to supervise control and manage the marketing activities. The Food Corporation of India (FCI) is the biggest procuring agency in the public sector. It deputes its staff to procure cereal food items, jute and cotton for its buffer-stocks. The network of mandis is widespread in the country. Farmers get full value for their produce.

However, vegetables, fruits, flowers and other perishable items have to be transported to private mandis. The Azadpur Vegetable and Fruit Mandi in Delhi is the biggest mandi is Asia. It is managed by private traders. New arrivals at the time of harvest are purchased by private traders at low prices. Most of the produce is stored in warehouses. After the harvest, the prices usually rule high at the expense of the farmers as well as the consumers. In the long run, this acts as a disincentive to undertaking extensive cultivation of vegetables and fruits. Co-operative societies have yet to show their competitive strength in perishable items. The problem is amenable to solution through provision of warehousing facilities by the cooperative sector. Setting up warehouses being expensive, individual fanners may not find it easy to finance it. Besides, farmers are not conversant with the organisation and management of warehouses.

Rural economic development is thwarted by the illiteracy and lack of technical know-how. The adult literacy programme and some community projects have the twin object of eradicating illiteracy and developing teclmical know-how.

New Dimensions of Indian Rural Marketing

New problems are emerging due to the invasion of corporations to take over the rural economy. One of them is opening up the rural sector to real estate development corporations, insurance companies, banking and transport, tele-communication, and power to give a surge to investment in rural industry. The Tatas have already established plants for preservation of perishable vegetables. They have installed micro-processing plants for eradicating bacteria from fresh vegetables to ensure longer shelf life. These are examples of big business houses taking advantage of their position of vantage in acquisition of advanced technology.

At present, agriculture is contributing 40 per cent of GDP, and showing a growth of 11 per cent. The capital industry is experiencing a much higher growth-23 per cent in 1994-95 (April end). The share of the rural sector is 35 per cent in the total investment of the private sector. Factories for production of fertilizers and pesticides, farm implements and machinery, and motorised trollies are being located in the rural regions. Development would have been faster than. at present, if power and telecommunication facilities had been developed.

A rough estimate of income in rural areas puts it at 1.6 lakh crore per annum, with 11 per cent average growth. Till recently, it was strongly believed that the rural consumption pattern is traditional. The assumption led to the conclusion that the rural economy is static and devoid of dynamism. The awareness created by electric media began to change the traditional pattern of consumption. Watches, soaps, toothpastes, brushes, sewing machines fridges, TVs, transistors, record players, Hi-fi musical gadgets, allopathic medicines, fancy clothes, care, motorcycles, jeeps and gypsies are common durable consumer items in villages for the upper classes. The members of the growing opulent class in the rural sector are educated. They are managing farms on commercial lines and have acquired a state for an urban life-style. The houses, interior decoration, designs, architectur furnishing and fixtures resemble those of urban villages. The farmhouses have the guest rooms and servant quarters and poultries and dairies for the kitchen. The rich farmers are very rich. The economic activities have been vastly diversified from farming to real estate development. Access to big money has come in handy for lavish spending by rich farmers in casinos and elite clubs in cities.

On the contrary, landless workers, forming the major chunk of rural society, are finding it difficult to make both ends meet. Illiteracy, ignorance, deprivation and unemployment are major problems. They can hope rise only if the state comes forward with bold and ambitious plans to fight poverty. Training and transfer of technology are the only means of rehabilitating landless workers, through providing jobs in industries in rural areas. In the near future, poverty can be turned into prosperity for the masses. NOIDA in Western UP and Unnao in Eastern UP can be cited as examples. The leather footwear industry established in Unnao is a successful exporter. It employs local workers and pays a steady wage of over Rs. 100/- a day. It takes one week for a worker to learn operating modern machines. NOIDA in Ghaziabad district has developed into a vast industrial zone for electronics. Multinationals are running manufacturing units at NOIDA.

The marketing centres are growing side by side industrial units. Hightech information systems, efficient transportation and steady power supply are going to reduce the physical isolation of villages. There is mounting pressure on industries to disperse from cities. Infornmtion-based marketing will take over the traditional marketing system. Purchases being traditionally confined to spices, salt, tobacco and textiles is no longer relevant. It is unfortunate that rural wealth goes into land and gold. Banks are gaining acceptance among the rural-rich to han le and manage their investments. A family budget allocates 50 per cent of the income to food, clothing and health. Durables consumer goods claim 30 per cent of the annual incomes, and 10 per cent is saved in the case of the upper classes The new middle class, which has created by modern institutions, spends 30 per cent of the income on this kitchen and 30 per cent on education and clothing. A substantial 15 per cent goes to health care. A negligible 5 per cent is saved in the form of compulsory contribution to provident fund. It is the white collar working class.

IMPORTANCE OF RURAL MARKETING

1. Size of the Rural Market. An analysis of National Sample Surveydata shows that of the total expenditure on manufactured consumer goods, 75 per cent is spent in rural India. The percentage has remained almost unchanged since 1960-61. Though per capita consumption and expenditure on manufactured consumer items is low in rural areas, the market is approximately three times larger. On the assumption that ill persons or families above the poverty line form the market for some branded consumer goods, this market has a size of 42 million households. If we take Punjab, Rajasthan, Gujarat and Andhra, the target market of 72 million people is larger numerically than France, U.K. or West Germany.

2. Rural Market in Value Terms. For non-food consumption items the size of the market (estimated by apply NSS proportions to central statistical organisation data) in current prices was Rs. 5,500 crore in 1970-71, Rs. 9,500 crore in 1974-75 and 13,500 crores in 1979-80. Assuming these items are mainly consumed by the rural population above the poverty line it represents an annual expense of Rs. 5.6 per head per annum. In real terms, however, the growth has been very modest at 2.5 per cent per annum due to a number of factors such as:

(a) Lack of concerted effort by the organised sector to penetrate the rural market.

(b) Averages are misleading in this type of analysis as peak opportunities which occur in certain pockets may not be funy realised.

(c) If the market for consumer products is considered as a whole it overshadows the opportunities that exist for selected products which may be growing at a much faster rate.

3. Rural Target Population. Wealth distribution in rural India is uneven and the top 13 per cent of the farmers' land holdings account for 37 per cent of cultivated area. Further, NSS data show that the top 10 per cent of the rural population accounts for above 37 per cent of the expenditure on consumer goods. Not surprisingly the potential market is at the top of the spectrum. However with the increasing spread of the rural income, consumer goods are expected to make substantial penetration into the lower income strata by the normal percolation effect. Then there is an increasing cross flow of population between urban and project town centres which act as conducts for cross flow of products and ideas thus supplementing the demand for such products.

4. The Market for Agricultural Inputs. There is a very rapidly expanding demand for agricultural inputs in rural market. This is borne out by the compound rate of growth in the off take of agricultural inputs between 1970-71 and 1980-81;

—Fertilizers	10 per cent	—Pesticides	12 per cent
—Area under high Yielding Variety	12 per cent	Tractors	15 per cent
		Pumps and tubewells	11 per cent

A recent survey in Andhra, Punjab and Haryana revealed that over 90 per cent of the farmers interviewed felt that they should use more and more new farm practices. The study established that in these areas the farmers are eager to use newer agricultural technology for improving profits and are prepared to take calculated risks.

5. Sources of Rural Purchasing Capacity. Following are the factors which contribute to purchasing capacity in rural areas:

(a) **Marketable Agricultural Surplus and Rural/Urban Terms of Trade.** So far as manufactured consumer goods are concerned, regression analysis indicates that there is a 0.7 per cent rise in consumption for every one per cent increase in marketable surplus of foodgrains. As the surplus is increasing every year, there will be increasing purchasing capacity with farmers.

(b) **Remittances.** The traditional remittances from within the countty are now being supplemented in several states by remittances from overseas. In 1978 total inward remittances in the state of Kerala were estimated at Rs. 400 crore. This creates new consumption and purchasing patterns.

(c) **Dispersal of Industry.** The investment in the development of backward areas will greatly speed up the income generation process in rural areas.

(d) **Government Expenditure.** Investments in flood control and irrigation facilities will be around Rs. 12,000 crore in 1983-1985 and central sector outlay for rural development and associated programmes will be Rs. 2,300 crore: These will generate income, and increased purchasing power of rural areas can be expected to support consumption of manufactured items. Further, these investments are expected to augment the income generation process from land in future years, which in turn, will accelerate the growth of rural markets. The investment proposed during the VII plan for developing village and khadi industries is of the order of Rs. 2,000 crore. This too will encourage the income generation process.

6. Helpful in the Food Processing Industry. India is a land of agricultural, horticulture, sericulture which produce a number of varieties of foodgrains, fruits, vegetables, commercial crops and flowers. The government of India making its efforts to develop the food processing industry while giving a number of benefits including tax benefits, incentives, subsidies, transportation and marketing facilities.

Food manufacturers or processors are primarily engaged in adding farm utility to raw farm products. Wheat is milled into flour, livestock is converted into meat products, fruits and vegetables are canned or frozen. These firms play a vital role in transforming bulky, raw, perishable farm products into storable, concentrated, and more appealing good products. In so doing, food processors become involved in several supportive marketing functions, such as transportation storage, and financing. Thus, food processors occupy a strategic position in the food industry. Through the purchase of farm commodities, their activities are closely linked to farmers. As the source of many food product innovations and as the major brand advertisers in the food industry, they are also in close contact with consumer markets. Punjab, Himachal Pradesh and Jammu & Kashmir are the main producers of fruits and vegetables, in south Gujarat, Kerala and Karnataka, Maharashtra are the producer of coconut, groundnut, bananas, cashewnuts and certain other products like tea and coffee. Government is developing food processing industries in these states, which is being responded as per the expectations.

7. Helpful in Economic Development. Rural marketing plays an important role not only in stimulating production and consumption, but in accelerating the pace of economic development. Its dynamic functions are of primary importance in promoting economic development. For this reason, it has been described as the most important multiplier of rural development. The development of an efficient marketing system is important in ensuring that scarce and essential commodities reach different classes of consumers. Marketing is not only an economic link between the producers and the consumers; it maintains a balance between demand and supply. The objectives of price stability, rapid economic growth and equitable distribution of goods and services cannot be achieved without the support of an efficient marketing system.

8. Increase in Farm Income. An efficient marketing system ensures higher levels of income for the farmers by reducing the number of middlemen or by restricting the commission on marketing services and the malpractices adopted by them in the marketing of farm products. An efficient system guarantees the farmers better prices for farm products and induces them to invest their surpluses in the purchase of modern inputs so that productivity and production may increase. This again results in an increase in the marketed surplus and income of the farmers. If the producer does not have an easily accessible market-outlet where he can sell his surplus produce, he has little incentive to produce more. The need for providing adequate incentives for increased production is therefore very important, and this can be made possible only by streamlining the marketing system.

9. Optimization of Resource Use and Output Management. An efficient rural marketing system leads to the optimisation of resource use and output management. An efficient marketing system can also contribute to an increase in the marketable surplus by scaling down the losses arising out of inefficient processing, storage and transportation. A well-designed system of marketing can effectively distribute the available stock of modem inputs, and thereby sustain a faster rate of growth in the rural sector.

10. Growth of Agiro-based Industries. An improved and efficient system of rural marketing helps in the growth of agro-based industries and stimulates the overall development process of the economy. Many industries depend on agriculture for the supply of raw materials. So many producers have installed their industrial units near the village side and are also interested to instal the units in the rural areas so as to minimise the transportation cost, easily availability of raw materials and some benefits which are specially meant for rural producers. So growth of agro based industries constitute one of the most important segment of rural marketing.

11. Widening of Markets. A well-knit marketing system widens the market far the products by taking them to remote corners of the country, *i.e.*, to areas far away from the production points. The widening of the market helps in increasing the demand on a continuous basis, and thereby guarantees a higher income to the producer.

12. Price Signals. All efficient marketing system helps the farmers in planning their production in accordance with the needs of the economy. This work is carried out through price signals. The government is announcing the minimum support price of the agriculture produce every year and also emphasising the importance of a particular farm products. For examples during the past 5 years the government is stimulating the farmers to produce more commercial crops like sugarcane, soyabean, sunbean, groundnut, tobacco and tobacco products, sericulture products, fruits and vegetables, cotton and oilseeds. To fetch a good price the farmers are directed to produce as per the requirements of the economy.

13. Adoption and Spread of New Technology. The marketing system helps the farmers in the adoption of new scientific and technical knowledge. Past experience shows that our rural areas were totally under-developed and under-utilised because of the lack of mechanisation of agriculture. With the advancement of technology, mechanisation, introduction of high yielding varieties, development of fertiliser and pesticides and proper government policy has increased the agriculture production to a greater extent which is the back bone of rural industries.

13. Employment. The marketing system provides employment to millions of persons engaged in various activities, such as packaging, transportation and processing. Persons like commission agents, brokers, traders, retailers, weightmen, hamals and regulating staff are employed in the marketing system. A number of employees are working in the marketing system which is three tier system ranging from primary marketing society, central marketing committee and state marketing board. Side by side cooperative marketing system provides employments to a number of employees. Storage, warehousing, transportations, middlemen, provides employments to a number of prospects.

15. Better Living. The marketing system is essential for the success of the development programmes which are designed to uplift the population as a whole. Any plan of economic development that aims at diminishing the poverty of the agricultural population, reducing consumer food prices, earning more foreign exchange or eliminating economic waste has, therefore, to pay special attention to the development of an efficient marketing for food and agricultural products.

16. Contribution to National Income. Marketing activities add to the nation's gross national product and net national product. An estimate indicate that 14% of the gross national product comes from the rural sector and 11% is derived from rural industries. Moreover there are number of activities which are called allied activities to rural sectors are also giving a reasonable contribution to the national net worth. Rural development means the development of the country cannot be over emphasised.

17. Utility Creation. Marketing is productive, and is as necessary as the farm production. It is, in fact, a part of production itself, for production is complete only when the product reaches a place in the form and at the time required by the consumers. Marketing adds cost to the product; but, at the same time, it adds, utilities to the product. The following four types of utilities of the product are created by marketing.

(a) **Form Utility.** The processing function adds form utility to the product by changing the raw material into a finished form. With this change, the product becomes more useful than it is in the form in which it is produced by the farmer.

For example, through processing, oilseeds are converted into oil, sugarcane into sugar, cotton into cloth and wheat into flour and bread. The processed forms are more useful than the original raw materials.

(b) **Place Utility.** The transportation function adds place utility to products by shifting them to a place of need from the place of plenty. Products command higher prices at the place of need than at the place of production because of the increased utility of the product.

(c) **Time Utility.** The storage function adds time utility to the products by making them available at the time when they are needed.

(d) **Possession Utility.** The marketing function of buying and selling helps in the transfer of ownership from one person to another. Products are transferred through marketing to persons having a higher utility from persons having a low utility.

CHARACTERISTICS OF SCIENTIFIC RURAL MARKETING SYSTEM

Agriculture is the back bone of the Indian economy. Industrial growth and development can only take when there is constant and dynamic agriculture growth. Both are complimentary and not competitive. Rural marketing is based on Indian agriculture which is developing area. It should satisfy the objectives of marketing systems for all the persons associated with marketing in the process of the movement of produce from producer to the consumers. The following are the characteristics of good marketing system:

1. One of the conditions of an efficient agricultural marketing system is that there should not be any government interference in free market transactions. The methods of intervention include restrictions on foodgrain movements, restrictions on the quantity to be processed or on the construction of processing plant. price supports, rationing, price ceiling, entry of persons in the trade, etc.

When these conditions are violated, the inefficiency in the marketing system creeps in, and commodities pass into the black market. They are not then easily available at fair prices.

2. The marketing system should operate on the basis of the independent, but systematic and orderly, decisions of the millions of the individual consumers and producers whose lives are affected by it.

3. The marketing system should bring demand and supply together and should establish and equilibrium between the two.

4. The marketing system should be capable of developing into an intricate and far-flung marketing system in view of the rapid development of the urban-industrial economy.

5. The marketing system should be able to generate employment by ensuring the development of processing industries and convincing the people to consume more processed foods, consistent with their tastes, habits and income levels.

6. There should not be any sort of pressure on the consumers to buy products from a particular trader or class of traders.

7. A good market should provide commodities which the consumers want and are ready to pay for.

8. The information on the presence of goods in the market and their relative merits should be available to all the prospective consumers.

9. There should not be any inefficiency or waste in the market.

10. Prices should be fair and uniform for the products for all categories of consumers.

11. It should provide a wide variety of products to consumers so that they may easily choose for themselves. The variety should not be so wide as to create a confusion for him.

12. The retailing services should be available in the market (together with wholesale facilities) for small consumers.

13. No harmful products should be offered for sale in the market. Precautions should be taken to protect consumers.

The tendency among the farmers to market their produce has been increasing. Production is complete only when the product is marketed at a price remunerative to the producers. Increasing specialization in production, higher marketable/marketed surplus of the produce and alternative channels of marketing have increased the importance of the marketing activity for the producers.

Difference between Rural Marketing and Marketing of Manufactured Goods. The marketing of agricultural Commodities from the marketing of manufactured commodities because of the special characteristics of the agricultural sector (demand and supply) which have a bearing on marketing. Because of these characteristics, the subject of agricultural marketing has been treated as a separate discipline and this fact makes the subject somewhat complicated. These special characteristics of the rural sector affect the supply and demand of rural products in a manner different from that governing the supply and demand of manufactured commodities. The special characteristics which the rural sector possesses, and which are different from those of the manufactured sector, are:

1. Perishability of the Product. Most farm products are perishable in nature; but the period of their perishability varies from a few hours to few months. To a large extent, the marketing of farm products is virtually a race with death and decay. Their perishability makes it almost impossible for producers to fix the reserve price for their farm-grown products. The supply of rural products is irregular; the price of the crop therefor fluctuates both during the year and from year to year. The extent of perishability of farm products may be reduced by the processing function; but they cannot be made non-perishable like manufactured products. Nor can their supply be made regular.

2. Seasonality of Production. Farm products are produced in a particular season; they cannot be produced throughout the year. In the harvest season, prices fall. But the supply of manufactured products can be adjusted or made uniform throughout the year. Their prices therefore remain almost the same throughout the year.

3. Variation in Quality of Products. There is a large variation in the quality of agricultural products, which makes their grading and standardization somewhat difficult. There is no such problem in manufactured goods, for they are products of uniform quality.

4. Bulkiness of Products. The characteristic of bulkiness of most farm products makes their transportation and storage difficult and expensive. This fact also restricts the location of production to somewhere near the place of consumption or processing. The price spread in bulky products is higher because of the higher costs of transportation and storage.

5. Irregular Supply of Agricultural Products. The supply of agricultural products is uncertain and irregular because of the dependence of agricultural production on natural conditions. With the varying supply, the demand remaining almost constant, the prices of agricultural products fluctuate substantially.

6. Processing of Product. Most of the farm products have to be processed before their consumption by the ultimate consumers. This processing function increases the price spread of agricultural commodities. Processing firms enjoy the advantage of monopsony, oligopsony or duopsony in the market. This situation creates disincentives for the producers and may have an adverse effect on production in the next year.

7. Small Size of Holdings and Scattered Production. Farm products are produced throughout the length and breadth of the country and most of the producers are of small size. This makes the estimation of supply difficult and creates problems in marketing.

COMMANDMENTS OF SCIENTIFIC MARKETING

The farmers can gain more if they follow the following commandments of scientific marketing:

1. Avoid Immediate Post-harvest Sales. Farmers should avoid sales immediately after a harvest. The prices ofthe produce touch the lowest level in the peak marketing season. Farmers can get better prices by availing themselves of the warehousing facilities existing in their area. Studies have shown that the price advantage to the farmers by selling in the later part of the year is more than the cost of storage. Farmers can meet their cash needs by pledging the warehouse receipt to nationalized banks.

2. Carry Bags/Pucks of Standard Weights. Farmers should weigh their produce and till each bag with fixed quantity before moving to the market for sale. A majority of the farmers do not weigh their produce before taking it for sale and suffer loss by way of a possible malpractice in weighing; or they may have to make excess payments in transit (octroi, transport costs).

3. Patronize Co-operative Marketing Societies. Farmers can get better prices by sales through a co-operative marketing society and can avoid the possibility of being cheated in the process of marketing their produce. The cost of marketing, particularly the transportation cost for producers having a small quantity of marketable surplus, is minimized, for transportation is arranged co-operatively by the society, and the profit earned by the, society is shared among its members.

4. Sell the Produce in Regulated Markets. The farmers should take their produce for sale to the nearby regulated markets rather than sell them in village or unregulated markets. In regulated markets, farmers are either not require to bear, or have to bear, marketing charges on a very few items. They get the sales slips in the regulated markets, which show the quantity of the produce marketed and the amount of charges deducted from the value of the produce. Sale slips protect farmers against the malpractice of deliberate erroneous accounting or unauthorised deductions.

5. Keep Abreast of Market Information. The farmer must keep in touch with market news in order to know the prices that prevail in different markets. Price information helps him to take decisions about when and where to sell the produce so that a better price may be obtained. Farmers who go to the market for sale without prior knowledge of the prevailing prices repent later. By and large, they agree to sell at a price which is lower than the price expected by them because it is difficult and cumbersome for them to postpone the sale or take the product to another market.

6. Sell Different Qualities of Products Separately. The produce of different varieties should be marketed separately. Many farmers mix the lots. It has been observed that when different varieties of products are marketed separately, the farmers get a higher price because of the buyer's preference for specific varieties.

7. Bring the Produce for Sale After Cleaning. The produce brought by the producers for sale in the market must be clean and free from such impurities as dirt, sand and pebbles, and should be unmized with produce of another quality. Impurities, when present, lower the price offered by the trader-buyer in the market. The fall in price is more than the extent of the impurity present in the produce would warrant. Many buyers are interested in buying only clean produce, and are ready to pay a higher price for it. Clean produce attracts more buyers.

8. Sell the produce After Grading. It is always advantageous for the farmer to market the produce after grading and standardizing it. Graded produce is sold off quickly. Studes have shown that sellers get a higher total income generated by the adoption of grading and standardization is more than the cost incurred on the process of grading and standardization. This shows that there is an incentive for the farmers for the production of good quality products.

RURAL MARKETING

Marketing is concerned to participation manifests itself in the form of consumer behaviour towards marketable products. An important achievement of the economic development in recent years is the conversion of a seller's market into a buyer's market; in the case of product like textiles, electricals, household goods, bicycles, transistors, torch lights, watches, soaps, detergents, soft drinks, etc. In recent time the development has been the concentration of the business executives attention on the customers in place of their products. Present the marketing executives try to understand their customers, study their responses and arrive at the basic conclusion.

Marketing may, aptly be described as the process of defining, anticipating and creating customer needs and organising all the resources of the company to satisfy them. The consumers' behaviour comprises the acts, processes and social relationships exhibited by individuals, groups, and organisations in the obtainment, use of, and consequent experience with products and services. An understanding and knowledge of the motives underlying consumer behaviour helps a firm in seeking better and more effective ways to satisfy its customers; it help to select tile appropriate rules and advertising strategies, and to plan its marketing programme in a more efficient manner so the products can move to the final consumer.

The rural market of India started showing its potential in the 1960s. The 70s and 80s witnessed its steady development. And, there are clear indications that the 2000 are going to see its full blossoming in our country, where research on consumer behaviour has been nominal, not much systematised information is available about the rural consumers. But, by and large, one has still to understand the rural buyer, his habits, attitudes and behaviour, particularly from the marking point of view.

Assumption of Rural Marketing

1. Many assumption prevail about rural marketing. For instance, one assumption is that the rural buyer is not very discriminating. Once he is persuaded to buy a particular product, he develops a strong affinity for it, and if satisfied, becomes brand loyal. As a result, Indian manufacturers are generally known to prefer selling fewer items at higher prices than selling more items at lower prices. A contrary view is that the rural buyer. being suspicious of the marketer's hardsell techniques, is quite discriminating, and is not easily persuaded.

2. Yet another assumption is that the rural buyer is not particularly been about quality and packaging.

3. Some other assumption can be quoted. But all these need deep probing for assuring at valid and reliable conclusions. Consumer' research, thus, is indispensable for entering the rural segment of the market. The pace of urbanisation has brought into existence new markets for pronumerous consumer goods. The rural market consists of two segments, *viz.*

(i) The market for consumption goods including consumer durables, and

(ii) The market for investment goods, including agricultural inputs. Rural consumers in both these segments are far less homogeneous than their urban counterparts, and also differ from region to region. A number of research studies have been made on the behaviour of rural consumers towards agricultural inputs like fertilizers, pesticides, sprayers and foodgrains.

The rural markets are green pastures for any marketer, provided his marketing plan are attuned to the specialities of rural markets. The rural market is estimated to be growing faster, compared to urban market. Being a new market, it could be easily manipulated, provided the manufacturers develop an insight into the behavioural patterns of rural consumers. The potential of rural markets is said to be like that of a woken up sleeping giant. This is substantiated in a study of market growth conducted by the Operations Research Group (ORG) during a six year period (1983-89). The study revealed that the offtake of rural markets for packaged consumer products accounted for Rs. 2,083 crores in 1989. The growth works out to 184 per cent, compared to the figure for 1984. Against this, the increase in urban market off take was from Rs. 1,855 crore in 1984 to Rs. 3,628 crore in 1989, working out to a 96 per cent crawl.

SIGNIFICANCE OF RURAL MARKETS

Every sales executives today if asked which market he would prefer to serve, the immediate answer would be, "Rural Markets" . A number of factors have been recognised as responsible for the rural market boom. Some of them are:

1. Population Increase. Increase in population, and hence increase in demand. The rural population in 1971 was 43.80 crore, which increased to 52.50 crore in 1981, and 72 crore in 1994 and it is about 78 crore in 2000.

2. Addition in the Rural Increases. A marked increase in the rural income due to agrarian property.

3. Development of Villages. Large inflow of investment for rural development, programmes from government and other sources.

4. Development of Educational Facilities. Increase in literacy and educational level among rural folks, and the resultant inclination to lead sophisticated lives.

5. Increasing Contract. Increased contract of rural people with their urban counterparts due to development of transport and a wide communication network.

6. Role of Foreign Goods. Inflow of foreign remittances and foreign made goods into rural areas.

7. Prosperity. The general rise in the level of prosperity appears to have resulted in two dominant shifts in the rural consuming systems. One is conspicuous consumption of consumer durables by almost all segment of rural consumers, and the second, the obvious preference for branded goods as compared to non-branded goods of rural origin.

8. Change in Buying Behaviour. Changes in the laud tenure system causing a structural change in the ownership pattern and consequent, changes in the buying behaviour.

Factors Contributing to the Change in the Rural Markets. While a variety of factors, acting in concert, have brought about this change, three factors deserve special mention.

Concerted Efforts at Rural Developments. As a part for planned economic development, the government has been making concerted efforts towards rural development. Plan after plan, it has been committing large outlays to sectors like agriculture, animal husbandry, irrigation, flood control, and khadi and village industries. They have generated new employment, new income and new purchasing power among the rural people.

2. The Green Revolution. The green revolution has been the next major factor. A technological break through took place in Indian agriculture. Rural India derived considerable benefit from the green revolution. Today, rural India generates 170 millions tonnes of food grains per year and' an equally substantial output of various other agricultural products. It produces 14 billion eggs, 80 millions broilers and 40 million tonnes of milk per annum obviously, rural India is acquiring a new power.

3. The Expectation Revolution. The expectation revolution among the rural folks completed the process. More than the green revolution, the revolution of 'rising expectations' of the rural people influenced the marketing environment of rural India. While the expectation revolution did not in itself result in any additional purchasing power, it brought about a powerful change in the environmental dynamics. It enlarged the awareness of the mral people; it kindled their hopes; it strengthened their motivation to work, earn and consume. Political and social changes taking place in the country strengthened this phenomenon. The rise in income resulting from the new farming strategy has added meaning and substance to the growing aspirations of the rural people.

STRATEGES IN THE RURAL MARKETS

While the rural markets of India certainly offers' a big attraction to marketers, it would be totally native to think that any firm can easily enter the market and walk away with a sizeable share of it. The firm has to grapple with these problems and provide innovative solutions to them. In fact, only because a few pioneering firms properly understood the peculiar problems of the rural market and came up with innovative solutions to them, we are now seeing a welcome trend to growth and change in the rural market.

1. Addition in Purchasing Power. Prosperity in rural areas is reflected in the buying and consumption habits of rural folks. Their inclination to spend on modern gadgets has increased as a result of the increase in their purchasing power. This necessitates an appraisal of the rural marketing environment which is an outgrowth of various socio-economic and cultural forces for evolving an appropriate and effective marketing strategy.

2. Understanding the Rural Environment : It is essential. Recently, attempts were made to define the specific differences between urban and rural markets, on the basis of various socio-economic factors. The dominant economic peculiarities of rural India may be recognised in tenus of the sources of income (agriculture), the frequency of receipt of income (unstable because of the dependence on mins), the seasonal nature of income (normally two seasons in a year) and the consumers (mostly farmers). These distinctive features affect the consumption pattern of rural consumers.

Factors be taken care while attending Rural Marketing. The opportunities in rural markets in contrast to the urban markets, are conditioned by the following factors:

(a) **Spatial Factors.** Low density of population, low mobility, low infrastructural level and low literacy level, but the market is contiguous.

(b) **Social Factors.** Intimate understanding between individuals and hence individuals better known, social norms more dominant and caste influence strong. Marketing communications better passed through so-called leaders-Initiating tendency more.

(c) **Marketing Factors.** Low product exposure, retail outlets lower in number—Difficulty in changing beliefs.

(d) **Economic Factors.** Seasonality of income receipts labourers' category receives income on daily or weekly basis changes in frequency and quality bought wider.

The Main Problem of Rural Marketing. The problem arise basically out of the peculiar dynamics of the rural market of India the uniqueness of the rural consumer, the uniqueness of the structure of the rural market, and the peculiarities of the distributional infrastructure in the rural areas. These are special to the rural market; and these require unique handling.

Practically, in every aspect of marketing, rural markets post certain special problems, but the following are found to be important from the point of view of marketing management.

(a) **Transport.** Distribution logistics, storage, transport and handling.

(b) **Location.** Location and degree of concentration of demand;

(c) **Attitudes.** Dealer's attitude and motivation;

(d) **Habit.** Mass communication media, their reach and influence;

(e) **Media.** Mass communication media, their search and influence; and

(f) **Arrangements of Products.** Organisational alternatives.

For any marketer, covering the 5.75 lakh villages of the country is a formidable task. Many villages are not connected by rail or road. Further, storage facilities in rural areas are inadequate and of poor quality. One also faces a high degree of conservatism and reluctance on the part of rural people to take major risks. Another problem is their low level of literacy which makes if difficult to communicate with them through various media.

The rural market of India is fascinating and challenging at the same time. It offers large scope on account of its sheer size. And it is growing steadily. Whereas the urban market is highly competitive, the rural market is relatively quiet. In fact for certain products, it is totally virgin market. The market pioneers can certainly reap rich rewards from the market.

Simultaneously, the market also poses several problems and hurdles. The firms have to encounter them squarely and put in a great deal of effort, if they have to get a sizable share to the market.

It is often said that markets are made, not found. This is especially true of the rural market of India. It is a market for the truely creative marketer.

SHIFTING OF RURAL MARKETING FROM CITIES TO VILLAGES

A Hindi poet has rightly said "Bharat Mata Gram Vasini", which means mother India lives in her villages. According to the 1991 Census, India's population was 850 million of which 75 per cent lived in villages. This is the average. There are states like UP, MP, Rajasthan, Kerala, Bihar and Orissa where the rural population varies from 80 to 90 per cent. The spread of population in 4200 cities and towns is to the extent of 25 per cent and of the remaining 75 per cent is in 5,76,00 villages. Of these 15,00,000 villages have a population ranging between 200 or less, 3,16,800 villages are in the range of 5,000 or more and the remaining 1,02,900 villages in the range of 5000 or less, but more than 500. As for the age-wise distribution of the rural population, 65 per cent is made up of adults, 29 per cent children and teenagers and 6 per cent of old persons above the age of 60 years. Fifty per cent of total national income is generated in the rural sector. Agriculture and agricultural wages account for 60 per cent and 17 per cent respectively, of the rural income, indicating that the prosperity of rural population depends on progress and prosperity of agriculture. The size of our rural market 1992 was of the order of Rs. 40,000 crore, made up of 22,000 crore for non-food items and 18,000 crore for food items. It is projected to be Rs, 1,00,000 crore by 2000 AD. Non food items include toiletries, readymade garments, dress materials, consumer durables, packaged food stuffs, baby-care products, and agricultural inputs like seeds, fertilizers, pesticides, pump-sets, tractors tillers, sprayers, harvesters, etc. The share of the rural market is 80 per cent, 70 per cent and 55 per cent of the sales of bicycles, razor blades and books and stationary respectively.

Between 1975-91, the consumption of packaged tea had increased by 50 per cent, and the demand for detergent washing powder and soap cakes had gone up by 75 per cent and 85 per cent, respectively.

According to a study of the growing of rural market for consumer products made by the Operations Research Group (ORG), the share of rural market in the All India Market was 59 per cent of washing soaps, 58 per cent of batteries (dry cells), 50 per cent of razor blades, 42 per cent of glucose powder, 40 per cent of packaged tea, 33 per cent of condoms (retail), and 26 per cent of premium soaps. The contribution of rural markets to the all India markets of packaged products increased from Rs. 733 crore (28 per cent) in 1984 to Rs. 2083 crore (37 per cent) in 1989. Thus, in the case of some consumer products, the rural market has outstripped the urban one. The rural market's contribution to the total national market has gone up from 28 per cent in 1985 to 40 per cent in 1990.

A survey conducted by the Indian Market Research Bureau (IMRB) revealed that in the upper income group (monthly household incomes ofRs. 1,000) 74 per cent own some form of transportation, 82 per cent own some means of entertainment, and 86 per cent own at least one household appliance.

Another survey by the National Council of Applied Economic Research (NCEAR) found that it is the low income group which now comprises an overwhelming majority of consumers for mass consumption products, as almost 90 per cent of the goods surveyed were purchased by people earning less than Rs. 18,000 per annum.

During the five years from 1985 to 1990, the demand for consumer products in rural India grew at a faster rate than in urban centres, where growth has flattened out. For example, the demand for toilet soap grew at 14.7 per cent in rural markets, while in the urban sector, in actually declined (0.6 per cent. Till 1987, rural demand for consumer products was growing at 17 per cent, but by 1989 it leapt to 41 per cent. It has largely been because of the boom in the rural income due to the green and white revolutions, changing life-styles of the villagers, increasing literacy, and greater exposures to TV and other advertisement media.

According to a study made by the Centre for Monitoring Indian Economics, mumbai, out of a staggering three million plus retail outlets, more than 78.9 per cent were located in rural areas. Pressures in the urban Market are forcing many to move into the rural areas. For instances earlier, white goods marketers ignored the rural consumers, now with the growing awareness and demand for their goods, companies are going rural.

In fact, a silent marketing revolution is sweeping the Indian countryside. It has forced marketing whizkids to abandon the airconditioned comfort of their Nariman Point skyscrapers and hit the dirt tracks leading to the remotest villages. Whether it is multinational companies like Procter & Gamble and Hindustan Lever, family owned business like Godrej or Balsara, or newer, aggressive, market-smart entrepreneurs like Karsanbhai Patel of Nirma fame, more and more marketers are being compelled to go rural.

Reports produced by research organisations like IMRB, ORG and NCEAR have reeled out a lot of impressive data and information, which can allure even a marketer who is hesitant and indifferent to enter the rural markets. But, marketing to the rural consumer is no cakewalk, though the rural market is attractive and enchanting due to its greed potential revealed by the studies conducted by the research institutions. Rural Marketing is fraught with many dangers and risks, and the road to the rural markets is full of pitfalls. The marketers, venturing into them should, therefore, be cautions and have to evolve and use appropriate marketing strategies. Capturing the rural market is possible for a marketer if he is able to communicate effectively with the rural people, and more his products to their doorsteps.

This article aims at a brief discussion of the marketing strategies adopted by a few big players in the Indian rural market and an examination of the specific problems that the marketers may have to face in the rural sector.

STRATEGIES OF BIG COMPANIES FOR RURAL MARKETING

Big companies, which were reluctant to enter the rural markets and completely ignored this sector a few years ago, have started making a bee line for the villages now, each offering its brands of different consumer products. The strategies adopted by them to sell their products to the villagers from the beginning of the 1990s are discussed in the following paragraphs.

1. Onida. The colour television giant, Onida, decided to make a pitch for the rural market when it faced a recession in the industry that showed no sign of an upswing. Their initial foray was disastrous due to their high priced models, and wrong, urban-oriented, communication packages. The black and white segment gave them an entry point, and they were able to make their presence felt in the rural markets. Onida's rural foray has taken on the shape of a full-fledged war campaign christened Gramin Bharat. Its urban-oriented ad campaign, starring the devil, was drastically altered. Though the devil was retained partially (only its eyes appeared in the print advertising), the punch line was changed to Onida ka black and white jadu. This was essential because its earlier urban aesthetics did not strike the right chord with rural consumers. It has also upgraded its distribution network.

2. HMT Ltd. The premier watch manufacturing company in the public sector, the Hindustan Machines Tools Ltd. (HMT Ltd.) whose brands like Sona, Janata and Kanchan have a presence already in the rural market is increasing its promotional pitch. During 1991-92, HMT spent Rs. 1,00 crore on advertising aimed at resident of semi-urban towns and rural areas. Their focus, of course, is on distribution, and they have established a well integrated distribution network of dealers and distributions and company-owned showrooms to co-ordinate the distribution.

3. Godfrey Philips India. Godfrey Philip India (GPI), a cigarette manufacturing company, found that its brands were not reaching rural outlets. Non-availability of Mass Media like TV and radio made it all the more difficult for GPI to reach out to its target audience. To counter this GPI put five Toyata vans on the road, fitted out with TV sets. Their routine stops in the villages were followed by an entertainment programme interspersed with ad messages. Their rural activity has increased, and the video vans help in creating awareness, encouraging sampling of brands, and monitoring the market.

4. Hero-Honda. One of the leading automobile companies with Japanese collaboration *viz.* Hero Honda, has introduced a new concept in motorbike marketing the extension counter. This came soon after it launched its CDSS 100 for the rural segment. There are small counters which are extensions to dealers in the bigger cities. The company had identified by April, 1992, 40 such locations for extension counters all over the country. Mobile workshops too is another area on which the company is laying stress. It has gone in for special video films on servicing maintaining that are shown on video vans, when the mobile workshops make their stops. It is an exercise in building the confidence of their dealers and local mechanics.

The Hero Honda CDSS 100 Campaign has been exclusively targeted at rural audience through wall paintings, hoardings, local vernacular newspapers, and radio. The idea is to give the brand a rural orientation further, Hero Honda CDSS 100 is being plugged through Hindi, Marathi and Gujarati campaigns, but there is none of the gloss and slickness that is normally associated with Here Honda name.

5. Procter & Gamble. The multi-product multinational company. Procter & Gamble, realised that packaging could make or break a brand in rural markets and therefore, adopted user-friendly sizes for the rural markets and made available. Their Vicks cough drops in single strips, instead of the regular cartons of 20. Earlier available at Rs. 4 for a 15 ml. Sachet, its sales were, at best, stagnant. But, the company re-launched it in 10 ml. packs for Rs. 2, and the offtake increased manyfold in smaller villages and towns.

6. Colgate-Palmolive (India) Ltd. Realising that offering products at the lowest unit price was necessary to enter the rural market, Colgate Palmolive (India) Ltd. designed 10 gm. sachets of their toothpastes. Further, keeping in view the rural consumers, the company dispensed with the age-old Sing of confidence'ad campaign, which had a distinct urban bias, and opted for a specially created 27 minute promotion film to woo the rural consumer.

In this way, the big marketers are finetuning their products, sprucing up their distribution channels, working out winning advertisement campaigns, and making a serious pitch for the rural sweepstakes.

PROBLEMS FACED IN RURAL MARKETING

The main problems are as:

The Indian rural market is characterised by

(a) Lack of proper communication *(b)* Transportation and *(c)* Distribution facilities. *(d)* Low Literacy level *(e)* Lack of extensive banking facilities *(f)* Highly dispersed *(h)* Thinly populated. *(i)* Scattered markets *(j)* Low per capita income. *(k)* Poor standards of living. *(l)* Strikingly diverse religions, languages *(m)* Social customs and traditions. *(n)* Seasonal demand for goods and services. As such, it poses a number of complex problems and the main problems and difficulties arising out of these characteristic features of the Indian rural markets that a marketer may face in cultivating the rural market are examined in the following paragraphs.

1. Lack of Proper Communication. Transportation and Modern means of fast communication, *viz*, telephone facility, is yet to reach our villages. Hence, marketer cannot easily contact or communicate with the rural folk. Most of the villages are inaccessible, particularly during the rainy season, as they are yet to be linked to the main roads with pucca link roads.

2. Low Literacy Level. Most of the villagers are still illiterate and, therefore, it is very difficult to convince them of the utility or usefulness of a product. Advertisement through print media is of little use in rural areas. It many be noted here that success in the American rural market was achieved through main order, which was possible because of the high literacy level. About 85 per cent of 200 rural persons, interviewed at the Hyderabad city bus station for the purpose of a study, could not distinguish between a commercial and a programme.

3. Distribution Problems. Supply of goods becomes difficult due to this. Retailers serving as distribution outlets in the villages are unable to stock goods due to inadequate working capital, and favour those products on which they get higher margins. Moreover, retailing is only a side business for many of them, who are money-lenders, beedi makers, bicycle mechanics or farmers.

4. Highly Dispersed and Thinly Populated Markets. Indian's rural market is very vast spread throughout its length and breadth dotted by about six lakh villages. About 81 per cent of these villages have a population of less than 500 each. As such, rural markets are viewed as uneconomic and unmanageable by both manufacturers and middlemen. In Uttar Pradesh, 27 percent of villages account for 65 percent of the population. In Madhya Pradesh, 40 per cent of the villages account for 71 per cent of the population. In other words, if 65 per cent of the population needs to be covered in any state, it will be possible to do so by reaching out to a quarter or one-third of the villages.

5. Different Religions, Languages, Cultures, Social Customs and Traditions. The numerous religious, languages and cultures of the tradition bound rural folk in different regions of the country present a colourful mosaic of their varied tastes, likings, preferences and buying behaviour. Culture, of course, has a great impact on spending by people and even the poorest think it culturally obligatory to be lavish spenders on socio-cultural occasions. This many be exploited by a progressive and dynamic marketer.

6. Lower Per Capita Income. Most of the consumers in the villages are very poor and their standard of living is very low. They are more price conscious than quality conscious, and measure quality 'in terms of price. The poor consumers buy very small quantities of goods, and that too not very frequently, rendering the distribution of many goods in rural areas uneconomical. Under these circumstances, no businessman can thinks of hiring or owing a retail store in many of the villages.

7. Seasonal Demand. The demand for goods and services in rural India depends heavily on agriculture, which accounts for more than 60 per cent of the rural income. Agriculture being seasonal. demand for various goods and services is also seasonal, peaking at the end of the two main harvests, *vis.* Kharif (October-November) and Rabi (March-April) and falling to low levels during the remaining month of the year. The peaks and the valleys in the demand-sender demand supply synchronisation by marketer pose a difficult and uphill tasks.

The foregoing examination of the problems and difficulties and threats and opportunities posed and offered by the rural markets makes it clear that entering final markets for different products and services and by grabbing a sizeable share thereof is a challenging task. Indeed, it is hard work, identifying cultivating and harvesting these markets, which calls for constant monitoring of the ever-changing rural environments. In order to be successful in rural marketing. A marketer has to clearly understand the needs, wants, desires, aspirations and dreams of the village as well as their linkings and preferences with regard to different products and services, with the help of appropriate marketing research techniques.

SUGGESTIONS FOR MARKETING STRATEGIES FOR RURAL INDIA

A marketer can fruitfully adopted the following strategies in respect of the different ingredients of the total marketing mix.

(1) Product. A marketer should offer the right product to the rural people, *i.e.*, a product which they realiy need and can afford. I am tempted to quote here a Hindi couplet, written in the sixteenth century *"Kar le sughi sarahi ke bhalo bakhane tahin, Aai gandhi matinand tum ita dikhawat kahin."*. In these lines, the poet is addressing a seller of scents, who is trying to sell his product to the poor people of a remote undeveloped village, by pouring drops of the perfume on their palms, free of any charge. For them it is a luxury beyond their reach. Of course, things have changed since then, and villagers of today may buy even scent.

The product should not only be needed, but should also be according to the taste and liking of the rural consumers. The design, colour, shape, size, features, taste, brand and, packaging of a product popular in urban areas need not necessarily be acceptable to the rural consumers. Hence, necessary modifications in the various attributes of a product should be made before taking it to the rural areas.

(2) Price. In view of the low income and purchasing power of the rural consumers, it is advisable for the marketers to offer a comparatively low quality brand or a smaller size of his product at a low unit price affordable for them. While doing so, the marketers must be watchful and take timely action against unscrupulous local makers of products which imitate the national brands and palm off their fake, me-too products to the ignorant and gullible rural buyers as standard products.

(3) Place (distribution). Even a product which exactly matches the needs and wants of the rural consumers will fail, if it is not easily made available to the rural customers at convenient points, preferably at their doorsteps. But the right type of agents, dealers and retailers are not readily available in the rural marketers. Under these circumstance, marketers can fruitfully utilise the services of the oldest type of itinerant retailers, *viz.*, the hawkers who are still quite popular in both rural and urban areas. They sell a very wide range of products at a very low price, and that too at the doorsteps of the consumers. It can be a very economical channel of distribution, as hawkers take a low margin. A hawker can be used both as a means of distribution and also as a medium of communication. But, in spite of all this, no big company has given enough thought to this type of retailing on an organised basis. It is high time that the big marketers made use of hawkers on a large scale for selling their products to the rural buyers.

(4) Promotion. Promotion stands for the activities that communicate the merits of the product and persuade target customers to buy it. It consists of four ingredients advertising, sales promotion, public relations or publicity and personal selling. A judicious mixture of all these ingredients of the promotion mix, which is basically communication, is essential for selling any consumer product in a competitive market.

As mentioned earlier, advertising on to the through print media is only of limited usefulness and not very effective in the rural markets in our country. The marketers should, therefore, try to communicate with rural people more and more through wall posters, hoardings and paintings on walls, showing pictures and symbols in bright attractive colours and shades.

Personal media have a greater effect than the impersonal ones in the rural marketing context. Rural consumers fall for sales-promotion activities such as 'Buy one, get on free' or one unit of product free for every three units bought free gifts and reduced prices.

The marketers should, therefore, more make use of there tools of promotion.

FACTORS AFFECTING THE GROWTH OF RURAL MARKETING IN INDIA

India is a land of agriculture and basically she resides in the villages. According to 1991 census more than 63 per cent of the population lives in villages. That this population makes its both ends by cultivating, selling the agricultural product, working on agriculture which is called agricultural labours, some are involved in the processing of agricultural products and allied activities. Some are rendering the services to the villagers by providing them seeds, fertilizers, pesticides and some are doing the job work on agriculture. The conclude rural marketing has taken place only ftom the agricultural field. There are some factors which are responsible for the growth of rural marketing in India. They are:

1. **Professionalisation or Specialisation of the Marketing.** Marketing has been recognised as profession in the early 1950. People are now preferring the jobs in the marketing department and accepting the challenges of the marketing management. People are now more interested to acquire knowledge of the marketing and apply it in the field of marketing. The tendency towards increasing specialization by persons in certain jobs has resulted in an increase in their efficiency and the breakdown in the self sufficiency of the family unit. Specialization, thus, has resulted in increased production, which is the base for the growth of marketing. The government is also motivating the people who are the graduates in marketing and also the institutions which are providing marketing education by allowing fellowship to the graduates and a huge amount of grants to the institutions.

2. **Urbanisation.** In the 1981 census the rural population was 69 per cent of the total population which fell down to 63% in the year of 1991. This indicates that the rural population is moving to the urban areas for the purpose of acquiring education seeking employment, business purposes and selling the agricultural and rural products in the urban areas. As the demand of rural products in urban areas is more and by selling these products in the areas they can earn their livelihood. Urban people are the main buyers of agricultural commodities. The urban population of India and increased from 33.5 million in 1931 to 62.9 million in 1951, to 109.1 million in 1971, to 181.9 million in 1981 and 217.2 million in 1991. This has necessitated a faster growth of agricultural marketing.

3. **Development of Transportation and Communication.** The modern means of transport and communication is the most important tool of developing the size of rural marketing. Transportation and communication is just like a life blood in the human life. Transportation and

communication make and help the process of marketing and minimizes the distance between the different centres. The increasing transportation and communication facilities have widened the market for farm products. The length the breadth of the market to which a product is taken from the production areas have increased. In the absence of these facilities, the movement of produce from one area to another was limited, and the consumption of a product was restricted only to the areas of production or at the most to nearby area.

4. **Technological Change in Agriculture.** Technological developments in agriculture, such as the evolution of high-yielding varieties of seeds, increased use of modem inputs and cultivation practices in the agricultural sector, has resulted in substantial increase in farm production. The marketed surplus of tbe agricultural produce has therefore increased. Production conscious farmers have also become income/price conscious. This has resulted in the growth of the marketing system. The importance of an efficient marketing system as a vital link between the farmer and the consumer was recognised way back in 1928 by the Royal Commission on Agriculture. Since then, a good deal of progress has been made in organising agricultural marketing by the adoption of the various administrative and legislative measures by the Government from time to time. The establishment of the Directorate of Marketing and Inspection in 1935, the enactment of the Act for the grading and standardization of agricultural commodities, the conduct of commodity market surveys, and the establishment of regulated markets in the country-these are some of the measures which have been taken upto improve the marketing situation and to make agricultural marketing as efficient as possible.

During the First and Second Five Year Plans, agricultural marketing did not receive importance. Whatever development that took place in the sphere of marketing was due to the gradual progress towards the commercialization of agriculture, as a result of its own dynamic nature, and not because of any specific Government efforts. The National Commission on Agriculture (the first commission which suggested measures for the development of agriculture in the post-independent period) remarked: "There is an increasing awareness that it is not enough to produce a crop or animal product, it must be marketed well. Increased production, resulting in a greater percentage increase in the marketable surplus accompanied by the increase in demand from urban population, calls for a rapid improvement in the existing marketing system."

5. Cooperative Marketing and Government Efforts. Marketing Committee system and cooperative marketing are the two parallel institutions framed for the purpose of rural marketing. The marketing system is working under the direct control for the respective state governments having its three tier system, the apex institution is state marketing board, at district level central marketing committee and at block level primary marketing committees are functioning. The cooperative movement as it was envisaged by the father of nation Mahatma Gandhi, in every state we are having the producer, commission agents, government nominees and the representative of local areas. These markets are working very successfully and as a result it has increased the share of sales of rural products in the regulated markets. By this system we mean one for all and all for one. It teaches the principle of cooperation and fraternitism. Moreover it is increasing the spirit of the producers as their interests are protected through the marketing system in India. So this is the main reason that rural marketing is gaining more and more attention in the Indian market scene.

❑

2

Rural Development and Marketing of Consumer Durables

Rural development has been on the main agenda of the Five year Plans of the country. These plans are formulated for the most effective and planned utilisation of the country's resources. Beginning with First Five-year Plan in 1951, we are getting ready to launch the Eighth Five-year Plan shortly. During this period, several changes have taken place in the policy framework. of rural development. In the beginning our development planing it was sought to initiate a process of all round balance development to ensure a rising national income and a steady improvement in living standards of the people over a period. The aim was not merely to plan within the existing socio-economic framework but to change it progressively through democratic methods. It was to be achieved through full participation of the people. For achieving these objectives the programmes of community development (CD) was started as a pilot project in selected areas in 1953 which was extended to the entire country during the next eight years. The programme aimed at agricultural extension, supply of inputs animal husbandry, fisheries, cottage and village industries, education, health nutrition, development of women and youth, etc.

The programme soon assumed the form of a movement. Later in 1959 Panchayati Raj Institutions (PRIs) were created to facilitate popular participation in decision making. But when the evaluation studies were conducted a decade later it was found that the CD movement concentrated mainly on agriculture development which was from time to time supplemented by special agriculture production programme. The other programmes received lukewarm attention in the programme. Thus, the efforts in rural development became synonymous to agricultural development. Though the country made remarkable progress on the agricultural front through adoption of new agricultural technology and achieving green revolution, the developmental energies created imbalances in the society. The general observation was that the resulting benefits of new agricultural technology by way of increased returns were not equally shared by the different farm size groups. It also added to the inequality in-incomes between irrigated and non-irrigated regions of the country. The studies conducted by UNRISD and ILO corroborated in fact that the increases in agricultural production benefited mostly the rich, specially the landlords, the merchantsand the owners of tractors and tubewells, while the poor and landless gained less or did not gain or lost. As a result, the gap between the rich and the poor increased. Another study reporting on the reasons for inter-regional disparities concluded thus:

"Because the new (agriculture) technology has, so far, been confined largely to irrigated and assured rainfall areas and requires good infrastructural development to facilitate input distribution and output marketing, inter-regional disparties were accentuated during the period following the green revolution".

In such a situation, raising the standard of living of people, especially of the less privileged section of the society and removing interregional disparities became the prime concern of the government. Development planning was to result not only in the integrated process of increased production but also in the rational distribution of the added wealth. The overriding inspiration had to be a burning sense of social justice. Development with social justice then assumed the paramount importance in the policy framework of development planning. The strategy adopted to meet the requirements of the new policy was special programmes of rural development which included developing alternative occupations for small and marginal farmers and agricultural labourers, supplemented by consolidation of gains of development through institutional meassres and infrastructural development. However, two important aspects which deserved attention were left out from the policy frame. These were:

(i) the need for correction of regional imbalances, and

(ii) the necessity of meeting the minimum needs of the poor people.

Taking into account these aspects of development policy was further modified and it was made explicit that removal of poverty and attainment of self-reliance were the two major objectives that the country had set out to accomplish.

But this time, most of the equity-oriented special programmes that were initiated earlier began to take shape. In the Prevailing situation it became possible for the government to enlarge the scope of earlier programmes so as to result in achieving growth with social justice and eliminating unemployment and underemployment. Thus, the nation-wide Integratel Rural Development Pragramme and National Rural Employment Programmes were started. The objectives of these programmes included growth in production, benefits to identified target groups in disadvantaged sections of the rural community, arid full employment within a given time frame. Side by side, the scope of the minimum basic needs programmes was expanded and more emphasis was given to the development of small scale and cottage industries. The current Seventh Five-year Plan document clearly, recognizes that the removal of poverty remains a central concern of planning in India. The development strategy which is currently in operation encompasses:

(i) coordinated approach to village life as a whole,

(ii) generating the maximum possible employment opportunities specially for the weaker sections of the population,

(iii) improving the quality of life in rural areas by the provision of basic amenities and families, and

(iv) ensuring people's participation in the planning and implementation of rural development programmes through existing rural institutions.

The task set at present before the government is to achieve the started objectives of rural development throuhh decentralised planning process.

Evolution of Decentralised Planning

The constitution of Planning Commission in 1950 by Government of India heralded a new era of planned development of the country. Though the Indian planners and policy makers from the beginning were conscious of the fact that centralised planning may not prove to be the most effective means of promoting rural development and alleviating poverty and that the human and material resources had to be mobreised through administrative structures and planning procedures that were more decentralised, due to obvious reasons it was not possible to start the planning process effectively at the lower level until the beginning of Seventh Five year Plan in 1985. Meanwhile, the planning exercises have passed through several stages.

The first stage covers the period of First and Second Five Year Plans (1951-56 and 1956-61) when the planning process was completely centralised and the Planning Commission had adopted uniform strategy for bringing about natioaal development. It was evident from the fact that the national short-term, medium-term and long-term plans were formulated, the plans were disaggregated, into, sectoral components" and the States were assigned the responsibilities for implementing the projects. The schemss relating to rural development were taken up under the Community Development Programme and formed a part of the schematic budget of the central plan sector. The authorities at the State and lower, levels were allowed to make, certain aggregation exercises for budgetary purposes. However, while preparing the First Plan, it was thought that the Planning Commission will take into account special development needs and resource position of federating states by ass ciating them in the planning process. But as the; state governments were new, poorly equipped with statistical information and without planning machinery worthy of name, the adminis rative infrastructure at the implementation (district) level were inadequate and they were financially and technologically dependent on the eentral government, they (the states) could not be involved in the planning process.

The second stage covers the period of Third Five-year Plan and three Annual Plans (1961 66 and 1966-67,1967-68 and 1968-69). It was here that the idea of decentralised planning started taking shape. By the end, of the Second Plan the States had strengthened the administrative machinery at the district level and established below the district a new administrative unit called Block for implementing Community Development Programme, equipped themselves with statistical information and started insisting for participation in the planning process. Realising the capabilities of the state governments, the Planning Commission initiated the process of involving the states in plan preparation. The states were asked to compile data in respect of their developmental performance, indicate their developmental priorities, show their resource position and suggest the ways for bringing the gaps between developed and underdeveloped regions. The plans, as emerged, were made flexible so as to allow the states to adopt such strategies which suited to the circumstances imposed by geography, climate, traditions and customs. This was evident from the fact that the central government changed its procedures of giving schematic grant to block grant from the Third Plan.

The third stage covers the period of Fourth Five-year Plan (1969-74) when the call for decentralised planning came into prominance. When the preparation of the Fourth Five-year Plan started, the attention of the government was drawn to the widening of inter-personal and inter-regional disparities result ingfrom the adoption of new agriculture technology and thus the need for shifting to the newer concept of equity and social justice. It was also pointed out that the states were not able to strengthen their own planning apparatus because of the shortage of financial resources. This led to introduce certain important departures both in the planning process as well as in the concept of planning. These changes were related to:

(i) the pattern of devolution of plan funds to the state level embodying in it a measure of weightage to backward states,

(ii) emphasis on wide diffusion of initiative, decision making and participation, and

(iii) initiative for strengthening the planning apparatus at the state level, through a centrally sponsored scheme, so as to enable them to share the responsibilities.

The last stage covers the period from Fifth Five-Year Plan till the current Seventh Five-Year Plan (1985-90) when it became possible to consolidate the gains of previous efforts for decentralised planning. By this time, it became clear that isolated efforts for decentralised planning would not be sufficient and that to make it functional it would need to be strengthened by organisational support. The capabilities for decentralised planning have to be constantly built up, the right procedures. and suitable structures have to be evolved and necessary administrative and technical changes have to be affected. The impertant actions related to:

(i) expanding of the centrally sponsored scheme for strengthening planning machinery at appropriate levels,

(ii) emergence of a broad consensus that the district should be the functional unit for decentralised planning

(iii) establishment of appropriate budgeting and reappropriation procedures, and

(iv) strengthening of Panchayati Raj Institutions (PRIs) for facilitating people's participation in plan formulation. and implementation.

Thus the evolution of decentralised planning process In India is based on gradual step by step approach. One significant point that emerges from above analysis is that it was the Government of India in the Planning Commission which took the initiative for decentralising planning process so as to enable the state governments to share the responsibilities. Though the state governments have started preparing their own Five-year and Annual Plans, it is national planning that occupies even now a pre-eminent position in the planning process and the commission (in effect the Government of India) influences the planning priorities of the states.

SCOPE OF DECENTRALISED PLANNING

The main arguments as advanced in favour of decentralised, planning for rural development are four-fold:

(i) Rural development requires coordinated approach to village life as a whole; decentralised planning enables various activities to be organised in a mutually supportive manner;

(ii) It facilitates optimum use of locally available resources and thus makes it easy to identify programmes for development of the region/area which aims at making full use of local authorities;

(iii) It helps to ensure that economic opportunities are created for those groups who were neglected in earlier efforts and also makes it easier to assess the financial, technical and administrative resources needed to implement the plan; and

(iv) It offers the best possible ways for enlisting people's participation in the process of planning and implementation of development programmes.

OPERATIONAL REQUIREMENTS

The operationalisation of decentralised planning process in India as elsewhere involves various policy decisions. These include among others:

(i) delineation of compact unit for planning;

(ii) creation of viable planning machinery for formulation of local plans;

(iii) decentralisation of financial and administrative powers to appropriate authorities; and

(iv) strengthening of existing rural local institutions for facilitating people's participation.

How far the operational requirements have been met? How such remains to be provided? An analysis of the above aspects presented below in that order provides the answer.

Delineation of Compact Unit. What should be the unit of decentralised planning? This question has been examined by several Commissions/Committees appointed by the Government of India besides the Planning Commission itself. The recommendations of the Administrative Reforms Commission (ARC) and the National Commission on Agriculture (NCA) are precise and clear. The ARC reporting in 1967 suggested district as the unit of planning. It said "The district is a compact area in which conditions are generally more homogeneous than in the larger regions or the whole stage and is a readily available administrative unit for plan implementation." The NCA reporting a decade later in 1976, reaffirmed the view that "Only a strong planning organisation at the district level will be able to translate the regional/area approach to development..." The Government of India generally accepted the recommendations of the ARC and the NCA to make district as the unit of local level planning. There was also a broad consensus among experts, policy makers and planners that the basic unit forpolicy planning, project formulation and implementation at the sub-state level should be the district. But rural development programmes (like Integrated Rural Development Programmes) which were grounded during the later half of 70s as a part of special equity programmes insisted for block level planning. With a view to examine the feasibility of block level planning, the Government of India again constituted a working Group on. Block Level Planning in 1978. The Working Group agreed that it would be ideal to build up necessary planning capabilities both at the district and block levels but considering the existing shortages of technical planning personnel and cost of providing these, it suggested to pool together the available planning skills at the district level instead of scattering this scarce resource in several blocks. The Working Group further visualised the district planning team as peripatetic team which will move down to the selected blocks and prepare the block level plans in association with concerned persons at that level. In the opinion of the Working Group this, would have the following advantages:

(i) it would ensure the optimum deployment of the personnel resources available for area planning and also enable' the planning team to take a broader perspective of resources potential and constraints, and

(ii) it would ensure better coordination, integration and harmonization of block plans with district plan.

Taking the report of the Working Group (1978) in its stride the Government of India appointed a Working Group on District Planning in September 1982 to suggest elaborate organisational arrangements with a view to making planning effective at the district level. The Working Group submitted its report in May 1984. It suggested several organisational changes with a gradual approach towards this goal. These suggestions Formed the basis for operationalising the process of decentralised planning under the Seventh Plan proposals.

Creation of Viable Planning Machinery. After accepting the district as unit of planning, the next task set before the government was to take decisions about an appropriate inter-dependency mix. and proper function sharing between the state and district levels. After this exercise, the following functions are to be performed at the district level:

(i) Breaking up the policy directives from the state or even the central level into suitable action programmes;

(ii) Resource inventory and data collection including analysis of prevailing levels of development, potential for further development, and identification of constraints in development;

(iii) Identification of priorities, formulation of programmes/ projects for development and establishment of their spatial and temporal linkages within an integrated framework;

(iv) Devising a plan for fuller utilisation of man-power resources; in other words, a plan for augmenting employment;

(v) Assessment of availability of financial ,resources from various sources-district budget, banking system, private sector and mobilising the same; and

(vi) Monitoring and concurrent evaluation of the programmes and their modification in the light of experiences.

It has been decided that following units which have been created at the state level could be replicated at the district level to form the nucleus of planning machinery:

(i) Perspective Planning Unit;

(ii) Plan Formulation, Monitoring and Evaluation Unit;

(iii) Projects Formulation Unit; and

(iv) Plan Coordination Unit.

The Working Group on District Planning has suggested that the District Planning should be conceived as a single holistic operation and all planning activities at the level of district would vest with a single District Planning 'Body' who would determin the priorities and allocate funds accordingly among the various development sectors. With regard to its constitution, the Working Group suggested that the District Planning Board should consist of a Chairman, Member Secretary and a reasonable number of members of about 50. In addition, it would be desirable to have a smaller executive body which will be in the nature of a Steering Committee. District Collector may he the Chairman of this Committee and the Chief Planning Officer may be its member-Secretary. The idea behind this suggestion was to minimise the organisational distance between the point of decision and the point of implementation. However, the Working Group was of the firm view that ultimately the Zilla Parishads should assume all the planning functions at the district level.

As at present the creation of District Planning Body has received considerable attention in most of the states. But due to different levels of their infrastructural development which are due to historical reasons, size of population and economic and social factors, an uniform administrative pattern has not been possible. As a result, different organisational set-up has come up in the states to carry out the task without detracting from the basis policy of the decentralised planning.

DECENTRALISATION OF FINANCIAL AND ADMINISTRATIVE POWERS

Finance is the scarce resource which influences the overall fanctioning of any system. So is the case with the systems associated with decentralised planning. If the control over finance remains with the state governments, the decentralised (district) planning will be ineffective. Hence, it—is necessary that there should be adequate and genuine devolution of financial powers to the district planning body. This task is being accomplished in two stages:

> First, to determine and divide the plan outlay between the district and state plans, and second, to determine the shares of the individual district from the total financial outlay earmarked for all the district together. Once this has been done the districts are given full freedom to prepare the plan, select the catalytic programmes and formulate the projects. In all the states more or less this. task has been achieved. However, in determining the shares of the individual districts, different states have adopted different criteria. Some states take the criterion of backwardness of the districts The other states consider the number of ongoing projects, special needs for area development, etc., of the districts for determining the shares of individual districts.

Decentralisation of administrative powers to district bodies is another important aspect which has received considerable attention. It has been considered necessary in this context that the apex body responsible for approval and review of the plan should have full administrative control ever the planning staff either directly or through. the coordinating officer. On the basis of experience gained so far, this will be possible only when adequate powers are delegated to the district body and that the states should satisfy themselves with the powers of ensuring that the district plans together fit in overall frimework of the state plan and meet the inter-sectoral consistency conditions. This is being attempted by all the states in varying degrees.

Strengthening of Rural Local Institutions

One of the basic assumptions of decentralised planning is that the planning machinery being nearer to the people, it will facilitate their (people's) participation in the planning process. Earlier, with a view to enlisting people's participation in the implementation of Community Development Programme, the Panchayati Raj Institutions (PRIs) were created during the years 1959-64 in all the states in India. But as it took time in making decentralised planning effective and in the meanwhile the PRIs also could not come up to the expectations for which they were created, the idea of people's participation could not become effective. In fact when the scheme of PRIs was suggested by the Study Team of Committee on Plan Projects headed by (late) Balwantray Mehta in 1958,13 the state governments adopted the scheme, passed the legislation and created these institutions in the hope that these, (the PRIs) being democratically elected bodies can mobilise local resources for local schemes, help utilise the unemployed manpower in rural areas, can generate popular enthusiasm for development programmes and above all secure people's participation. A perusal of the Panchayati Raj Acts of State Governments would ieveal that planning of development programmes was an essential function of the PRIs. But they could not emerge as an effective vehicle of change and there was general disappointment with the working of the PRIs. The PRIs remained dominated by economically or socially privileged sections of the society and as a result the benefits of productive activities were distributed unequitably and the poor were denied access to inputs and services. Most of the states, therefore, preferred to keep these institutions in a dormant stage. After initiating decentralised planning process the steps are being taken to activise PRIs. However, with a view to ensuring that the PRIs do not meet with the earlier results, the state government are visualising suitable amendments in their. Panchayati Raj Acts. Recently the Government of India also introduced a Panchayati Raj Bill (64th Constitution Amendment Bill) in the Lok Sabha with a view to provide constitutional status to the PRs. A clear picture in this respect to yet to emerge; broadly the modifications are being thought of on the following lines:

(i) In order to avoid the dominance of rich and affluent sections and to ensure the representation of all sections of the society, it is on the anvil to provide reservations in the PRIs, to the weaker sections and various occupational groups in proportion to their population.

(ii) With a view to ensuring the equitable distribution of benefits to all the sections, the system of constituting. Social Justice Committee in each tier of PRIs as is prevalent in some states, may find favour of the states.

(iii) It was found that these institutions became ineffective, because all the powers were vested in the presiding officers at the respective levels. Their powers might be diluted by spreading responsibilities, by introducing social audit system, and by organising training programmes for the members.

Although there was general disappointment with the working of the PRIs, wherever these institutions maintained continuity and were allowed to function with adequate executive powers and resources, they (the PRIs) showed positive results. It is expected that in the emerging situation the PRIs will play their role effectively.

Emerging Scenario

A good plan alone cannot bring the desired results unless followed by careful implementation. In India, normally those incharge of preparation of sectoral plans are responsible for their implementation also. This has been more so at the district level and below. Now by providing with a nucleus staff for planning at the district level an attempt is being made to keep these two organs independent of each other. It is hoped that ill the modified set-up the implementors will concentrate on achieving the results.

Some of the remarkable achievements of the grassroots delivery systems in India have been to make the rural people aware of developmental programmes, to raise their level of aspirations and to prepare them to participate in their developmental efforts. In the emerging situation it will not be a waste of developmental energies if the implementors give the proper direction to the people, are ready to help them at the right time and provide the preferred govemmental assistance.

Earlier with some proposed economic reforms (like land reforms) could not yield the desired results, the government was accused of running with lack of political will. But in the case of rural development, the government has demonstrated sufficient will power and in the policy statements the government has reaffirmed in no uncertain terms about their commitment for rural development through taking the planning machinery to the local level. With a clear policy enunciation full political support, and needed administrative infrastructure, it is expected that the goals of rural development will be achieved.

MARKETING OF AGRICULTURE PROCEDURE

Probably there is no village in the country where one cannot find soaps like Lux, Hamam or Lifebuoy or detergents like Rin or cigarettes like Scissors, Blue Bird, Charminar or small tea sachets from Brooke Bond or Lipton. Similarly the shops in most of the taluk, towns, block headquarters towns and Nandi towns stock electrical goods, torch lights, dry cells, cosmetics, sewing machines mopeds and other durable items where the rural consumers go for selling the agricultural produce and also make purchases of durable items mentioned or above.

Traditionally many rural shops have been stocking and selling packaged products like tea, soaps and other similar items. Unfortunately, data on rural consumption of many packaged items is not easily available. Companies have definite distribution arrangement in rural areas and keep such information confidential to safeguard their interests in terms of market share in rural areas. Organisations like ORG (Operations Research Group) regularly conduct retail shop level audit to know brand wise off-take of packaged goods in rural market. The rural audit survey conducted by the Reserve Bank of India in 1951, described the agricultural produce marketing system as Insufficient and exploitative. A proper and efficient agricultural produce marketing system is imperative for the development of rural market for manufactured consumables, durables and services. The income of Rural Consumers depends upon the efficiency of agricultural- produce marketing, irrespective of the technology adopted in production. Any technological innovation should go hand in hand with efficient marketing. The peculiar features of agricultural produce are as:

(a) Bulkiness goods.

(b) Perishability commodities.

(c) Wide varietal differences.

(d) Dispersed production.

(e) Processing needs for consumption.

(f) Seasonality output.

(g) Comparative advantage.

The above characteristics make the agricultural produce marketing a complicated system. Generally the farmers market only the raw agricultural produce (as harvested) without any processing. At the farm level processing of raw produce is generally not done, rather the value addition to the produce is very minimal. Since only raw produce is marketed there arises a need for many intermediaries to operate between the producer and consumer. Too many intermediaries between the producer and the consumer depresses the ultimate price realisation by the farmers. From the characteristics mentioned above, it is obvious that there are many functions to be performed by the intermediaries in the marketing of agricultural produce. The major functions to be performed are:

(a) Assembling or collection

(b) Equalisation

(c) Dispersal.

In fact the share is much lower in the case of perishable produces like fruits and vegetables. Agricultural production being seasonal, most farmers produce the same crop at the same time. Further, the producers lack withholding power, and are forced to bring the produce to the market soon after the harvest, creating a glut in the market, which depresses price realisation. This problem is much more acute in the case of perishable products like vegetables, fruits and flowers.

The farmers do not have any knowledge about the demand and supply conditions. They also do not have organisations which can protect their interests. In the process, they are exploited by the intermediaries. The marketing expenses are also borne by the producers unlike in the case of manufactured goods. In the case of manufactured goods all the marketing charges including the advertising expenses are included in the ultimate price paid by the consumer.

Thus, the agricultural produce marketing system requires attention with a view to improve it, so that the price realisation are higher to the farmer producers. By and large some improvements have been brought about in the system, which have proved beneficial to the producers but a lot still remains to be done.

Regulated Markets. Presently there are about 500 Primary and secondary agricultural produce wholesale assembling market functioning in the country. These markets are meant for the farmers to take their produce for sale. In the past, these markets were controlled by local bodies: Panchayats or municipalities. All the states have now enacted an Agricultural Produce Markets Act, which has empowered the state to control these markets in several ways. These acts provided for regulating the existing markets and also creating new ones wherever necessary. Today all the states either have a state agricultural marketing board or a department of agricultural marketing and the control of these markets are vested with them. The salient features of the act are:

(a) An elected market committee is constituted to administer these markets. It consists of representatives from all interests like farmer producer commission agents wholesalers and some government nominee like registrar of co-operative society, director of state agricultural marketing board and others. This helps in any arbitration being decided in favour of farm producers.

(b) All the functionaries in the market (commission agents, wholesalers, weighmen, loaders) have to obtain a licence from the market committee to operate.

(c) The sale proceeds have to be paid to the farmer-producers on the day of sale itself.

(d) The sales have to be conducted very transparently, generally by open auction. No secret deals are allowed.

(e) The charges to be collected for the services rendered by the functionaries in the market are fixed by the market committee called Arbitration Committee.

(f) The market charges incurred in effecting the sales have to be borne either by sellers or buyers or shared equally between the sellers and the buyers. This varies from state to state. While in some states the market charges like commission, weighmen charges, loading/unloading charges, etc. are totally borne by the farmer-producers, in some others by the buyers and in yet others equally between the sellers and buyers.

(g) Any dispute arising during the process of sale has to be referred to the arbitration committee whose decision shall be final.

(h) The market-intelligence has been strengthened. The licensed functionaries are required to submit complete details of all transaction taking place each day. This enables the committee to know the exact quantity of arrivals, sale, stocks and the prices of different commodities which are published or exhibited on notice boards everyday. This information is further disseminated to the hinterland villages of the market, which helps the farmer in judging the best time to go to the market when he can obtain best possible prices.

(i) Physical facilities like rest house, canteen, drinking water, cattle shed, etc. are provided in the regulated markets for the benefit of the farmers and their cattle.

(j) Facilities for grading and standardisation of the produce brought for sale by the farmer-producers are provided.

(k) The packing sizes for various commodities are also stipulated by the market committee, *e.g.* 75 kg bag for paddy or 180 kg bales for cotton, etc.

(l) The Central and State warehousing Corporation are expected to establish godowns near the market for the benefit of the farmer-producers. In the eventuality of the prices being low or if the produce cannot be sold on the day of arrival for any reason, they can store it in these godowns at the charges fixed by the warehouses. The receipt issued by the warehouse authorities is supposed to be a negotiable instrument, for purposes of getting loans from any bank if needed. The loan can be cleared when the produce is sold at a later date.

In short, 'Regulation of markets' has really helped the farmers in cutting down the marketing charges and to an extent exploitation also. Studies conducted on the impact of regulated markets revealed that, the number of farmers selling the produce in such markets has increased in addition to realisation of better prices. Thus, the establishment of regulated markets bas conferred tangible and intangible benefits on the farmers in terms of avoidance of malpractices and better price realisation.

FORMATION OF CO-OPERATIVE MARKETING AND PROCESSING SOCIETIES

One of the major improvement for real producers is the formation of Cooperative Marketing and Processing Societies. The farmers with common interest form Cooperative Societies, so that some of the functions performed by the intermediaries are taken over by these societies. These societies shoulder the responsibility of processing and marketing the produce for the member farmers. To increase the incomes of the farmers, it is important to involve them in processing. The processed agricultural produce becomes a 'value added' product and the benefits accrue to the farmers only. A number of cooperative societies are engaged in this activity. A good example of such an activity is the Sugar Cooperatives of Maharashtra which is very powerful both economically and politically. There are similar examples in other states also for other agricultural commodities.

A real beginning was made in the integration of Production, Processing and Marketing of milk—a highly perishable product-with the initiation of 'Operation Flood programme. This was followed by Operation Flood II and III programmes. Under this programme the dairy farmers in villages are organized into village level cooperative societies called the Dairy Cooperative Societies (DCSs). In turn the DCSs in a district form a Milk Producers' Cooperative Union at the district level. These Unions take the responsibility of collecting milk from the DCSs. processing it in their dairy and marketing it. In addition, the unions also take the responsibility of supplying the necessary inputs required for milk production to the dairy farmers. The inputs could be feed, fodder slips, health care, artificial insemination facilities, purchase of milk at an assured price and other related services. The Unions at district level form a Milk Producers Cooperative Federation at the state level. The federation renders the necessary help to the Unions and in turn to the DCSs for production, processing and marketing of milk and milkproducts, These types of organizations are popularly known as 'Amul' pattern societies. Diagrammatically, this can be represented as follows:

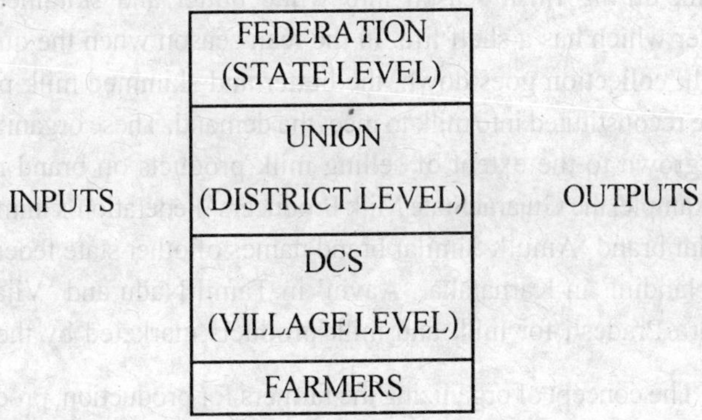

'AMUL' PATTERN ORGANIZATION

The system is functioning satisfactorily, since all the inputs required for milk production are supplied with an assurance that irrespective of the quantity of milk supplied, the pre-announced, assured prices will not change. This type of arrangement is in vogue in most of the states in the country and it is estimated that about eight million litres of milk is collected every day through these societies. The fact to be reckoned here is that the dairy farmers are the shareholders of the organisation. Hence, the value addition through processing of milk into butter, ghee, ice-cream, milk based sweets and other milk products stays within the organization. The payment for the milk supplied could be on a daily, weekly or a fortnightly basis.

At the time of payment, the cost of inputs provided is deducted. Despite being successful and widely followed throughout the country, the proportion of milk handled by this system is hardly 20 per cent of the total production of about 50 million tonnes in the country. The initial aid for this scheme was provided by the European Economic Community in the form of skimmed milk powder and butter through National Dairy Development Board set up by the Government of India, Operation Flood I concentrated on flooding all the metropolis with milk, while Operation Flood II and III concentrated on flooding the state capitals and district headquarters. By and large this scheme has proved a success. This system also provides for the conversion of milk during flush season into white butter and skimmed milk powder which has a shelf life. In the lean season when the quantum of milk collection goes down, the butter and skimmed milk powder can be reconstituted into milk to meet the demand. These organizations have grown to the extent of selling milk products on brand names. For example, the Gujarat State Milk Producers' Federation's immensely popular brand 'Amul'. Similar brand names of other state federations are 'Nandini' in Karnataka, 'Aavin' in Tamil Nadu and 'Vijaya' in Andhra Pradesh for milk and milk products marketed by them.

The concept of organizing the farmers for production, processing and marketing of agricultural produce has been accepted because of its success in the case of milk. Similar efforts are on in the area of edible vegetable oils. Here again most of the states have already established Cooperative Oilseeds Growers Federations with processing facilities and are marketing edible oil under their own brand name. Since the organization is viewed as a commercial venture, they follow modern management practices. In the case of vegetable oils also, brands like 'Safal' (Karnataka) and 'Dhara' are popular.

Similarly the Horticultural Producers Cooperative Marketing and Processing Society Ltd. (HOPCOMS) at Bangalore, is engaged in the collection of vegetables and fruits from their members for sale in Bangalore city. This started in the year 1959 as Grape Growers' Cooperative Society and then diversified itself into all horticultual produce. This society is now operating in about four districts of Kamataka and will shortly cover the entire state. The society has opened purchase centres at important locations that purchase vegetables and fruits from the farmer-producers. The produce thus collected is immediately transported to Bangalore city on their own trucks. The society has opened about 150 retail outlets in Bangalore city for sale of these vegetables and fruits to the ultimate consumers. In addition to retailing, they also undertake bulk supply to institutions, industrial canteens, etc. Here again, the intermediaries are rendered redundant as their functions are taken over by the society, keeping service as the prime objective and a very low margin to cover the costs. The members producing vegetables and fruits are only happy to sell their produce to the society. The society operates on the following lines.

(a) the price is fixed as per market conditions.

(b) up to Rs. 2,000 the payment is made immediately in cash and if above Rs. 2,000 by cheque.

(c) there are no malpractices in weightment and no unnecessary deductions are made for quality since the produce is graded before sale.

A similar arrangement exists in Andhra Pradesh also, under the name 'Fresh Marketing Society', the seven ensure the consumers that the vegetables sold to them are always fresh. From the consumer point of view also these societies are popular, as quality products can be bought at fixed prices and accurate weightment.

The present policy of the Government is to encourage establishment of food processing industries, since these are considered foreign exchange earners. This has given impetus to many an entrepreneurs and multinationals to invest in food processing industries. Already companies like Marico industries, ITC Ltd, Lipton, etc are in the edible oil manufacturing and marketing field. There have been new entrants like Pepsi also. Entry of Pepsi has given a boost to tomato cultivation in four districts of Punjab. They need about 600 tonnes of tomatoes everyday for the manufacture of tomato puree and paste for export. They have signed contracts with the farmers for growing and supplying tomatoes which they process. The farmers are given high yielding tomato seedlings and other necessary inputs for cultivation, and are supervised by agronomists and extension staff of the company. The agreement with the farmers stipulates that they sell 60 per cent of their production to Pepsi at a fixed price and they are free to sell the balance anywhere they like. The average yield of tomatoes, which was 19.5 tonnes per hectare, has now boosted to 47.5 tonnes per hectare and certain individual farmers have even obtained yield as high as 75 tonnes per hectare. During the year 1992, they procured about 43,000 tonnes of tomatoes and disbursed Rs. 8 crore to the tomato supplying farmers. This type of integration of production-processing marketing is required in the case of agricultural produce marketing.

Another example is that of 'Mahagrapes' in Pune. Mahagrapes is an organization of a number of Grape Growers Cooperative Societies in the Pune-Nasik region. To meet the stringent quality requirements of export market, this organization imported an equipment for harvesting, packing and pre cooling of grapes at a cost of Rs. 75 crore from the USA. This has enabled the Mahagrapes to effort seedless grapes to UK and West Asia. During 1991-92, they exported 2,000 tonnes of worth Rs. 8 crore. Their future plans are to reach.an export target of about 12,000 tonnes valued at about Rs. 30 crore. There are about 12,000 farmers involved in this activity. Again, this is a case of a farmers/producers' cooperative directly handling exports. All the middlemen and intermediarites are avoided and the margins at each level of operation accrue to the society, thus increasing the incomes of the farmer producers.

There are many more such examples in our country. The returns to the farmers can increase substantially if the farmer producers unite and take more initiative in processing and marketing. While the support or procurement prices have to be increased to commensurate with the increase in input prices, this may not offer a long term solution for achieving higher incomes. The farmers should be in a position to participate in processing and marking, where the value addition to the raw produce takes place.

The recent liberalisation measures initiated by the Government should have a significant impact on farm income. The Dairy industry, hitherto reserved for the cooperative sector only, is now thrown open to private sector also. With the private sectors clout of marketing, this should be a boon to the dairy farmers. The decontrol of molasses is a step in the right direction. The price for sugarcane is normally fixed in relation to the recovery of sugar, which is the main product. The molasses was almost ignored since this was under the control of the government and released at a very nominal price. But molasses, when distilled into alcohol, attains a high value. This alcohol forms the basis for Indian Made Foreign Liquor (IMFL) and acetates. From acetates one can derive the numerous chemicals for pharmaceutical industry. But this aspect is totally ignored while fixing the price of sugarcane and only the sugar output is taken into account. Since the sugar mills will be free to sell alcohol at the market price, the realizations will be more, and further passed on to the farmers, at least in the case of Cooperative Sugar Factories. Since sugar is a controlled commodity and the releases are dependent upon the government directives (65 per cent production is procured by government for distribution through the public Distribution System and only 35 per cent is allowed to be sold in the open market), as of today many factories owe money to sugarcane farmers. The immediate impact of molasses decontrol could help in clearing of dues to the farmers by the factories.

In addition, many byproducts which were of no value earlier are now being used economically with the necessary technology being available. For example, rice bran, which was normally fed to cattle, is now being used to extract rice bran oil and the de-oiled cake is fed to the cattle. Paddy straw, husk, cotton stalks are now being used for manufacturing hardboards. Bagasse, (the fibre left behind after extracting the juice from sugarcane) till now used as a fuel is now being used for the manufacture of paper, a high value product. Such technological innovations in the utilization of by-products are necessary to ensure better income to the farmers.

Traditionally our country has been importing raisins from overseas. 'Mahagrapes' mentioned earlier, is now perfecting the technology for manufacturing raisins from grapes. If the raisin-making technology is perfected, the prices of grapes during the harvest season can improve, since shelf life can be given to this perishable product. This effort of Mahagrapes has given impetus to mango farmers in Maharashtra also to think in terms of conversion of mangoes into mango powder. This powder can be remixed with water to make mango paste and then mango juice.

The impact of the development of Modern Marketing concepts, tools and techniques has been very minimal on agricultural produce marketing with liberalisation policies of the government laying special emphasis on food processing industries and thrust on exports, the scope for improvement in the system of agricultural produce marketing is enormous. This should help ensure better and higher incomes to the rural populace and consequently result in the growth of rural market.

IMPORTANCE OF RURAL AND COTTAGE AND ARTISAN INDUSTRIES

Rural and cottage industries and rural artisans are very significant to the rural economy. These have proved a source of employment and income generation for the landless population and also to the rural artisans who posses certain skins and talents acquired through generations. Most states have specialised in products like lacquer ware, bidriware, rose wood in lay and ivory items of Karnataka, meal craft and brassware of Uttar Pradesh, Bandhani and jewellery of Rajasthan, carpets and shawls of Kashmir, bell metal lamps of Kerala and bronze idols of Tamil Nadu and so on. Most of these skills are family oriented and passed on to the younger generation by elders. These products have aesthetic value are highly priced and have a good export market.

The significance of rural/cottage industry and rural artisans products can be enumerated as follows:

(1) Provides a subsidiary occupation to the rural population.

(2) Enables the rural population to supplement their slender incomes.

(3) Provides employment during off season, drought and famines.

(4) Develops rural talent and helps uphold our culture.

(5) Reduces evils of urban industrialisation.

(6) Suits a country like ours very well.

Broadly the rural/cottage industries and rural artisans products can be enumerated a follows:

(a) **Agro-based.** Ghani oil, processing of cereals and pulses, cane, gur and khandsari, pahn gur, beekeeping, coir, fruit processing and preservation and scriculture.

(b) **Textiles.** Handlooms, polyvastra, khadi.

(c) **Metal Wares.** Aluminium vessels, brassware, black smithy and agricultural tools.

(d) **Wood Related.** Match industry, carpentry bamboo and canework and hand made paper.

(e) **Leather.** Leather processing.

(f) **Pottery and ceramics.**

(g) **Chemicals.** Inks and dyes.

(h) **Fishing.** Dried fish.

(i) **Miscellaneous.** Non-edible oil soaps, lime, gobar gas, minor forest produce, shellac, gums and resins.

There is tremendous scope for developing such rural village and cottage industries which can go a long way in augmenting the employment and income of the people in rural areas.

To help such rural/cottage industries and rural artisans, produce and market their production, a number of central and state level organisations help the rural folk in:

(1) technology upgradation.

(2) Organization for the artisans.

(3) Getting credit from institutions.

(4) Procurement and supply of raw material.

(5) Establishment of works heads, where the artisans can work and use upgraded technology and equipment.

(6) Domestic marketing through retail outlets.

(7) Export marketing wherever possible.

These incentives have helped the artisans to stay in their profession and also profitably practice the trade known to them for ages without migrating to the urban areas.

These apart, there are Khadi Gram Udyog Bhawan which also render necessary help to the rural industries and artisans. Their retail outlets styled as Khadi Gram Udyog Bhandars are found all over the country. They sell a wide variety of products ranging from honey, toilet soaps, washing soaps, khadivastra, khadi silk vastra, leather shoes, and chapples, papads, match boxes cotton clothing and several other items. Basically being small producers they require support for marketing their products which such organisations are able to provide.

The All India Handicrafts Board and State Handicrafts Development Corporation also play a significant role. These organizations encourage the rural/cottage industries and artisans by providing necessary help as mentioned earlier, opened sophisticated showrooms in all metros, cities and towns for marketing the rural produce. The All India Handicrafts Board's showroom at Janpath in New Delhi attracts numerous foreign tourists. The range of products in the showroom is wide ranging. Similar showrooms are also owned and operated by State Handicraft Boards, in the country, also try to give a brand image to the products sold by them in these showrooms. For example, 'Cauvery' of Karnataka, 'Pumpuhar' of Tamil Nadu, Leepakshi of Andhra Pradesh, Gujari of Gujarat and others.

The rural handlooms sector has received a very special treatment: Since the number or people dependent on handlooms for livelihood are very large. The States have fonned state handloom weavers cooperatives for the handloom weavers in rural areas. These cooperatives also have a number of showrooms throughout the country. Since the cloth is much low-priced than the mill made cloth, the lower and middle income segments of urban population prefer to buy them. These organisations also try to promote a brand image to their products like. Cooptex of Tamil Nadu, Priyadarshini of Karnataka, Apco fabrics of Andhra Pradesh, weaver of Haryana and others. At the National level also there is a handloom development corporation which organises 'handloom fairs'.

At the national level also there is a Handloom Development Corporation which organises 'Handloom Fairs' in different parts of the country. It is not uncommon to find these organizations offering rebate on purchases during fairs and festival seasons like Deepawali or Sankaranthi to increase the sales. The marketing efforts put forth by these organizations are quite commendable. By organizing the weavers into cooperatives, assisting them in production and arranging for marketing the end products, these organisations have helped the rural people to earn more incomes.

If the rural market has to expand and grow, it is not enough to simply concentrate on marketing of manufactured goods, but it is necessary to pay attention to the marketing aspects of the rural production. *viz.,* agricultural produce aud products of rural cottage industries and rural artisans. Such an organisation will help the rural population in generating more disposable income for the purchase of manufactured goods. In other words the marketability of rural produce has to be improved significantly to ensure a market for consumables, durables and services.

❑

3

Attitude and Behviour of Rural Marketing

BACKGROUND OF RURAL MARKETING

In a country like India for a long time marketing has been used for urban marketing, but these days the scene is different. These days rural marketing is being widely used and discussed topic among researches. The composition of population shows that nearly 70% of the population is still living in villages and 40% of total Gross National Product (GNP) emanating from agriculture, 93% million consumers are classified as rural middle class. The rural development is fuelled by government policy which covers 50% of the plan outlay be available for agricultural or rural development.

The Government is giving assured support price for agricultural produce, remittances flowing from within India and abroad, and the programme of Industrial dispersal in backward rural areas. These resulted in the process of rural agricultural markets for consumers as well as for products boosting agricultural yields, thus, rural marketing in India is fast growing in all its dimensions. There are two important aspects of Indian Rural Marketing:

(i) These provides vast opportunities, and

(ii) These displays intimidating Challenges.

The rural markets is totally new markets involving new customers and new marketing situations. Here an attempt is made to face some challenges of Rural Marketing which further has two broad ways to action:

(a) Broad dimension of rural markets,

(b) Point out (high light) tile thrust and challenges.

(a) Broad Dimensions of Rural Markets. Indian rural consumers vary tremendously in their age, income, educational level, mobility pattern and taste.

The size of India's rural consumers is shown in the following table:

POPULATION OF INDIA: RURAL—URBAN 1971-1991

	1971	*1981*	*1991*	*Increase over previous decade in absolute numbers*	
				1981	*1991*
Rural Population (in crores)	43.90	50.20	60.21	+ 6.30	10.01
Urban Population (in crores)	10.91	15.62	24.18	+ 4.17	8.56
Total	54.81	65.82	84.39	+ 11.01	17.57

Source: Rural Development Statistics. National Institute of Rural Development. Hyderabad.

The above table shows that more than 70 per cent of the total population was rural according to the 1991 Census. It shows that while in absolute terms the total population of the country had gone up sizeably from 54 crore to 84 crore, the rural-urban proportions remained more or less the same as in 1971-1981. During two decades the size of rural markets had increased from 44 crore to 60 crore. Apparently, therefore, in terms of the number of people, the Indian rural market is almost twice as large as the entire market of the USA and the former USSR.

The state level picture, shows that in several states like UP, MP, Rajasthan and Kerala, the rural population constitutes more than 80 per cent of the total population. There are also states like Bihar and Orissa where as much as 90 per cent of the total population is rural.

Location Pattern of Rural Consumers. The 60 crore rural Indian consumers are scattered unevenly.

This is shows in the following table:

DISTRIBUTION OF RURAL CONSUMERS

Size of Villages (based on population)	*No. of villages in group*	*Population in the group ('000)*
Less than 200	1,50,072	15,246
200—499	1,68,561	56,628
500—999	1,32,990	93,412
1000—1999	87,973	1,13,162
2000—4999	36,005	1,04,547
5000—9999	4,974	32,717
1000 and above	1,358	22,334

Source: Rural Development Statistics.

It can be seen from the above Table that out of the 5,76,000 villages, only 6,300 villages have a population of more than 5,000 persons each. More than three lakh villages or 55 per cent of the total are in the class of 500 persons or less and more than 1.5 lakh villages or 25 per cent of the total in the class of 200 or less. Thus, generally, villages with a population of less than 2,000 will have higher components of lower income consumers. Such villages would primarily be markets for daily necessities like matches, cooking oil, salt etc.

Literacy Level of Rural Consumers. It is estimated that rural India has a 27 per cent literacy rate compared with 50 per cent of the whole country. The adult literacy programmes launched by the government in the rural areas are bound to enhance the rural literacy rate to some extent in the years to come. Literacy is one of the important variables that determine the consumption patterns and buying styles.

Age-wise Distribution of Rural Population is as:

AGE-WISE DISTRIBUTION OF RURAL POPULATION

Age group (in year)	*Share of total 1971*	*Population 1986*
0—4	15.8	10.6
5—15	25.6	22.7
15—59	53.4	60.5
60 & above	5.2	6.2

Source: India Basic statistics, published by Ministry of Government of India, Information and Broadcasting.

It can be seen from the above Table that by 1991 more than 60 per cent of the total rural population constituted adults, and that only 10 per cent belonged if the 60 years + group. This gives an idea of the emerging youth market in rural market.

Return Income Pattern. The source pattern of rural income is shown as:

SOURCE PATTERN OF RURAL INCOME

Source of Income	*Proportion to total %*
Agriculture	58.8
Agricultural wages	16.1
Business and Crafts	8.8
Non-Agricultural Wages	7.2
Salaries	2.5
Current Transfer	1.9
Others	4.7
Total	100.0

The income pattern shown in the above Table reveals that nearly 60 per cent of the rural income is from agriculture. Evidently, rural prosperity and the discretionary income with the rural consumer are directly tied up with agricultural prosperity, which directly results in increased income for the rural people and a consequent increase in their capacity to spend. The predominance of agriculture in the income pattern has one more dimension; rural income and therefore rural demand are relatively more seasonal.

Consumer Expenditures in Rural Areas. The rural consumer generally uses 40 per cent of his total spending on non-food items.

CONSUMER EXPENDITURE IN RURAL AREAS
(Value in per person for a period of 30 days)

	Amount	*Percentage to Total*
Food	110.25	64.1
Non-Food	61.82	35.9
Total	172.00	100.0

Source: Rural Development Statistics.

Media and Media Reach in Rural Markets. The following table speaks about media and media in rural markets:

MEDIA AND MEDIA REACH IN RURAL MARKETS

	Percentage of Rural Adult Population	*Total Number (million)*
Press	9	32
Radio	32	113
TV	31	108
Cinema	36	125
	Total Adults	352

The TV Satellite Expansion Programmes launched by the government are bound to enhance to some extent the media reach in rural areas. This will help in building a national market for a product.

Statistics on saving patterns reveals that, in recent years, the rural consumers have been drawn into the saving habit in a big way. Commercial banks and co-operative have been marketing the banking habit in rural areas for quite some years.

To sum up, broadly, it can easily be seen that the winds of change are blowing and transforming the rural market appreciably. The revolution of rising expectation is gaining ground, incomes are increasing, literacy level is going up, transport and communication facilities are improving, and transport and credit facilities have increased substantially in rural markets.

(b) Thrust for Developing New Cousciousness About Rural Marketing. The broad emerging profile of rural marketing, indicates that in future marketing in rural markets is a challenging task. In the coming future, in order to meet the expectations and aspirations of rural consumers, the business practitioners, marketers, marketing. scientists and scholars, will all have to encounter the realities of such expanding rural markets.

Indian rural economy is characterised by several features, *viz.*, large but dispersed; erratic seasonal and yearly variations; poor transport facilities; inherent resistance to change and irrational geographical variations owing to differences in life-style beliefs, consumption pattern and purchasing power. An understanding and analysis of these factors needs a new approach to the study of the dynamics of rural marketing.

Study of rural marketing in India will have to be approached as a competitive general marketing system. The marketing system is not synonymous with the functioning of the economy. In view of rapid adoption of liberalisation, privatisation and free economy policies adopted by the Government of India, it will be a mistake to conceptualise the marketing system or even market economy as capitalism. Instead, the character and capacity of the market system must be conceptualised in terms of the historical background and drift, the traditional legal system, and social and political goals and value system of society.

If the marketing practitioners/scholars desire to contribute to rural prosperity, they will have to widen the scope of the study of rural marketing and treat it separately-keeping aside the present principles of marketing, which have exclusive orientation to urban marketing.

The questions they will have to answer may be listed as below:

1. What is the domain of rural marketing as a field of study?
2. What are the boundaries and the areas of business practices?
3. What is the role of marketing in modern rural society?
4. What about marketing ethics, values, responsibilities and Marketing—Government relationships?

In coming decades, it is hoped that rural marketing as a function of business will possess a social role, distinct from the personal role. This can be achieved by developing Rural Marketing as a distinct discipline.

RURAL PRODUCTS

The commodity approach refers not only to the manufactured goods *i.e.*, both consumer goods and industrial goods, but also the study of goods made by the art of rural. Rural goods require more of natural conveniences than of human efforts. No doubt, human efforts are required to produce them, but nature plays a vital role in determining the quality and quantity of the crops grown and harvested. In this chapter, we concentrate our study on the characteristics and marketing considerations in general and rural marketing in India in particular.

Rural products are the result of the art of agriculture and allied activities. In a narrow sense, rural products refer to the products arising out of the cultivation, namely various crops, vegetables and fruits etc. In a broader sense, agricultural goods arise out of cultivation, dairy farming, poultry farming, pig farming etc. Thus eggs, butter, cheese, fluid milk, meat etc., are also the rural products and also handloom, weaving, spinning, fisheries, gur products etc.

Types of Rural Goods

These rural products are classed into two categories *viz.*, 'industrial' goods and 'consumer' goods. 'Industrial-rural' goods are those used for further industrial processing, *e.g.*, tobacco, fibre crops like cotton and jute; eggs, and butter used in bakeries, vegetables and fruits canned and pickled, wheat and gram used by flour mills to grind them. On the other hand the 'consumer-rural' goods are meant for direct use, like all foodgrains, dairy products, poultry products, vegetables and fruits. This classification is not rigid, as some of the rural goods become both consumer goods and industrial goods, depending upon the use to which they are put *e.g.*, in the case of fruits especially, if they are consumed directly by the consumers, they become 'consumer goods', and if the same fruits are used in canning factory, they become industrial goods. Another best example can be cited is that of groundnut. If used for home consumption, it becomes consumer good and if used for production of oil, it becomes industrial good. This point is to be borne in mind.

Characteristics of Rural Products

1. Small Scale Production. The production of rural goods is carried on a very small scale as compared to the production of manufactured goods, The techniques and principles of large scale production are not applied to a greater extent. This is particularly true in case of developing countries, like India; and where 75 per cent of the total supply comes from small scale producers even in sophisticated countries like U.S,A., Japan, etc, In India, it is still higher. Such small production is mainly due to the small size of farms of land holdings, The marketing of such small production creates certain problems, Marketing cannot be effective, because grading and standardisation are not possible, There is no economy in transportation, As a result, the farmers are unable to influence the market price by individual actions. Therefore, they have to depend upon the middlemen or co-operative societies in the marketing of their goods.

2. Scattered and Specialized Production. Scattered production of rural goods is a univesal truth. The natural conditions like quality of the soil and climate make rural production scattered and specialised. Moreover, every piece of land and every type of climate does not suit the productions of all rural goods. The fertility of the land varies, from place to place and particular climate and contents of the soil, and rainfall go to determine the crops to be grown. Different areas are suitable for growing different crops, *e.g.* sugarcane is mainly grown in Uttar Pradesh, Karnataka, Maharashtra in India; Jawa, and Cuba, are other world tends to specialise in the production of certain commodities. Thus, geographical localisation and specialisation are common.

3. Variation in Quality. The quality and quantity vary invariable from area to area, time to time, depending on the changes in climate, fertility of the soil, rainfall, are of cultivation etc. It is beyond the control of producers to assure the quality and quantity. Number of natural, calamities come in the way of rural production. Flood, frost, drought, hail storms, animal and plant diseases, insects, are some of the natural threats which affect rural production. Though, attempts are being made to climate and prevent certain diseases of the natural threats which affect agricultural production. Though, attempts are being made to eliminate and prevent certain diseases of the plant and animals, still man is not having control over the quality and quantity of crops that are grown. Because of these variations, there are effects even on the storage and transport facilities. Sometimes, when bumper crops are yielded, there is more demand for storage and transport facilities and reverse is the case when there is no or less yield.

4. Seasonal Production. Production of rural goods is seasonal. They are not grown throughout the year. They grow only during certain months of the year, depending upon the rainfall and climatic conditions. Bnt the demand for them is spread throughout the year, *e.g.*, paddy, cotton, jowar, etc. are harvested from December to March but are demanded continuously. Therefore, the goods move from the producing centres to the consumption centres because of this, there usually occurs a 'peak load' in their sale, and lience, on storage, transportation and financing. These services tend to increase the cost of marketing relatively.

5. Bulky and Perishable Products. Rural goods are bulky in nature. The intrinsic value is quite low as compared to their bulky appearance and size. This makes transportation and warehousing costly. Majority of the rural goods are perishable. That is, they cannot last long. Fruits, vegetables, milk eggs, flowers, etc., are prone to perishability high order. Therefore, they need recent improvements in refrigeration and transportation. The foodgrains like wheat, jowar, rice and cotton, tobacco, which are to be stored for a considerable period of time without deterioration, do require proper storage facilities. This, again increases the cost of marketing.

6. Inelastic Demand. Inelastic demand is a special feature of the rural goods. Inelastic refers to unchanged demand. That is, whether the prices rise or fall, the demand for agricultural goods, remains more or less the same; there is no change in the demand. Neither it falls, nor it increases with the variation or fluctuations in price. If a product in short supply its price rises automatically, If the supply increases the price falls. That is why, rural goods always face the problem of price stabilisation.

LATEST TRENDS IN RURAL MARKETING

There have been developments even in the field of rural marketing as there are developments in research and technology these days. The traditional system of rural marketing have been left off and new methods of marketing have made their beginning. The recent trends in rural marketing may be classified under two heads namely decentralisation of marketing and development in the system of input and output of rural products.

1. Decentralisation of Rural Marketing. First of all, the rural goods used to move through the channel of local market, central, jobbing market or secondary market and ultimately to either consumers or industrial usrs. But now, this trend has changed and decentralisation has poked its nose even in this field of marketing. The central market is left aside and the goods move directly either from the producers, or from the middlemen in the focal market, to the jobbing market or consumers or industrial users.. This means that there is a market change in the distribution channel; and marketing of rural goods is decentralised. This decentralisation is due mainly to the following factors:

(a) **Development of Modern Facilities of Transportation.** Development of modern facilities of transportation have helped to cover the wide area, for the collection of agricultural goods. This is true, especially, in case of agricultural raw-materials like sugarcane, which is collected by the manufacturers directly, from the farms producers and some consumer goods like fruits, vegetables etc.

(b) **The Improved Warehousing Facilities and Cold Storage Arrangements.** The improved warehousing facilities and cold storage arrangements have succeeded in reducing the deterioration of quality of the products.

(c) **The Modern Communication System.** The modern communication system makes it possible to collect information about prices and supplies in the market and thus, reduces the reliance on the middlemen, in the central market.

(d) **Standardization Grading.** Standardization and grading, speak of the quality of the products and hence, the buyers do not feel like observing and inspecting the goods.

(e) **The Tendency of Eliminating the Middlemen.** The tendency of eliminating the middlemen has reached its peak, when we look at the establishment of certain large scale retail organisations, like departmental stores, super markets, chain stores etc.

(f) **Rise and Development of Co-operative Marketing Societies.** Last, but not the least, the rise and development of co-operative marketing societies and regulated markets have ensured the decentralisation process.

2. Development of Specialised Services. Since 1965 the government of India has been making its sincere efforts to provide specialised services in the field of rural marketing. On the basis of the recommendations made by Dr. Rajender Sachher an institute of standardisation and grading was started in 1965 at Pune having its local centres in Cherni, Calcutta, Mumbay, and Delhi also having 17 regional centres. These institutes provide training to the marketing employees regarding standardization and grading. The development of transportation facilities has also been a stimulating factor in the development of rural marketing. The Warehousing, FCI and Central Warehousing Corporation have also contributed towards the growth of rural marketing. Banking, insurance companies and tetiaty sectors has also paved a way towards the growth and development of rural marketing.

3. Classification of Marketing Functions. Various authors have classified the functions of marketing in different ways. Thompson has classified the marketing function into three categories. First may be regarding primary function which includes assembling of the products, processing of the product, distribution of the products. It covers a long range or a wide network that how the products are reached from producers to consumers. This is the basic objective of the marketing. The second function of marketing is relating with the secondary type of functions. It may include packing or packaging, transportation, standardisation and grading, quality control, storage and warehousing, price determination, risk bearing, financing, creating of demand and supply of market information system. These are the secondary type of functions without which the process of marketing cannot take place. These functions are the supporting functions, which make the process of marketing a specialised and perfect market. These are deemed as aids to marketing structure. The third type of functions may include banking, insurance, and communications. It also includes the facilities of post and telegraph and energy and powers. Banking and insurance works just as the life blood in the meal system insurance covers the different types of risks and protects the interest of the producers and buyers. Communication may be defined as the transmission of the message from senders to receivers and receiver receive the messages in the same sense and same spirit. Communication plays an important role in the development of any marketing system. With the help of communication marketing information system can be better known. With the up-to-date, current and accurate marketing information system, the system of marketing can be used and worked out effectively, efficiently and smoothly.

One more expert in marketing management Huegy and Mitchell has classified the function of marketing into three types. The first type of function may include storage, packing, transportation, grading, and distribution. Again the first function of marketing relates with the specialised services. The second function of marketing is defined as ownership movements functions which may include creating demand, finding out buyers and sellers, negotiation of price, rendering advice and transferring the title to goods. The second function explain the process of marketing when the subject matter of the goods is reached from sellers to buyers. The third function is classified market management functions. These functions are advisory and staff in nature which may include auditing, supervision, accounting, formulating policies and procedures and lastly securing information regarding the marketing. Thus we can say that different authors have explained the functions of marketing management in different way from the different point of view.

OBJECTIVES OF STUDYING THE RURAL MARKETING

The objectives of studying the Rural Marketing are listed as:

1. Wide Coverage. Rural Marketing has attracted a great deal of attention in recent times in all areas of trade and industry and Government circles, and evoked discussions among marketing men because of its pre-eminent position in the Indian economy. The Rural Marketing, has always been seen as an unmanageable territory, because of its vastness and scattered nature.

2. Shift in Market Strategy. Producer while producing a product, pay little attention to the Rural Section of the society. Most of the production is set for an urban target market though the percentage population in urban areas are comparatively low. To a layman, such a strategy may sound surprising. Thus, it needs revision in the views of buyer behaviour in the urban and the rural segments.

3. Disposable Income. The general level of disposable incomes among rural consumers, as compared to urban consumers is low. They purchase products which not only meet their needs but also give a fair exchange for their money. Rural consumers may be illiterate but they are not naive. They have a fairly good feel' of the real value of money worth of a product.

4. Change of Attitude. The rural buyer in India shows a tremendous range of contradiction and paradoxes which baffle marketing people who have lived mostly in urban areas, and even more the new entrants, *i.e.* foreign multinationals. In the rural areas, most of the products consumed are in the nature of basic wage goods, such as soap, cooking oil, tea, kerosene etc.

5. Rural Marketing Needs Communication. Communication with the people in these areas is difficult as only a small percentage of them are literate. There are variations in the type of products demand in different areas because of climatic conditions, attitude towards living, level of literacy, income etc.

6. Quick Awareness. Rural marketing has generated quick awareness about consumer products in villages. The rapid expansion of television during the last decade has contributed significantly to educate the rural consumer about availability of convenience products.

7. Addition in Knowledge about Quality of Products and After-sales Services. With the process of economic development at a high speed the totally new market of the rural areas has been thrown open. The rural population values quality and after sales services as much as urban buyer, even when Indigenously made local products are much cheaper. The marketing to the rural consumeris no cake-walk, more and more marketers are waking up to this home truth. The comparative figures to prove are as : The rural contribution to the total market has gone up from 28% in 1985 to 40% in 1990 and market size is estimated to be in the range of Rs. 5000 crore.

8. Addition in Purchasing Power. Rural marketers have realised that the purchasing power of the rural population and changing marketing strategies will bring about changes in advertising n the near future. People in crores are rising above poverty-line as well as becoming literate. The purchasing power has increased, a new and large middle class has emerged in all areas, urban, semi-urban, and rural.

9. Big Entrants to Rural Markets. The contribution of big multinational players like Hindustan Lever, Colgate-Palmolive and Proctor & Gamble, to name a few, continue to rule the roost in rural areas, and the new entrants follow in their footsteps to emulate their success.

10. Knowledge of Buying Period. One should take into account the buying period of villagers which is in general: Diwali, Dusshera, Baisakhi, Onam and Pongal are the periods of buying household articles. The buying habits of the rural consumers tend to be subject to local, religious, cultural and social pressures, and vary greatly from one region to another. One of the keys, to success in the rural markets is taking these regional variables seriously in formulating, designing, packaging and advertising of products.

The entry of the marketers posses relatively more expensive than entering into urban markets, of course there are huge potential in rural markets in Indies.

Factors Responsible for Rural Marketing Development/Growth

Since the mid-eighties, a silent revolution has occurred in rural India, the bumper crops, increasing purchasing power and accessibility, the most powerful and cost effective communication media in the form of television. Acceptance and adoption of new agronomic practices, selective mechanisation, multiple cropping to include non-food crops, and growth of dairying have resulted in a substantial increase in the disposable incomes of rural consumers.

Following is the list of examining the impact of the following key factors inherent in the emergence, growth and development of rural marketing in India:

1. Infrastructure. Development of infrastructure and communication links resulting from the growth of the information-technology industry has resulted in the rural buyer having enhanced access to product offerings in the marketplace.

2. Electricity Supply. More than 70 per cent of the villages in India have been electrified. It allows wider and cheaper utilisation of ground water removing dependence on rain for irrigation, which has a direct impact on the cropping pattern. Farmers are now well-equipped for and experienced in developing an economic mix of long and short duration crops. This flexibility in cropping pattern has stabilized their income, eliminating the factor of seasonability in income receipts, and also increased their disposable incomes.

3. Literacy. Since independence, literacy has been a thrust area of successive governments. We have witnessed a shift towards non-agricultural income-generating activities among young literates of rural India. The movement and migration of rural literates to nearby urban areas for employment and settlement have also influenced the disposable income levels of rural families. Rural literacy has also facilitated better brand recognition and retention in rural markets. The buying behaviour has changed from male heads of families exclusively making decisions to active involvement and participation of other family members with increased access to product-market information, made possible by wider media options available to advertisers.

4. Road Networking. Road networking has added to and improved the mobility and communication links among the rural consumers. It has increased their exposure to innovative and fast-moving products and services. It has also enabled them to collect the most recent updates on agronomic practices to improve crop yields for higher returns. This has a direct significant impact on price realisation by them also. Road networking has facilitated moving of produce and monitoring of its prices in towns, maximising their returns.

More than 40 per cent of villages today are connected by all weather roads. This, in turn, has increased communication links. The reach and exploitation of rural markets by Indian companies have become feasible. This has resulted in systemised product distribution upto the village unit level. It has brought about it modified and improved distribution system whereby an increasing number of companies are now servicing village markets directly. The objective is product promotion, pushing customers to buy non-durables, and pulling them to dealer-points in case of durables.

5. Change in Social Values, Norms and Structure. Improved infrastructure, interaction with media, greater and diverse influences of urban markets on rural consumer, emphasis on education, borrowing, buying process, savings and investment patterns have brought about significant changes in socio-economic values, bringing individual behaviour and action to the centre-stage from the social fabric and influence of village groups or rural consumers. Their adaptability to a new offering has become quicker and more responsive due to changes inutility and usage perception of products and services. The time gap in converting a potential rural buyer into an actual buyer is gradually declining. The savings and investment patterns of rural consumers have change in favour of consumer durables, and their participation has become positive in banking and capital market activities of the country. An irrevocable process towards consumerism has been activated in a large part of rural India.

6. Rural Consumption. The changing social system, increase in the number of earning family members, access to credit facilities, new product innovation, demonstration effects, status value attached to products etc., have led not only to a growing rural market but also to a shift in the consumption pattern. The rural market presents an exciting opportunity to develop brands into generic product association.

The total size of the rural market for packaged consumer goods today is estimated at over Rs. 2,100 crore, which is barely 1.14 per cent of the net rural income. Rural consumption gives every indication that the past has been a mere precursor to high-profile rural marketing in the future. According to a National Council of Applied Economic Research (NCEAR) report in . 1987-88 the rural sector will have a major share in the rising and changing, durables market. In specific categories, such as portable radios, bicycles and wrist-watches, the rural share exceeds 70 per cent. Nearly 56 per cent of the total market for dry battery cells, 53 per cent of the popular toilets soaps market and 50 per cent of the razor blades market, were accounted for in the mid-eighties, by rural markets. In washing powder, the rural share exceeds 40 per cent.

With the urban markets for toilets soaps, washing powder and talcum powders fast reaching saturation levels, marketers cannot afford to look down upon the rural markets. The rural market is vibrant, discerning, and at the current rate of growth will outstrip the urban market.

The vast potentiality of the rural market, like a gold mine, has raised issues related to the role and attitude of the industry and the Indian marketers in creating new marketing opportunities and developing the rural market rather than merely exploiting those that already exist. Are they able to achieve it? Can they take sales for granted? Effective rural marketing should be consumer-centred, but unfortunately, the industry sees itself as merely a beneficiary of the changes and developments taking place in the countryside, and not as a catalyst of or contributor to the changes. Industry associations have merely become for a for hackneyed platitudes on rural marketing. Sustained growth and development of rural markets are possible only if there is constant improvement in the living standards of rural consumers. A Development Marketing Approach which could nurture the rural markets of India could be as follows:

Development Marketing Approach. The emphasis of industry and marketers should be on development marketing rather than conventional marketing because of following considerations:

(a) It would help in promoting the incomes and living standards of rural consumers.

(b) If industry contributes to developing relevant communication links, it will enable them to understand the rural markets better.

(c) The industry should identify, develop and promote campaigns like those of National Literacy Commission, National Immunisation Commission, Ecology, Family Planning etc.

(d) The industly should make social marketing an integral feature. The only way to create marketing awareness is to have a kind of public relations approach. It could further help companies to cash in on the "goodwill" created among the public as well as the government.

Planning and Participation in Developmental Schemes. The industry and the government should join hands to make development efforts more meaningful. The industry should contribute to the development effort py participating in schemes like Jawahar Rozgar Yojana (JRY), as they offer employment, and thereby create instant purchasing power. The industry is more than capable of promoting rural development as can be seen from the successful efforts by GSFF, GNFC, KRIBHCO, in developing model villages. Setting up of agro-service centres and information service centres by GNFC and IFFCO; development of demonstration farms by GNFC, Union Carbide's Eveready's Jeevan Sathi campaign, and ITC's film for promoting Honeydew cigarettes, group-meetings of farmers by GSFC, village fairs, festivals and melas are a few such developmental activities.

On the other side, if we take the entire industry into consideration, its efforts in this direction, instead of serving as replicable models for development, have remained mere showpieces of a few industrial enterprises,

Professional bodies and associations could bring success stories to the notice of planners and help the cause of development. Lastly, the industry will have to be a watchdog of such developmental programmes.

The industry must recognise that rural marketing is out and out developmental marketing. It is often said that markets are made, not found. This is especially true of the rural markets of India.

RURAL MARKETING SCENARIO

There are about 5,76,000 villages in India, 75% of our population lives in villages. A rural market is any market that exists in the rural areas with a population less than 10,000.

Rural Market Scenario. The rural consumer the Important features of rural consumers are as:

1. Price Policy. Mostly village people do not understand the trade and price policy followed by traders or Government.

2. Education. The villagers are not well-read. They are ignorant about their rights because of low level of education. They are mostly disorganised and do not create enough pressure on traders or Government to bother about their interests.

3. Seasonal Demand. The purchasing levels of the rural consumers vary on a seasonal basis. For example, during harvests and festive seasons, purchases increase abnormally.

4. Poor Savings. The villagers have poor purchasing power. They consider bargaining and comparative shopping as necessary techniques for buying.

5. Size of Rural Consumer Group. The census data reveal a clear picture of the size of the rural consuming group. Though the urbanisation percentage had increased, according to the 1991 census, by 2.4, the rural population constituted 74.3 per cent. Of course, inter-state variations exist. In several states like UP, MP, Rajasthan and Kerala, the rural population constitutes more than 80 per cent of the total population.

5. Pattern of Rural Income. Nearly 75 per cent of the rural income comes from agriculture and agricultural wages taken together. Hence, the prosperity and the discretionary income with the rural consumer are directly tied up with agricultural prosperity.

Life Cycle of Rural Vs Urban Markets. Table-1 gives a picture of the stage of the Life Cycle (LC) by-products of both urban and rural markets in India.

TABLE-1

Production	*Urban*	*Rural*
Population Soaps	Maturity	Growth
Soap Cakes/Bars	Decline	Maturity
Batteries	Decline	Growth
Talcum Powders	Maturity	Growth
Washing Powders	Late Growth	Early Growth
Premium Soap	Late Growth	Early Growth

Source: ORG Data Base, A& M, January, 1991

7. Size and Composition of Rural Demand. Value of non-food items at current prices gives some idea about the potentiality of the rural market. This was in the range of Rs. 18,000 crore in 1987-88. The annual growth rate since 1970-71 is around 2.5 per cent.

8. Composition of Rural Market. The rural market can be divided into two major segments for the purpose of analysis of the nature of its composition. They are:

The market for consumption goods including both fast moving consumer goods and durables, and

The market for agricultural inputs and other investment goods.

Market for consumer goods. It is estimated by the National Sample Survey that, of the total expenditure on manufactured consumer goods, 75 per cent is spent in rural India. There is an unprecedented expansion, particularly in the range and sophistication of the consumer products. The rural market for non-food items, which was Rs. 5,000 crore at current prices in 1970-71, stood at Rs. 18,000 crore in 1987-88. There has been a marked change in the rural expenditure pattern with the ratio between food and non-food items going down from 71 : 21 in 1976 to nearly 60 : 30 in 1989. A number of varieties of products have already been well-established in the rural markets. (See Exhibit-1).

Exhibit-1

Consumer Non-Durables	*Consumers Durables*
* Washing soaps	* TV-Colour & B & W
* Premium soaps	* Bicycles
* Packaged tea	* Electric irons
* Condoms	* Pressure cookers
* Talcum powder/cosmetics	* Wrist watches
* Educational stationery	* Portable radios
* Readymade garments/	* Ceiling fans
* Dress materials.	* Two-wheelers
	* Power tillers
	* Harvesters.

Thus, the perception that the rural consumers consume only some essential items and traditional produce, and that they constitute a small segment of the rural market is not true. At present, they occupy a large area, compared to the share of the urban market. The new product adoption process has become faster. There has been a shift from a shave by the village barber to individuals buying and using razors and shaving cream. The saving and investment pattern of the rich is shifting from gold and land to tractors, harvesters, VCRs, and even stocks and shares. This is evident from the data presented in Table-2.

TABLE 2

Products	*Purchase per 1,000 Households* *Top 1%**	*Bottom 60%***
B & W TV	38	3
Portable radio	70	18
Ceiling fans	71	8
Bicycles	70	32
Electnc irons	41	3
Pressure cookers	69	5
Mechanical wrist watches	141	32
Quartz wrist watches	128	13

* With income per household per annum of over Rs. 50,000/-.
** With income per household per annum of up to Rs. 11,000/-
Source: The Economic Times, Calcutta, October 22, 1992.

The rural share in packaged consumer goods had grown 28 per cent in 1984 to over 42 per cent in 1992. In specific product categories such as radio sets, bicycles, wrist watches, detergent cakes and cigarettes, the rural share exceeds 70 per cent.

Market for agricultural inputs: Progressive agriculture demands among other things, improvement in inputs and methods of irrigation, improved seeds,better manures and fertilisers, plant protection, use of mechanisation, etc. The new agricultural strategy protection, use of mechanisation, etc. The new agricultural strategy is based on increased use of fertilisers. A wide market for fertilisers exists in the rural sector. The production of nitrogenous fertilisers rose from 11,000 tonnes to 4 million tonnes (approximately) between 1950-51 and 1992-93. During the same period, production of phosphatic fertilisers rose from 16,000 tonnes to 1 million tonnes. So, the fertiliser consumption rate among the farmers is increasing very fast. All these lead to a good market in rural areas.

The Marketing Research Department of Hindustan Lever Ltd., in a survey of farm practices in AP., Punjab and Haryana, observed that farmers are showing more and more interest in using advanced agricultural technology for raising profits, and are prepared to take up a challenge. Naturally, more and more agricultural inputs have come to the rural areas to meet the needs of the farmers. The manufactures of various agricultural inputs and implements take a lot of pains to demonstrate the use and application of the same. For example, IFFCO has taken several agricultural fields for demonstrating the technique of fertilizer application and the advantages of such application. .

India has shown impressive advances in the areas of dairy products and fisheries. There are, at present, 238 dairy plants comprising 126 liquid milk plants, 47 milk product factories, and 75 pilot milk projects. India has now become the fourth largest producer of milk in the world.

Indian farmers are now aware of the importance of improved seeds. They enable them to produce more and more high quality crops. With the introduction of the High Yielding Varieties programme, the need for stepping up the production of better seeds has grown considerably. The government is also taking the initiative for direct marketing of seeds through several agencies like National Seeds Corporation. There are also Seed Development Corporations in some of the states.

❑

4

Retail Trading

HISTORY OF RETAILING

The early peddler with his trinkets had to go from tribe to tribe and from village to village either on foot or by donkey as fast moving transport vehicles were not available. In the orient, the camel was used and long caravans loaded with only luxury goods like spices, silks etc. The earliest traders were the Cretans who sailed the Meditarraneans and carried on trade with the people of that area. The Phoenicians followed the Cretans as the traders of this region. These merchants Specialised in shipping, during this period. These shipping merchants sold goods in retail and wholesale to other regions. Tyre and Sidon became the great market cities of the world. Phoenician traders succeeded by the Romans. The first middlemen who specialised in marketing were probably retailers, but they had no allegiance to consumer sales. They used to sell to producers, other merchants or consumers.

During the time of Roman Empire, shops became numerous in Rome and other cities of the empire. Numerous small shops were set up within veritable shopping centres. Roman ruins indicate that the world's first departmental store was in Rome. The fall of the Roman Empire marked the collapse of retail trade also.

The period following the Roman Empire was known as 'dark ages' in the history of retailing. During this period, the chief means of retailing was only peddlurs, who with their stores on their backs used to go from village to village to sell their goods. Dishonesty in trading was not uncommon and the traders used to deceive the villagers by offering inferior quality goods for higher prices. This was the reason why the rulers, scholars and priests looked down the retailing profession. There were instances of penalising the traders for their malpractices. This is clear from the Magna Charta when it reads, "merchants shall have safety to go and come, to buy and sell without any evil tolls, but by ancient and honest customs". During the tenth century, trade began to revive in a number of Italian cities.

The centre of the resurgence of trade was England and other Italian cities. Merchant middlemen developed by 1000 AD and specialists like smith, tailor, cobbler, miller, baker etc., emerged. They were among the first of the modern retailers, though their basic function was production. These producer retailers sold directly to consumers, by hawking their goods from village to village or street to street.

During 13th century, markets and fairs, assumed greater importance. These early markets and fairs had a religious foundation. On festival days, people used to gather at religious places and exchange their goods besides worshipping. Later, it became customary for people to gather at religious places for the exchange of goods. Therefore, it was said "there is no great festival without a fair, no fair without a festival". These markets and fairs were to be held with royal sanction. The king promised peace and security to the life and property. There were number of laws to regulate these markets and fairs such as, no fair can be allowed within 7 miles of the previously established fair, no selling can be carried out before or after the fair, no false rumours can be spread. Forestalling, regrating and engrossing were prohibited.

In the early period of history, they have no permanent establishments at one place. The larger markets were called fairs and which lasted for longer period. They were very few in number. Merchants from all over the country and even from foreign countries used to attend these fairs, for selling their goods. Though barter was the order of the day, gold and silver was also used as a medium of exchange, to some extent. Gradually, fairs became places of amusement as well as trading centres. The practice of holding the fairs can be seen even today, in rural areas, in the form of jatharas or melas and in urban areas, in the form of trade fairs, exhibitions, etc. The recently held trade fairs in the name of India Fair by Indian Government in countries like the U.S.A., France, Germany etc., come closer to this concept. The markets of short duration (lesser than that of fairs) by a week or so are popularly known as weekly markets. Though there are no evidences of these weekly markets in Western countries, it was very much practiced in backward countries. It is strongly believed that since the time gap between the fairs was much longer, in some cases years and months, the fairs could not satisfy the consumers' desire for more goods in frequent intervals. This must have prompted the merchants to hold markets with a shorter gap of time-say a week or fortnight. These weekly markets are prevalent in almost all the backward countries of the world including India. Those who were unable to go to the fairs and weekly markets were served by the peddlers who procured goods from fairs and weekly markets.

By about 15th century, a new development in the history of retailing occurred. Artisans and tradesmen no longer depended solely on fairs and markets or hats for selling their goods, but opened small shops. This was also necessitated by the fact that the consumers wanted goods in more frequent intervals on daily basis and that too at the vicinity of their residences. This shopping culture was the result of unlimited wants of modern age and also increased purchasing power. In the beginning, there used to be a wooden frame in front of the house called 'stall' upon which goods were displayed for sale. Later these were developed into a permanent stacking equipment called sbop. The early English shopkeeper had his home and his shop under the same roof in which front served as shop and the back part for residence. In order to identify the type of shop, some signs were to be put in front of their shops. To promote sales, someone used to be kept outside the shop to cry the articles available in the shop. The shop system had become quite successful in England. Their importance can be observed from the Napolean's reference to the English as a "nation of shopkeepers". Though in America, the retailer has reached the highest levels in the business and social life, most of the American retailing institutions originated only after 1850. Prior to that, most Americans lived in rural areas and were self-sufficient. Transportation was poor in rural areas. Itinerant peddlers and general stores were popular.

As the frontier of trading moved on, many of the trading posts developed into general stores-characteristic of American, institutions. The retailer or shopkeeper kept a general stock of merchandise like calico and other cotton and wollen goods, household and farm hardware, staple groceries, stationery and medicines, breweries, etc. As the customers were few with limited wants and limited purchasing power, the retailer used to stock only necessities that too of one variety. Lack of variety of stock was also due to lack of capital. As people's income increased, their desires increased and accordingly the retailer increased not only the size of the stock, but also the variety of goods. The luxuries of one age became the necessities of the next. Very often goods were to be exchanged with the agricultural goods like wool, wheat, meat, etc., brought by the farmers. The retailers also extended credit to the farmers for longer periods which generally coincided with harvest season. The store used to serve even as Post Office.

Improvement in the means of transportation, people could move to greater distances for shopping and as a result the business of small towns was shifted to larger towns. However, the large and prosperous general stores did their business well. Many of the modern general stores adopted up-to-date methods of retailing and forged ahead in the face of competition. By rendering continuing service to their farming communities and giving good values, they built up a large and loyal clientele. There is a certain kind of competition between general store and chain stores. For shopping and speciality goods people are inclined to go to a nearly city where they can purchase in larger stores carrying more stocks of merchandise while convenience goods are shoppen in local general stores. The general store has an advantage in its location close to its customers and this led to personal relationship between the retailer and his customers.

Emergence of Modern Retail Institutions

Through the centuries, the retail trade tried to provide goods and service to satisfy consumers' wants. The agencies it used to accomplish this purpose have been not static but rather kaliedoscopic, changing constantly with the advent of new ideas and new conditions. The industrial revolution which began in 18th century with large scale production accompanied by mass scale, marketing, improvement in the quality of life, changing buying behaviour, the growth of cities and the increasing concentration of population in urban centres were instrumental in the emergence of new patterns of retailing methods and institutions.

Classification of Retail Institutions

Now, an attempt is made to briefly describe the various types of retail institutions that exist today, in the world over, in order to present a broad field of retail trade. In order to understand, in a better way, the various kinds of present-day retail institutions, it is better to classify them into groups. The grouping of retail stores depends, to a large extent on the basis that is used for classification. However, because of their constantly changing characteristics, it is not only difficult to classify into distinct types, but also different classifications overlap to some extent. Each of these types has certain characteristics, merits and demerits. The most important bases for classifying retail institutions are depicted in Annexure. It includes the following:

1. On the basis of merchandise/product-line carried.
2. On the basis of functions performen/level of service offered.
3. On the basis of ownership.
4. On the basis of legal forms of organisation.
5. On the basis of pricing strategy.
6. On the basis of store Cluster.
7. On the basis of nature of business premises (Non Store Retailing).

8. On the basis of scale of operation, and
9. On the basis of geographical location.

1. Retailers Grouped on the basis of Merchandise Handled

This classification, groups retail institutions according to the types of merchandise offered for sale. On this basis, these can be classified as grocery stores, furniture stores, hardware stores, drug stores, etc. But, on the basis of the length and breadth of the merchandise assortment, the retail stores can be categorised as following:

(i) One-line store or speciality store,

(ii) Departmental store,

(iii) Convenience store.

A brief description of these categories of retail stores is presented in the following paragraphs.

(i) Single Line Store or Speciality Store. As communities became larger and trade increased it paved the way for stores to specialise in a single line of goods instead of a general merchandising business. This resulted in the emergence of single or one-line stores such as, grocery, hardware, drug, book stores, foot-wear stores, etc. These stores have three important characteristics, *viz.*, *(i)* owned and operated by independent units, *(ii)* they handle a fairly complete assortment of a single line of merchandise, and *(iii)* they usually do not have an elaborate departmental organisation. Independent retail stores are owned and operated independently and without affiliation. Speciality store can be further classified by the degree of narrowness in their product line. For example, if a store carries on clothes business, it is a speciality store, but if it continues its business only in women clothes, it will be a limited line store and further if it restricts its stock only to men's shirting, it will be called as super-speciality store. The independent retail stores are spread over in towns, cities and suburban areas.

(ii) Departmental Store. A Departmental Store is a largescale retailing institution selling under one roof and single Control a variety of goods divided into separate department which specialises in one type of product line like furniture, home-appliances, hardware, medicines, clothing, etc. Each line is operated as a separate department which is managed by separate-sales force. These departmental stores will be of large size with a large volume of annual sales.

Departmental stores evolved in several ways. Some departmental stores owe their origin to the growth of villages and small towns into cities and consequently, a local general store expanding itself into a department store by taking on new lines of products. A few grew out of a single line store that handled one speciality product. Still other independently owned shops who were under common management merged into a centralised operation with a single owner. Sometimes, it so happened that those who were wholesalers in the beginning added retailing to their old business later. Subsequently, they abondoned wholeslings and concentrated on retailing and developed them into department stores. Whatever may be the source of their evolution the department stores became giants of 20th century retailing which exerted considerable impact on the retailing industry. These department stores introduced several innovative principles such as low mark-ups and rapid turnover, marking and displaying the prices of goods, encouraging customers to visit the shops without pressurising them to buy, and liberal redressal of complaints, etc. In India, the department stores have not made much dent in the retailing industry. The sahakari bazars or super bazars are the latest development in department stores in India which are established only in big cities while these stores spread to suburban areas in western countries.

(iii) Convenience Stores. The antithesis which began to emerge in the late 1960s and early 1970s has taken a variety forms, one of which is the convenience store. Important features of these stores include; closeness of location, longer hours, self-service, narrow assortments, higher prices, and convenient location near residential sub-division. Convenience food stores are relatively small in size. These stores resemble the single line grocery outlets that were in existence before the emergence of super markets.

2. Retailers Grouped on the Basis of Functions Performed or Services Rendered

Retail institutions, particularly in developed countries have come to recognise that their survival is very much dependent upon their level of service to the affluent consumers. The products offered for sale by retailers should have a product service mixture that will yield satisfaction to the consumer. On the basis of the service rendered, retail institutions can be classified as following:

(i) Self-service and self-selection stores,

(ii) Super Markets,

(iii) Super store, combination store and super market,

(iv) Service stores.

They are briefly explained in the following paragraphs:

(i) Self-Service and Self-Selection Stores. The main objective of this method of retailing is to encourage customers to visit all parts of the store, selecting goods as the customer proceed, and to transport them to the check-out for payment. The goods in a self-service store are so arranged that the goods must sell themselves. Goods are attractively wrapped, and the packing bears the information on all matters of interest to the customer like, composition of contents, methods of preparation, and instructions for storing. Customers in these stores are drawn in the desired direction of customer-flow by means of a logical sequence of merchandise, so that each group of goods is followed by related group of items. In self-service stores, baskets are provided to the customers to transport goods around the store. In this type of stores, all goods are on display, there is no pressure from sales staff, customers can quickly shop. This will result in better utilisation of staff and low cost of sales. However there may be a problem of shop-lifting in this type of stores.

(ii) Super Markets. Cundiff and Still defined super market as "a large retailing business unit selling mainly food and grocery items on the basis of the low margin appeal, wide variety and assortments, self-service and heavy emphasis on merchandise". The super market is the most recent retail institution to rise to the prominence. The super market emerged in the early 1930s and was largely the result of the consumers' increased mobility brought about by automobile ownership and his urgent desire to reap price advantage. A super market is a highly departmentalised establishment with adequate parking space, dealing in foods and other household merchandise, either wholly owned or with some of the departments leased out to concessionaires. At first super markets handled only packaged grocery goods, but later spread to wide variety of merchandise including drinks, drugs, hardware, dry goods, etc. According to MC Cammon, the super market concept involves self-service and self-selection, displays, centralization of customer services, usually at the checkout counter, large-scale physical facilities, a strong price emphasis, and a broad assortment and wide variety of merchandise to facilitate multiple item purchases. The self selection and self-servicing-the most important characteristic of super market was developed with an objective of increasing the volume of sales and reducing the overhead expenses. Moreover, help and advice will be provided to the customers in making a decision. Therefore, super market was defined as "one which is relatively large, low-cost, low-margin, high volume, self-service operation designed to serve the consumers. total needs for food, laundry and household maintenance prodocts". There are over 37,000 super markets in operation in America accounting for 76% of total grocery sales. Some of the super markets are independently owned stores, other are independently owned chains of super-markets, while some other are operated as units of the usual type of chain stores.

(iii) Super Store, Combination Store and Hyper Market. These three types of retail institutions are of recent development and found in most advanced countries like Germany, France, the U.K. and the USA. These are examples of adaptive behaviour of retailing institutes. All these three types are larger than conventional super markets in terms of selling, space and sales volume. It is an upgradation of super market. The important objective of super store is to meet consumer's total needs for routinely purchased food and non-food items. They also offer services which include laundry, dry cleaning, shoe-repair, bill paying, etc. Combination stores are generally found in medical Profession. It is the application of super market philosophy to the drug and prescription field.

The hyper market is a combination of discount store, super market and a warehouse under a single roof. Typically it sells both food and non-food items at 10-15 percent below normal retail prices and stacks merchandise as high as 10ft. These stores are larger than super stores and combination stores. These stores are generally situated in the outskirts of towns or cities as they require much space.

The emergence of most sophisticated and large-scale retailing institutions like super stores and hyper markets were on account of the fotlowing two important reasons:

1. From the point of view of retailers, it is to reduce the distribution costs by diversifying their product lines both within the super markets and in other types of operations,
2. Consumer pressure for an ever-expanding variety of products and services in both food and non-food under a single roof.

(iv) Service Srores. The business enterprises whose main product line is service are called service retail institutions. This category of retailers include banks, insurance companies, hotels, restaurents, clubs, associations, hospitals, theatres, repair services, barber and beauty shops, laundries, dry-cleaners, etc. Bankers, health organisations are revolutionising the way in which they can promote their service sales. Some organisations applied franchise and chain organisation principles in their endeavour to promote their service sales.

3. Retailers Grouped on the basis of Ownership and Control

Under this, the classification of retail institutions is based on the ownership and control. On this basis, retail institutions can be classified as: *(i)* Independent retailers, *(ii)* Voluntary chains, *(iii)* Chain Stores, *(iv)* Franchise organisations, *(v)* Consumer co-operatives, *(vi)* Fair Price Shops A brief description of these stores is presented hereunder.

(i) Independent Retailers: The most common form of retailing is the small, independent retail store. These stores played historical role in the distribution of goods in the past even in the advanced countries. However, in recent years, much of its field is taken over by the new and more sophisticated larger stores like department stores, chain stores, super markets, etc. Numerically, the independent retail stores constitute the largest group in almost all the countries. In the U.S. A. according to a census of Business conducted in 1972, there were about 85% independent stores accounting for 53% of all retail sales. In Britain, it is estimated that there were about 3,90,000 retail shops of which about 90% were small. In India, according to non-official estimates, the number of retail outlets is in the order of 33 lakhs of which the vast majority are small.

(ii) Chain Stores. The chain stores has been defined as a group of two or more reasonably similar stores in the same field of business, under one ownership and management, merchandised wholly or largely from central merchandising headquarters and supplied from one or more distributing warehouses or directly from the manufacturer or on orders placed by the central buyers. From the above definition, it is clear that a chain store has *(i)* a group of retail stores, *(ii)* located at different places, *(iii)* one ownership, *(iv)* centralised management, *(v)* similar layout and other external appearance and *(vi)* considerable uniformity in operating policies of all the units as the important characteristics.

The basic objective of this type is to get as nearer to the consumer as possible and cater to the large number of customers. Bata's and Caron as retail outlets are the living examplee of chain stores in India. Chain stores are widely prevaleut in the U.S.A. The census of Business revealed that chain stores which are only 11% of all retail stores did 31% of the total retail business in the U.S.A. These stores have many advantages in terms of economies of large scale buying, promotion, management and also integration of wholesaling with retailing.

(iii) Franchise Organisation. The term 'franchise' refers to the right to market a product or provide a service in a specified area. Such right is provided by a manufacturer or a wholesaler to a retailer through a written agrement. In other words, it is a licensing system by which the owner of a product, method or service identified by a brand name obtains distribution at the retail level through affiliated dealers while maintaining control over how the product is merchandised. The automobile and pertroleum industry has pioneered in this type of retailing. It is estimated that there are over 5,00,000 franchine outlets in the U.S,A. accounting for nearly 25% of the aggregate retail business of that country. For the services, the franchiser provides to the franchisee, include charges like initial fee, a royalty on gross sales, rental and lease fee on equipment and fixtures supplied, a share of profits and sometimes a regular license fee etc.

(iv) Voluntary Chains. The voluntary chains were emerged to counter the competing chain stores. There are two types of voluntary chains. The first type comists of a wholesaler sponsored group of independent retailers engaged in bulkbuying and common merchandise. The second type consists of a set of independent retailers who set up a central buying organisation and promotional efforts to avail the large scale economies of these operations. These chains are a form of co-operative society.

(v) Consumer Co-operatives. A consumer co-operative store may be defined as voluntary society formed by low or middle income consumers for selling consumer goods among themselves at low prices, run on low-cost, low profit basis and generally managed by an executive committee of the members themselves elected on the principle of 'one member one vote'. From this definition, important characteristics of a consumer co-operative stores can be stated as under:

(a) Each member has one vote only which he exercises at the general meting of the store to pass accounts, elect members of the executive committee.

(b) The store buys articles for selling to the members from either the manufacturers directly or the whole saler.

(c) The store is managed by an executive committee elected by members.

(d) Stores are run by professional managers.

(e) Sells goods to members at fair prices.

(f) They do not make high profits.

In brief, it is a retail outlet owned by the consumers themselves. These stores were established as a protest against the failure of the distributive system in adopting fair business practices to serve its customers. The idea behind these stores is based upon the conviction that consumers working cooperatively and running the stores can get quality goods at cheaper rates and with continuity of flow of goods.

In India, these consumer's co-operative stores are called differently in different states apart from a common name of Super Bazar. In Maharashtra. Rajasthan, Madhya Pradesh, these are known as Vishal Sahakari Bhandar or Sahakari Bazar, and in Andhra Pradesh, as Kalpalatha, Apna Bazar or Naya Bazar in Uttar Pradesh, Delhi, Punjab, Bihar and Gujarath, in Kerala as Super Market.

(vi) Fair Price Shop. Public distribution of essential commodities has become the important feature of the developing economies. In India, it is a retailing system supervised and guided by the State. The important objective of this public distribution system is to provide essential commdities to the vulnerable sections of the society at fair price. It attempts to reduce the overall costs and tries to extend maximum benefit and satisfaction to the public at large. The retail shops which are established to serve this objective are called fair price shops. In India, at present, the public distribution system is composed of government-owned fair price shops, consumer co-operative stores and licensed private sector members. As these stores have a limited purpose of supplying only a few articles, they are not in a position to compete with pdvate retail outlets even within the limited area of their operation.

4. Grouping of Retailers Based on the Legal Forms of Organisation

Based on ownership and control of the firms, the retail stores may be classified into three types, *viz.* *(i)* Sole proprietorship, *(ii)* Partnership, and *(iii)* Corporation/companies. A brief description of each type of retail unit is presented hereunder.

(i) **Sole Proprietorship.** It is the most popular form of legal organisation in most of the countries. Personal initiative, relatively small capital are some of the important features of this form of organisation.

(ii) **Partnership.** In these stores, the entrepreneure combines in himself all the functions of good management. He is entrepreneure, manager, proprietor and seller of goods. There will be personal touch with customers. However, on account of small scale operation, modern techniques cannot be limited. In order to overcome problems inherent in sole proprietorship partnership has emerged. It provides complementary business skills, capital, confidence in the joint effort, etc.

Company or Corporation form of retail outlets are confined mostly to advanced countries and urban area of developing countries.

(iii) **Corporation.** The retail stores of this form provied benefits such as limited liability, perpetuality of existence, access to a wide range of talents, better access to sources of capital, etc.

5. Retailers Grouped on the basis of Pricing Strategy

Here, the basis of classification is the pricing strategy of retail outlets. Some stores offer normal prices, some other medium, while a few others offer high prices and also less that normal prices. Major types of retail stores under this category include: *(i)* Discount store, *(ii)* Warehouse store, and *(iii)* Catalogue show-room. A brief narration of each type of the retailer under this group is presented.

(i) Discount Store: This is also one of the recent addition to the field of retailing. It is originated in the U.S.A. after World War-II and later spread to the U.K. and other European countries. The presence of this type of retail stores is not felt in developing countries like India. According to William Stanton, discount houses are large stores, freely open to the public, advertising widely, carrying a reasonably complete selection of well-known brands of hard goods such as, appliances, furniture, etc., consequently selling below nationally advertised list prices and offering minimum customer services. Important characteristics of discount store are: *(a)* they are large-sized stores, *(b)* low price is their major appeal, *(c)* customer service is maximum, *(d)* hard goods are the major lines of goods offered by them, *(e)* generally sales will be for cash, *(f)* store emphasizes national brands, *(g)* the location of stores tends to be a low-rent area and draws customers from relatively long distances, *(h)* normally only cash transactions. It is estimated that there are about 8,500 discount stores with 80 billion sales in America. In recent times, discount retailing moved from general merchandise into special merchandise stores like discount book stores, discount retailing moved from general merchandise into special merchandise stores like discount book stores, discount drug stores, etc. However, as there is stiff competition among discount houses and also between discount stores and department stores, they are forced to spend much on decoration, good locality, promotion, etc., as a result of which prices offered by them are also moving up.

(ii) Warehouse Store. The main objective of this type of store is to sell in huge volumes and obtain economies of large seale. They offer goods for low prices and located in suburban low-rent areas. The space of selling will be very large. This type of operation is targeted to buyers of medium priced brand name furniture who are interested in discountries and immediate delivery.

(iii) Catalogue Show-Room. The catalogue show-room grew at a rapid rate during the 1960s and early 1970s. During the early 1960s, the management had to work exceedingly hard to earn a 1% or 2% net return on sales. Location, sector and service had become almost as important as price. The catalogue show-room thus emerged offering a wide assortment of merchandise name brands, low prices and the opportunity for a time-conscious consumer to make purchases from a catalogue rather than having to travel to a series of individual outlets to purchase merchandise. The low overhead cost results in offering low prices. The rapid growth of catalogue show-room indicates that customers are most saving conscious and are willing to accept less service. These types are rarely found in developing countries like India.

6. Retailers Grouped on the basis of Store Cluster

Under the conventional classification system, it is customary to group retail stores according to the number and nature of neighbouring stores. In the early stages of retail trade, retailers started their stores at the convergence of rivers, land trails and transportation intersections. The main objective behind clustering of stores is to provide different types of goods to consumers through one-stop shopping. On the basis of store cluster, the retail stores of modern world can broadly be categorised into four types. They are: *(i)* Central business district, *(ii)* Regional shopping centre, *(iii)* Community shopping centre, *(iv)* Neighbourhood shopping centre. A brief narration of these types is presented.

(i) **Central Business District.** In developed countries like the U.S.A., France, the U.K. and in urban parts of developing countries like India, these central business districts are found. Till 1950s, these were dominant in towns and cities in America containing departmental stores, speciality stores, banks, cinema theatres, etc. But due to heavy traffic and expensive parking, consumer preferred to visit shopping complexes developed for the purpose in suburban areas which are known as small business districts.

(ii) **Regional Shopping Centre.** A regional shopping centre has been defined as "a group of commercial establishment planned, developed, owned and managed as a unit related in location, size, and type of shop to the traders that it serves and providing on-site parking in definite relationship to the types of sizes of stores it contains". Size of regional shopping centre may differ with number of stores ranging between 40 and 100. This cluster of store serves one lakh to ten lakhs population staying within 30 minutes driving time. At the two ends of this cluster, there will be departmental stores and speciality stores set-up in between.

(iii) **Community Shopping Centre.** Community shopping centre will serve a population ranging between 20,000 and 1,00,000. People within a distance of 1 to 1½ miles are attracted to these centres. Generally, there will be 15 to 50 retail stores in these centres of which one will be a department store or a branch of it and others include a super market, convenience goods stores and professional offices like a bank.

(iv) **Neighbourhood Shopping Centre.** This type of stores will be larger in number in any country to serve neighbourhoods. These centres contain 5 to 15 stores to serve a population below 20,000. Generally these centres will be away by 5 minutes walk. Most of the stores at these centres will be convenient shopping centres such as, dry-cleaner, laundry, shoe-repair, beauty shop, pan dabba, etc.

7. Grouping of Retailers on the basis of Nature of Business Premises

It is also customary to classify the retail trade broadly into two categories, *viz.*, *(i)* Store retailing, and *(ii)* non-store retailing. The various types which have already been discussed belong to the former category. In fact, the store retailing dominates the retailing industry in terms of sales volume, investment, etc. However, the role of non-store retailing is also not insignificant, In the U,S.A. non-store retailing amounted to $57 billion or 12% of all consumer purchases in 1977. Some observers foresee a greater role for this non-store retailing in future, due to heavy traffic and as a time saving device. Non store retailing which is also known as remote retailing is one where there will be no permanent business premises or establishment to make purchases by the customers. The important types of non-store retailing include: *(i)* Mail/Telephone Order Retailing, *(ii)* Door-to-Door Selling, *(iii)* Street Traders, *(iv)* Cheap Jacks, and *(v)* Automatic vending. All these types of non-store retailing units are discussed briefly in the following paragraphs:

(i) Mail/Telephone Order Retailing. Initially it was only a mail order business which had its origin in the 1900s in the U.S.A. Later, on account of improved communication facilities, telephones are also being used on large-scale in place of mail for the purpose. It is a business by post or telephone. Through mail or telephone orders are placed by customers and executed by the retailers and the goods are sent to the customers through Post Offices. Customers need not go to shops, but goods are supplied at their very door. Particularly in advanced countries and urban parts of developing countries this type of retailing is booming. The reasons contributing for success of this business include: Women joining the work-force leaving no time for shopping, higher costs of driving, traffic congestion, parking problems, etc. There are 11,000 mail and telephone order houses with total sales of over $ 8 billions.33 Sears, Roecbuck and Company and Montgoney Wardand Company are pioneering in the field. Poor road facilities to villages also contributed for the development of mail order business.

In India, where there are more than 5,000 remote villages not connected by good roads and not having retail outlets worth signifying, the mail order business has got a good future. But the main bottleneck in the process is poor communication facilities and also the illiteracy among the rural masses. Added to this, there are several languages as a result of which advertiserment becomes costly. However, there are several mail order houses doing a good business. The most popular include Mail order Sales Pvt. Ltd., (which sells bull-workers) Ramon services Pvt. Ltd., Ross Morak a, etc. Now-a-days, this business Spread to education field on a very larger and unexpected scale. British Institute of Educational Technology, Open University system introduced by several State Governments are the best examples. Some spurious mail order houses dealing in commodities taken advantage of the illiterate villagers by cheating them and lost their credibility in India.

(ii) Door-to-Door Selling. Modern door-to-door selling sales persons of modern companies owe their vision to 'Yanke peddlers' of earlier stages who, on foot or horse-back used to travel from farm to farm and village to village to sell their goods. The main difference between the earlier people and modern door-to-door selling personnel is that the former used to carry business on their own while today's peddlers are agents of manufacturers or distributors. The most popular company dealing in door-to-door selling in the U.S.A. is Avon Products Co., which has more than 3,50,000 sales personnel, mainly women.

In India, in recent times, this type of business is gaining ground. The multinational companies like HLL and Procter and Gamble Co. Ltd.. are approaching their consumers through this method particularly to promote the sales of washing powders like Rin and Ariel respectively by employing most of the female members. In villages and also in towns the traditional hawkers and peddlers who carry business on their own play a significant role in retailing. They move from locality to locality and house to house dealing in a particular line of products, say utensils, plastic goods, spices, vegetables, fruits, clothes, etc. Generally the goods in which these peddlers and hawkers deal will be of low quality and low prices. Sometimes, peddlers accept the consideration in kind also. However, peddlers and hawkers also lost their credibility due to some unscrupulous and unfair trade practices in rural India.

(iii) Street Traders: Those who run their business on the pavements of busy towns and cities, particularly at bus stops, railway stations, government and commercial offices, educational institutions, etc., are known as street traders. Though these were earlier confined only to cities like Hyderabad, Madras, Delhi, etc., now found their way to district and taluq headquarters. It can be observed that this business takes place every day in cities while it will be on holidays in smaller towns. Sultan Bazar of Hyderabad, Chandini Chowk of Delhi are good example of this business who generally deal in garments, bags, plastic goods, cosmetics, leather goods, etc.

(iv) Cheap Jacks. Those who maintain a shop temporarily in a busy locality and shifts it to some other locality when the former locality proves to be not profitable are known as Cheap Jacks. The Chief difference between the cheap jack and the street trader is that the former maintains a shop temporarily and moves from one locality to the other, while the later does not maintain any shop but moves from one locality to the other with goods.

(v) Automatic Vending. Selling through automatic machines which is called robot selling involves the sale of goods to the consumers through coin operated mechines and without help of any salesman. There are slots in such machines through which a specified type of coin is inserted. Soon after, the desired product comes out through another slot. Generally, impulse goods with high convenience value such as candy, coffee, soft drinks, cigarettes, newspapers, beverages, hosiery, cosmetics, food-snacks, T. shirts, etc., are sold. Automatic vending is gradually becoming popular in advanced countries like the U.S.A. and the U.K. According to the National Automatic Merchandising Association, there are more than 6 million machines doing a business of $ 1.3 billion accounting for 1.5% of total retail trade in U.S.A. This type of retailing offers 24 hours selling self-service. But it is costlier and frequent machine break-downs, high pilferages cause much inconvenience to consumers. In India, automatic vending machines are installed in almost all the important railway stations. In metropolitan cities and exhibitions, vending machines are used to sell candy, ice-cream, fruit-juice, coffee, etc.

8. Grouping of Retailers on the Basis of Geographical Location

In a developing country like India which has a vast majority of villages, it is also customary to classify the retail stores on the basis of their geograpbical location. On this basis retail stores may be classified broadly into two types, *viz.*, *(i)* Urban retail stores, and *(ii)* Rural retail stores. As usual a brief introductory narration is presented about these two groups of retailers.

(i) Urban Retail Stores. These are located in urban areas with a population of more than 20,000. Whatever type of store tbat is found in these areas can be called as urban retail stores. They may range from general store to super market, department store, hyper market to automatic vending.

(ii) Rural Retail Stores. Retail Stores operating in villages with a population of less than 20,000 are called rural retail stores. Most of the stores found in rural areas are of general stores in nature apart from a few speciality stores, street traders, peddlers, co-operative stores.

9. On the Basis of Scale of Operation

One of the most popular bases of classifying retailers is the scale of their operation. On this basis, the retail stores can be broadly categorised into two types. They are: *(a)* Large-scale retailing, and *(b)* Small-scale retailing. A brief note about these is presented below.

(a) **Large-Scale Retailing.** It is becoming extremely popular in big towns and cities. The number of benefits and large-scale economies such as benefits of bulk purchase, specialised management practices, sound financial position, adequate financial resources, effective personal selling, grand display of merchandising, latest advertising techniques, benefits of specialisation, etc., associated with this type of retailing have contributed for its popularity. These include department stores, chain stores, mail order, super market, discount house, automatic vending, etc., which have been already dealt with under different classifications.

(b) Small-Scale Retailing. The retail stores which are found in most of the developing countries. particularly in rural areas, belong to this category. Due to inadequate capital of the retailers and poor purchasing power of consumers on rural front, the business operations will be on small scale. The retailers follow only the traditional methods of operating to run their business. Some prominent types of retail stores coming under this category are: unit stores, speciality shops, street traders, hawkers, peddlers, etc. There are very powerful economic factors at work to maintain small units.

The small-scale retailer cannot compete with large-scale retailer in economies of buying, in specialisation of function, in heavy outlay on lease in main street sites, and many other advantages. But, the small-scale retailer had a number of advantages which are as under.

1. As a business unit, small-scale retailing is far more flexible than the retailing units of the large-scale organisation.

2. They do not have fixed expenses like rental, employees' salaries, fixtures and layout of shop, and other overhead charges.

3. The small scale retailer with no minimum limit as to the size of turnover could enter and serve these very small markets. The small-shop still retained a definitely favourable position where nearness to the home of the consumer is important. "Buying round the corner" by no means displaced the big department or multiple store.

4. They have no minimum size. From the parlour shop based on the part-time services of the wife or opened to eke-out

an old pension to the street barrow and to the lock-up shop employing assistants, all sizes of independent retailers existed and were able to operate in areas and sections of markets closed to large-scale retailers as uneconomic.

5. The acquisition of small shop has always been, and remain, a particular attraction to many people.

6. The possession of small shop remains a great attraction to the small venturists. For so long as a small shop provides a return of the present order, people will be tempted to set up business for themselves although many may fail through the lack of ability and experience. They need not pay any provident fund, gratuity to employees.

7. The small unit has more survival value. The possession of a small shop means an independent livelihood though, such independence may mean any amount or worry, drudgery, vexation and insecurity. There are traditional techniques attached to the small business which have been left by grand-fathers to their sons and grand-sons. There is a feeling of pride in the possession which may obscure financial consideration.

8. The small independent shop is not the only one which is liable to uneconomical expansion.

9. Small shops provide an opportunity to inter-connect the artisan's activities with that of shop-keeping.

10. Another advantage of the small-scale retailer is the quality of personnel service and the skill the retailer could give his customers in contrast to the impersonal service of the branch manager or assistant of the large-scale undertaking.

11. Another significant advantage of the small-scale retailer is the variety of different goods stocked. The large retailers from the very nature of their trading methods could not compete with the small mixed retailer in the range of different goods stocked.

12. There are certain products which cannot be traded on a large-scale. For example, fish, fruit, vegetables. milk, etc. In some cases, particularly, for women-wear and jewellery, they prefer only small shop retailer who is known to them personally.

The problem is to discover the most economical retailing unit for a given community of consumers. Making the distance from the shop to the consumers as short and speedy as possible is what individual consumers might prefer. But, if this aim can only be achieved by having a multiplicity of retailing units, involving an increase of retailing costs which otherwise might be available, the customer is certainly not well served. In practice, the task is to strike the right balance between concentration for economic reasons and what is generally called the convenience of the shopper, and the balance must be so struck that the supply of a great diversity of qualities and varieties is not endangered.

As there are different bases for classifying the retail stores, 'it is quite natural that different classifications overlap. For instance, one independent retail store may sell only groceries, serve only a neighbourhood, and operate on a small scale and in a rural village. Though there exists considerable competition among different types of retail stores, different stores with different appeals to the public may have different clientele of their own. In some cases, there may be heavy competition, while in some cases it may be of no significance. For instance, there appears heavy competition between a mail order and general stores, but little competition between a general store and a department store.

Importance of Retail Trade in Indian Economy

After having explained the concept and allied matters of retailing, now an attempt is made to analyse its importance in Indian context.

Next to agriculture, retail trade is the most important economic activity in terms of number of establishments-big or small, public or private to serve the consumers spread over the vast rural and urban areas of the country. In terms of the size of the market, India is the second largest consumer market in the world with about 150 million households and more than 84 crore population. As at the end of 1981 there were nearly 1.95 lakh wholesalers and 32.98 lakh private retail outlets apart from about 3 lakh fair price shops and 52,000 consumer co-operative stores. The estimated turnover of private retail outlets alone was to the tune of Rs. 15,000 crores and investment of Rs. 5,000 crores. Therefore, India is said to be the world's largest private retail distribution system. Further, the retail trade sector being more labour-intensive, is relevant in our economy, which is suffering from heavy unemployment on one hand, and scarcity of capital, on the other. Retail trade provides employment to more than 58 lakh persons as at the end of 1471.

The market for consumer goods in India has experienced a real boom in recent years. It has grown in size, range and sophistication. Sizewise, the consumer products market of India, which was of the order of Rs. 2,400 crore in 1960-61 and Rs. 13,000 crore in 1976-77, has now become a Rs. 30,000 crore market. By 1985-86, cosmetics and toiletries had become a Rs.200 crore business, bathing soaps a Rs. 550 crore bnsiness, and washing soaps and detergents a Rs. 1,000 crore business. ORG's retail audit on forty-four packaged consumer' products, including toiletries cosmetics, packaged food items blades, torches, batteries, etc. has estimated the total market for such products at Rs. 3,572 crore in 1986. In consumer durables, the production of bicycles in 1986-87 was more than six million, production of sewing machines nearly 3,50,000, production of two-wheelers nearly a million, production of electric fans nearly 5.2 million, production of radios around 1.3 million, mixer grinders was nearly 5.00 lakhs, TVs 1.5 millon. Twenty years ago, only 500 Indians owned TV sets.

Two Segments of Indian Retail Market

Indian retail market can be broadly categorised into two segments on the basis of location - urban retail market and rural retail market. The urban retail markets are those which cover relatively high density of population nexuses with a developed infrastructure which include metropolitan cities, towns, district headquarters and industrialised townships. Urban retail markets are well developed and well integrated in terms of communication, transportation, organisational forms, and dimensions and also the elite consumers. Urban retail markets are comparable to the retail markets of developed countries.

Rural Market Defined

As the present study forms part of a broad area of rural marketing, now, an attempt is made to define 'rural market'. In the process of defining rural market, for the purpose of clarity, it has been attempted to firstly, deal these two terms 'market' and 'rural' separately and then combine them into one, later.

The term, 'market' is used in many contexts. For example, the urban market, the rural market, the agriculture market, the commodity market etc. Thus, market as a concept is most confusing. According to economist's view, market is a physical place where buyers and sellers get together, and a transfer of title takes place as goods are exchanged. Thus, markets include the people who sell the goods and services and also those who purchase them. Another view is that market refers to the people with buying power and willingness to buy. In the present study, both the views have been taken into account.

With regard to the term 'rural area' also there is no unanimity among the authorities. A few authorities defined a geographical place as a rural area with a population of 10,000 while few others defined - place with a population of 20,000 as rural area. But, for the present study, the criterion adopted by the census of India, 1981 for defining an urban area has been taken as the basis for defining the rural area. Accordingly, rural area is defined as a place with human habitation of 5000 and below with agriculture as the main economic activity and with a density of population less than 400 sq. km. Some areas with a population more than 5000 are also classified as rural area in view of the agriculture being the main economic activity of a vast mojority of population in that area.

On the basis of the definitions of the above two terms, the rural market may be defined as any market that exists in the rural area with a population less than 10,000 where the areal density of population at any population nucleation is low without any significant infrastructure. In other words, total market of India excluding the urban markets can be called as rural market. These rural markets are mostly unintegrated, very small in size and rudimentary in nature.

Composition of Rural Markets

The rural market in India is made up of two broad compartments with difierent dimensions altogether. These are:

1. Rural retail markets which deal with marketing of consumer goods (both durable and non-durable) and services of which mostly produced in urban areas in villages, and

2. Agricultural markets which deal with marketing of agricultural and allied goods produced in rural areas and also agricultural inputs produced in urban areas.

Rural Retail Market

Of the above two, the former compartment of rural market is relevant for the present study. And as such. an attempt is made here to define 'rural retail market' with the help of the definitions already given for terms-retail trade, market and rural area. Rural retail market may be defined as that market which deals with goods and services at the ultimate consumer level, in rural areas. Viewed from this point, rural retail market and rural retail trade can be treated interchangeably.

Types of Rural Retail Markets

Again, the rural retail markets can be broadly classified into three types (Annexure Chart 1.A): *(i)* periodic markets, *(ii)* mobile traders (peddlers), and *(iii)* permanent retail outlets.

The periodic markets like hats (which are called 'peta' or 'angadi' in Telugu) and fairs are the chief institutional feature of the rural markets in India. In spite of the development of permanent shops, these play an important role in rural economy as an institution of marketing. These are the oldest forms of trading institutions in the process of evolution of today's permanent shops which used to provide an opportynity to exchange surplus goods occasionally, such as weeks, months, or years etc. These markets provide an oppportunity of not only purchasing the consumer goods, but also selling their surplus agricultural and allied produce.

When the need for exchanging goods was felt in between the periodic market days, this gap was filled by the mobile trader. Usually those traders who participate in weekly markets will visit the adjoining villages when there is no weekly market.

As far as rural marketing is concerned, the permanent retail outlet is the final stage of evolution of marketing institution. When a need to exchange goods on permanent or daily basis was felt and there was enough surplus production, and also when operating a shop was feasible the mobile trader started the permanent retail outlet.

Functions of Retailing

The work of distribution of goods and services is a gigantic task and it would not be possible for the manufacturers to serve all the consumers directly. It is in this context, retailers render a yeomen service to the different segments of our economic institution Retailers' functions are unavoidable link between consumers and the manufacturers. Thus, retailing has an economic justification.

The various functions performed by retailers to customers can be broadly categorised into two *viz.*, essential functions and optional functions. The functions such as providing merchandise from which consumers select their purchase, providing accommodation (place, location) and providing staff and equipment to assist customers in selecting goods, etc., which are unavoidable and whose provision is a must are called essential functions. There are certain other functions which the retailer can choose to provide to help customers in buying their goods such as delivery and credit, discount and provision of amenities such as cloak-rooms, parking places, etc., which have no direct connection with the purchase of goods but which make shopping more attractive, comfortable and convenient. In what follows, the functions-essential and optional, of retailing are discussed in detail.

I. Essential Functions are again classified into: *(i)* Provision of merchandise, *(ii)* provision of accommodation, and *(iii)* provision of services. For the purpose of indepth understanding, they are briefly discussed.

(i) The Provision of Merchandise. The primary function of any retailer is to make goods available to the consumers. Retailers purchase goods of different varieties from different suppliers and present them in a place convenient for customers. Suppliers are generally scattered throughout the country and sometimes from outside, Thus the retailer enables the customer to tap the goods of the world. Further, in view of the variety of goods available in different product lines, retailers want to specialize continuing their activities to a particular type of merchandise. That is the reason why there will be number of shops in the same line of business in the same street, but each offering within that range a selection of goods which is markedly different from that offered by other shops. In brief, the retailer's important job would be to provide right goods, in the right quantity at the right time, in the right condition and at the right price. A brief explanation of an these "rights" will provide an insight into the retailers' functions with regard to merchandising. The goods offered by the retailer should be appropriate to the needs of the people in the area and should reflect their tastes, preferences, living conditions, etc. Keeping in view the competition, retailer may concentrate on a particular section of the consumers in terms of their incomes, sex, age, etc.

The right quantity refers to the fact that the retailer should be able to satisfy the consumer with the sizes of goods of their choice. No customer should return from the shop without purchasing goods in the quantity which he wants.

The right time refers to making available goods when consumers want them. The manufacture or production of goods may not be uniform throughout the year or may be seasonal, but retailer must purchase and store them in anticipation of demand till they are purchased by consumers.

Offering goods in right condition refers to the fact that goods should be in perfect condition, which will create confidence in the minds of cosumers that goods are standard and not of inferior quality.

(ii) The Provision of Accommodation. The accommodation which refers to the building in which retail shop is to be housed should be able to protect goods, consumers and staff from the weather, dust, damage, thefts, etc. This apart, building should also reflect proper layout, attractive presentation and ease of operation. The decision of the retail building varies with factors like type of goods to be sold, the method of service to be used, the anticipated volume of trade, the market to be served and the type of organisation for whom the premises are to be built, etc. For example, the importance of hygiene in food trades necessitates buildings which can be thoroughly and quickly cleaned.

(iii) The Provision of Service. There are three important methods of service, to assist customers in selecting their goods: *(a)* Personal service in which staff of the retailer assist the customer in the selection of goods, *(b)* self-selection in which customers select merchandise from a counter and hand it to the staff at that counter for wrapping and payment, and *(c)* self-service in which customers select their goods and pay for them near the exit at a check out. The method of service used depends on the merchandise and the type of customer. Personal service is necessary where goods are expensive and complex, while self-service can be used for cheap, protable necessities like food, etc. and self-section for wide-range of inexpensive items.

II. Optional Functions are again considered as the provision of: *(i)* services, *(ii)* amenities, and *(iii)* information. They are discussed as under:

(i) The Provision of Services. For certain types of goods like soft furniture the provision of service is a must. Services are facilities which are necessarily part of a sale or which directly encourage a sale. These services include delivery, credit, fitting rooms, installation, maintenance and repairs, etc,

(ii) The Provision of Information and Communication. The retailers provide a great service to both-producers, on one hand, with regard to likes and dislikes of consumers and also to the consumers with regard to the products available, forthcoming or new products, their features, prices, advantages. etc., on the other.

(iii) The Provision of Amenities. These amenities are meant for improving the customer comfort and also to attract the customers. These include the provision of lifts and escalators, chairs and restrooms, telephones, cloak-rooms, crechas, cafes and restaurents, parking places, etc.

Stages of Evolution of Retailing

After having learnt about the economic justification and functions of retailing, now an attempt is made to know about its evolution. The purpose is to analyse the qualitative growth of retailing in the context of rural economy. This aspect is discussed in three stages as under.

In the primitive stages of economic development, there were only self-contained economic systems, wherein all the members of the family/community used to provide for their own needs and did not interact or trade in any way with other families. Thus there was absolutely no trade at all. People were concerned more with their limited wants of necessities.

Decentralised Economic System

In the later stages of economic development, exchange emerged as a means of satisfying individual needs. When households were able to effect small purchases of different products, a basis of exchange developed. As households found their needs satisfied by an increased quantity of variety goods, the importance of exchange increased. Thus, there was an emergence of trade in a small and limited measure.

There is a belief that trade was developed for slightly different reasons in different points of time. There is a group of six factors that have direct bearing on the emergence and development of trade. They are as following: *(i)* Socialisation, *(ii)* Specialised production, *(iii)* Surpluses, *(iv)* Control over property, *(v)* Appreciation of values, and *(vi)* Ordered markets.

Socialisation refers to the interactions based on communication that takes place between individuals and groups. Specialisation allows the producer to become proficient in his work because full time can be devoted for perfecting his task to the exclusion of other duties. As a result of increased specialisation, output of a limited number of goods increassed, which in turn increased interdependence among people. This interdependence ultimately led to the exchange of goods (trade). Control over property contributed much for the development of trade. The desire to control over goods or property led to socialisation in the form of warfare or predation. In the beginning, it is believed that it was owned jointly by the family or community. The goods that were at the disposal of the community elders were given as gift, in the beginning. Trade might have developed on account of dissatisfaction of the individuals with the manner in which the property was managed and their desire to have greater control to dispose their goods. Thus private control came into existence. Control over property may lead to appreciation in the value, as it creates imperfections in the distribution process. It is quite natural to think that there must be some appreciation of value in order to initiate the idea that goods can be traded. However, in gift giving this may not be the case. In order to appreciate the value of goods, the trade was developed on a large scale.

Ordered markets are those in which there will be assurance that market interactions will take place under predictable circumstances. As some order is necessary for all social interactions for trade also orderliness is a must. This orderliness of markets has led to development of the trade.

Under this decentralised economic system, exchange took place directly between producer and consumer and there was no central marketing agency to facilitate movement of goods between these two points. Every consumer should have to seek the producers of different goods spread over a large area to procure his requirements.

With the growth of decentralised system of exchange, specialisation and division of labour led to more production. But the efficiency was confined only to the production, while the distribution was not considered as a specialised activity. Non-specialisation of marketing led to various difficulties like affecting excessive number of transactions by wasting too much time in travelling and negotiations. Thus, this resulted in loss of time, which otherwise can be used for increasing their production. Thus, ultimately marketing inefficiency led to the inefficiency of production and the entire system was adversely affected.

Evolution and Development of Retail Trade in India

Though, the development and growth of trade in different parts of the world was different due to differences in demographic, economic, socio-cultural and geographic factors, and the timing of development and growth, there seems to be some commonness in almost all the countries of the world including India. The evolution, development and growth of retail trade in India is discussed broadly in three stages: *(a)* ancient period, *(b)* pre-modern or medieval period, and *(c)* modern period.

Trade in Ancient India (Vedic Period)

In ancient times, the population of India like any other country, was nomadic which moved from place to place in search of food. At a subsequent stage. they discovered and learnt the use of seeds, cleared patches of forests and started rising crops. At a later stage of development of human civilisation, people gave up their nomadic habit. The tribe settled down in one place, made dwelling houses of permanent nature and raised crops on a permanent basis. When these settlements were not able to provide the required food due to increased population they migrated to some other places nearby forming subsidiary settlements. This led to the development of villages and hamlets. Over a period of time each village became self-contained unit. The cultivator produced agricultural commodities and the artisan provided the other simple necessities of the villages. The scope of trade was very much occasional and limited during this period. In Rigvedic period, there are some direct hints to show the state of self-sufficiency of wealth in the early Aryan community. Before the rise of caste system in the Indian society, every family sufficiently produced for their food, clothes, equipment, etc, by adopting occupations relating to agriculture and industry. The Indo-Gangetic river basins were the cradles of earliest human civilisation. The rivers made the soil fertile and that influenced the agricultural production. The origin of markets can be traced to surplus production by farmers. Roads and carts came into existence in the wake of these developments. Boats along the rivers and coasts also came to be employed for the purpose.

Emergence of Varna Dharma and its Impact on Trade

The advent of Varna dharma in Indian society which divided the duties or occupations (known as dharma) broadly into form types, *viz.*, Kshatries, Brahmin, Vaishyas and Shudras, disturbed the state of self-sufficiency considerably. According to Varna dharma, one must practice only that occupation which is meant for that, particular varna and should not encroach upon into other occupations. Consequently, Kshatries confined themselves to ruling. Brahmins to advise and guide Kshatries, Vaishyas for trading, leaving the occupation of production like agriculture, cattle breeding and household industry to shudras. Production of certain commodities and services was restricted to certain classes of communities.

The division of labour influenced commerce and trade in India in a big way. This brought the exchange goods among those who undertook production of different commodities and such exchage, in turn, brought the phenomenon of the value of money and price, Gradually. trade became popular among vedic Aryans. There are evidences to show that both internal and external trades were at their height in ancient times. This is evident from the archaeological findings of Mohanjodaro and Harappa. With urbanisation of the Indus culture, the trade became vitally connected with economic life of society. Trade during this period made considerable progress and much of cultural and colonial contact of Indian people with other countries seems to be the results of commerce. All this tells that trade became popular among Vedic Aryans.

The Gupta period is regarded as the golden age in Indian trade and cultural history. This period made a great impact on Central Asia and Malaysia. The political unity during Guptas and Mauryas gave; a great impetus to Indian trading and markets in the country. Indian trade also spread to Indonesia, Burm, Indo China and other parts of th Far-Eastl2. In the first two centuries of Christian era, there was a considerable increase in trade between Rome and India. The intermediaries in the Indo- Roman trade were the Alexandrians, the Greeks, the Syrians, the Jews, the Phoenicians, the Arabs and the Parthicans. Indian shipping was in a much developed state by the first century A.D. Even in ancient times, Indian ships used to sail to Malaysis, Eal't Africa and the Persian Gulf.

After having a brief feeling of the retail trade in Ancient period, let us now consider its basic features which are as under.

(a) **Philosophy of Trading.** Kraya-Vikraya (Purchase and sale) was the marked feature of Indian business. A trader carried the business for profit (Labh) which was earned on the capital (mulya) invested by him. In the Rigveda the root Kri occurs for purchase, venik or vanijya for trading.

In Kautilyan terminology, a retail trader was called Vaijya Vrtya. It is clear from Kautilya's Arthasastra that there was contractual relationship between wholesale dealer and retail trader and the basis of contract was perhaps commission or a share in profit. It is also clear that there was a system of modern dealership existing during that period in retailing. Besides, there were commission agents, servants to sell the commodities on behalf of the employer for a wage or pay. These middlemen had to sell goods and remit the same to the employer without taking any profit. Similarly, they were not responsible for any loss due to fall in prices.

(b) **Methods of Trading.** In the early stages of development, of trade, there were neither trading in stitutions nor markets. Most of the business was carried on through hawkings Hawkers used to sell goods not only procured from wholesalers, but also those they either produced or procured directly from the producers. During the days of Jataka, hawkers not only sold goods in local areas but travelled to distant places for selling their commodities. They used to carry goods either on their person or on donkeys. In the process of giving publicity and to promote their sales, they used to shout the names of commodities in the central place of the village.

(c) **Medium of Exchange.** Originally, in ancient India, it was barter that constituted as the medium of exchange of commodities. But, keeping in view the inconveniences attached with barter system, metal pieces and coins were introduced.

(d) **Places of Business:** Besides, long-term of permanent markets, there were some temporary or short-term markets. Temporary markets were meant for perishable goods and were located outside the towns at the city gates. According to Jataka stories, every village had its own resident traders and most of the business was done directly in the individual shops or in the market place. The towns were having streets especially earmarked for different products. The dantakara, vithi 'rajaka', 'vithi', tentavita were the specialised markets for ivory groups, dyed cloths or the wover products respectively. There were also the markets for flowers, perfumes or rice. In milltrade parts, markets are mentioned as one of the essential elements of a city.22 In the Ramayan, the markets of Ayodhya were vividly described.

(e) **Trading Facilities.** Even during ancient times, retail trade was given its due place in the matter of administrative facilities. This is clear from Kautilya's Artha Sastra in which he commended that merchants trading with scents, garland grains and liquid should settle in the eastern quarter of the town. Traders in cooked rice, liquor and flesh should live in south and artisans, manufacturers are worsted threads, cotton threads, bamboo, mats, skins, armors etc., in the west. Gold smith and other workers in precious metals and stones had their place in the north.

(f) **Trading Communities.** As a result of strict adherence to the Varna-dharma, Vaishyas as a trading community emerged. They stood third in the order of the social class after Brahmins and Kshatrias. People belonging to this class were performing many duties such as trade and commerce, banking including agriculture, cattle breeding, etc. The nature of their vocation made this community subservient to other two upper Varnas. The Vaishyas were considered to be an object of exploitation for the Brahmins and Kshatries, who were encouraged by the sastra to subsist upon this class either by way of dakshina (sacrifical fees) or exorting 'bali' (tax) from them. The rise of big monarchies and structures of their state was having a direct bearing on this community.

(g) **Trading Practices.** The following are the trading practices that were popular with the retailers of ancient India.

(i) **Merchandising.** The process of buying and selling in ancient times was very interesting, resembling present day practices of tribal people. Hawkers used to attract the attention of consumers by crying the names of commodities. This is clear from the Seri Vanja Jataka which explains as to how a trader in the city of Anuradhapuram used to sell pots and pans by crying out the names of commodities. Before enquiring about the price, the consumers used to examine the commodities thoroughly and only after getting satisfied with it they used to ask the price. If the price was found satisfactory, they used to pay for it and take deliverry of the goods. Magging was also on a large-scale in the process of buying by consumers.

(j) **Price Fixation.** Similar to that of the present day welfare governments of different countries, in ancient period also, the Kings used to exercise their control in fixing the prices of commodities. Kautilya advocated two types of prices customary price and statutory price. The former was to be fixed as a matter of tradition in that region for different commodities while the latter was to be fixed by Kings. In Manu smrithi, there are evidences of fixing prices by the Kings. Manu says that Kings should settle prices publicly with the hely of merchants every fifth or every fourteenth day. Yagna Valkya also upheld the power of Kings in this regard and said that purchase or sale should be conducted at the price fixed by the Kings, and the surplus alone could be the legal profit of the traders.

(k) **Control and Regulations of Trade:** In ancient period, state exercised control over the spread of market, location of market and regulation of market of different trading practices. Adulteration was an offence punishable under the law. The Jataka stories reveal that adulteration was a crime and the traders who sold grains mixed with chalf went to Tantaulas hell. Kautilya specified the articles in which adulteration was a crime. Adulteration of grains, oils, alkalis, salts, scents and medical articles with similar articles of low quality shall be punished with a fine of 12 pannas. Yagna Valkya recommended a fine of 16 pannas to be imposed on a trader who adulterated articles such as, medicines, oil, salt, perfumes, grains, sugar, etc. For goods of high price such as iron, wood, cloth, gems, etc., the fine was eight times the amount of the sale price. Manu too condemned traders who indulged in adulteration to gain profit.

Regarding other malpractices, Kautilya said, middlemen who causes a merchant or a purchaser the loss of the 1/8th panna by substituting with tricks of hand, false weights or measures, or other kinds of malpractices shall be punishable with a fine of 200 pannas. Fines for greater loss shall be proportionately increased commencing from 200 pannas. In the Mauryan administration, there used to be one official called 'Panya-Adhikari', who used to check the genuinity, ownership and weights and measurements of commodity before it was sold.

During the seventh and Eighth centuries A.D. Indian trade developed further. The Guptas gave an honoured place to the earning of wealth by sea trade. There is ample evidence to testify the existence of Roman merchants and trading colonies in Madurai and other places in South India where large finds of Roman coins were unearthed.

However, after the downfall of the Mauryas, the Gupta and the Kushan empires, there was a decline in trade because of lack of security on the trade routes. The caravans faced many difficulties such as, robberies and attacks from wild animals.

Trade During Medieval Period

Medieval period which is marked by surpluses and degnity necessitated the multi-faceted commercial activity. The pattern of trade during this period was full of complexities. Broadly, there were two types of markets *(i)* Rural Markets and *(ii)* Urban Markets.

(i) Rural Markets. The rural market was a feature of intra-local trade of the period. It is evident from the writings of Tavernier when he states that "even in the smallest village, rice, flower, butter, milk, vegetables, sugar and other sweemeats dry and liquid can be produced and provided in abundance". In large villages, most of which were under a Muslim official, sheep, and pigeons were sold. In Hindu villages, there were only flour, price, vegetables and milk. On account of the provision of food items available everywhere, travellers did not carry food with them in journeys. In Bengal, as literary evidence reveals that good Rajas or Zamindars used to establish markets for the periodic hat, In some places there were two to three markets and some times more days in a week. There were two types of markets in the country side *(a)* Bazars consisting of mainly retail markets, and *(b)* Mandis with only wholesale markets. Epigraphic evidence from South India shows wide range of commodities like food grains, vegetables, fruits, butter, salt, pepper, spices, oil, camphor, cotton thread, fabrics, metalware, etc., were traded in these markets.

(ii) Urban Markets. The trade of towns and cities was more complex and varied when compared to the rural market. As observed by Tavernier, it is the custom in India when they build a public edifice, to surround it with a large market place. As a result, most major towns had several markets or bazars, one of which was the chief or great bazars. For example, in Surat, there was a crowded bazar between the customs house and the mint. Fryer wrote that "there were high streets with shops on each side, unlike in Europe, where there were more peddler stalls. Describing the Surat bazars, Ovington remarked that it was difficult to "pass through the multitude of Banians and other merchants that expose their goods. The merchants used to stand with silks and stuffs in their hands and on their heads selling goods to the consumers. Compland commented that "Surat seems like another Ezypt, or to say better, a terrestlal paradise, as there was abundance of all earthly things. In Goa, also there were innumerable shops offering both domestic and foreign goods of all kinds. In Hugli and Bombay these markets were prevalent. In most urban centres, there were artisans and specialised manufacturers. Some producers, particularly of textile weavers used to market their own products. But most of the urban trade was inter-local rather than intra-local offering commodities of other places. Most urban markets not only catered to the needs of local consumers, but also acted as emporia and entre pots from where the dealers of other places procured their supplies. In what follows main features of trade of Medieval period is presented.

(a) Inter-local Trade. A major feature of the inter-local trade was the predominantly one-way flow of commodities from the villages to towns. The paddler, the hats and the mandis used to mediate the distribution of goods to villages. Intervillage trade was extremely rare prior to the eighteenth century. To a larger extent, the economic needs of the precolonial village in India were mostly met from its own produce distributed through customary arrangements rather than through exchange. This pattern of economic organisation was peculiar in India.

The inter-local trade—both rural to town and inter-town flow of commodities was a short-distance version of the inter-regional trade. The villages and towns were inter-dependent. The practice of collecting revenue in villages generated pressure to sell the agricultural and manufactured goods and the towns provided necessary demand for these goods. There was a very good response from villages to the demand from towns in the matter of food stuffs.

(b) Inter-Regional Trade. Coming to the inter-regional, trade, traders preferred waterways to land routes as the former was cheaper. This inter-regional trade was mostly of highly priced products including textiles and foodstuffs. The flow of goods between Gujarath and North India was served mainly by-two routes: The first linked Surath with Agra through Western Rajasthan *via* Ajmer, Merta, Jodhpur, Jalor, Ahmedabad, Cambay and Broach. The second, move easterly passed through Malwa and Khandesh connecting Gwalior, Sironj, Ujjain, Mandu, Burhanpur, Tapti and Surat. There were also alternative routes linking interior regions. The trade links between the two coasts were also maintained along more than one route. One route went from Surat South-eastwards to Aurangabad and then through Asthri and Golkonda to Masulipatnam. Other routes known as Debul-Goa route linked Goa with Bijapur. The Masulipatnam-Paliacatta route hugged the coastal line most of the way, passing through Nellore. These routes land and water—alongwith other infrastructural facilities provided an opportunity to integrate market covering extensive parts of Hindustan, Bengal, Rajasthan, Gujarath, Malwar and the Deccan, both east and west.

Inland emporia like Agra, Lahore and Burhampur developed as commercial towns on a large-scale as they were on cross-roads for inter-regional trade. The port towns developed as entry points for the imported and coastal trade goods and exit points for the produce of inland territories. Every emporium included three types of market-local market serving the needs of the resident population; a wholesale spot market to cater to retail trade and inter-regional trade and finally the latter's off shoot a wholesale forward market. Towns like Bombay, Madras, Calcutta, Malbar were most important port towns of that time.

Despite the diversity and the spatial range of the inland trade, the scale of its markets was, of course, small by modern standards. Distant parts of the sub-continent also had a wide range of mutually independent economic institutions. Weights, measures, currency, systems of taxation varied from place to place.

Markets in Pre-Modern Period

The markets of India during medieval period discharged two distinct functions: Firstly, they brought together commodities for the consumption of the local buyers or for distribution among consumers in distant markets. Secondly, there was a hierarchy of scales in markets ranging from the miniscule rural hat to the emporia of international trade like Surat or Agra.

Combining these two categories, the Indian markets were classified broadly into four types. They are: The emporia, the small scale bazars, periodic fairs and isolated rural markets. The emporia dealt with long distance trade, inland, and overseas. Where goods were gathered from places within a short radius primarily for purposes of local consumption and wandis or wholesale markets were called small-scale bazars.

For periodic fairs, traders met together to sell and replensih their stocks, but consumers were not excluded the local surplus produce was exchanged among the producers-cum-consumers in isolated rural markets. The difference between the above types of markets was of scale rather than economic function.

The merchants of this period were also heterogeneous in terms of their functions and wealth. Broadly, they can be classified into three types: *(i)* Corporate merchants; *(ii)* Independent traders; and *(iii)* Small merchants.

For every emporium there were rich merchants and the large port towns had merchants comparable to Europe's merchants, princes in terms of wealth and power. Virji Vora of Surat was the wealthiest man of his time. Mir Jumala, Golkonda Kiogdom, Malay Chetti, Kasi Veeranna and Sunca Rama Chatti of Southern Coromandel were masters of extensive commercial empires. Their trade covered a wide range of commodities and many branches of the inter-regional trade. Some of them owned large fleet of ships. Some of them, like Kasi Veeranna, exercised monopoly powers over certain commodities. Though wealth of such merchants was mainly obtained from trade —both inland and foreign, links with political authorities as financiers and tax-framers also contributed much for accumulation of wealth by them. For instance Hirmand Sahu, a Marwari banker from Amber, came to Bihar in the 17th Century as Maharaja Man Singh's banker-purveyor. His son Manik Chand, the first Jagath Sets (literally, Banker to the world) acquired enormous wealth and power. His sons collected taxes and remitted the revenue of Bengal to Delhi through their banking houses, gave credit to Zamindars and further profited from trade in produce paid as revenue. Their wealth was estimated at Rs. 100 million. Similarly, the notorious adventurer Omichand started his career as a petty 'dadni' merchant, but rose high through unscrupulous practices and also by greasing the right palms. He became mint 'minister of Patna in 1941. But the fortunes of great trading families were short lived and their failures owed much to the political rather than commercial reasons.

Independent traders, who were next to the traders of emporia, were trading with their own and borrowed capital. The range of their activities—both in terms of commodities and geographical area of operation was limited when compared to the first type. They employed their own agents and sometimes had a dealer network.

The typical small merchant operated within a limited area. They used to move from one locality to the other. They used to sell different types of commodities like butter, rice, straw, vegetables, etc. There were partnerships also. One small merchant, *viz.*, Banarsi of Jain community set-up a partnership.

Political conditions in Southern India were unsettled and just before 1750 large part of it had been involved in wars in which both the English and the French participated. These conditions led to a general decline in trading and other economic activities in trading and other economic activities. Madras, because of its protected position was an important centre in the coastal trade. It was also important centre of external trade, especially in relation to the countries, further to the east. The chief articles entering into the trade on the Coromandel coast in which Madras held a central position were grains, cloth, cotton, indigo and pepper.

Bangalore was the largest and most active centre of internal trade. The Malabar coast containing such important ports as Cochin, Calicut and Mangalore had been extremely active in foreign trade since the advent of the Portugese and the Dutch. There was considerable coastal trade between Surat, the Konkan ports and the Malabar coast, the imports into Malabar being chiefly grains, pulses and sugar and the exports of teak wood and coconut.

Hyderabad was at this time an important centrally situated place which was also the capital of a powerful and comparatively a stable kingdom. Its trade was largely oriented towards Madras and Masulipatnam. The Godavari River was an important channel of trade for a part of this Hyderabad territory and important supplies such as of timber came down of the Godavari from the region surrounding its banks. The Circar region comprising in the main the deltas of Godavari and Krishna had a long coastal line and a comparatively well developed system of internal water transport.

Modern Indian Retailing

Due to industrialisation and revolution in agricultural sector on one hand, and the increasing level of income and better standards of living on the other, there has been a spurt in the demand for consumer goods and its consequential impact on the distributive trade in modern India. There is a vast potential for consumer goods market in India as it is the second most populous country in the world. Its population is nearly three times the population of the U.S.A., eleven times that of the U.K., twelve times that of France and six times that of Japan. Levels of income of the indian population and their standard of living have also gone up very significantly over the years. As a result of these changes, Indian consumer market developed from centres of small-scale exchange of goods to the present day modern large scale trading organisations, particularly in urban areas. However, the rural areas still retain, to a larger extent, the characteristics of markets of primitive stage with fairs, periodic markets and also small-scale general stores dominating in the distribution of consumer goods.

An attempt is made to examine analytically the Indian consumer market, its characteristics, weaknesses and trends, in Indian retail marketing.

❐

5

Distribution Channels of Rural Marketing

Marketing channels for rural products vary from product to product, country to country, lot to lot and time to time. For examples, the marketing channels for fruits are different from those for foodgrains. Packagers play a crucial role in the marketing of fruits. The level of the development of a society or country determines the final form in which consumers demand the product. For example, consumers in developed countries demand more processed foods in a packet form. Wheat has to be supplied in the form of bread. Most eatables have to be cooked and packed properly before they reach the consumers. Processors play a dominant role in such societies. In developing countries like India, however, most foodgrains are purchased by consumers in the raw form and processing is done at the consumer's level. Again, the lots originating at small farms follow different route or channels from the one originating in large farms. For example, small farms usually sell their produce to village traders; it mayor may not enter the main market. But large farms usually sell their produce in the main market, where it goes into the hands of wholesalers. The produce sold immediately after the harvest usually follows longer channel than the one sold in later months. With the expansion in tninsportation and communication network, changes in the structure of demand and the development of markets, marketing channels for farm products in India have undergone a considerable change, both in terms of length and quality.

1. Marketing Channels for Foodgrains. Marketing channels for various cereals in India are more or less similar, except the channel for paddy (or price), where rice millers come into the picture. For pulse crops, dal mills appear prominently in channel. Some common marketing for wheat have been identified as follows:

(i) Farmer to consumer;

(ii) Farmer to retailer or village trade to consumer;

(iii) Farmer to wholesaler to retailer to consumer;

(iv) Farmer to village trader to wholesaler to retailer to consumer,

(v) Farmer to co-operative marketing society to retailer to consumer;

(vi) Farmer to a government agency (FCI, etc.) to fair price shop-owner to consumer;

(vii) Farmer to wholesaler flour miller to retailer to consumer.

The channels for paddy-rice and pulses are broadly the same, except that the rice millers or dal millers come into the picture before the produce reaches retailers or consumers.

2. Marketing Channels for Oilseeds. Marketing channels for oilseeds are different from those for foodgrains, mainly because the extraction oil from oilseeds is an important marketing function of oilseeds. The following flow chart reveals the movement of oilseeds from producers to consumers in India:

The most common marketing channels for oilseeds in India are:

(i) Producer to consumer (who either directly consumes the oilseeds or gets it processed on custom basis);

(ii) Producer to village trader to oil retailer to consumer;

(iii) Producer to oilseed wholesaler to processor to oil wholesaler to oil retailer to oil consumer;

(iv) Producer to village trader to processor to oil consumer;

(v) Producer to government agency to processor to oil wholesaler to oil retailer to oil consumer.

3. Marketing Channels for Fruits and Vegetables. Marketing channels for fruits and vegetables vary from commodity to commodity and from producer to producer. In rural areas and small towns, many producers performs the functions of rural areas and small towns, many producers performs the functions of retail sellers. Large producers directly sell their produce to the processing firms. Some of the common marketing channels for vegetables and fruits are:

(i) Producer consumer;

(ii) Producer to primary wholesalers to retailers or hawkers to consumer;

(iii) Producer to processors (for conversion into juices, preserves. etc.)

(iv) Producers to primary wholesalers to processors;

(v) Producers to primary wholesalers to secondary wholesalers to retailers or hawkers to consumers;

(vi) Producers to local assemblers to primary wholesellers to retailers or hawkers to consumers.

Marketing Channels for Eggs. The prevalent marketing channels for eggs are:

(i) Producer to consumer;

(ii) Producer to retailer to consumers;

(iii) Producer to wholesaler to retailer to consumer;

(iv) Producer to co-operative marketing society to wholesalers to retailers to consumers;

(v) Producers to egg powder factory.

Sometimes, the wholesaling and retailing functions are perfonned by a single firm in the channel.

4. Marketing Channels for Live Poultry. A study conducted in the Punjab has identified the following movement path for live poultry:

Most of the studies on the identification of marketing channels for rural commodities have concentrated on a concept of marketing channel which defines the flow of the produce from the producer (farmer) to the consumer.

But as the commercialisation (market orientation) of agriculture, is increasing and as the producers and consumers are located in different states or different countries, the marketing channels that are emerging go across state or even national boundaries. This apart, unless quantities flowing into various channels are estimated, the relative importance of alternative channels cannot be assessed. Such an analysis was done by Acharya for gram grains in Rajasthan. According to this study, there are three points of entry of gram grain in the marketing channel viz., farmer level, wholesaler level (from outside the state) and processor level (also from outside the state). There are 28 marketing channels, village traders appear in 8 channels, grain wholesalers appear in 5 channels and retailers appear in 15 channels, dal (split) wholesalers appear in 5 channels and retailers appear in 15 channels. Assuming the farmers' surplus entering the marketing channel as 100 units, the entry from outside the state at wholesaler and processor level was 4.24 per cent of the producers surplus.

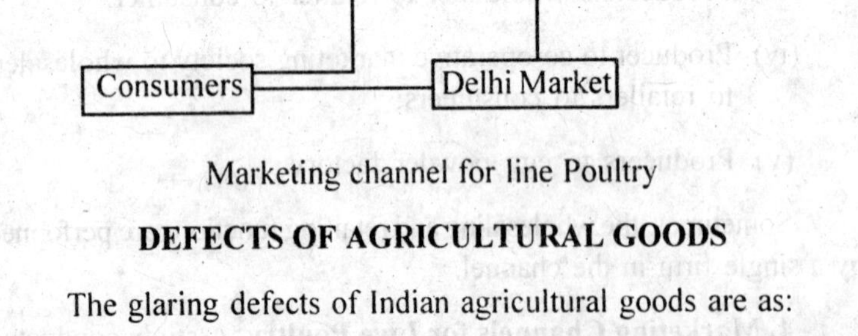

Marketing channel for line Poultry

DEFECTS OF AGRICULTURAL GOODS

The glaring defects of Indian agricultural goods are as:

(1) Lack of Organisation. This is a very serious defects that various producers are not collective in their approach for marketing their products. Main reason can be: wildly scattered, uneducated and believes in freedom and secrecy.

Of course producers union can have positive impact to have limited action in the market, where as the buyers have unity. Farmers must understand this "united we stand and divided we fall".

(2) Forced Village Sales. The farmers generall sells his produce in villages, at an unfavourable place and time, and gets the lowest price. Nearly, 75 per cent to 80 per cent of the total output is sold in villages. Main reasons are as:

(a) ***Indebtedness of Farmers.*** Indian fanner is destined to take birth in debt, to live in debt and to die in debt. He is in need of money for purchasing seeds, manures, and to meet expenses of other agricultural operations. The ready made source of finance is the village money-lender who force the fanners to sell to him at an agreed rate which is the lowest possible. As soon as the harvesting is done, agricultural produce moves automatically to the godowns of village money-lenders. Thus the farmer is not at all in a position, to clear off the debts and the. same is extended to generations together.

(b) ***Unsatisfactory Conveyance System.*** Even the nearest market, lacks good road system. At times, he is not having even his own bullock or cart to move the produce to the market. Further, he does not have time to go personally to the market.

(c) ***Lack of Waiting Capacity.*** Since, many cultivators are hard pressed for cash to meet the claims of creditors *i.e.*, money lenders and other obligations, they are forced to dispose of the produce immediately after harvest. Thus, glut is created in the market, which results directly in the fall of prices by at least 20 to 25 per cent. Thus, the farmers get lower prices:

All the above mentioned factors make the farmers to sell the produce in villages, reducing their resistance power, to hold the stocks of goods and to reap the advantages of the market in the off seasons.

(3) Excessive Middlemen. Indian agricultural marketing is characterised by the existence of excessive middlemen or intermediaries between the producers and consumers. Such a large army of middlemen which operates in the market cuts the bits both from producers and consumers. They cut off larger share of the cake, and as a result, neither the producers nor the consumers are happy. It is estimated that 50 to 60 per cent of total value of commodities; goes to the middlemen like wholesalers, agent middlemen, jobbers etc. In case of paddy, it is 80 per cent of the price. As we have already observed, the number of markets and middlemen through which agricultural goods move ire superfluous and unwanted. To quote the example of paddy, if flows through the following channel.

Paddy from tanner → village agents → local market → central market → wholesalers → retailers → sub-retailers → consumers.

(4) Multiple Market Deductions. Numerous deductions are made out of the price of the produce. To get better prices, the farmer carries his produce to the distant markets, where he is again cheated by the merchants. In order to dispose of the produce to the merchants. Agent middlemen, called as 'dealers' are to be employed, who charge what is known as 'dalali' or 'arhat'. While weighing the produce the dealer cuts for weighment or what is called as 'tulai'. The persons who help in loading and unloading and holding the bags and scale-pans, to charge for their services, which is talled 'palledari'. The wholesaler deducts heavily for impurities in the produce in the form of garda'. Again, as the produce is not seasoned he cuts for possible loss in the weight in the form of 'dalta'. Further, his sweepers, watermen, watchmen, get the share in the form of 'dalta'. Lastly, the farmer is shaved cleanly for the purpose of charity to be given to the dispensary, gowshala's, chool etc. On in average, 20 per cent goes to them, in the form of various market deductic 15 of course, these vary from state to state.

(5) Defects (Malpractices) in Markets. Various defects mischief are being played in the markets for agricultural goods which are mostly unregulated. These malpractices may be analysed as follower only a few samples:

(a) The producer-seler is being doomed by the buyers or middlemen in the market by using the non-standard weights and measures. To quote the experience of many villagers 'the middlemen use different measures and weights while buying and different measures and weights while selling. This itself is a sufficient proof of the manipulation of weights and measures by the merchants. Of late, this is disappearing. It is an exception than a rule.

(b) As have already noted, number of arbitrary deductions are made for religious and charitable purposes. This again, reduces the share of the producer-sellers, in the price he, gets for his products.

(c) Sufficiently large portions of the produce are withdrawn as 'bangi' or sample. Usually 1-10 seers per cartload are taken away for which nothing is paid.

(d) The brokers, who are negotiating between the buyers and sellers, have a tendency. favour the buyers and cheat the sellers by way of 'cover' dealings.

(e) The buyers are in a position to dominate, in case of any disputes to price, quantity, quality etc. The farmers are not protected by anybody. They are at the mercy of dealers in the market. Even if they try to protest, the farmers are fooled by shrewd business people.

(f) These and some other malpractices are experienced by the farmers, in the unregulated markets. From the following data, it will be crystal clear that farmers face many difficulties in selling their produce as middlemen's share in the sale proceeds is exorbitant.

Items	*% Share of middlemen*	*% Share of producers*
Grapes	73.60	26.40
Mosambi	71.40	28.60
Orange	67.60	32.40
Guava	66.40	33.60
Papaya	63.10	36.90
Potatoes	57.72	42.28
Tobacco	43.87	56.13
Eggs	17.50	62.50
Rice	33.20	66.80
Wheat	31.50	68.50

(6) Adulteration in Agricultural Goods. Adulteration and admixturing in agricultural products have very bad effect on trade. Adulteration is commonly resorted to, by the middlemen and farmers. This is because the refraction allowed amounts to 5 per cent. This has become the minimum rather than the maximum. Thus the farmers who bring good produce to the market, tend to lose the percentage as impurities. This has encouraged the adulteration and admixture. Many tricks have been played, now-a-days, to sell such products. New-rice product is being sold as 'old-rice'. Many stone crushers and grinders are working to supply I'izeable pebbles, to be, mixed. Damping of cotton, chillies, groundnuts, is common in order to enhance the weight. In case of wheat, barley, the clay balls, pebbles etc., are mixed. Spices are adulterated with the soil, dust, sand, sheep and cattle dung. Tea powder is mixed with saw dust. In case of chilli powder, oxide is used to brighten the colour. In case of pepper, 'papaya' seed are mixed. This may increase the profits of the traders, but at the cost of the health of the people. As a result, our name in intemational markets is spoiled.

(7) Poor Storage Facilities. The storage facilities available with the fanners are deplorably low. In most of the villages, the farmers store the produce in open space, in bags, earthen vessels, or underground ditches or pits. These indigenous methods of storing the agricultural produce are adopted in villages and markets are not capable of protecting the produce from dampness, weevils, and other vermins. The loss to the farmer is estimated to be 5 to 15 per cent in weight and quality. Again, there is a loss due to fungi, insects, mites, rodents, birds etc. The total loss in terms of rupees comes to Rs. 400 million every year. Enemy number one is rodent. In India, there are 2,600 million rats. It is calculated that 20 rats eat the food of an individual per day. The total consumption, by rat population, amounts to 24 million tonnes.

(8) Poor Means of Transportation. Transport system of our country is not satisfactory and developed even today. Though, ours is a nation with wide distances, we lack the means of transport. The development of different means of transport is very disheartening. The bad roads, and trucks which connect the villages and markets, not only increase the loss of transportation, but also aggravate the strain on bullocks and other pack animals; and results in the multiplication of small dealers and intermediaries. To take the instance of construction of railways in India, the considerations which are given more weight are the administrative and strategic aspects, but not the needs of the farmers. Wherever there are railway facilities, there the feeder services are not adequate and proper, as the bad roads prevent such services. The following table indicates the position of road mileage in different countries:

Country	*Road mileage per 100 sq. miles of area*
France	650 miles
U.K.	320 miles
Germany	225 miles
U.S.A.	200 miles
Japan	100 miles
India	100 miles

(9) Luck of Proper Information. Unfortunately farmers have practically no contact with outside world. They depend on the hearsay reports, of village's petty merchants who are least interested in supplying correct information. Even if the information is available by hard efforts, it is unreliable because, prices are differently enforced in kilograms, mounds, tons etc. The amount of refraction differs from market to market. As a result of this, the farmers feel to sell in villages at the prices ruling there which are mostly determined by the money-lenders or village banias. Again, the villages of India are not covered by a network of communication system, which is a must. The only sources are radio and transistor sets which are used as entertaining media than to give market information.

(10) Poor Grading and Standardisation. The agricultural goods are not standardized and graded. The reputation of our agricultural goods, in the world market is not encouraging. In spite of the efforts of the government, even today, there is adulteration mixing, damping, wetting etc. The cotton of long staple is mixed with short staple. The position of oilseeds is satisfactory except the groundnuts which are vetted to increase the weight. All these mischiefs owe their origin to the non-development of grading and standardization facilities in required measure. There are no common standards and grades accepted on all India basis. This is another important factor which gives the farmers low prices. Central Banking Enquiry Committee has pointed out "the price paid by the consumers in Europe for these products is based largely on reputation and this reacts unfavourably upon the price received by those cultivators who have improved their quality."

(11) Poor Finance Facities. The village farmer is financed by the money lenders called-either the 'sahukars' or 'shettys'. These people charge exorbitant rates of interest to the extent of 18 to 40 per cent. They take security, of either gold ornaments or farms and follow compound and not simple interest method. He plays mischief by taking under advantage of illiteracy of the cultivators. This is why, it is always stated that he is born in debt, lives in debt and dies in debt.

DISTRIBUTION OF PRODUCT IN RURAL MARKETING

The producer's chief aim is to make goods available to its valued consumers as soon as possible. All commodities cannot be grown in all areas due to variation in agro-climatic conditions. Thus, consumers are to get these products, only two main routes:

(i) Direct Route, and

(ii) Indirect Route.

(i) Direct Route. In this process commodities passes from producers to consumers, no middlemen but its area is limited.

(ii) Indirect Route. Here products move from producers to consumers through middlemen. It is network between producers—Wholesale dealers Retailers.

MARKETING AGENCIES

In the marketing of rural commodities, the following agencies are involved:

1. Producers. Most farmers or producers, perform one or more marketing functions. They sell the surplus either in the village or in the market. Some producers; especially the large ones, assemble the produce of small producers, transport it to the nearby market, sell it there and make a profit. This activity helps these producers to supplement their incomes. Frequent visits to markets and constant touch with market functionaries, bring home to them a fair knowledge of market practices. They have, thus, an access to market information, and are able to perform the functions of market middlemen.

2. Middlemen. Middlemen are those individuals or business concerns which specialise in performing the various marketing functions and rendering such services as are involved in the marketing of goods. They do this at different stages in the marketing process. The middlemen in foodgrains marketing may, therefore, be classified as follows:

(a) Merchant Middlemen. Merchant middlemen are those individuals who take title to the goods they handle. They buy and sell on their own and gain or lose, depending on the difference in the sale and purchase prices. They may, more over, suffer loss with a fall in the price of the product. Merchant middlemen are of two types: *(i)* wholesalers *(ii)* retailers.

(i) ***Wholesalers.*** Wholesalers are those merchant middlemen who buy and sell foodgrains in large quantities. They may buy either directly from producers or from other wholesalers. They sell foodgrains either in the same market or in other markets. They sell to retailers, other wholesalers and processors. They do not sell significant quantities to ultimate consumers. They own godowns for the storage of the farm produce.

The wholesalers perform the following functions in marketing:

(a) They assemble the goods from various localities and areas to meet the demands of buyers;

(b) They sort out the goods in different lots according to their quality and prepare them for the market;

(c) They equalize the flow of goods by storing them in the peak arrival season and realizing them in the off-season;

(d) They regulate the flow of goods by trading with buyers and sellers in the various markets;

(e) They finance the producers so that the latter may meet their requirements of production inputs; and

(f) They assess the demand of prospective buyers and processors from time to time, and plan the movement of the goods over space and time.

(ii) ***Retailers.*** Retailers buy goods from wholesalers and sell them to the consumers in small quantities. They are producers' personal representatives to consumers. Retailers are the closest to consumers in the marketing channel.

Itinerant traders and village merchants also come under this group. Itinerant traders are petty merchants who move from village to village, and directly purchase the produce from the cultivators. They transport it to the nearby primary or secondary market and sell it there. Village merchants have their small establishments in villages. They purchase the produce of those producers who have either taken finance from them or those who are not able to influence the market. Village merchants also supply essential consumption goods to the producers. They act as financiers of poor producers. They often visit nearby markets and keep in touch with the prevailing prices. They either sell the collected produce in the nearby market or retain it for sale at a later date in the village itself.

(b) Speculative Middlemen. Those middlemen who take title to the product with a view to making a profit on it are called speculative middlemen. They are not regular buyers or sellers of produce. They specialise in risktaking. They buy at low prices when arrivals are substantial and sell in the off-season when prices are high. They do the minimum handling of goods. They make a profit from short run as well as long-run price fluctuations.

Processors carry on their business either on their own or on custom basis. Some processors employ agents to buy for them in the producing areas, store the produce and process it throughout the year on continuous basis.

They also engage in advertising activity to create a demand for their processed products.

(c) **Agent Middlemen.** Agent middlemen act as representative of their clients. They do not take title to the produce and, therefore, do not own it. They merely negotiate the purchase and/or sale. They sell services to their principals and not the goods or commodities. They receive income in the form of commission or brokerage. They serve as buyers or sellers in effective bargaining. Agent middlemen are two types:

COMMISSION AGENTS OR (ARHATIAS)

A commission agent is a person operating in the wholesale market who acts as the representative of either a seller or a buyer. He is usually granted broad powers by those who consign goods or who order the purchase. A commission agent normally takes over the physical handling of the produce, arranges for its sale, collects the price from the buyer, deducts his expenses and commission, and remits the balance to the seller. All these facilities are extended to buyers-firms as well, if asked for.

Commission agents or arhatias in unregulated markets are of two types, Kaccha arhatias and Pacca arhatias. Kaccha arhatias primarily act for the sellers, including farmers. They sometimes provide advance money to producers and itinerant traders on condition that the produce will be disposed off through them. Kaccha arhatias charge arhat or commission in addition to the normal rate of interest on the money they advance. A Pacca arhatia acts on behalf of the traders in the consuming market. The processors (rice miller, oil millers and cotton or jute dealers) and big wholesalers in the consuming market employ Pacca arhatias as their agents for the purchase of a specified quantity of goods witllin a given price range.

In regulated markets, only one category of commission agent exists under the name of 'A' class trader. The commission agent keeps the establishment—a shop, a godown and a rest house for his clients. He renders all facilities to his clients. He is. therefore, preferred by the farmers to the co-operative marketing society for the purpose of the sale of the farmers produce. Commission agents extend the following facilities to their clients:

(a) They advance 40 to 50 per cent of the expected value of the crop as a loan to producers to enable them to meet their production expenses;

(b) They act as bankers of the producers. They retain the sale proceeds, and pay the producers as and when the latter require the money;

(c) They offer advice to producers for purchase of inputs and saie of products;

(d) They provide food and accommodation to the producers and their animals when the latter come to the market for the sale of their produce;

(e) They provide empty bags to enable the producers to bring their produce to the market;

(f) They provide a storage facility and advance loans against the stored product upto 75 per cent of its value;

(g) They help the producers in times of personal difficulties. and

(h) They arrange, if required by the producers, for the transportation of the produce from the village to the market;

Brokers. Brokers render personal services to their clients in the market; but, unlike tile commission agents, they do not have physical control of the product. The main function of a broker is to bring together buyers and sellers on the same platform for negotiations. Their charge is called brokerage. They may claim brokerage from the buyer, the seller or both, depending on the market situation and the service rendered. They render valuable service to the prospective buyers and sellers, for they have complete knowledge of the market of the quantity available and the prevailing prices.

Brokers have not established in the market. They simply wander about in the market and render services to clients. There is no risk to them. They do not render any other service except to bring the buyers and sellers on the same platform. In most regulated markets, brokers do not play any role because goods are sold by open auction. Their number in foodgrain marketing trade is decreasing. But they still play a valuable role in the marketing of other rural commodities, such as gur, sugar, oil, cottonseed and chillies.

(d) Facilitative Middlemen. Some middlemen do not buy and sell directly but assist in the marketing process. Marketing can take place even if they are not active. But the efficiency of the system increases when they engage in business. These middlemen receive their income in the form of fees from those who use their services. The important facilitative middlemen are:

Hamals or Labourers. They physically move the goods in market place. They do unloading from and loading on to bullock carts or trucks. They assist in weighing the bags. They perform cleaning, sieving, and refilling jobs and stitch the bags. Hamals are the hub of the marketing wheel. Without their active co-operation, the marketing systems would not function smoothly.

Weighmen. They facilitate the correct weighmen of the produce. They use a pan balance when the quantity is small. Generally the scale-beam balance is used. They get payment for their services through the commission agent. The weighbridge system of weighing exists only in a few big markets.

Transport Agency. This agency assists in the movement of the produce from one market to another. The main transport means are the railways and trucks. Bullock carts or camel carts or tractors are also used in villages for the transportation of foodgrains.

Graders. These middlemen sort out the product into different grades, based on some defined characteristics, and arrange them for sale. They facilitate the process of prices settlement between the buyer and the seller.

Communication Agency. It helps in the communication of the information about the prices prevailing, and quantity available in the market.

Sometimes, the transactions take place on the telephone. The post and telegraph, telephone, newspapers, the radio tend informal links are the main communication channels in rural marketing.

Advertising Agency. It enables prospective buyers to know the quality of the product and decide about the purchase of commodities. Newspapers, the radio, and cinema slides are the main media for advertisements.

From the discussion we had so far, it is clear that the channel of distribution for rural goods in more lengthy than that of the manufactured consumer goods. Normally they move from the producer to the resident buyers, co-operatives and auction companies in the local market to the wholesale receivers, and agent middlemen in the central market to the jobbers in the jobbing market and then to the retailers and consumers. But the channels that are in use for these consumer goods, differ from producer to producer, depending on the distance between producing and consuming centres. However, the channels through which the rural consumer goods move are:

1. Producer-Wholesalers-Retailers-Consumers. As we have observed earlier, the rural goods move generally through this channel. Majority of the goods are sold *via* this channe. in this channel, the products move from producer to one of the wholesalers dealing in the local market, central market and jobbing market. Thus, it is lelieved by jobbers from jobbers to retailers, who in turn sell to consumers. Since the channel is the longest one, the cost of distribution would be definitely high. Sometimes the agent middlemen may also be employed. This again, adds to further cost of marketing.

2. Producer-Retailers-Consumers. Some rural consumer goods such as fruits, eggs, milk, butter and vegetables are being sold directly to the retailers in jobbing market. Thus, the producers bypass the wholesalers in the central and local markets. The retailers directly enter the local market and buy from the farmers or producers and sell them to the consumers. Certain merits accrue to the producers by selling through this channel; they are in a position to get higher price for their produce. The small producers can perform the functions of grading and standardisation. But it is very difficult and cumbersome to assume such functions if the produce is large. Particularly, this channel is not an alternative for the producers at long distance from the markets. It is possible to deal with large retailers like chain stores.

Similarly, the retailers also enjoy the advantages of sure supply, fresh/stock, lower prices. At the same time, they are to face the problem of collecting the supplies from different producers located at great distances. Moreover, the retailer himself has to assume certain marketing functions like storage, grading and standardisation.

3. Producer-Consumers. Some rural consumer goods are also sold directly by the producers to consumers by eliminating both the wholesalers and retailers. A very small portion of the rural goods are sold through this channel. The products such as eggs, butter, milk, fruits, vegetables are being sold directly to the consumers. Following methods are used to sell directly:

(I) House to House Selling. The products like milk, eggs, are sold in this way. Home delivery of the products is given. Again, the selling of fruits and vegetables by hawkers is an instance of house to house selling.

(ii) Retail Public Market. Retail public markets are the open markets where the buyers and sellers meet. The farmers carry the goods to the particular market places and sell the consumers who visits them with the purpose. In India, we call them as 'bazars' or 'hats'. In western countries, they are commonly called as 'farmers market' or 'farmers retail market.'

(iii) Road-side Selling. The producers sell their products like fruits, vegetables by the side of the road, where their farm is located. Even the poultry products like eggs are sold in this way. Here, the consumers come to the farm and make purchases. This is exactly opposite of house to house selling.

(iv) Selling Through Post. In advanced countries, this method is followed. But this is of little importance for selling agricultural consumers goods, where there is no direct touch between the consumer and producers, contacts are being made by means of post. According to the orders placed, goods are packed and transported. It is very difficult way of selling, involves heavy cost of packing, the problem of collection and keeping of accounts. From the point of view of rural producers, to get higher prices for their produce they may prefer to sell directly to the consumers. This is a practical and worthwhile proposition, if the producers are in close proximity to the thickly populated areas. However, very negligible portion of the rural consumer goods are sold in this fashion. Moreover, they will have to spend lot of time and energy to sell directly, in which they are interested. Therefore, they decide to sell either through the wholesalers or through the retailers. About 90 per cent of the total rural produce moves through the two channels. On the other extreme, consumers are also not interested in buying directly as they believe and rely more on middlemen than on the producers. In order to enjoy higher prices, they will have to store the goods for longer time, but they do not have the proper warehouses to store them. So all these factors make it almost an impossible to sell directly to consumers except a few dairy and poultry products.

The rural raw materials pass through different channels as the consumer goods do. The only difference between the two is that there are no retailers in the picture, in the channels of raw materials. The raw materials such as jute, cotton, tobacco, sugarcane, groundnuts, etc., are marketed through anyone or more of the following channels:

1. Producer-Local Market-Central Market-Secondary Market Industrial user.
2. Producer-Central market-Secondary market-Industrial user.
3. Producer-Secondary market-Industrial user.
4. Producer-Industrial user, directly.

The bulk of the raw materials are sold through the midalemen in local market, central market or secondary market. However, direct selling is an exception.

FACTORS AFFECTING DISTRIBUTION CHANNELS

In the words of Prof. W. Stanton, *"It is route taken by the tite to the goods as they move from producer to the ultimate consumer or industrial user."*

Richard M. Clewett, in his article "Checking your marketing Channels" states, "A channel is the pipeline through which a product flows on its way to the consumer. The manufacturer puts his product into the pipeline or marketing channel and various marketing people move it along to the consumer at the other end of the channel.

John A. Howard, an authority, defines as, "Marketing channels are the combination of agencies through which the seller who is often, though not necessarily, the manufacturer, markets his product to the ultimate user.

Wrote Alderson, described, a marketing channel as, "A group of firms that constitute a lose conditions engaged in exploiting a joint opportunity in the market, " a marketing channel or trade channel is the mean through which goods move from the producer or manufacturer to the ultimate consumer. To put it in other words, the channel is opened with the producer's and ended by the ultimate consumers. However, the persons and institutions who render specialised services to bring about change in the title of the goods, such as banks, transportation agencies, insurance companies and warehousing organisations are not included. The channels of distribution include producers, wholesalers, retailers and agents and consumers. Selecting the channel or channels of distribution for letting out the products and placing them either in the hands of consumers is the most difficult problem faced by the manufacturers or producers. For determining, a particular channel(s) number of factors are to be taken into account, as this is a part of the policy decisions of manufacturers. Now, let us examine these factors.

Marketing channels for rural products vary from product to product, country to country, lot to lot and time to time. For example, the marketing channels for fruits are different from those for foodgrains. Packagers play a crucial role in the marketing of fruits. The level of the development of a society or country determines the final form in which consumers demand the product. For example, consumers in developed countries demand more processed foods in a packed form. Wheat has to be supplied in the form of bread. Most eatables have to be cooked and packed properly before they reach the consumers. Processors play a dominant role in such societies. In developing countries like India. However, most foodgrains are purchased by consumers in the raw form and processing is done at the consumer's level. Again, the lots originating at small farms follow different route or channels from the one originating in large farms. For example, small farms usually sell their produce to village traders; it may or not enter the main market. But large farms usually sell their produce in the main market, where it goes into the hands of wholesalers. The produce sold immediately after the havest usually follows longer channel than the one sold in later months. With the expansion in transportation and communication network, changes in the structure of demand and the development of markets, marketing channels for farm products in India have undergone a considerable change, both in terms of length and quality.

1. Product Analysts. First and foremost aspect, in order to choose a channel, is to take account of the classification of products either as consumer goods and their sub-classification. As we have noted already, that the consumer goods are classified into three categories, *viz.,* convenience, shopping and speciality goods. The other factors which require mention, are uses of the product, frequency of purchase, fashions, habits, perishability etc. Sometimes, service plays a significant role in selling certain shopping and speciality goods. In this case, the manufacturer is decided through whom the goods must be sold. The middlemen that he selects should be properly qualified. That is why, the manufacturers themselves as a strategic point, open their own retail shops. Seasonal purchases of goods, low priced, goods, and large scale retailers, necessitate services of middlemen like wholesalers, retailers etc., to shift the risk of storage and thus, manufacturers can reduce the marketing costs.

2. Firms Size and Financial Position. Is the marketer well financed and large, or is he small and without adequate financial backing? If a concern is in a strong financial position, it can support a programme of direct distribution that requires the spending of money for sales effort, the longtime investment of funds in branch warehouse facilities, and the trying up of working capital in inventories and accounts receivable. On the other hand, if a firm lacks adequate capital, it must sell its output as quickly as possible after it is produced, get paid for it as soon as it can, and carry on the entire process of distribution at the least possible cost. The use of distributors or agents helps to achieve these ends. Only a few salesmen are needed to sell to distributors; such outlets vary most of the stocks necessary to serve the trade; and they usually discount their bills. The agent offers the great advantage that while the firm that uses him must generally carry he stock needed to service his customers, it incurs no selling expenses until after the has sold some of its goods and the amount of its selling cost varies with the volume of sales made.

3. Nature and Extent of Market. Lazo and Corbin remark, "Marketing management select channels on the basis of what the customer wants, how, where and under what circumstances." In other words, as the products are manufactured for, selling, a clear cut idea, as to the nature and extent of market is very essential. Understanding the market implies finding out the potential buyers, their location, their habits, fashions, likes, dislikes, preferences, prejudices, the motive behind the purchase etc.

4. Review of Channels used by Rivals. Number of channels are being used by the competitors to move their products. The important channels used are:

(i) Manufacturers-Consumers

(ii) Manufacturers-Retalers-Consumers

(iii) Manufacturers-Wholesalers-Retailers-Consumers

(iv) ManufacturerAgent Middlemen-Retailers-Consumers

(v) Manufacturers-AgentMiddlemen-Wholesalers-Retailers-Consumer.

Now the manufacturer has to review these channels used by his rival and then decide, which channel or channels should be used to distribute the products. The merits and demerits, services rendered by Wholesalers, Retailers, Agent-Middlemen etc., are to be considered.

5. Dynamic Nature of Channels. The channels that are to be used are dynamic in nature, which means that a single store may deal in variety of products like, departmental store, chain stores or super markets. Thus, it is left to the sweet will of manufacturer to decide through which channel, he wants to market his products. Similarly, the wholesale organisations also deal in number of commodities both of rivals as well a of different lines of products.

In short, we conclude, that selecting the channel or channels of distribution, though seems easy, is not so. The above factors *viz.*, product analysis, nature and extent of markets, review of channel used by rivals and dynamic channels etc., are going to decide and influence the decision of the manufacturers. Selection of the best channel will depend on a balance of factors and the relative importance which the management attaches to each of the factors in any particular set of circumstances. There is none 'best' channel for all the manufacturers of a single class of products.

❑

6

Marketing Structure and Performance

The concept of marketing and its influential role in the transformation of market, consumer and Indian economy is increasingly felt. It is a pervasive element in contemporary life of everyone. Marketing provides an opportunity to contribute to society as well as to an individual company. In the context of present competitive environment, marketing has become the key in deciding the success and the health of a corporate. Corporates in India have recognised this fact and thus are laying a greater emphasis on marketing.

The growth of an economy is indicated by an increase in the Gross National Product (GNP) and per capita income. Increase in gross national product and per capita income in a country requires an increase in the production of goods and services. Hence, the level of production is significant in determining the level of income whether of an individual economic unit or of the economy as a whole.

Marketing has both micro and macro aspects. In its micro aspect, an efficient system of marketing enables the producer of commodity to get a higher price for the product and thereby enables him to earn larger income and helps him maintain a higher standard of living. In its macro aspect, it enables society to get different products which its members need at reasonable prices and thereby enables them to improve their consumption standards and levels of living. It avoids waste of economic resources by mobilising goods from places where they are in plenty, and hence do not have much value in terms of human satisfaction, to places where they are scarce and hence have a great value in terms of such satisfaction.

The Concept of Marketing

The term 'marketing' connotes different meanings to different people; to some it is shopping, to others it is selling and still others understand it as purchasing as well as selling. Marketing is the activity undertaken by the companies to make an exchange transaction, a consummate and adding on bring out greater output at a minimum cost. Marketing in its most general definition "is the directing of the flow of goods and services from the producer to consumer or users".

Marketing is the set of human activities directed at facilitating and consummating exchanges. Marketing is human activity directed at satisfying needs and wants through exchange prices. Marketing is also referred to as the process of discovering and translating consumer needs and wants into product and service specification, creating demand for these products and services and in turn expanding this demand. Paul Mazur defines marketing as the creation and delivery of standard of living. Marketing is a matching process, based on goals and capacities by which a producer provides a marketing mix (product and services, promotion, pricing and distribution) that meets consumer needs within the limits of society?

Marketing is a total system of business designed to plan, promote and distribute want-satisfying products and services an? ideas to target markets in order to achieve organizational objectives. Marketing is the process of planning and executing the conception, pricing, promotion and distribution of ideas, goods and services to create exchanges that satisfy individual and organizational objectives. In simple words, marketing may be defined as the process of providing the right product in the right place, at the right time and at the reasonable price to the consumer.

Marketing has moved away from the selling of basic necessities to selling specific facilities. The application of marketing concepts makes a company to view consumer needs as focal points for identification, analysis, and development of strategies which are evolved out of a clear understanding of customer needs. To be precise, target market needs are identified, and attempts are made to develop marketing programmes in order to increase consumer satisfaction. All marketing starts with the consumer and ends at his satisfaction. The consumer understanding is therefore indispensable to marketers for the effective planning and execution of their marketing strategies at all levels.

Rural Marketing

The definition of rural as given by the Census of India is not being Urban. There could be several approaches to understand the rural market. It will not be an exaggeration to state that if the whole of India excluding the metropolitan cities, various district head-quarters and the large industrial townships is considered as the rural market.

Rural market is not an independent entity by itself. In fact, there are sociological and behavioural factors which affect the economy of rural market. By and large, markets may be described as an environment of the country side and the habitants thereof. People are the market for marketers. In that sense, India is the second market in the world. As per 1991 Census, the population of India is 844 million. It is growing at the rate of 2.00 per cent every year. The rural population of the country is at 627 million, accounting for 74.3 per-cent of total population.

The Indian rural market, with its vast size and demand base, does offer great opportunities to marketers. More than three-fourth of country's consumers live in rural areas and more than half of the national income is generated by them. It is only natural that rural India should occupy an important position in the total market of India. The rural market is made up of two broad components: *(1)* the market for consumer goods which includes both durable and non-durable goods, and *(2)* the market for agricultural inputs (fertilizers, pesticides, seeds, etc.) and other investment goods. The market for agricultural inputs is predominantly rural and relatively well established.

Marketing in rural areas has a varied conceptual dimension as the events occurring in markets are necessarily taking place in a set of conditions affecting the rural dwellers and institutions hinterlands. Many marketers seem to take rural market as agricultural marketing, but it is a wrong view of the subject. In fact, by rural market, we mean the performance of business activities that direct the flow of goods from urban to rural areas (for manufactured goods) and vice versa (for agricultural produce) and products manufactured by rural non-agricultural workers. Therefore, rural marketing has two major areas:

(a) marketing of agricultural products, and

(b) marketing of manufactured products in rural areces.

Rural and Urban Markets Distinction

It may be of relevance to present the salient features of rural market and the difference between rural and urban markets. The urban markets are a large contiguous settlement of towns or urban agglomerations whereas the rural markets are small contagious settlement units of villages far from cities. The rural consumers are far less homogeneous than their urban counterparts and differ and that has gȯ important implications for the marketers. To begin with the "rural-urban" construct (rural being defined as "not urban", says the Census) is born out of convenience and the availability of data. words, it is not vigorously characterised.

Chart-1

Distinction Between Rural and Urban Markets

ATTRIBUTE	*RURAL*	*URBAN*
Density of population	Low	High
Literacy	Low	High
Occupation	Agriculture & Cottage Industries	Trade, Industry and Service
Exposure to media	Low	High
Mobility	Low	High
Family structure	Joint family	Nucleus family

Attitude to modernisation	Tradition-bound	Ready for change
Infrastructure	poor and weak	Abundant and strong
Economy	Closed and less magnetized.	Open and magnetized
Distribution outlets	Fewer	More
Dependence of outlets	Fewer	More
Dependence of employment	High on natural factors	Low on natural factors
Social norms	More visible	Not visible
Manufacturing activity	Low	High
Exposure	Low product exposure low brand awareness High exposure to make unbranded goods.	High product exposure High brand awarenss High Market reach.

Source: Ramana Rao, "Assessing the Rural Market".

Second, even if we were to work with this definition, the rural setting is fundamentally different from the urban. From the marketing angle, clear distinction between urban and rural centers can be made taking the attributes shown in Chart 1. The contrast between the rural and urban consumers can be made clearer by the factors such as sociological, economic; psychological and exposure factors. These factors contributing in their own way to the awareness of rural people by putting them to greater exposure and providing them with information about the happenings in the world outside. The rural consumer, unlike his counterpart, is frugal and does not consider the daily chores of life a physical exertion. Things of utility are more likely to attract his attention. A rural consumer, as a rule, wants to be very sure of the quality of the product and expects the product to spell out its use at the outset. He will purchase only that product which would give him the satisfaction of having got his money's worth. Upon buying the product, he should feel that his has been a wise choice and that he has not been taken for a ride by a fast talking city salesman.

The urban and rural consumers differ with regard to brand loyalty too. The urban consumer, being discriminative, generally has a try at any new product or the same product with a novel feature or plus attraction. In that sense, we could call an urban buyer flexible and dynamic. Not so the rural consumer, once the rural buyer is induced to buy and use a particular product and once he is satisfied with it, he becomes a staunch supporter and loyal user of that brand and may even make efforts to get the whole village to use it.

CHARACTERISTICS OF INDIAN RURAL MARKET

The rural market of India consists of about seventy-five per cent of the population of the country spread over nearly 6.30 lakh villages, some developed and many underdeveloped. The important characteristics are discussed below.

A Steadily Growing Market

The rural market has been undergoing a considerable change over the last three decades. The growth has not been only quantitative but also qualitative. This was the result of new employment opportunities and new sources of income made available through rural development programmes which have resulted in green and white revolutions and a revolution in rising expectations of rural masses. The rural market in India is with full of contradictions and paradoxes. Rural ,consumers are far less homogenous than that of others and differ from region to region. The rural markets are by and large less explored, less exploited and largely agricultural oriented. It is generally made up of market for consumption groups and the market for agricultural inputs. Green revolution and the resultant prosperity is confined to a few select areas in the country. As a result, the effective demand for consumer items is confined to select pockets only. The income generated and sent by the members of their families employed in towns and abroad also contributed to increase the purchasing power of the rural people.

In spite of the increasing rate of growth in urban population through migration and other channels and the consequent increase in their purchasing power, the rural market still offers opportunities which are vast and yet relatively untapped. A study made by the Operations Research Group (ORG) in 1989 estimated that the contribution of the rural market at Rs. 2,083 crores was as high as 37 per cent of the all India market. In countries like India the rural market centers are the farmers' first contact points with the marketing channel. Therefore, rural markets may be considered as the nerve centres of the economic social and cultural activities of the rural life of the country.

Vast and Scattered Market

India's rural market is vast, encompassing 627 million consumers. In terms of value, it crosses Rs. 40,000 crores of which Rs. 22,000 crores is for non-food and Rs. 18,000 crores for food items. It is scattered and widespread over 6.30 lakh villages, unlike the urban market confined to a handful of metros, cosmopolitan cities and towns. Hindustan Lever Limited (HLL) was perhaps the first of the marketing giants to realize the tremendous purchasing power of rural consumers. As early as in 1983, the then HLL chairman devoted his entire speech at the AGM to this issue. And over the past decade, the company has developed a highly penetrative distribution network that reaches practically every nook and corner of this vast Indian rural market. Other multinational and corporate giants like Colgate-Palmolive, Escorts, Bajaj Auto, Godrej Soaps, Asian Paints, VIP Industries, Video con, Nirma, and Proctor & Gamble have also committed significant human and material resources towards conquering rural markets.

Seasonality of Demand

The demand for goods and services in rural India depends heavily on agriculture as it accounts for more than 60 per cent of rural income. Thus the demand for products including consumer non-durable and durables is seasonal and therefore uneven in a year.

Low Living Standards

The rural consumer's purchasing power and per capita income being very low, clubbed with a high sense of savings, low literacy level, resulting in low standard of living. Added to this the traditions, religious pressures, cultural values and deep-rooted superstitions are the hindering factors for an upward social mobility.

Sources of Purchasing Power

The purchasing power of the people in rural areas is dependent on several direct and indirect factors related to the rural economy. Marketable agricultural surplus and rural urban terms of trade are the main sources of purchasing power for rural consumers. For everyone percent increase in marketable surplus of food grains, the consumption of manufactured consumer goods increases by 0.7 per cent. To a large extent, Indian agriculture is dependent on rainfall. Therefore, the rural demand for consumer goods is indirectly Influenced by the rainfall.

Government spends huge amounts of money on irrgation, flood control, infrastructure development, antipoverty schemes, fertilizer subsidies, etc. This governmental expenditure directly generate income in rural people ultimately leads to increased consumption of manufactured items. Further, these governmental investments are expected to augment the income generation process from land in future years, which in turn will accelerate the growth of rural markets. Due to government policies encouraging the rural industrialisation, growth of small scale and khadi industries, industrialisation in backward areas and the policies governing industrial licensing have resulted in the spread of industries to backward and rural areas. This process generates more rural income, which means more purchasing power in rural areas.

Regional Variations in Demand

Income distribution in rural areas across the country is not uniform, mainly due to uneven agricultural development. Impact of green revolution is more pronounced in the areas where assured irrigation is available. For instance, in Punjab, Haryana, Coastal Andhra Pradesh, and western Uttar Pradesh where agricultural productivity is higher due to assured irrigation, purchasing power of the rural people in the above regions is higher.

Skewed Income Distribution

Income distribution is more skewed in the rural areas. The lower 90 per cent of the rural households account for two-thirds of the total rural household income while 1/3 of the income is accounted by the top 10 per cent. Due to this skewed distribution of income, demand patterns for manufactured goods differ widely in the rural areas.

Media Habits

Media habits of rural consumers are likely to be different as compared to urban consumers. As illiteracy is more in rural areas, print media cannot reach large number of people. Market research studies on the media habits of farmers in Andhra Pradesh and Haryana/Punjab showed that over 30 per cent read newspapers regularly and over 70 per cent listen to radio. About 65 per cent of the farmers in Andhra goes to cinemas while it is only 26 per cent in Haryana and Punjab. This shows that media habits significantly in rural markets differ from region to region across the country.

Buying Behaviour

The rural consumer is more of an adopter than an innovator. If the product is of good quality and gives value for money, there is a higher probability of adoption and brand loyalty. Older generation and male members of rural households have decisive role in the purchase decisions as they are the frequent visitors of near by urban markets and weekly shandies. However, this phenomenon is changing as the youth in rural households, who are more educated and better informed, have increasing influence in buying decisions. Major purchases by rural households are made, particularly durable and trousseau items, during festivals, harvests and ceremonies such as marriages, births, deaths, etc.

Credit Requirement

Unlike their urban counter parts, the source of income for the rural consumer is agriculture, Cash income accrues at the time of harvests only. In one crop season, the farmer gets his income only once a year and he spends it throughout the year. This necessitates credit purchases of consumer goods. It therefore, seems necessary to introduce credit in marketing programmes. Production credit has already been introduced, but the need now is to introduce consumer credit. This may end up, perhaps by altering in a great measure, the existing mix of marketing elements.

Rural Market—Some Issues

Manufacturers and marketing experts have to pay special attention to the question whether rural consumers constitute a distinct market from urban consumers. It is clear that the rural market as a whole has different features from the urban market. Differences seem to arise mainly on account of certain external factors that shape the rural market rather than due to the real tastes of consumers themselves. In what follows, an attempt is made to present some of the issues concerning the rural market:

Product Planning

One of the prevailing beliefs is that the rural buyer imitates his urban counterpart. Does this mean that the same products can be sold in two different markets? Some manufacturers who tried to enter the rural market have however, found to their utter dismay that this is not the case. Goods have to be specially designed to meet the tastes and preference of the rural consumer. Before one embarks on a programme of rural marketing, one should have a sound idea about rural consumer attitudes, habits, social standards, important festivals, marriages, crop seasons, significance of astrology, local institutions which have an impact on daily life, and importance of gold, etc. An understanding of these would help in designing the marketing strategies effectively for rural areas.

Retail Outlets

Most marketing managers believe that rural families mostly buy their manufactured consumer goods in towns or mandi markets. While in the case of some durables this might be true. It is not necessarily true for consumer products which have a high frequency of use like soaps, hair oils, tea, tobaccos, biscuits etc. For products which cannot be taken up for sale by either the general stores or the kirana stores, mandi markets became the most suitable place to locate the retail outlets. For radios, transistors, cycles, kerosene stoves, etc., which call for a degree of servicing and stocking of spare parts, it seems essential that retail outlets are not located away from the consumers, though the costs of penetration will have to be taken into account.

Branding

Some marketing analysts believe that no special branding is required and that sophisticated brand names will catch up in rural areas. This is seldom true. Therefore, marketers may have to give their products names which can be easily remembered and pronounced with wrappers printed in local languages. On account of high proportion of illiteracy and lack of persistent publicity, branding carries practically little importance in remote villages. The rural consumer does not make brand discrimination but once induced to buy and use a product he becomes loyal to the brand, provided he is satisfied about the functional utility.

Promotion and Advertising

Yet another belief that exists is that strategies adopted in promotion and advertising for urban consumers can be replicated with only minimal changes for use in the rural areas. For instance, manufacturer deals without regard to the difference between market segments. Today, even the biggest rural marketers service just upto the block town level, with the village coming out not reaching there. The marketers who swear by their marketing have singularly failed to exploit rural India's traditional selling system their near-obsession with just duplicating the urban type net work and that to with vary limited success, has kept the find to the obvious. Till now corporate India has based itself just catering to the needs of the affluent rural elite, paying no attention whatsoever to the marginal/small former. No one ever thought of landing a brand specifically for the rural market. let alone liked seriously at the marginal rural classes as consumers.

Firms are increasingly realizing the importance of weekly markets, fairs and melas, and mobile publicity vans. For certain consumer products, market experts have successfully tried to use mobile publicity vans as sales outlets with the idea of making these self-paying, thus reducing the burden of the additional expense on promotion.

Size of the Rural Market

The size of rural market can be studied from the angle of market for consumer goods and market for agricultural inputs.

The Market for Consumer Goods

The per capita consumption and expenditure is generally low in rural areas yet, the expenditure is very high due to the larger size of the market. An analysis of NSS shows that of the total expenditure on manufactured consumer goods, 75 per cent is spent in rural India. And notably, the percentage has remained unchanged since 1960-61. In this segment, the market is approximately three times larger. On the assumption that all persons for families above the poverty line form the market for some branded consumer goods, this market has over 50 million households.

Wealth distribution in rural India is uneven and the top 13 per cent of the farmers land holdings account for 57 per cent of cultivated area. Further, NSS (1991) data show that the top 10 per cent of the rural population accounts for about 37 per cent of the expenditure on consumer goods. Not surprisingly, the potential market is at the top end of the spectrum. However, with the increasing spread of rural income, consumer goods are expected to make substantial penetration into the lower income stratum.

The Market for Agricultural Inputs

In line with the increase in demand for manufactured consumer good there, is also a complementing demand for agricultural inputs in rural areas. This can be seen from the compound rate of growth in the off take of agricultural inputs and equipment fertilizers 12 per cent, pesticides 15 per cent, area under high yielding varieties 15 per cent, tractors 18 per cent and pumps and tube wells 18 per cent.

Importance of Rural Marketing

The role of marketing, influencing the level of rural consumers and thereby on rural development, is still greater. It is due to the fact that the rural sector is the main suppliers of inputs for agricultural and also for the consumer goods. Hence, an efficient system of marketing in the rural areas, which acts as a link between the rural and the urban sectors, is necessary for the rapid development of the rural markets in the country. In the recent past, the rural sense has been undergoing a sea change. The green revolution has a sweeping effect over the rural sector; transport and communication systems have improved; the market intelligence system in the villages has assumed better quality; retail outlets have expanded; fashions and tastes of the urban elite have visited the villages with a greater demonstration effect; and more funds are now being pumped in by financial institutions.

Any economy, developed or underdeveloped, is a market oriented economy. Marketing is a critical factor at all stages of economic development. The contribution of an efficient system of marketing to the rural development of a country like India is great. In developing economies like India the study of the evolution of rural consuming system is highly relevant, in the context of spurt in economic prosperity occurring through agricultural and rural development, because it reveals how the consuming system adjust to such spurt in material prosperity.

The survey conducted by National Council of Applied Economic Research (NCAER) suggest that 1992-93 was a year which saw increased inequality, with rise in population having income below Rs. 18,000 per annum. The trend towards a faster increase in the proportion at higher levels of income in rural India as against urban India continued. Some change in occupation in rural India is visible from cultivation to wage earning. Education and especially literacy seems to be rapidly increasingly and more so in rural than in urban India.

In rural households, there appears to be a change in character of the heads of households with somewhat greater education and more participation of rural households in the purchase of household amenities. The contribution of the rural market to the all India market in certain categories of products clearly shows the importance of the rural market in India.

It has been noted that the rural consumer is discerning and the rural market vibrant. At the current rate of growth it may even outstrip urban market. Surveys and audits for a number of consumer products and services have, over the years, clearly highlighted the emerging importance of this sector. The rural market is not sleeping any longer. "Go-rural" seems to be latest slogan. Rural consumption of all products is growing by leaps and bounds, since the urban market has reached near saturation levels in a number of categories like washing powder, toilet soaps, batteries and talcum powder.

Chart 2

Per Capita Consumption

PRODUCT	*URBAN*	*RURAL*
Soap	5339	2199
Premium Soap	1379	209
Toothpaste	1229	129
Shampoo	20 ml	1.2 ml
Talcum Powder	46 g	4g

Source: Mehr Mehtha, "Rural Marketing: The new buzzword," Indian Express, 23 Aug. 1993.

If a marketer takes rural consumers on the path of change, even products that are more urban in nature will see rural market volumes increasing. The rural market at present is almost as big as urban, if not bigger. Mr. Keshub Mahindra, well-known businessman says, "with the break-through in agricultural sector and the rise in rural incomes, as a result of the outlay of crores of rupees on irrigation, fertilisers, and other agricultural inputs, the face of the countryside is changing. The villagers will need and are asking for a variety of goods which were beyond their ken two decades ago. Bicycles, radios, fountain pens, soaps, watches, furniture, better clothes, and many other new products are now in demand in the rural areas."

The size of the rural population will serve as a large potential demand base for a variety of products. The revolution in agricultural sector will certainly result in increased generation of wealth, increased productivity, increased income and increased consumptions. The presence of the increased consumption can be felt in household goods, household durables, agricultural inputs, agricultural capital goods etc. The rate of growth of the rural market will depend not only on the increasing rural income but also on a policy on the part of the manufacturers for developing national markets.

If penetration of rural areas is thus necessary from the point of view of business for finding new outlets for their products, widening of marketing horizons beyond urban and semi-urban areas is also imperative for raising the standards of living of the rural masses as well as their productivity. Marketing of both consumer and capital goods therefore needs to be expanded considerably.

Problems of Rural Marketing

In the Indian context, rural marketing is a complex subject. For a business organisation, rural marketing is beset with a number of problems. The process of rural marketing poses many problems due to the vastness of the country and a high potentiality for providing an effective marketing system. Besides, a few other problems stem from the underdeveloped markets and illiterate and gullible people constitute the major segments of the markets.

The rural markets in India have some peculiar problems compared to urban markets. These problems arise basically out of the peculiar dynamics of rural market of India—the uniqueness of the rural consumers, the uniqueness of the structure of the rural market and the peculiarities of the distributional infrastructure in the rural areas. The rural market is a case for the introduction of traditional marketing activities of promotion, distribution, sales and servicing, by introducing appropriate innovation, selection and adaptation. There are about 5,79,000 villages in India, 77 per cent of them with a population of less than 1,000 each.

The major hurdles in tapping the rural markets can be summarised in the following Chart 3.

Chart 3

Hurdles in Tapping the Rural Markets

1. High distribution costs
2. High initial market development expenditure
3. Inability of the small retailer to carry stocks without adequate credit facility
4. Generating effective demand for manufactured goods
5. Lack of wholesaler and dealer network problems
6. Mass communication and promotion problems
7. Banking and credit problems
8. Management and sales managing problems
9. Market research problems
10. Inadequate infrastructural facilities (physical distribution roads, warehouses and media availability)
11. Highly dispersed and thinly populated markets
12. Low per capita and poor standards of living social, economic and cultural backwardness of the rural masses
13. Low level of exposure to different product categories and product brands, and
14. Cultural gap between urban based marketers and rural consumers.

The development of the rural market will involve additional cost both in terms of promotion and distribution. In rural marketing, often it is not promotion of brand that is crucial but creating an awareness concerning a particular product filed, for instance fertilizers and pesticides.

Undeveloped Road Network

It is hardly understressed that the development of rural markets depends on a rigorous network of roads to connect the villages to towns, and to transport products to the rural hinterland. However only 40.7 per cent of the villages *i.e.* 2,34,400 villages, are connected by all weather roads. Development of all weather roads, to link all the 5,79,000 villages, will give a fillip to economic development and employment in the rural areas. It will also make household necessities and convenience products of daily use freely available in the villages.

Inadequate Communication Facilities

Market development in rural areas will receive tremendous fillip if infrastructure, facilities for communications are strengthened. Growth of telecommunications has been tardy in India with only around fifty lakh telephones at the end of 1990s. The studies by United Nations and world bank indicates that the number of telephone connections in India is low. The population per telephone ratio in India is the highest in the world, even when compared to the less developed countries. There has to be a concerted effort to boost the number of telephone connections in the villages. The means to communicate freely will lubricate the wheel's of trade, commerce and marketing. Travelling in the hinterland is extremely tedious and stay is a big problem. It is necessary to build more circuit houses or small motels in the interior villages.

Orthodox and Conservative Consumer

The orthodox and conservative views are also major players in selection of product in the case of rural consumers. It has at times, even happened that a consumer product been outrightly rejected for it was considered a bad omen. The villager has been very conservative in his attitude and approach and highly reluctant to change his traditional way of thinking and doing things. His attitude, in many respects, is that "home-made" is the best. Many of these antiquated attitudes are changing although, the rate of change is sluggish.

Inadequate Rural Market Study

Research on rural market is very less and reliable quantitative data about the total size of the market for specific durable and non-durable products is not available. In the absence of adequate data and information about rural market, the marketer finds it difficult to evolve strategies and specific plans for rural markets. There is a greater need to study: the total size of the rural market for specific durable and non-durable products by geographical, income and occupational segments. The consumer behaviour in the light of traditions, culture and the impact and influence of media on rural markets.

Limited Reach of Media

Studies conducted by the National Readership Survey and ORG reveal that only 9 per cent of the rural adult population read any newspapers or magazines, 31 per cent watch TV regularly, 36 per cent listen to the radio and 29 per cent watch cinema. Added to this low level of literacy is also an hindering factor. for the reach of the printed word to rural areas.

Inadequate Outlets

There are around two million retail outlets in rural areas selling consumer products, toiletries and household necessities to a rural population of round 625 million. Which is 6 times lower than urban outlets. The number of outlets in a village primarily depends upon the level of economic prosperity, purchasing power of the villagers, population of the village and the awareness of consumer goods and the general pattern of the number of shops per village.

Presence of Spurious Products

The imitation is another major problem in rural marketing. As soon as a brand becomes popular in rural areas, at least 10 to 15 imitations and spurious products prolife rate the market. Loosely defined, spurious brands are look-alike products with similarity in packaging and minor alterations in name. The primary motive is to capitalise on the trust built by established brands. No sooner does a brand find a comfortable placement, than there is a deluge of spurious replicas elbowing the original for shelf space. Each of these motto's offer higher margins to the retailer and has lower end consumer prices as compared to the real thing. To counter this unhealthy competition, companies need to create a clear brand identification and strong pull from the rural consumer. Local promotion in individual village markets could be an effective route to educate him.

REGULATED MARKETS

Regulated markets occupy a place of paramount importance in the process of rural marketing scenario in a country like India. The institution of regulated markets has today emerged as the most powerful instrument to revamp and radicalise the age-old and tradition bond system of rural marketing. The remarkable growth of this institution over the last three decades speaks volumes of its fast-growing popularity. From a bare 268 at the outset of the First Plan, their number touched an impressive figure of 6,996 at the end of March, 1994. The "Quantitative Explosion" in their number, has been made possible primarily on account of the rapid strides made by this institution for streamlining the system of rural marketing in India. In addition to this protective function, the regulatory apparatus has also helped in making the marketing system more efficient.

The Royal Commission further observed, "the defects and chaotic conditions, prevailing in the markets for rural goods, could be removed only by the establishment of properly regulated markets. The overall aim of establishing the regulated markets, is to prevent the exploitation, to make the market system effective and efficient. To improve marketing conditions with a view to creating fair competitive conditions to increase in the bargaining power of producer-sellers was considered to be the most important prerequisite of orderly marketing. Most of the defects of, and malpractices under, the marketing system of rural products have been more or less removed by the exercise of public control over markets, *i.e.*, by the establishment of regulated markets in the country.

Creation of long cherished marketing infrastructure, introduction of standardised marketing practices, predetermined, reasonable and standardised market charges, correct payment, open auction system of sale and so on are some of the causes of their successful functioning.

The working of Regulated Market is not absolutely free from limitations. Studies into their working have revealed that these are yet to bring about substantial charges in the traditional system of rural marketing. The findings of these studies may be debatable, but it can hardly be disputed that the operational efficiency of Regulated Markets is not without criticism.

The working of Regulated Markets is beset with a number of shortcomings, some of which have now started assuming serious proportions. The role that Regulated Markets is to be assigned in our forthcoming developmental plans depends remove the major problems in their working. Hence, it is high time that the problem areas of Regulated Market were carefully identified and suitable remedial measures initiated before it is too late.

Regulated Markets in India at a Glance. Going back to the history or regulated markets, it was in 1897 that the regulation of markets was brought about by the passing of Berar Cotton and Grains Market Act. However, the real regulation started from the year 1927 when Bombay Cotton Market Act was passed. It covered only, the then, Bombay province. Later on similar acts were passed by other central provinces like Madras, Mysore, and Punjab. The number of regulated markets, started increasing rapidly after independence when the Planning Commission stressed the need and emphasized the importance and realised the effectiveness in eliminating and remedying the defects of agricultural marketing. The following figures give the picture of regulated markets:

Plan-years	*No. of regulated markets registered (cumulative)*
In 1939 per plan period	122
During 1951—1956 1st plan	470
During 1956—1961 2nd plan	725
During 1961—1966 3rd plan	1600
During 1966—1969 (Plan holidays)	N.A.
During 1969—1974 4th plan	2640
During 1974—1979 5th plan	4000
During 1979—1980 Annual plan	4050
During 1980—1985 6th plan	5695
During 1985—1990 7th plan	6275
During 1990—1992 Annual plan	6780
During 1992—1997 8th plan*	7800

* Expected to reach.
N.A = Not available.

MAIN FEATURES OF A REGULATED MARKETS

Such regulated market has certain characteristics of its own. These are as:

1. Market committee.
2. Area of operation.
3. Methods of sales.
4. Licensing the functionaries.
5. Market levels.
6. Settlement of disputes.

(i) Market Committee. As per the requirement of Act a market committee is to be constituted with companies of representative from different sections of society, representatives of farmers, agents, traders, Government, local bodies, and co-operatives. These representatives may be either elected or nominated by the Government. The Market Committee enjoys certain rights and powers. It can prescribe the conditions of fair trading. It also has the right to bring about improvements in marketing methods by necessary actions and to facilitate the farmers, at the time of marketing. Moreover, it has the power to penalize those, who contravene or break the rules and regulations.

2. Methods of Sale. The main objective of regulated markets is to ensure fair trade practices, by eliminating malpractices and unauthorised deductions. In order to avoid these ills of unorganized markets, the regulated market provides for 'open auction' sale methods. A representative of the market committee is to be present on the auction spot and to take note of the quantity sold, the price at which sold and the names and addresses of buyers and sellers. Thus, the 'private negotiations' are discouraged and 'underhand dealings' are prohibited.

3. Area of Operation. The State Government, first issues the notification in the newspapers of its intention to exercise its control over trade practices in a specified area. Such an area of operation of the regulated markets is laid down either as municipal limits, districts or even larger. Separate 'market yards' are necessary for effective regulation which many of the regulated markets do not possess in India.

4. Licensing the Functionaries. Those who work within the 'market yard', must seek proper licence from the market committee. The functionaries, who operate in the market yard, may be traders, auctioneers, farmers, weighmen and other labourers. Separate licences are issued to deal, in different commodities. They have to procure the licences after paying certain amount offees. The act also provides the rate of commission, allowances, and other charges payable to the functionaries in the regulated markets.

5. Settlement of Disputes. The regulated markets provide a separate machinery for setting the disputes. The usual disputes that arise in the course of transactions, are prices to be paid, allowances to be given to the middlemen and the quantity of the products etc. A separate committee called 'Arbitration Committee' is being formed to settle the differences and disputes. Its decision is final and binding on the part of both the parties.

6. Market levels. Market "cess" or 'fee' has to be given by growers as well as dealers. This levy may be calculated on the basis of value or volume of the goods bought or sold or it may by on the basis of 'cart load' or 'truck load'. The licence fees, fines and market cess are the only source of income to meet the expenses of managing the affairs.

Regulated markets are as:

1. Reduction in Village Sales. The establishment of regulated markets has led to the decrease in village sales. The grower-sellers are made aware of the fair practices in the regulated markets. Now, they bring the saleable produce to these markets. The agricultural goods brought to the markets have risen from 20% to 95%.

2. Fair Prices. The prices determined in the regulated markets are fair and reasonable to both the producers as well as dealers and not one sided. Thus, the farmers are assured of getting higher share in the price. The farmers are having kindling of the candle of incentive to grow more and earn more.

3. Reduction in Market Charges. Payment of commission, weighing charges, brokerage, hamali, charity etc., are prescribed by the Market Committee. Thus, all the unauthorised deductions are prohibited. Thus, the farmers, share in the actual price has increased. Prior to regulation, these marketing charges varied from market to market, with an average of 3.41 %, now have come down to 1.79%, resulting a saving of 1.62%.

4. Correct Weighmen. There was manipulation is weighing, prior to the establishment of regulated markets. But now, they have introduced correct weights and measures in the markets; weighing is done by licensed weighmen. Hand balances are replaced by beam balances and weights bridges. Metric system of weighment is adopted. The weights are also standardised now. This assures correct weighment to the farmers and thus, eliminates manipulation in weights.

5. Marketing Facilities. Number of facilities are being provided by the regulated markets like drinking water facilities for both men and animals, parking arrangements, storage, cold storage, auction sheds etc. All these amenities are available only in the regulated markets.

6. Marketing Services. Grading of agricultural goods has been accepted, as one of the important functions of regulated markets. It solves many problems like better prices, continued market etc., 'Agmark' standards have been accepted by all. That is why, today we find this mark on packages of many products like, grains, honey, ghee, vanaspati, etc., which speaks of the quality. It becomes easy to determine the price.

Market News. The dissemination of market information and news, has been regarded as an important service functions to be performed by the market committee. The prices ruling in various markets are exhibited on the notice board. Now, the price of the commodities are being announced through broadcasting on all India or regional level.

To conclude, the regulated markets play a vital role in removing, majority of the defects and malpractices and, therefore more and more regulated markets are to be established and operated on proper lines, in those areas where they are present by their absence.

What is Regulated Market?

Regulated market is a wholesale market where dealings or buying and selling are regulated or controlled by the State Government through a 'Market Committee', which consists of representatives of producers, traders, agents, local bodies, co-operative societies and Government. It is a market where the activities are to take place under set rules and regulations and the malpractices like incorrect weighment, unnecessary deductions are curbed. Moreover, the regulated markets provide for settlement of disputes, if any, amongst the sellers any buyers. A regulated market is one which aims at the elimination of the unhealthy and unscrupulous practices, reducing marketing charges and providing facilities to producer-sellers in the market. Any legislative measure designed to regulate the marketing of rural produce in order to establish, improve and enforce standard marketing practices and charges may be termed as one which aims at the establishment of regulated markets.

Regulated markets have been established by State Governments and rules and regulations have been framed for the conduct of their business. The establishment of regulated markets is not intended at creating an alternative marketing system. The basic objective has been to create conditions for efficient performance of the private trade, through facilitating free and informal competition. In regulated markets, the producer is able to sell his marketed surplus in the presence of several buyers through open and competitive bidding. The legislation for the establishment of regulated markets does not make it compulsory for the producer to sell his produce in the regulated market yard. Instead, voluntary action on the part of the producers to take advantage of such a market is assumed. The basic philosophy of the establishment of regulated markets is elimination of malpractices in the system and assignment of dominating power to the producers or their representatives in the functioning of the markets.

Important Objectives of Regulated Markets

(a) To Safeguard the Interests. Regulated market works under a business code of conduct framed by the 'Market Committees' to be followed by producer and traders. Producer is interested in getting higher prices for his produce. On the contrary, traders are prepared to buy more only at a low price. This may result in misunderstandings or disputes. To bring about compromise or to settle the matter the regulated market works well and tries to protect the interests of both parties but, particularly, the interests of producers who are ill organised.

(b) To Create Conditions of Fair Competition. Existence for fair competition is quite essential for the healthy growth of markets so that the fair prices can be determined. It is possible when purchases and sales are regulated by a statutory body. This is a 'fair deal' in marketing the produce at an acceptable and fair price, so that the producer is not hit hard. The facilities offair dealings are provided in the regulated markets.

(c) To make the marketing system most effective and efficient so that producers may be better prices for their produce and the goods are made available to consumers at reasonable prices;

(d) To prevent the exploitation of producers by overcoming the handicaps in the marketing of their products;

(e) To provide incentive prices to producers for a better production programme, both in quantitative and qualitative terms; and

(f) To promote an orderly marketing of rural produce by improving the infrastructural facilities.

Important Features of Regulated Markets

Under the provisions of the Agricultural Produce Market Act, the state government gives notice of its intention to bring a particular area under regulation by notifying the market area, market yard, main assembling market and sub-market yard, if any, under the principal regulated market. The meaning of these terms is explained in the following paragraphs:

(i) Market Area. The area from which the produce naturally and abundantly flows to a commercial center, *i.e.*, the market and which assures adequate business and income to the market committee.

(ii) Sub-Market Yard. It is sub-yard of the principal assembling market. This is a small market and does not generate sufficient income to be declared as a principal assembling market.

(iii) Principal Assembling Market. It is the main market which is declared as a principal market yard on the basis of transactions and income generated for the market committee.

(iv) Market Yard. This is a specified portion of the market area where the sale, purchase, storage and processing of any of the specified rural commodities are carried out.

Some of the important features of regulated markets are:

1. Market Committee. In accordance with the requirements of the Act, a 'market committee' is to be constituted which comprises representative from different sections of society *viz.*, representatives of producers, agents, traders, Government, local bodies, and co-operatives. These representatives may be either elected or nominated by the Government. The Market Committee enjoys certain rights and powers. It can prescribe the conditions of fair trading. It also has the right to bring about improvements in marketing methods by necessary actions and to facilitate the producers, at the time of marketing. Moreover, it has the power to penalise those, who contravene or break the rules and regulations.

2. Area of Operation. The State Government, first issues the notification in the newspapers of its intention to exercise its control over trade practices in a specified area. Such an area of operation of the regulated markets is laid down either as municipal limits, districts or even larger. Separate 'market yards' are necessary for effective regulation which many of .the regulated markets do not possess in India.

3. Method of Sale. In regulated markets, the sale of rural produce is undertaken either by open auction or by close tender method. These sales methods ensure a fair and competitive price for the produce and prevent the cheating of farmers by market functionaries. By these methods, the sale is carried out under the supervision of an official of the market committee, and the signature of the buyer are taken as soon as the auction is over. The business is done during fixed hours. Generally, different commodities are traded at different times of the day. Bidding is kept open to all authorised traders, and the highest bidder is given the produce. The producer has the option to refuse to accept the sale even at the highest bid, if he so desires.

4. Payment of the Value. It is obligatory on the buyer to make prompt payments for the produce without deductions of any muddat. In unregulated markets, the payment of the price of the produce is made by the buyers after 3 to 15 days of the sale of the produce in accordance with local market rules. In the past, if the seller insisted on cash payment, the buyer would deduct muddat (cash discount) to the extent of Rs. 0.50 for the produce worth Rs. 100 while making the payment. This practice has been stopped with the regulation of markets.

5. Licensing of Market Functionaries. All the market functionaries, from the hamals to traders working in the regulated market, have to obtain a license from the market committee, after paying the prescribed fees, to carry on their business. The licenced traders have to keep proper records and maintain accounts in accordance with the bye-laws of the market committee. This facilities the exercise of a proper control on the accounts of the traders and the collection of the correct amount of the market fee by the market committee. Any violation of rules by middlemen may lead to the cancellation suspension of the license by the market committee or to the filling of challans in a court of law.

6. Market Charges. With the regulation of markets, such market charges as darmada, charity, kanla, dhalta and muddat, were abolished, while the rates of other market charges, such as commission, brokerage, hamali and weighing charges, were specified in proportion to the extent of the service rendered by middlemen. Recently, the market charges payable by sellers have been transferred to the buyer; the seller have to pay only for the activities undertaken prior to marketing of the produce, *i.e.*, for transportation and hamali only. There is, thus, some saving for the producers. The extent of saving varies from market to market and from commodity to commodity.

7. Weighment of Produce. Weighment of the produce is done by a licenced weighman with standard weights and a platform scale. In some markets, a weighbridge has been installed. This eliminates short weights and malpractices which arise out of weighing with a hand balance. Now-a-days computerised weighment system and instruments are used which are totally free from all the defects.

8. Market News Service. In regulated markets, there is an arrangement for a proper and correct dissemination of market prices through various media, such as loudspeakers and notice boards. However, the dissemination of price information is not perfect in most markets because of the non-existence of these facilities. Sometimes, farmers are unable to take advantage of this facility either because of the illiteracy or the non-availability of information when they require it.

9. Standardisation of Grading. Standardisation of grading plays a vivid role in the successful functioning of the rural marketing. In the primary marketing societies this system was totally absent. Regulated market is the step in this regard to establish standardisation and grading facilities. It means the produce in the regulated markets is sold only after grading; but because of the absence of facilities, such as space, funds for the employment of technical experts for grading and the purchase of grading equipment, the grading scheme could not be implemented in all the markets in the country. The scheme is in operation only in some markets. According to the National Commission on Agriculture, only 13 per cent of the regulated markets have grading facilities. There is, therefore, a need for the extension of grading facilities to all the markets in the country.

10. Supervision. The day-to-day functioning of regulated markets is supervised by the officials of the market committee, *i.e.*, the secretary, auction clerks, and other staff. The administrative decisions are taken by the nominated/elected market committee. The market committee consists of representatives of all sections, *i.e.*, producers, traders, co-operative marketing societies, co-operative or commercial banks, autonomous bodies (panchayat samiti and Municipal Board of the area), and government officials. Prior to the establishment of regulated markets, the rules for the conduct of the business in the market were framed by traders without any consideration of interests of other groups of persons *i.e.*, farmers and consumers. The composition of the market committee varies from state to state. Some states have a smaller number of the members and some have larger. The maximum number of the members as prescribed by the government should not exceed 20. The members are the representatives of producers, traders, co-operative organisation, local bodies, government nominees, weighman and labourer. This market committee nominated for the first time a period of two years. Subsequent committees are elected for the period of three years. Out of the members a chairman and deputy chairman is elected or selected or nominated.

The administration and management of the market committee is undertaken by the elected or selected nominees of the market committee with the assistance of government officers. To meet the expenditures and to create an infrastructure of the market committee it gets funds from the following sources:

1. Market fee on the produce brought for sale in the market yard/marked area. The rate of this market fee varies from State to State. In the past, the rate of market fee was Rs. 0.20 to 0.30 for produce valued at Rs. 100. At present, the rate is from one to three per cent of the value of goods.

2. Licence fee/renewal fee of market middlemen functioning in the area.

3. Subsidy from the government.

The functions of the market committee vary from State to State. Its important functions are:

(i) To manage the main and sub-market yards and run them in the interest of the agriculturists and traders;

(ii) To prescribe the hours of trading with a view to controlling and regulating transactions;

(iii) To issue renew or withdraw licences of market functionaries with a view to regulating the entry of persons in the market;

(iv) To fix market charges for various functions and services;

(v) To realise markets fees from buyers and sellers;

(vi) To collect and disseminate market news among cultivators and buyers;

(vii) To provide facilities for grading and standardisation and to take steps for the prevention of adulteration of rural produce;

(viii) To bring, prosecute and defend any suit on behalf of the market committee;

(ix) To settle disputes, which arise out of the sale and purchase of notified rural commodities, among producers, traders and other market functionaries;

(x) To control and regulate the behaviour of those who enter the market for transactions;

(xi) To create amenities in the market yard as well as in the market area which are necessary for the smooth functioning of the marketing of rural committees.

11. Settlement of Disputes. Settlement of disputes is one of the factor which must be considered at grass roots level. When there are more than two persons are dealing in the proceedings, there may be differences or disputes, which must be solved promptly, effectively and efficiently. Disputes arising between producer-seller and traders by reason of the quality of the produce, accounts and deductions of unauthorised charges are solved by the sub committee of the market committee. This avoids the legal complications and unnecessary expenditure. Prior to regulation no such facility existed. If a farmer was not satisfied, he had to go to a court of law to get his due share, which involved a lot of expenditure and wastage of time.

12. Eliminating Malpractices. Regulated markets were formed with a primary objective to remove malpractices which are prevailing in the rural market system. With the existence of regulated market, it has tried to achieve this objective and to a greater extent it has been successful. These regulated markets have brought a general awakening among the members and they are also co-operating and coordinating to the full of their extent. Now the sales slips of the produce sold are given to producers. Showing the details of the quantity sold, the rate of sale and deductions, if any. A copy of the sales slip is supplied to the market committee for purposes of checking. The malpractice of the taking away of samples by the bidders has also been stopped.

13. Provision of Amenities in the Market. The market committee provides the amenities required for a smooth and efficient marketing of the produce of producer-sellers. These amenities are indisponsable for the successful and result oriented rural marketing system. These amenities may include the provision for infrastructure such provisions of roads, transport, drinking water, staying arrangements and certain other facilities. These facilities encourage the producers to bring their produce for sale in the regulated market, and check the tendency on their part to sell locally. There is also a check on the tendency to aversion of city markets for one reason or the other.

The various amenities provided by the market committee are:

(i) Link roads and culverts in the area;

(ii) A spacious market yard;

(iii) Rest houses, cattleshed and water troughs;

(iv) Light, watchman, drinking water and parking space for carts in the market yard;

(v) Infrastructure facilities, such as banks, canteens and post offices in the market yard.

The amenities vary from State to State and from market to market depending upon the financial status of the market committee. Most of the regulated markets lack these amenities to the extent of the norms that have been formulated. It is essential, therefore, that the government should see to it that the necessary facilities are created in accordance with the norms that have been laid down.

BENEFITS OF REGULATED MARKETS

The following are the benefits of regulated markets:

1. Reduction in Village Sales. The establishment of regulated markets has led to the decrease in village sales. The grower-sellers are made aware of the fair practices in the regulated markets. Now, they bring the saleable produce to these markets. The rural goods brought to the markets have risen from 20% to 95%.

2. Market News. The dissemination of market information and news, has been regarded as an important service functions, to be performed by the market committee. The prices ruling in various markets are exhibited on the notice board. Now, the prices of the commodities are being announced through broadcasting on all India or regional level.

3. Correct Weighment. There was manipulation in weighing, prior to the establishment of regulated markets. But now, they have introduced correct weights and measures in the markets; weighing is done by licenced weighmen. Hand balances are replaced by beam balances and weighbridges. Metric system of weighment is adopted. The weights are also standardised now. This assures correct weighment to the producers and thus, eliminates manipulation in weights.

4. Marketing Facilities. Number of facilities are being provided by the regulated markets like drinking water facilities for both men and animals, parking arrangements, storage, cold storage, auction sheds etc. All these amenities are available only in the regulated markets.

5. Reduction in Market Charges. Payment of commission, weighing charges, brokerage, hamali, charity etc., are prescribed by the Market Committee. Thus, all the unauthorised deductions are prohibited. Thus, the producers, share in the actual price has increased. Prior to regulation, these marketing charges varied from market to market, with an average of 3.41% now have come down to 1.79%, resulting a saving of 1.62%.

6. Fair Prices. The prices determined in the regulated markets are fair and reasonable to both the producers as well as dealers and not one sided. Thus, the producer are assured of getting higher share in the price. The producer are having kindling of the candle of incentive to grow more and earn more.

7. Marketing Services. Grading of rural goods has been accepted, as one of the important functions of regulated markets. It solves many problems like better prices, continued market etc. 'Agmark' standards have been accepted by all. That is why, today we find this mark on packages of many products like, grains, honey, ghee; vanaspati etc., which speaks ofthe quality. It becomes easy to determine the price.

8. The regulated markets play a vital role in removing, majority of the defects and malpractices and, therefore more and more regulated markets are to be established and operated on proper lines, in those areas where they are present by their absence.

DEFECTS OF REGULATED MARKETS OR PROBLEMS OF REGULATED RURAL MARKETS

The constraints retarding the effective performance of regulated markets are varied and multi-dimensional. While a good number of the handicaps emanate from the faulty working of the institution itself, sprung up in the wake of tremendous charges in the pattern of production and marketing consequent upon the recent globalisation of Indian economy.

The problem of Regulated Markets in India are as:

1. Undue Emphasis on Fee Collection. The foremost problem associated with the working of regulated markets appears to be the faulty approach to the every concept of market regulation. A regulated market is a facilitative and service-oriented organisation. Ţhe fee levied by these markets is a sort of quid pro-quo a charge, regulated directly to the services rendered by the imposing authority. However, the actual working of regulated markets seems to be at variance with the much acclaimed service motive of the institution. Market regulation in most of the states has proved to be a source of additional state revenue. To quote the findings of a study of the Birla Institute of Scientific Research, "In Hissar, the charges 1.5 per cent commission on the value of Kutcha Arhati goods bold through him, and his services include supervision of unloading of produce, its cleaining and display, finding and collection the buyers, auctioning the produce, weighment, and making payment. In their bid to expand their income-net, Regulated Markets in most of the state impose matket fees on a number of such commodities as for which they hardly render any service worth the name, sugarcane, ghee, vanaspati, timber, etc. to mention just a few.

Thus, it is clear that the statutory regulated marketing system has become a mechanism of additional revenues. "The general impression is that Market Committee officials act only as additional middlemen, and like all middlemen add to the cost of marketing by charging market fee".

2. Defective Formation of Market Committees. The institution of Regulated Market is administrated and managed by a market committee which is a representative body of various interests associated with the process of Agricultural Marketing. Since regulation of market is a state subject, there is great heterogeneity in the composition and construction of market committee as provided in the various sets. The numerical strength of the market committee varies from 9 in Himachal Pradesh to 20 in Madhya Pradesh.

A peculiar feature of the statutory provisions as noticeable in the various state acts is that while in a few states the numerical strength varies from market to market, in most of the states it has been fixed for all the markets alive. Such fixity in the numerical strength of the market committee seems to be a faulty proposition. The size of market committee must vary according to the area to be served, the volume of business to be transacted, the number of sub-yards to be managed, the number and types of commodities notified for regulation, and so on.

3. Lack of Autonomy in Working. Autonomy and accountability are two essential prerequisites of a successful and purpose-oriented organisation. Autonomy of working assumes particular significance in institutions like regulated markets which have to deal with a whole gamut of agricultural marketing, the actual practices of which vary from region to region and from market to market. They generally aim at ensuring uniform and cohesive working on the part of regulated markets. But, while doing this, the marketing boards are expected to see that regulated markets continue to exist as independent entities with meaningful autonomy left with them. However, an objective appraisal of inter se relationship between the two institutions shows that with all pervasive powers of the marketing boards, Regulated Markets today are divested of their working autonomy to a large extent, so much so that no decision taken by the market committee is supposed to be final until and unless it is approved by the Marketing Board. Possibly on this account, a study about the working of regulated markets in Bihar has gone to the extent of observing that "Market Committees are purely autonomous bodies.

4. Lack of Continuity in Administration. A sound and effective administration is essential far the successful functioning of any organisation. The functions falling within the purview of administration are generally performed by a person known as the chief executive. Since most of the policy decisi.ons are taken and implemented by the chief executive, his tenure bears a direct relationship to the continuity in the decisi.on-making process which, in turn, affects the quality of management in a big way.

The market secretary happens to be the chief executive officer of regulated markets in mast of the states. Hence, the efficient working of a regulated market calls for a reasonable tenure of his office. An in-depth study into the average tenure of market secretaries in many states, however, reveals a gloomy picture. The average tenure of market secretaries in Bihar, for example, has roughly been two years, against a standard period of three years. Conditions obtaining in Andhra Pradesh, Uttar Pradesh and Gujarat are not very different. The success story of wholesale markets in Europe clearly establishes the close inter-relationship between the continuity of office of the administrator and the multidimensional achievements of the market concerned.

5. Grading. While the need for grading at producers level has been well realised, progress on this score has been rather tardy. The pathetic state of affairs can be judged from the fact that out of 6,996 regulated markets in the country, only 2,028 had set up grading units till March 30,1994.

6. Ineffective Implementation of Regulatory Reforms. The basic objectives of market regulation in our country *inter alia*, include *(i)* to regulate the trade practices; *(ii)* to increase marketing efficiency through the introduction of grading and market intelligence services; and *(iii)* to protect the interests of the producer-sellers through open auction system of sale, reduction in market charges, and prompt payment of sale proceeds.

SUGGESTIONS

The National Commission on Agriculture in its twelfth report, emphasised that, with the increase in production and in development facilities for rural, there willbe about 30,000 markets by 2000 AD. in each of these markets (assembly and sub-markets, the following minimum facilities must be provided:

(a) Physical facilities for grading, weighing and storage;

(b) An agency which should take charge of the farmer's produce, advance money for his immediate needs, process the produce, arrange far further marketing at the next point and make final payment;

(c) An alternative for the personal dealing and disposal;

(d) Inter-village and intra-village road communication in the market area;

(e) Shops for inputs and domestic necessities in the same market area for easy purchase by producers;

(f) Means of communication of marketinformation in the market area.

Though the market regulation scheme has been implemented in the country, its benefits to the different, classe are not uniform. Studies have pointed out that it has a high benefit-cost ratio. Nevertheless the fact remains that many improvements are needed to make it deliver goods in an efficient manner. It is a socio-economic reform. There is, therefore, a need for bringing home its advantages to the cultivators and market functionaries. To make farmers conscious of their rights in the management and control of the market is a *sine qua non* of the success of the scheme. Producers should not submit *meekly* to the practices of market functionaries when these are contrary to their interest. Market functionaries, too should be convinced that the market regulation scheme has not been designed to eliminate them but to bring to book those unscrupulous traders who defame the entire trading community by their anti-social and dubious activities. It is with the co-operation of all these agencies-producers, consumers and market middlemen-that the market regulation scheme can make the marketing system of rural produce an efficient system. The main recommendations bringing about improvements in the efficiency of regulated markets are:

(a) The list of rural commodities notified by the market committee should be enlarged to include commercial products, horticultural products, vegetables, livestock products and minor forest products in addition to foodgrains.

(b) Farmer-growers should have major representation on the market committee; the chairman and vice-chairman should be representatives of the growers.

(c) Recognising the importance of widening the network of marketing institutians, the National Cammission on Agriculture has recommended the establishment of intermediate level markets, to be known as shanties. Following additions to the list of suggestions made by the National Commissian on Agriculture with a view to improving the efficiency of regulated markets in the country need to be made.

(i) Primary co-operative marketing societies, which are functioning at the base level, must be strengthened and properly integrated with the regulated market.

(ii) Adequate extension effort must be made in rural areas to educate the producers about improved marketing facilities, such as grading, storage and market information.

(d) The officials of the market committee, *viz.*, the Secretary, the Market Supervisor, the Market Intelligence Inspect, the Grading Supervisor and Auctioneer, should belong to the State Marketing Department.

(e) Facilities in the regulated should be improved in such a manner that each market must have a market yard, an administrative block, a bank, a trading for grading weighting and storage of all commodities.

(f) A minimum market fee may be levied uniformly on *ad valorem* basis.

❐

7

Marketing of Agricultural Inputs

The agriculture and allied activities are the mainstay in rural India in as much as they account for 75 per cent of rural income with 72 per cent of to rural population directly engaged in this activity, agriculture inputs marketing has been a big business. In traditional or subsistence farming, there was no need for any externally produced inputs and all the requirement was produced on the farm or in the village itself. A number of corporate bodies are engaged in the manufacture and marketing of agriculture inputs like fertilizers, pesticides/insecticides, seeds, oil engines, electric motors and pump sets, tractors and other related equipment. It is estimated that the agricultural inputs business is approximately of the order of about Rs. 1,20,000 million per annum.

The agricultural inputs can be classified into two categories- consumable inputs and durable inputs. Consumable Inputs include fertilizers, pesticides, seeds and the like, which are required for farming, season after season. Durable inputs include tractors, motors and pumpsets, major farm machinery items like harvesters, threshers, winnowers, which are probably purchased once in the life time by a farmer.

The various inputs which fall under these two categories are listed below:

CONSUMABLE INPUTS

1. Plant food (manure and fertilizer)
2. Soil amendments (calcium and gypsum)

3. Plant protection chemicals (for pests and diseases)
4. Seeds (high yielding, hybrid and improved varieties)
5. For power generation (diesel, oil, petrol and electricity)
6. Simple hand-held farm tools (pavada, sickle, hand hoe, crowbar)
7. Packing material (gunnies, rope, twine)
8. Feed (for cattle, poultry)
9. Veterinary medicines (prophylactic and curative)
10. Others (bamboo articles like baskets etc.)

DURABLE INPUTS

1. Farm implements (tractors, harvesters, threshers, power tillers)
2. Construction materials (cement, bricks, zinc/asbestos, sheets for roofing)
3. Irrigation equipment (motors, pump sets, sprinklers)
4. Transportation equipment (bullock carts, tractor trailers, mini trucks)
5. Farm animals (bullocks, cows, poultry, goats, sheep)
6. Others (tyres, tubes, spare parts)

An approximate estimate of value of consumption of some major in puts are presented in Table 1.

Table 1: Approximate Value of Major Agricultural Inputs Consumed

(Value in Rs million)

Sl. No.	*Name of Inputs*	*1981-82*	*1991-92*
1.	Fertilizers	25,000	75,000
2.	Pesticides/Insecticides	2,000,	10,000

3.	Tractors and Agricultural Machinery	1,500	10,000
4.	Pump Sets, Oil Engines and Electric Motors	1,500	5,000
5.	Seeds	14,000	20,000
6.	Total	44,000	1,20,090

Table 1 gives the size of the rural agro-inputs market. It would be interesting to study and understand the marketing of these agro inputs since the marketing practices vary widely. Some of these inputs have to be marketed as per the directions of the government while others enjoy a free and unrestricted market. The marketing mix adopted by the manufacturers and marketing men for some of the important inputs are described below.

FERTILIZERS

Over the years, the market for fertilizers has developed significantly. In the early fifties, fertilizers were not acceptable to farmers because of wrong notions. The expansion efforts of the Government and fertilizer companies have ensured a phenomenal growth. Today about 13 to 14 million tonnes of fertilizers nutrients valued at about Rs. 75,000 million are absorbed. The target is to reach a consumption level of 20 million tonnes by 2000 AD.

Fertilizer market is a typical example of exploitation of the potential of rural market. During the year 1951-52, when fertilizer was totally a new input to farriring, the consumption was only about 66,000 tonnes, which grew to 3,38,000 tornes. In 1961-62 fertilizer consumption showed further increases in 1971-72, when it touched 2.66 millions tonnes and during 1981-82 the consumption was 6.07 millions tonnes. The market is still growing and consumption was 6.07 millions tonnes. The market is still growing and the consumption was 13 millions tonnes in 1991-92. This further expected to grow to 20 millions tonnes by the end of 20th country.

The fertilizers consumption depends upon several factors like:

* Profitability of farming
* Availability of irrigation facilities
* Introduction of new technology
* Availability of fertilizers
* Prices of fertilizers

Fertilizers are classified into three different groups depending upon the nutrients they supply to the crop like Nitrogenous (N), Phosphatic (P) and Potassic (K). The fertilizers which supply only a single nutrient like N or P or K are called straight fertilizers. Examples of such fertilizers are ammonium sulphate, urea, calcium anunonium nitrate (which upply only the nutrient of nitrogen) and single super phosphate, triple super phosphate (which supply phosphate). For example, Di-Ammonium Phosphate (DAP which is quite popular now) is a complex fertilizer which supplied both Nitrogen and phosphate. In addition there are fertilizer mixtures which supply all the three nutrients in proportions required by different crops and different regions.

Marketing of fertilizers is higwy controlled by Government regulations. Fertilizers are governed by both essential commodities act (ECA) and Fertilizers control order (FCO). What the companies normally do is to add their company name to the generic name, like Mangala Urea (Mangalore Chemicals and Fertilizers Ltd.), SPIC Urea (Southern Petro Chemical Industries Corporation Ltd.) In addition, they also use a symbol or a logo so that the rural consumer can recognise the brand Mangalore chemicals and fertilizers Ltd. uses a 'Poorna Kumbha' which as a symbol is identified with the company.

Under the Essential Commodities Act (ECA) and Fertilizers Control Order (FCO). the Government is empowered to allocate the quantum and territories to various manufacturers. The manufactureres are obliged to sell only such allocated quantities in allocated territories only. Each type of fertilizers should contain a specified percentage of the nutrient. For example, Ammonium sulphate should contain 26.6 per cent of Nitrogen and Urea 46 per cent of Nitrogen. This has to be clearly indicated on the bag itself. This could be tested by the agricultural department of different states under FCO.

Fertilizers have to be sold at a uniform price throughout the country and selling prices are notified by the Government for different fertilizers. Since the government fixes the price of fertilizers, a fixed return on investment is guaranteed to the fertilizer manufacturers which is given as subsidy. The government also prescribes the transport/cost/equated freight payable for the fertilizers produced and transported by different manufacturers. The manufacturers are expected to transport the production within the equated freights fixed by the government. If they exceed these limits, the excess cost will cut into their profits/Margins. The specified transportation model include rail and road for transit of fertilizers from factories to allocated marketing territories. The policy also prescribes that rail transportation should be full rake loads up to a single destination and from this point road transportation can be used for further dispersal.

The government policy also prescribes the distribution margins payable to the channel members in respect of each variety of fertilizers. The government further insists that fertilizers shall be delivered freight paid up to block headquarters level. Since the government enforces several restrictions on fertilizer marketing the manufacturers are entitled for subsidies on many accounts. The subsidy on fertilizer distribution marketing has reached an alarming level of Rs. 5,000 crore per year during the Seventh Plan period.

Fertilizer imports from countries like Germany, Jordan, USA, former USSR, Japan and others take care of the gap between the demand and supply with all these controls on fertilizers distribution and prices, the fertilizer industry has done extremely well. This is mainly due to the coordinated extension efforts of the government (both central and state) and the fertilizer manufacturers.

FERTILIZER MARKETING MIX

The fertilizer marketing mix is as:

(a) Product

(b) Price

(c) Placement or Distribution

(d) Promotion.

(a) Product. Not much manoeuvrability is possible for the manufacturers and marketing men in product designing. At the most they can manufacture and market fertilizer mixtures which supply the three nutrients in a proportion that is required by certain types of soils or crops or regions. These are called paddy mixture or sugarcane mixture, but the bag should clearly indicate the proportions of the three nutrients *e.g.,* there could a mixture as 20 : 20 : 20 which means the mixtures contain N, P and K in that proportion. Thus the product manoeuvrability is very limited in the case of fertilizers. The basic purpose of any product under fertilizer category is to supply N. P & K nutrients.

(b) Price. Prices are totally controlled by Government including the margins for channel members and the companies may offer to their dealers volume discounts or off-reason discount at the most. This is very closely watched by the Government and any such rebates have to be borne by the company as the subsidy will not cover such discounts.

(c) Placement or Distribution. The government policies dictate the type, quantum and the area for distribution for each manufacturer. Therefore, the manufacturers do not have much say in distribution.

Most fertilizer manufacturers use distribution networks to reach the fertilizers to end users. Traditionally, the cooperatives and Agro Industries Corporations played a significant role, but oflate private trade has also taken to the fertilizer distribution in a big way because of affective margins. Earlier the proportion of fertilizer distributed between the co-operatives and private trade was in the ratio of 60 : 40. Presently the trend is reversed and private trade accounts for 60 per cent, while cooperatives and Agro Industries Corporations for only 40 per cent. A few manufacturers have their own retail outlets also—Fertilizers and Chemicals of Travancore (FACT) in Kerala, and GSFC in Gujarat. Sometimes the retailers pass on fractions of their margins to actual users.

(d) Promotion. In the case of fertilizers, the one element of marketing mix 'promotion' allows the manufacturers to use their ingenuity not only to sell the quantity allocated to them but also create a brand image. Various promotional measures are adopted by different fertilizer manufacturers and marketing men.

1. Inter-personal and Group Contracts. Right from house to house contract campaigns, to discussions with small farmer groups are adopted by fertilizer manufacturers. This is also combined with training programmes for the farmers.

2. Mass Media. Mass media has also been extensively used by fertilizer manufacturers to promote their product. Advertisements in vernacular press and journals, literature on crops and products in the form of pamphlets and folders are quite. popular. Radio has been very extensively used, especially before and after farm programmes like Krishi Darshan and farm and home programmes. Other measures include visuals like hoardings posters, paintings on the bullock carts in rural areas and point of purchase materials. They also take part in exhibitions and fairs.

In addition many manufacturers use their own audio-visual vans through which they screen films interspersed with fertilizers advertisements slide shows, puppet shows and other forms of entertainment like film, music and the like. Of late, advertising through television is also used by some manufacturers, especially when farm programmes are telecast. This appears to be important in as much as television is supposed to cover about 90 per cent of population.

3. Special Promotion Measures. Many fertilizer manufacturers resort to special promotion drives. These could be result and method demonstrations in the farmers' fields, arranging for field visits of farmers to research centres and progressive farmer's fields, free soil testing services through mobile soil testing laboratories, literature on agro techniques for special crops, farmer service centres, organizing farmers clubs for exchange of information on cultivation practices, visit to fertilizer factories and dealers training programmes. Some manufacturers even institute awards for farmers getting highest yields in specific crops on the lines of Krishi Pandit awards. The latest promotion measure is village adoption programmes. The manufacturers adopt villages with an aim to promote on all round development. Even the commercial banks involved in rural financing go in for village adoption programmes either independently or with some fertilizer manufacturers. Such programmes not only aim to increase fertilizer consumption but also other people related activities. This can be termed as 'Social Marketing' which is discussed in a subsequent chapter.

In short, the promotion measures adopted by fertilizer manufacturers are quite innovative and worth being emulated by other involved in marketing of consumables and durables also. The main advantage with fertilizers is that the Agricultural Departments of the centre and state governments do play a major role in advertising the farmers with regard to the usage, in addition to the cost-benefit advantage.

Changing Scenario in Fertilizer Marketing. Since 1991-92, the fertilizers market has undergone a phenomenal change, with the government's decision to slowly phase out the Rs. 5,000 crore subsidy given to fertilizers. Still the nitrogenous fertilizers have gone up substantially due to decontrol. This has pinched many manufacturers and sales have come down. This is expected to offset an increase in fertilizer prices. When fertilizer prices went up during the oil crisis in the year 1970-71 the demand declined initially, but picked up later. It is likely that the fertilizer industry may be totally decontrolled in the near future. The manufacturers and marketing men have to prepare themselves for such an eventuality when all the four Ps of marketing mix will be totally under their control. It is unfortunate that the fertilizer industry is unable to reach out to farmers. It is time the industry comes-out of such a mindset and thinks in terms of marketing and competition in a true sense.

As of now, there appears to be no threat to the ever expanding market of fertilizers. But research is underway to develop 'Bio-fertilizers', which are supposed to be more environment friendly and can be produced at lesser costs. Some bio-fertilizers like Rhizobium, Blue-Green Algae, etc. are. already in the market. The bio-fertilizers being cheaper, there is a likelihood of bio-fertilizer catching up and the market for chemical fertilizers declining. As of today, this appears to be a distant possibility, given the technology and need for accelerating agriculture production.

The scope for increasing fertilizer consumption in the country is enormous which is justified by the following facts:

First, there is a need for increasing the food grain production to 200 to 225 million tonnes by 2000 AD to feed the growing population with the income levels rising, there is always a switch from inferior food grains to superio. foodgrain like wheat and rice. Given the present level of technology, improved seeds, irrigation and fertilizer can only achieve appreciable increase in production while evolving new varieties and extension of irrigation facilities take a long time, fertilizers is the only alternative to achieve a quick increase in productivity and production. Hence the fertilizer consumption is expected to grow to about 20 millions fonnes from the present level of 13 millions tonnes.

Next, the present levels of fertilizer application to various crops are low not only when compared to the recommendations by research stations but also when compared to the levels of consumption in other developing and developed countries. The following table pres.nts the fertilizer consumptions in kgs hectare in selected countries.

Table 2 Fertilizer Consumption in Different Countries 1987-88

(Kgms/Hectare)

Sl No.	*Country*	*N*	*P*	*K*	*Total*
1.	Pakistan	49.7	15.3	1.7	66.7
2.	Bangladesh	48.6	18.4	5.3	72.3
3.	China	40.8	11.1	3.2	55.1
4.	Egypt	264.5	72.4	13.7	350.6
5.	Japan	125.3	143.4	112.7	381.4
6.	Europe	69.9	34.8	37.5	142.2
7.	Korea Repb.	202.3	95.2	108.7	406.2
8.	India	32.2	12.7	5.1	50.0

Source: The Fertilizer Association of India, Fertilizer Statistics, 1988-89, December 1989.

As is evident, our consumption is lower than even that of some Asian Countries. The scope for expanding the market is very promising.

These apart the fertilizer consumption in the country is not uniform and is concentrated in about 200 districts. Also, there are wide variations among states districts and even villages. Many districts which are arid region may not offer much scope for fertilizer consumption. Yet in irrigated areas, there is ample scope for increasing the same.

Table 3. Classification of Districts According to the Share in Total Consuption of Fertilizers 1988-89

SI. No.	*No. of Districts*	*Proportion to Total Consumption*	*Cumulative Percentage*
1.	8	10	10
2.	12	10	20

3.	15	10	30
4.	18	10	40
5.	22	10	50
6.	24	10	60
7.	30	10	70
8.	37	10	80
9.	22	5	85
Total	188	85	85

Source: The Fertilizer Association of India, Fertiliser Statistics, 1988-89, December 1989.

Out of about 400 districts in the country, 85 per cent of the total consumption of fertilizers is accounted for by 188 districts only. Thus, there is immense scope for extending the fertilizers to other districts in addition, the area under irrigation projects. This will also help increase fertilizer consumption. The proposed Sardar Sarovar project across the river Narmada is estimated to increase the irrigated area by about 19 lakh hectares in Gujarat, Madhya Pradesh and Maharashtra, which will offer vast potential for fertilizer consumption. Last, but not the least, is the proportion of fertilized area to gross cropped area and proportion of farms using fetilizers. This presents a very interesting picture.

Table 4. Fertilizer Consumption Pattern Farm Size Wise

Sl. No.	*Size Group in Hect.*	*Proportion of Holdings Using Fertilizers (%)*	*Proportion of Fertilized Area to Gross Cropped Area (%)*	*Fertilizer Input in Kgms per Hectare*
1.	Below 1	36.8	31.3	92.3
2.	1 to 2	44.8	32.7	85.8

3. 2 to 4	55.3	36.1	80.1
4. 4 to 10	55.4	35.2	71.1
5. 10 and above	58.8	34.2	59.0
6. All holdings	45.2	34.4	76.4

Source: The Fertilizer Association of India: Fertilizer Statistics 1988-89, December 1989.

It is seen that on an average only about 45 per cent of the agricultural holdings use fertilizers, which is again restricted, approximately to one third of the gross cropped area in the holdings (Table 4) Further, the consumption of fertilizers per unit area varies from 59.0 kg to 92.3 kg per hectare in different size groups. In typical marketing jargon, it can be said that there is scope.

(a) To bring in new holdings to use fertilizers (new accounts)

(b) To encourage more area to come under fertilizer application and increase the consumption where fertilizers are already being used (increase the consumption of existing accounts). The ever expanding market for fertilizers calls for innovative and effective marketing strategies with subsidy being withdrawn slowly, the manufacturers have to think and evolve innovative marketing strategies. It will not be wishful thinking if the fertilizer industry gets completely decontrolled in he near future. In such an eventuality all the elements of marketing mix will be under the control of the manufacturers and marketing men, which would necessitate evolution of appropriate strategies.

AGRICULTURAL CHEMICALS

The chemicals used for control of pests, diseases, rodents, virus, etc. are broadly termed 'agricultural chemicals'. The agriculture chemicals market can be classified as follows:

(a) Insecticides

(b) Fungicides

(c) Rodenticides

(d) Herbicides

(e) Fumigants

The agricultural chemicals market comprises insecticides that account for about 80 per cent, fungicides 15 per cent and the rest 5 per cent of the total market. The manufacturers of technical grade material and formulations.

There are about 79 licensed manufactures of technical grade material, out of which only about 51 are estimated to be active. Nearly 10 out of these 51 manufacturers alone account for about 80 per cent of the production of technical grade material. In 1985-86, the installed capacity for manufacture of tecnnical grade material was 1,02,328 tonnes out of which only 68 per cent was utilized. But the agriculture chemicals market has been growing steadily at about 7.5 per cent per annum. This is evident from the fact that the production of technical grade materials, which was only 19,280 tonnes in 1966 increased to about a lakh tonnes in 1985-86.

The formulators buy the technical grade material and prepare various formulations for the. ultimate users in different concentrations for different crops and also for different types of pests and diseases. These are about 800 formulators in the country. It is estimated that there are about 77,080 sale points for agro chemicals. Out of this 55,870 are privately run 16,237 are run by cooperativés and 4,973 outlets by respective state governments.

All the manufacturers and formulators have to register themselves with the Central Insecticides Board under the Insecticides Act of 1968. The banned insecticides should not be manufactured or sold, *e.g.* DDT was banned in the country in October 1989. Apart from this, the formulators are free-to adopt any trade or brand name for the products manufactured. Hence the same chemicals are sold on several trade or brand names by different companies.

Nearly 50 per cent of the sale points for agro-chemicals are concentrated in four or five states. *viz.* Andhra 'Paradesh, Uttar

Pradesh, Gujrat, Tamil Nadu and West Bengal. As in the case of fertilizers the consumption of agro chemicals is also concentrated in certain states. This is, of course dictated by the crops grown and their susceptibility to pests and diseases *e.g.*, cotton and paddy alone account for nearly 65 per cent of the agro-chemicals consumption.

The consumption of agricultural chemicals varies widely across different states.

Table 5. State Wise Share of Agrochemicals Consumption

Sl No.	*Name of States*	*Proportion to Total (%)*
1.	Andhra Pradesh	33.6
2.	Karnataka	16.2
3.	Gujarat	15.2
4.	Punjab	11.4
5.	Maharashtra	5.1
6.	Haryana	4.7
7.	Tamil Nadu	3.6
8.	West Bengal	2.9
9.	Orissa	2.0
10.	Uttar Pradesh	1.7
11.	Kerala	1.3
12.	Madhya Pradesh	1.0
13.	Bihar	0.8
14.	Assam	0.3
15.	Himachal Pradesh	0.1
16.	Rajasthan	0.1
17.	All States	100.0

In India the agrochemical consumption is dependent upon several factors-irrigation facilities, types of crops grown, concentration of plantation crops, susceptibility of crops to different pests and diseases. This can explained by the fact that the irrigated area is substantial in the state, dependence on paddy and commercial crops like sugarcane, tobacco and chillies, and intensity of cropping. Thus the market for agro-chemicals is not uniform. This is further substantiated by Table 6 which presents the data on proportion of agrochemicals consumption crop-wise.

Table 6. Agrochemicals Consumption: Crop-Wise

Sl. No.	*Name of Crop*	*Proportion of Area under the Crop to Total Area (%)*	*Proportion of Consumption to Total (%)*
1.	Cotton	5.0	27
2.	Rice/Paddy	24.0	27
3.	Plantation Crops	0.5	15
4.	Vegetables	1.7	12
5.	Sugarcane	1.8	4
6.	Oil seeds	10.0	4
7.	Wheat	10.0	3
8.	Others	47.0	8

Though a crop like cotton occupies only 5 per cent of the total cultivate area, it accounts for 27 per cent of the total agrochemicals consumption which indicates its high susceptibility to pests and diseases. The cotton farmers use large quantities of pesticides/ insecticides either to control the pests and diseases after the attack or as a prophylactic measure to prevent the occurrence of pests and diseases.

Thus the market for agrochemicals depends heavily on the region and the crops grown therein. Since there are no significant government controls as in the case of fertilizers, the elements of marketing mix are very much under the control of the manufacturers and marketing men of agrochemicals.

Product. The formulators are free to manufacture and market any combination or concentration of insecticides or pesticides from the basic chemicals. They are also free to use any trade or brand name for their product. In other words, flexibility available to the manufacturing or marketing men is very immense. Even though these applicators are not very expensive, most fanners do not possess them. They either borrow from their neighbours or hire from agro input vendors. Most cooperative societies at village level and the departments of agriculture of various state governments keep these applicators for custom hiring to farmers. This is a case of providing product related services without which the product cannot be used effectively.

Price. The prices of agro-chemicals are not controlled by the government. The manufacturers are free to fix the prices. The main consideration in pricing is the strategy of the competitors and the nature of insecticides/pesticides.

Distribution. This is the most crucial aspect in the marketing of agrochemicals: Appropriate chemical have to be made available at the time of pests/disease attack. This requires a reliable method of forecasting the seasons of attack of different pests and diseases depending upon the crop growing seasons. In addition, most chemicals have a definite shelf time. Fortunately, the chemicals are low volume and high value-products unlike fertilizers, which are high volume and high value products. This enables quick movement. This is one of the reasons why there are a number of small formulators who cater to local areas. This distribution arrangements for agrochemicals appear fairly adequate with about 75,000 retail selling outlets. Since most of the chemicals are poisonous and hazardous, packaging requirements are of at most importance along with instructions for the use of products in the field.

Promotion. The promotion measures adopted by agrochemical manufacturers and marketing men are nearly the same as for fertilizers. In addition, the agrochemical manufacturers maintain contracts with the departments of agriculture and agricultural research stations, since they recommend the farmers the specific names of pesticides/ insecticides to be used for different types of pests and diseases. This is highly productive promotion measures adopted by the agrochemical manufacturers.

Threats. There appear to be no immediate threat to the agrochemicals market, but this may not be so in the long run. The usage of chemical on crops results in effects in food consumed, which are supposed to be carcinogenic. Thus a need is felt to develop agrochemicals of biological origin. Neem-based chemicals and biological organisms are being widely tried. Hence the pesticide/ insecticide manufacturers and marketing men should think in terms of developing such eco-friendly products and be market leaders.

3. Seeds. Marketing of seeds is an important area wherein lies the key to future with the entry of multinationals in production and marketing of hybrid and high yielding seeds, the agriculture scenario is bound to change drastically from self sufficiency to exports. The liberalization and globalization policies also favour seeds marketing with the importance given to food processing industry. Traditionally the seeds market was in the hands of central and state seeds corporations. In addition, a few private seed companies were also in operation. The responsibility of evolving new varieties of high yielding seeds mostly rested with the government agencies like agriculture research stations and agricultural universities of central and state governments. The corporation distributes their seeds through co-operatives, private dealers and their own sales counters.

With the entry of several multinational seeds coinpanies like Cargill and Pet Seeds of USA, Pioneer Seeds, Hoechest, Harrison Vanderhave ITC, Indo-American Hybrid Seed Company etc., the scenario is fast changing. Simultaneously the Government is also encouraging the food processing industry through several concessions with a view to earn foreign exchange. For example, Pepsi has encouraged cultivation of high yielding tomato varieties in Punjab to meet their export commitmenis of tomato puree and paste.

In additior many public limited companies are also engaged in the business of cultivation, processing and sales of vegetables and fruit both internally and for exports. Max vorth Orchards, ITC, Hindustan Lever, Thapar's Reitgel India, etc. to name a few. Many such corporate bodies are also engaged in the processing arod export of fruit and vegetable products, flowers, mushrooms, prawns and cereals. The bodies either have their own captive farms or procure them from farmers on a contract basis. Such activities are expected to increase the demand for seeds considerably.

DURABLE INPUTS OF AGRICULTURAL MARKETING

1. Cattle, Poultry and Aqua Feeds. This is another area where a number of multinational and Indian companies also are very active (Hindnstan Lever and Godrej Agrovet). The milk production in the country got a boost with the implementation of operation food programmes. The strains of breeds they distribute require proper care and feeding. The farmers who have taken up dairy or poultry have to care for balanced nutrition. Aqua farms for being and harvesting shrimps is catching-up fast in the country due to expert possibilities. Considerable investment have been made in coastal areas of Andhra Pradesh, Tamil Nadu, pondicherry, Orissa to.establish shrimp farms. In fact the area under paddy is declining because of the establishment of shrimp farms. These activities will increase the demand for scientifically prepared, baianced feeds. Such animal based activities also create a demand for veterinary medicines, both for prophylacies and treatment.

2. Tractors. The country produces about 1.5 lakh tractors per annum, which are sold without. much difficulty. These tractors of different horsepowers 25 HP, 35 HP and above 35 HP are manufactured and marketed by major companies like HMT, Escorts, Eicher, Massey Ferguson, International, Punjab Tractors etc. Since the cost involved in the purchase of tractors and implements is substantial, the dependency is more on loans from the rural financial institutions. It has been estimated that nearly 90 per cent of the tractor sales is based on the loans advanced by rural financial institution like state land development banks and commercial banks. Since such loans are treated as long terms loans, the prospective bnyer of the tractor should be able to offer collateral security to the lending agency. Hence farmers with sizable land holdings alone can afford to apply for loans which clearly segrilents the agricultural machinery market.

While in the case of consumable inputs, all farmers, irrespective of the size of holding, will constitute the market, in the case of tractors and other agriculture machinery these is a need to clearly identify the segment offarmers which can own and use the tractors profitably. For example, in highly irrigated areas where three to four crops are grown in a year, even a farmer owing and operating in about 20 acres of land can efficiently use a tractor. Whereas in dry/ unirrigated/ rainfed areas farmers with more than 20 or 25 acres ofland alone can afford to use the tractor profitably. When the fanner approaches a bank for finance for purchase of a tractor, the bank not only takes into account the possible utilisation of tractor on his own farm, but also the possibility of hiring out the services of the tractors to the neighbouring farmers. Thus most of the farmers who do have large land holdings are able to obtain loans for purchase of tractors.

The most important criteria which count in tractor purchase are:

1. Area of land holding
2. Nature orland holding (irrigated/dry)
3. Types of crops grown and number of crops grown in a year
4. Availability of loan
5. Possibility of hiring out the.services of the tractor to others.

6. Requirements of tractor for transport of produce to market and inputs to the farm.

From the following point of view the factors which count for successful sale are;

1. Loan available from banks
2. Personal selling, identification of potential tractors users and approaching them
3. Trouble free service-less number of break downs.
4. Availability of spares for easy repairs
5. After sales service
6. Resale value of tractors.
7. Training on how to use Tractors
8. Fuel efficiency.

Most manufacturers and marketing men get themselves registered with the lending agencies as approved suppliers as and when the farmer is sanctioned loans, the approved suppliers compete among themselves to supply the tractor. The farmer in addition to his investment in tractor (which is only a prime mover) has to invest in implements which can be hitched to the tractors like disc ploughs, levellers, tailors, power sprayer etc.

The farmers require advice with regard to the choice of appropriate horse power of the tractor. This would depend upon the type of soil, purpose for which the tractor is purchased and the load it is expected to carry at the time of harvest. The marketing personnel should be in a position to advice the farmers on these aspects.

Farms machinery marketing mainly require the following:

1. Finance for purchase of Machinery
2. Personnel selling

3. Efficient after-sales service
4. Training in operation of the equipment

3. Irrigation Equipment. Compared to tractors, irrigation equipment are fairly low cost capital requirements. Here again the loan availability is an important factor. Most of the lending agencies prepare a list of approved suppliers of irrigation equipment and once the loan is sanctioned and well is dug, orders are placed with the suppliers by the lending agencies to install the pump set on the farm. This also requires training in operation and efficient after-sales service. Numerous manufacturers of irrigation equipment are in fray and competition is tough.

The opportunities available in marketing of irrigation equipments are enormous. The trapping of underground water has become necessary for commercial agriculture. These sophisticated systems economise on the water usage, so that the available water can be used to irrigate more area and also wastage can be avoided. Even though more costly, these new sophisticated irrigation systems are bound to prove popular because of economic usage of water which is fast becoming a scarce input.

4. Farm Machinery. There is other farm machinery like mould board ploughs, seed drills, winnowers, threshers, harrows etc. These are locally manufactured and marketed. They may be either power-driven or bullockdriven. Many of these are used by farmers regularly in their farming operations. These are readily available, easy to maintain and operate. Since these are locally manufactured and marketed, employment of marketing knowledge is somewhat minimal.

Apart from the above, there are simple farm tools like plough share, had hoe, sickle, phavada, etc. Which are also locally manufactured by the village artisans and blacksmith and sold: These tools have a short life. Hence there is not much quility consciousness among the farmers.

Another important farm machinery which came into being during early sixties is the power tiller. Several firms were licensed to manufacture power tillers and the demand forecast by the planning commission communicated great promise. The technology for power tillers was imported from Japan. Somehow this did not succeed much. As of today barring two manufacturers, the rest have ceased to exist. The two manufacturers who are still operating are Kerala Agro Machinery Corporation, and V.S.T. Tillers, Banglore, who produce 'Kubota' and 'Mitsubishi' tillers respectively. The production is very low, the prices are two high and the performance on the filed falls short of expectations. The kits imported from Japan were initially assembled and sold. This has not been totally indigenised to suit Indian soil conditions. The product has nearly failed. A case of power tillers is given at the end of the book. An analysis of this case would reveal the lacunae and problems with this particular farm machinery.

The marketing of major agricultural inputs have been discussed above. These are the inputs which contribute substantially to the value.

There are other inputs like electricity, diesel, lubricants etc. which are totally under the control of the central and state Governments. They take special measures to see that the rural areas get these inputs at a concessional price.

The marketing mix, marketing organisation and marketing strategies are decided based on three important factors in the case of agricultural inputs.

These are:

1. Product characteristics, 2. User characteristics and 3. Use characteristics.

The product characteristics in the case of agricultural inputs can be as follows:

(a) Consumable input or capital input. *(b)* High value or low value. *(c)* High volume or low volume. *(d)* High cost or low cost.

(e) Manufactured or locally produced. *(f)* High shelf life or low shelf life.

The user characteristics are:

(a) Planters and big farmers. *(b)* General farmers. *(c)* Dealers. *(d)* Blenders.

The use characteristics are:

(a) Irrigated forms or dry or rainfed farms. *(b)* Cash crop farms or food crop farms. *(c)* Progressive farms or traditional farms. *(d)* Market oriented or subsistence farms.

These characteristics play an important role in deciding upon the elements of marketing mix, the size of the marketing organization and appropriate marketing strategies.

❐

8

Selling in Rural Markets

SALES PROMOTION AND CUSTOMER SERVICE PRACTICES

After having examined the merchandising, selling and pricing practites of rural retailers, now attempt is made to analyse the sales promotion practices. The purpose of this discussion is to focus the importance or otherwise of the customer service practices in a competive environment.

Sales Promotion

Sales promotion is an important activity of retail trade. Because it represents different forms of communication between the retailer and the customer which provide information as to where is the store, what merchandise it caries, how its merchandise is priced, what range of special service it offers and why some stores serve their customer's need better than others etc. The purpose of sales promotion at the level of retailing has dual objective of creating image to the store and increasing sales of its merchandise. Therefore, sales promotion is said to have three important objectives: *(a)* to inform the consumers about the stores and products, *(b)* to persuade them as to why the consumers have to partronise their store and goods, and *(c)* to remind them as to how the store met their needs and that it can continue to do so. Therefore, promotion can be defined as all the activities of retailers to communicate with customers in order to sell more goods or services, create good will, build a desired image, and also to create a competitive advantage for the store.

There are many methods a retailer can use to communicate with a wide variety customers which can be arranged into certain groups such as advertising, visual merchandising, publicity, special incentives public relations etc. Strictly speaking this also includes customer services. Though customer services are part of sales promotion, it has been separately dealt with. The combination of communication methods that retailers use for promotion is called promotional mix.

Non-personal paid message by an identified sponsor about merchandise, services or ideas that retail marketers wish to communicate to customers and potential customers is called advertising. The tools that the advertisers use to communicate their messages are called advertising media. This includes newspapers, journals (print media), Radios, TVs, Cinemas, direct mail etc.

Under visual merchandising method of promotion retailers use imaginative methods of window and interior displays in a way which stimulate an interest in consumers, help them to make selections and also method of using the products. Publicity refers to the mention of a retail store's name, or its service, in the mass media in any form other than advertisement.

A few retailers may also want to improve their image by contributing to certain community welfare schemes like supporting community projects, instituting scholarships, supporting service clubs, like, Rotary, Lions, Jaycees, etc. Special incentives offered by retailers as part of promotion includes premiums, price reductions, coupons, trading stamps, contests, free samples, free gifts, issue of calendars and diaries, etc.

The combination and volume of the various promotional tools are a continuous problem to be coordinated continuously by the retailer. A sound promotional policy must consider the correct proportion of each element in the promotional mix. This depends upon factors like nature of the firms, market opportunity, the overall store image desired by the retailer, the nature of the goods assortment offered by the retailer etc. The first step involved in determining as to what image is best, consists of an analysis of stores' target market in terms of age, income, sex, family size, tastes, life style, place of residence, pay periods etc. Only after this, with regard to the customers to be served, retailer can decide as to what kind of image he wants to create through various promotional activities. In the light of the importance, objectives and various dimensions of different promotional tools, relevant data was collected from the rural retailers of sample villages with a view to analyses as to which method of promotional media was widely used be different trades. The responses of rural retailers with regard to sales promotional media used is analysed and given in Table.

It can be seen from the Table that most popular method of sales promotion among rural retailers was visual merchanding. An overwhelming majority of 64.71% of retailers, on the whole, adopted visual merchandising as a major sales promotion media. In the order of preference next came special incentives with about 21.57% of rural retailers adopting it. The proportion of 'other methods' which included personal selling was 10.46 %. Only a negligible fraction of retailers used advertising (1.96%) and publicity (1.31 %).

Those retailers using advertising as a media of sales promotion used this technique mostly through slides in cinema halls, hand bills. There was no single instance of advertisements, through other advertising media. The various methods used by rural retailers under special incentives included issue of calendars, gifts, good wrapping, etc. Reduction sales was very rare. The over-dependence on visual merchandising by rural retailers was due to the increasing sameness of merchandise and services among competing stores. It has become difficult for stores to create a competitive advantage. Therefore, this method offers a way for a store to create a distinctive image and attract customers. Most of these promotional methods were adopted by retailers operating in relatively bigger villages. The various techniques under this method included using colour, lighting, sign boards, and fixtures etc. Window displays were used only by a few cloth stores.

On the whole, the analysis reveals that the modern methods of sales promotion are not being used by rural retailers because of forbidden cost, on one hand, and illiterate customers, on the other.

Table 1.
Major Sales Promotional Media used by Rural Retailers

Trade type	Advertising		Visual merchandising		Publicity		Special incentives		Others		Total	
	Type of promotional media											
	No.	*%*	*No.*	*%*	*No.*	*%*	*No.*	*%*	*No.*	*%*	*No.*	*%*
Kirana	—	—	178	68.99	4	1.55	54	20.93	22	8.53	258	100.00
Cloth	6	27.27	12	54.55	—	—	4	18.18	—	—	22	100.00
General	—	—	2	25.00	—	—	2	25.00	4	50.00	8	100.00
Kangan	—	—	3	75.00	—	—	1	25.00	—	—	4	100.00
Medical	—	—	2	40.00	—	—	2	40.00	1	20.00	5	100.00
Footwear	—	—	1	20.00	—	—	2	40.00	2	40.00	5	100.00
Others	—	—	—	—	—	—	1	25.00	3	75.00	4	100.00
Total	6	1.96	198	64.71	4	1.31	66	21.57	32	10.46	306	100.00

Source: Questionnaire data.

Further, most of the manufactured packaged goods are regularly advertised by the manufactures through radio, TVs, Cinema screens etc. In case of smaller villages where there were only one or two retailers, they did not for the need for adopting any sales promotion media except personal selling. All this reflects the poor and backward state of retailing in most of the rural areas.

Personal Selling

Personal selling is the heart of retailing. This is more so in case of developing countries like India, particularly in rural areas where the self service concept has not yet been accepted the selling in rural retail stores most of which are very small in size, the work of selling in done mainly by retailer himself, his family members or his sales personnel in few cases. The face to face nature of retail store selling is an exceedingly important form of retail store communication which provides instantaneous feed back, in both the ways.

Other promotional methods like advertisements, window display etc., can attract customer to the store, but the face-to-face communication that occurs in personal selling provides unique opportunities of feed back on customers reactions and their needs. Personal selling is often required to convince customer of the merits of the goods in the light of other alternatives. To a great extent the salesforce is responsible for the successor failure of a store. It is the sales person who comes in personal contacts with the customer. A proper attitude on the part of salespersons is the key factor in the attempt of the store to serve its customers.

The main function of the retailing is to produce matched parallelism in which there will be a perfect match of many wants ar consumers with those of available goods that will satisfy those wants. The retailer should develop an understanding of consumer point of view, Customers are in many cases, particularly, in rural areas who are illiterates, ignorants, immobile, less-aware do not know the quality and prices of goods. They do not know the new lines of merchandise available in the market. They might suffer from misconceptions and prejudices about the goods. This fundamentally affects their buying behaviour.

In terms of the total retail merchandising strategy, the role and importance of personal selling will vary considerably from one store type to another and from one merchandise line to another. For example, with regard to convenience goods like, toothpaste, soaps etc., which consumers buy wherever and whenever they want, they do not want any information from retailer. But when the consumer purchases shopping goods like clothes, and other consumer durables, they want information and advice from the retailer.

There are number of studies which have established the fact that the behaviour of the customers in terms of merchandise selection and choice of store is influenced by the behaviour of the sales personnel. Therefore, a trained and experienced retailer and his sales personnel can contribute to the success of his stores.

There are three elements in every transaction between the retailer and the customers—the merchandise, customers needs of sales person. The basic task of retailer is to create and establish a link between the merchandise and customer needs.

Important objectives of personal selling are: *(a)* increasing volume of sales, *(b)* building up goodwill for repeated buying, *(c)* attracting more customers, and *(d)* knowledge of customer. The knowledge of customer psychology is basic to successful selling. The retailers perception of consumer behaviour will help him greately in influencing the purchases to be made by the consumer. Consumers buy goods to satisfy their needs and with different motives like, *(a)* satisfying physical needs like food, clothing etc., *(b)* recreation, and comfort, *(c)* imitation, *(d)* recognition and self-esteem *(e)* family affection etc. But in the process of satisfying, these motives consumers are concerned about factors like: *(a)* economy, *(b)* durability, *(c)* low maintenance cost, and *(d)* availability of maintenance facilities.

Knowledge of the customer's character, his behavioural pattern, mood and idiosyncracy will help the retailer in the process of identifying the customer and modify his approach to effect sales. This involves a study of nature and type of people their likes and dislikes. A customer will not be always of the same type every time, he comes to the store. However, on the basis of behaviour, customers can be broadly classified into five types. They are: *(a)* decisive customer, *(b)* indecisive customer, *(c)* silent customer, *(d)* talkative customer, *(e)* skeptical customer, and *(f)* self-opinionated customer.

Decisive customers are those who are with firm intention of purchasing a particular type of good and in a particular price range. He knows about the price and quality of the goods. They are quick in effecting sales and similarly the sales persons should also be quick in completing sales. Slowness on the part of retailer in attending to them will displease them.

Indecisive customers will be unable to reach a conclusion with regard to the goods to be purchased and price range. To such customers retailer has to provide information about the substitutes available to make up his mind. Further, customers of this type can be persuaded by giving them an option of returning goods, if he is not happy.

Silent customers will not give their mind to the retailer. They seldom speak and does not give any clue of his intention. Facial expressions, and remarks may sometimes provide an opportunity to the retailer about his interests. Otherwise, retailer should initiate talking by putting searching questions about quality, feature and price range of goods.

Some other customers may be opposite to the above type who are called talkative. Sometime, these customers, may distract the salesman from other customers. The retailer or salespersons should see that such discussion is avoided and try to centre it around the merchandise.

Skeptical customers are those who feel that the retailers are trying to cheat them in some way. Therefore, retailers have to inspire confidence in these customers with regard his store and merchandise by demonstrating various merchandise. If any printed data with regard to price or quality is available, that is to be shown to him.

Ability to deal with different types of customers comes partly through experience. By observing the customers actions, expression and appearance the retailer or salesperson can judge their characteristics.

It has been observed during the field survey, that in most of the small villages which have retail stores ranging from 1 to 3 and most of which are dealing in grocery and general items, the rural retailers perfectly know about the various types of customers of that village. These shops receive only customers of middle or lower strata of the village. Most of the retailers being native of the villages in which they are operating, know intimately about different traits, of their customers personalities, temperaments buying behaviour, the type of product they purchase, the price range etc. There were cases of coming across all the types of customers in rural areas but with varying degrees. But coming to the bigger villages, where the customers are large in number and where a significant portion of consumers are from nearby villages, it was somewhat difficult to know about the customers and their characteristics.

It has also been observed that to make the selling process more effective the following measures are suggested.

(a) Knowledge of the Purpose of Selling. Though the purpose of selling is to make sales, the retailer should be cautious in dealing with the consumers. Because, retailer cannot force or thrust goods on customers. A few customers may come only to collect some information. No pressure is to be exercised on them. But providing information as of now may bring him as a customer of tomorrow. Therefore, the purpose of selling should be to make sales now or in the future, alongwith other activities like, providing information with regard to product, price, manufacturer, etc.

(b) Knowledge of Retailer Himself. Self-knowledge is basic to breeding self-confidence. Self-knowledge comes from analysis of one's strength and weaknesses and understanding how they fit into the sales process. These retailers should have some basic qualities which are part of his personality. Therefore, about 9 essential qualities that a successful retail salesperson should possess: *(1)* enthusiasm, *(2)* courtesy, *(3)* loyalty, *(4)* attentiveness, *(5)* dignity, *(6)* tact, *(7)* poise, *(8)* honesty, and *(9)* imagination.

(c) Knowledge About the Product. Knowledge about the products in which the retailer deals is a must as it develops self-confidence in him in the process of advising the consumers. Knowledge about the product include, physical characteristics, distinguishing characteristics, service, warrantees, sizes etc.

(d) Knowledge About the Store. The retailer and his salespersons must also be familiar with the store's basic operating policies and procedures, credit policies, refunds, returns, delivery schedules etc.

Selling Process

Retail selling can be described as four-step process consisting of: *(a)* receiving customers *(b)* determining customer needs, *(c)* help consumers to make right buying decision, and *(d)* closing the sales.

Welcoming the customer to the store by retailer or sales person by greeting him with a genuine smile to realise that the retailers wants to be of service is the first and most important stage of selling process. Because no customer likes to be ignored. This will be more so, particularly with women customers who expect extra politeness.

Determining tbe customers needs is an essential second step and natural extension of welcoming in the sales process. Customer's needs can be identified quickly observing his interest in various products and also by getting clues from his comments or remarks.

But when a retailer offers multiplicity of products brands price lines and sizes, the task of determining customer needs is more difficult. However, asking some probing questions politely about the interests, purpose, style etc., of consumers will serve the purpose. The salesperson should be cautious in not asking questions like price. size etc., as they may hurt their feelings.

As a sequel to the determination of customer's wants retailer has to present merchandise that reflects what he believes will be satisfying customer's needs. The retailer should size-up the customer which includes observing such facts as sex, approximate age, dress, overall appearance and general behaviour etc. All this is to make it possible for him to serve the customer more effectively. The best price line to show first is often the middle one. Then depending on the customer's reaction, sales person can move up to a high-priced line called 'trading up' or 'down' to a lower-priced one.

The third important stage of selling process is to help the customer make the buying decision. The three important rules to be applied at this stage include: *(a)* showing only a few articles at a time to avoid confusion, *(b)* putting the merchandise into the hands of the customer to strengthen customer's interest, and *(c)* demonstrating the product to aid the customer to make ultimate decisions. Sufficient time is to be given to the customer to compare the quality, quantity, prices and other atributes of alternative products and finally deciding to make purchase.

Retailer should be able to meet the objections raised by customer in the process of selling very politely and with full knowledge, in a way which will inspire consumer confidence in the quality of the merchandise.

Once the customer made up his mind to buy a particular product, the retailers should make him feel that his choice is the best. The techniques for closing a sale are both physical and verbal. The sales person writes the bill, goods are wrapped, packaged, and made ready for the delivery. When the customer is about to leave the store, the retailer should thank him and wish him a good day.

As already pointed out, the importance of personal selling varied considerably from one store to another and from one merchandise line to another and also from one type of consumer to another in rural areas. In case of convenience goods like toiletries and cosmetics all the steps of selling process are not there. In majority cases the selling process was very routine. In case of groceries, most of the customers did not ask for the price, quality etc. Both in mornings and evenings consumers used to purchase them in a hurry to prepare food.

The customers ask for oil or rice of say Rs. 5 or 1/2 kg. After, taking all the items the retailer will total the customers purchases. Upper strata customers were treated very sincerely and cautiously by retailers when compared to the lower strata customers.

The selling process in its true sense in rural areas was used in shopping goods like clothes, utensils, footwear etc. As amost of the curtomers were known to the retailers sizing up the customers was not at all a problem to the rural retailers. As the sales persons of stores were not trained in personal selling the retailers used to pay much attention on all aspects of personal selling to attract the customers and to retain them in future.

Customer Services

Prompt, efficient and courteous performance of customer services is one of the most effective tool both in attracting the customers and holding their patronage. When the merchandise carried by more and more stores is becoming increasingly similar, and when prices and price policies of different stores are more and more alike, the need for store differentiation becomes more and more acute. Therefore, it has been aptly put that retail services which are non-price devices are used to help the retailer differentiate his offerings in order to achieve higher sales, and thereby maintain a certain segment of the market. Because, the customers choose that store which offers the services they want most. Retail services have been defined as activities, benefits or satisfactions which arc offered for sale or are provided in connection with the sale of goods. Retail services include: *(a)* accepting merchandise returns, *(b)* delivery of merchandise, *(c)* wrapping of merchandise, *(d)* providing convenient customer shopping hours, *(e)* servicing and counselling on the use of merchandise. *(f)* handling consumer complaints, and *(g)* offering credit. The services to be offered by retailers are influenced by the type of trade, type of merchandise handled, services offered by competitor, type of operation, location, financial strength and cost of each service, etc. Many retailers offer these services at cost, or at less than cost or free of charge in order to encourage customer patronage.

All these services can be broadly grouped into three type: *(a)* essential, *(b)* expected, and *(c)* optional. Alternatively, these services can also be grouped into other three types: *(a)* prepurchase services which include shopping hours, display etc., *(b)* post-purchase services like delivery, wrapping the merchandise, adjustments, returns, and *(c)* ancillary services such as repairs, credit etc.

Return of Goods (Merchandise Return)

The way in which merchandise return is bandled by retailers affect the store image. As it was rightly observed, the customer's goodwill is the greatest asset of the business. By cheerful, gracious handling of returns, this goodwill can be protected in the long run. Customers return goods for different reasons which include, wrong size, colour, defective merchandise, charging higher prices, purchase of merchandise by a person other than the consumer. These reasons for return may be due to retailer errors or customer errors. Since returns are part of retailing, stores should formulate return policies in between two extremeties like absolutely not accepting any return, or accepting every thing that is returned without any reservation. Goods returned will have additional cost in terms of mark-downs, taking it back, reselling the goods etc. However, retailers are obliged to accept these returns when there is a legitimate reason and as it is a part of retailing. The retailer should be sympathetic and listen to the consumer and try to take corrective action. There may be habitual customers who always return the goods. The retailer should be cautious and should not irritate the consumer through rude or impolite accusations. Thus merchandise return is an important service extended by retailer. The data collected from rural retailers of sample villages with regard to various merchandise return policies and procedures adopted by them are tabulated in Table 2. It may be observed from, the data that, on the whole, a great majority *i.e.*, about 75% of rural retailers were extending merchandise return facility to their customers. Barring cloth stores and utensils stores, the proportion of rural retailers offering return facility was more than 60%. When enquired about the important reasons as preceived by customers, 122 rural retailers revealed that it was due to charging of higher prices. Defective goods, poor quality goods, and short weighment as other important reasons for merchandise return was stated by 56, 48 and 46 rural retailers respectively. In case of footwear, under or over size were the reasons for return, and in medical stores, the non-prescribed brands of items by doctors was reported as an important reason. The cloth stores accepted only pieces and readymade garments but not the clothes once cut from thana (long cloth). In case of utensils, the items on which names of customers were written, were not accepted for return.

Table 2.

Mechandise Return Practices Adopted by Rural Retailers

Trade type	*No. of shops*	*Shops accepting returns*		*Mode of dealing with returns (No. of shops)*	
		No.	*%*	*Refund Cash*	*Buy other items*
Kirana	258	198	64.71	56	142
Cloth	22	6	27.27	—	6
General	8	6	75.00	2	4
Kangan	4	3	75.00	1	2
Medical	5	3	60.00	—	3
Footwear	5	3	60.00	—	3
Others	4	2	50-00	—	2
Total	306	221	72.22	58	163

Source: Questionnaire data.

Further, the data indicate that of the total 228 rural retailers who extended return facility, about 72% of them insisted that customers' should buy other items in place of returned goods, while 28% of them refunded the cash. However, there were instances of penalising the customers for mishandling of merchandise or any damage caused to them by the customers. When enquired about the important objectives of their return policies rural retailers revealed that satisfaction of consumers was their important objective. It was also revealed that since almost all the customers were known to them personally they were under obligation to accept the returns. Non-acceptance of returns would pose unnecessary problems, and customers may stop coming to their shops. In few cases there were heated arguments and disputes between customers and retailers on returns.

Customer Complaints

The way in which customer complaints are handled affects the store image. It gives an opportunity to the retailer to gain loyal customers on one hand, and satisfaction to the consumer on the other. Therefore, retailers should adopt adjustment procedures in such a way which will ensure that each dissatisfied customer receives proper and problem solving attention. Generally complaints arise due to faulty merchandise, incorrect delivery, damaged merchandise, mistakes in billing, resentment with credit collection methods and dissatisfaction with sales persons. The retailer is under obligation to make satisfactory adjustment when the consumer has a legitimate and reasonable complaints. Even if, there are habitual complaints, the retailer should listen to them and deal with them convincingly but he should not argue with them. Because, consumers satisfied with adjustments generally recommend the store to his friends, while dis-satisfied consumers advise their friends not to go to that stores. Retailer has to identify the reasons such as poor merchandise, credit and delivery procedures and performance of sales persons and take corrective action.

Field survey provided an opportunity to the researcher to observe the complaints adjustment procedure adopted by rural retailers of different trades operating in different types of villages. In small, remote and tribal villages most of the complaines were relating to poor quality merchandise, resentment with credit collection methods ano over-charging of prices and under-weighment of merchandise etc. Generally in villages, for most of the grocery items, customers' send their children for shopping who are not aware of these unfair practices. Only after inspection at home by the elders, defect was to be found out. There were cases of argument between retailers and customers in this connection. In spite of this, customers continued to visit these shops, because there was no other shop in the village. In villages, where there are more number of shops customers stopped going to that particular shop who did not comply with their complaints. In bigger villages, the retailers adopted good adjustment procedures. In case of cloth stores, kangan halls, utensils and footwear due to over-size and under size and poor quality, goods were returned. They dealt with customers very amicably. This was the case with other types of trades also.

Delivery Service

Offering delivery service by retailers, generally is influenced by factors like the size and weight of the merchandise, the distance covered, the speed of the delivery required by the consumer, the perishability of the merchandise, the frequency and volume of deliveries, and the type of customers. Barring a very few kirana shops, that too in case of few salaried and influential customers, home delivery was totally absent in rural stores operating in the selected villages. This was due to the fact that most of the rural consumers did not demand for this service.

CONSUMER BEHAVIOUR

The consumer behaviour is a psychological process leading to decision making. The consumer behaviour in decision making is governed by:

(i) Sources of information.

(ii) Role of family members (neighbours friends).

(iii) The role of retailers in the purchase process.

(iv) The price and quality of products.

The role of rural markets for many product is increasing if one looks to the data these are as 75 per cent bicycles and portable radios are sold in rural markets, 60 per cent of table fails, sewing machines and wrist watches were brought in rural India, 72 per cent washing cake (soap) share is of rural markets.

Items	*Year* 1989 to 1992-93	*Percentage*
Black and White T.V.		44% to 47%
CTV's		19% to 31%
Cassette Recorders		42% to 49%
VCP and VCR		5% to 8%
Cold and Vanishing Cream		24% to 26%
Tooth Paste		30% to 38%
Washing Powder		48% to 52%
Edible Oil		65% to 68%
Washing Powder		48% to 52%
Biscuits		46% to 49%
Tea		54%to 5%
Electric Tubes and Bulbs		34% to 39%

APPROACH PROCEDURE FOR CONSUMER BEHAVIOUR

Sample Design. In a research a sample of 2,000 consumers were selected, one thousand each from urban and rural consumers, these were taken from different levels of income groups. Consumer satisfaction is the soul of each producer, every producer should know the consumer requirements.

On the basis of consumers wants the manufacturer prepares its strategy, a producer who takes into account its valued consumers preference in mind are in general more successful. Marketing is described as engineering customer satisfaction.

"Marketing concept is a philosophy of business that states that customers want satisfaction that is, the economic and social justification for a firm's existence. Consequently, all company activities must be devoted to finding out what the customers want and then satisfying those wants while still making a profit over the long run." (Stanton J. William, 1984). The executives must think in terms of what benefits they market what needs (wants) they are satisfying.

The understanding of consumers has to come invariably from the consumer. The information relating to consumer behaviour has to be necessarily based on an enquiry into his purchase process. Each decision made by a consumer to boy a product or brand involves the problem solving process. Through the purchase, a consumer attempts reducing the drives. In the process, the consumer tries to reach maximum satisfaction.

Factors 'for Purchasing. "The purchase act by a consumer is governed by various factors such as. *(1)* economic, *(2)* social and *(3)* psychological. Consumers are. inherently concerned with meeting their needs, with living their lives witll all that implies in terms of cultural socio-economic and psychological influences." Since the purchase is a process, it is necessary for a marketer to analyse the factors involved in the process. The act of purchasing a product can be very complex. The consumer not only must collect information and determine the selection criteria, but also must make many decisions concerning style, size, colour, retail agent, and the like. "Buyers act like rational people, decide after applying themselves thoughtfully to problems. Only a few decisions are made as a matter of habit and generally buyers have an interest in the social as well as personal effects of their choices."

Sources of Information. In general consumers are not always sure of their preferences, availability of product more often these are based on persuasion. Marketing communication can help shape wants and beliefs. In general marketing analysis the consumer is tended a central processing unit (CPU) as in a computer, which receives, stores, process and delivers the output. In a sense, a consumer is exposed to the information created and transmitted by the marketers into the environment. The transmission (delivery) may be through different media available, such as radio, television, print, film, and outdoor. Though there are different media, it is possible that consumers may be receiving information only through one or some of the media, depending on the accessibility to media. It would, therefore, be of interest to study the source from which consumers gather the information relating to product offerings.

A consumer before buying needs information for the following purposes:

(a) Awareness about products.

(b) Interest in product.

(c) Evaluation-suitable or not

(a) Product Awareness. The consumer must be aware of a product before he can buy it. He needs information about the existence or availability of a product or brand, *i.e.,* awareness.

(b) Interest in Product. On the assumption that interest is a necessary precondition, considering the fact that consumer needs information which will give him a reason to become interested in a product. The consumer has three basic types of information sources to which he can turn in order to satisfy his information needs. Firstly, the marketer-dominated sources, which are under the direct control of the marketer, such as the product itself, packaging, promotion through different medical distribution, etc. Secondly, the consumer-dominated sources, *i.e.,* all interpersonal sources of information (family, friends and neighbours). Thirdly, neutral information sources, such as reports and magazines, and newspaper articles about products. (Birmill, 1966). It was revealed in one of the recent studies that "information to the poor generally passes through a zig-zag and a horizontal fashion. Most of our mass media, like television the press/ print/ad messages, transfer information in a vertical fashion to the rural and urban slums. This moves in a horizontal and non-linear fashion The information transfer among the poor households takes place through indirect mechanisms like gossip among men in tea and bidi shops and gossip sessions of women when they gather around the village well, pond, bathing ghat or temple.

Findings. The following are the findings of the study:

(i) Variation in Sources of Information. Has maximum reach in terms of providing information to rural consumers. For urban consumers, the most important source of information is television. Friends and dealers in rural areas and friends and radio in urban areas are the next important sources of information. Comparatively fewer consumers in urban areas gather information from retailers, compared to those in rural areas. It may be due to the exposure an urban consumer has through more media. Another revealing finding of the study is that about one-third of the rural consumers did not draw information from any of the sources listed. They are from lower and middle income groups, while there is no such case in urban areas. The one similarity between rural and urban consumers, as regards the sources of information, is that a majority of them draw information from friends.

(ii) Incomewise Source of Information. An income wise analysis reveals that for lower income rural consumers, the most important source is the retailer followed by friends, whereas for the same category in urban areas, the important source of information is radio and films. For both middle and higher income groups, in rural areas, radio is the most important source, whereas for those in urban areas television and print are the most important sources. The study tlms highlights further differences within different income groups in rural and urban markets.

(iii) Selection of Source of Information. Consumers vary in the types and number of sources of information they consult when they need information for reaching a purchase decision. The nature of information sources, consumers seldom find it necessary to consult the mass media. Often they find it necessary to supplement mass media information with information from sources they consider more complete, or more trustworthy. One of the most important published studies (Katz and Lazarafeld, 1955) in consumer behaviour showed that interpersonal communication among friends plays a major role in a great many consumer decisions, and thus some consumers, the "Opinion Leaders" have a more central role in this process than others. It is well accepted by marketing scholars and managers that non-marketing dominated sources of information are given substantial weight by consumers in forming opinions and making product decisions.

The study enquired about the source which was used most (the source acting as a great influencer) for the purpose of decision making by the consumer. Interestingly, friends and retailers are the major sources of information, in both rural and urban areas, and the consumer relied more on personal sources of information compared to market dominated sources.

Role of Advertisement. It is of importance to study the impact of advertisements released by marketers through mass media. The analysis is not made product-wise. The question asked was whether the consumers had taken the messages from advertisements into consideration in their purchasing process. The responses broadly indicate the perceptions of the fonsumers towards the reliability of the advertisements. Surprisingly, very few consumers felt that advertisement through mass media have made any impact. Though the primary objective of an advertisement is to increase awareness, it should also induce action on the part of consumers. Then only can the advertisement be said to be truly effective. The study shows that advertisements have been mainly playing the role of increasing awareness, but for the decision making, consumers appear to have been dependent mostly on their peer groups.

Inter-Personal and Social Influences. No consumer is an island. It implies the consumer's constant and frequent interaction with his immediate neighbours. Consumer behaviour cannot be fully understood unless consideration is given to the effects of inter-personal inriuence on development of attitudes, norms, values, aspirations and purchase behaviour. Consumer susceptibility to inter-personal influence is defined as the need to identify or enhance one's image with significant others through acquisition and use of products and brands, the willingness to conform to the expectations of others regarding purchase decision and/or the tendency to warn about products and services by observing others or seeking information from others. One's family is also an inter-personal determinant of consumer behaviour. The influence of household members is often significant in the purchase decision process.

The selection process of a brand may be primarily decided within the family. Roughly more than fifty per cent of the cases, family members (husband, wife, son and daughter) would select the brand in both rural and urban axeas. Rural consumers are influenced by neighbours in the selection of a brand, which is not that much cited social prestige. It is clear from the data that even in rural areas, higher income consumers are conscious of social prestige. It may thus be inferred that consumers associate brand use with social prestige, a factor to be reckoned with by marketers. This observation would be highly useful in the development of positioning strategies for various brands.

An interesting phenomenon was observed regarding the use of brand. It was found that 70 per cent of the rural consumers used the same brand used by their neighbours, whereas only 20 per cent of the urban consumers did so.

Price Consideration in Buying Process. On an average, for both rural and urban consumers, price is relatively more important in the use of durable products, and less important for non-durables. In one of the studies, it was found that price is the most important economic factor which affects the behavioural pattern of the textile consumer. (Sainin D.R. 1986) In the mral market, price is the most important element in the purchase decision. About 90 per cent of consumers in mral markets have the attitude that price is always important in case of consumer durables. The corresponding figure for the urban market is marginally low at about 80 per cent.

Price-Quality Relationship. There is much evidence that a relationship exists between a product's price and its perceived quality. Strong relationship for perceived product quality and price leads to the propensity to buy generic products. It was reported in a study that, "The findings, in conjunction with those of earlier studies strongly suggest that consumers rely heavily on price as a predictor of quality when there is a substantial degree of uncertainty involved in the purchase decision. (Boring and Gonsior 1964) However, no study has evidence that the price-quality relationship can be generalised to various products with varying prices and consumer purchasing patterns.

Consumers generally perceive a product to be of inferior quality when it is priced low. On the other hand, when a product is priced high, it is observed that the quality of the product is perceived to be very high. There are no mral, urban and income-wise variations found regarding this perception.

Price Increase and Change of Brand. It would be of interest to marketers to find the general attitude of consumers relating to the change of brand on account of price increase. A marketer would be able to analyse and set the pricing strategies for his product. A study on price theory showed during 1970 that consumers do have ranges of acceptable prices for products they want to purchase. Anything above or below the range is considered unacceptable. Another study revealed that there was no relationship between price consciousness of consumers and income level. The study, however, found inverse relationship between education and brand loyalty.

The number of consumers changing the brand on account of price increase from the higher income group is low. It implies higher income consumers are by and large, less price sensitive. The study finds that a majority of the higher income consumers in both rural and urban markets are fairly brand loyal. This conclusion is based on the fact that about 50 per cent of consumers in both the markets stated that they never changed their brand due to price increase. But in case of durables, it may be emphatically stated that the second purchase may be only to replace the product. That being the case, change of brand, as given by the consumers in the study, may not be a valid result.

Place of Buying. It is equally necessary for a marketer to find out the place where consumers buy their products. The place of buying has important implications to the marketers for designing the distribution network. The type of distribution network varies across products. In a country of the size of India, with a majority of the population living in a large number of w dely dispersed settlements, distribution has a crucial role in meeting the needs of the masses by making goods available in every part of the country. It often provides the key to the development of potentially large markets for various products. The reach of distributive trade varies from product to product. The widest coverage is for soap, tea, foodgrains and edible oil, which are carried by 63 per cent to 81 per cent of all the outlets. In rural India, a much larger proportion of outlets carry items of daily necessity than in urban India, for lack of specialisation in rural areas. However, the reach in urban India is better due to the larger number of retailers (per lakh population) that exist there.

CHANGE OF CONSUMER BEHAVIOUR AT A GLANCE

1. Radio Source of Information. Radio has maximum reach in terms of providing information to rural consumers, and TV is the most important source of information for urban consumers.

2. Source of Information. A majority of the rural and urban consumers draw information from friends and neighbours.

3. Role of Retailers. More rural consumers gather information from retailers, compared to those in urban areas.

4. Role of Friends. Friends and retailers are the most reliable sources of information, compared to other sources in both rural and urban areas, and retailers play a vital role in mral markets, particularly for convenience products.

5. Role of Advertisement. Very few consumers feel that advertisements through mass media have made any impact.

6. Brand Loyalty. In a little more than 50 per cent of the cases, family members would select the brand in both rural and urban areas.

7. Role of Price. Price is relatively more important in the case of durable products and less important for non-durables for both rural and urban consumers.

8. Quality Product. Consumers in both rural and urban areas generally perceive a product to be of inferior quality when it is priced low, and when a product is priced high, the quality of the product is perceived to be high.

9. Income Group. Middle and higher income consumers from urban areas and higher income consumers in rural areas are fairly conscious of brand use and social prestige.

10. Role of Neighbours. About 70 per cent of rural consumers use the same brand that is used by their neighbours, whereas only 20 per cent of the urban consumers do so. Among these, a majority are from the lower income group.

11. Place of Buying. A majority of the consumers buy the convenience products from the same shop, indicating high shop loyalty in both rural and urban markets; however, rural higher income consumers buy from outside the village.

CHANGE IN CONSUMER BEHAVIOUR

The market structure in India is dichotomous comprising rural and urban markets. In spite of the same needs, aspirations, beliefs and attitudes, certain specific characteristic features of rural consumer behaviour call for unique marketing strategies to be distinctively developed.

The sea change one finds in India is that material and multinational companies have started concentrating on rural markets to sell their products with multiple marketing inputs. The rural market's contribution to the total market has gone up from 28 per cent in 1985 to 40 per cent in 1991.

Pressure in the urban market are forcing many to move into ruml areas because of some reasons like demand for heavy promotional expenditure due to tough competition, decrease in product life cycle, increase in the awareness level of consumers, etc.

As a result, the rural markets are becoming green pastures for marketers. They are growing faster than the urban markets. The potentialities of the rural market are like a "woken up sleeping giant", and to tap these potentialities or opportunities, marketers need to have challenging marketing strategies.

However, for exploitation of this market its scattered nature and the changing behavioural patterns of consumers must be recognised and analysed, so that a better platform for the exploitation of the opportunities can be created.

Changing Behaviour of Rural Consumers. The life-style and purchasing patterns of rural consumers are undergoing significant changes. Widespread availability of consumer products in village during the last decade is changing the line and attitude of rural consumers. Exposure of TV and radio has made consumer more aware, which result in composite effect of change in the purchasing patterns and habits of rural consumers. This change has created a latent opportunity and demand calling for a unique developmental marketing.

The basic changes in the consumer behaviour can be highlighted as:

1. Better Quality of Life. Increase in income and improved awareness level have made villagers seek a better quality of life. This desire has led to significant changes in the market size of consumer products. Rural consumption now covers a variety of items, from food to electronic items.

2. Brand Awareness. Now rural consumers do not ask for just tooth paste or soap, but for specific brand such as 'Close-Up'

'Lux' or other brands. Sharpened brand awareness demands creative advertising and promotional strategies to create brand loyalty.

3. Desire for New Products and Fashion Consciousness. The rural consumers are willing to experiment with new products and a variety of brands without any hesitation. This makes it easier to get higher trial rates when new products are launched in the villages.

Increase in awareness of new fashions stimulates the demand for textile goods, readymade garments and cosmetics. The market for these products in the rural areas is growing at a much faster pace as compared to other products.

4. No Desire to Save. A new tendency is noticed among consumers; they are willing to spend money instead of keeping it. Today, they spend their surplus income on several products like clothes, entertaimnent items, insurance policies, etc.

5. Influence Through Demonstration. Rural consumers havc.greater faith in a product if they actually see it in use. It is therefore useful to conduct demonstrations with a new product to strengthen creditability. This type of promotional campaigning hastens consumer adoption.

6. Role of the Retailers. The rural consumer has always relied strongly on the recommendation of rural retailers. This factor can have an impact on the distribution network. The retailer can become a very useful link between the marketer and the rural consumer.

Some other changing factors also should be given due consideration while designing the game plan for rural markets. They are the increasing significance of women in the buying process, role of opinion leaders, effect of films and television, increasing interest in premium products, changing demand for packaged products, etc. Understanding the consumption pattern of rural people is helpful in developing efficient marketing strategies for exploiting the potentialities of the rural market. Managing this complex market calls for modification in each tool of the marketing mix and each step of procedure for marketing. These sequential strategies can be described in the following manner.

7. Selection of Target Market for Proper Penetration and Profit. Marketers, necessarily, will have to tap the rural market rigorously in the future. It will be necessary to segment the rural market in a structured manner. Here, identification of clusters must be made on a scientific bases.

Each segment of the rural market has to be judiciously evaluated for its total sales and contribution, after estimating the receptivity of the villagers to a new product, their level of satisfaction with existing products, current level of competition, and possible reactions of competitors.

8. Re-designing Product Front. Increased disposable incomes, raised aspirations and improved levels of general awareness have made consumers more demanding. They except value for money. Their aspirations are, in a way, comparable to those of urban consumers. While quality and packaging appeal to him, it will not influence his paying if the product is not perceived to be offering satisfaction at an affordable price.

9. Pricing Strategies. Pricing strategies must be framed keeping in mind the estimated rural market size, perceived value of consumers, target share of the market, and margin expected by retailers and distributors. In spite of the decreasing the role of pricing, as compared to other tools of the marketing mix, it becomes a critical detenninant of the fate or the product, its sales volume, and the market of the company.

10. Distribution Strategies. Considering the vastness of the rural market, the main problem is essentially that of distribution. The distribution cost of serving the rural market, tends to be high due to several factors, *viz.* poor communication facilities, less offtake, and high scattered distribution of outlets. Further, in spite of increasing awareness, there is a tendency among. rural consumers to buy those products, which are readily available at convenient retail outlets.

In farming distribution strategies, the importance of the retailer and the local staff should be considered. Being local, the dealer can feel the pulse of the market much better.

11. Promotional Measures. The right communication of promotional strategies make the difference between success and failure. Consumer education forms an essential part of brand promotion.

Technological advancement in the field of television has made it a powerful medium to expose products to rural people. In addition to formal organised media, a variety of non-fonnal media like mobile audio-visual publicity, public meetings, etc., have to be developed to meet the specific requirements of these areas.

Both the media and the advertising messages should be tailored to appeal to rural audiences. Urban aesthetic cannot always strike the right chord with rural consumers. To market a product effectively, we have to get off our high horses and understand rural ways.

In short, unique promotional strategies depend on correct identification of opportunities. Creating vehicles of communication for the local environment and experimenting with new media are essential steps towards reaching out to the unreached rural audience. Some other strategies like proper packaging can also work. In sales management, the company should take the help of local staff to handle the specialised market successfully. Understanding the consumer's needs properly is vital.

Further, reorientation and training progranunes are essential to reorient the attitudes of the sales staff. For successful selling, they must have grass roots knowledge of the concerned area.

PROBLEMS IN RURAL MARKETING

Agriculture is the life blood of the Indian economy. The most striking feature of the country's economic life is the preponderance of agriculture over other occupations. This is supported by the fact that 30% of the GDP is from agricultural sector and two third of the population depends upon this sector. To increase GDP a long term trend growth rate of 3% in Indian agriculture has been considered desirable, but to achieve the target a number of key problems in agricultural sector will need to be resolved. Of these various problems, the problem of proper marketing of agricultural produce is the most glaring one.

Rural Marketing is a time consuming affair and requires considerable investments in terms of evolving appropriate strategies with a view to solve these problems.

The major problems faced by manufacturing and marketing men in rural areas are described below:

1. Problem of Transportation in Rural Areas. Transportation is an important means in the process of movement of products from urban production centres to remote villages. The Transportation infrastructure is extremely poor in rural India. Due to this reason, most of the villages are not accessible to the marketing men. In our country, there are six lakh villages. Nearly 50 per cent of them are not connected by road at all. Many parts in rural India have only kachha roads. During the monsoons, even these roads become unserviceable. Regarding rail transport, though India has the second largest railway system in the world, many parts of rural India remain outside the rail network.

2. Problem of Proper Communication. Marketing communication in rural markets suffers from a variety of constraints. The literacy rate among the rural consumers is very low. Printed media have limited scope in the rural context. Apart from low levels of literacy, the tradition-bound nature of rural people, their cultural barriers and their overall economic backwardness add to the difficulties of the communication task, post, telegraph, and telephones are the main components of the communication infrastructure. These facilities are extremely inadequate in the rural parts or our country. In rural areas, the literacy percentage is still low, compared to urban areas. In India, there are 18 recognised languages. All these languages and many dialects are spoken in rural, areas. English and Hindi are not understood by many people. Due to these problems, rule consumers, unlike urban consumers, do not have exposure to new products. Upto 50's or' early 60's Radio was considered to be a potential medium of communication to rural people.

3. Problems of Warehousing. A storage function is necessary because production and consumption cycles rarely match. Many agricultural commodities are produced seasonally. Whereas demand for them is continuous. The storage function overcomes discrepancies in desired quantities and timing. In warehousing too, there are special problems in the rural context. The Central Warehousing Corporation and state warehousing, which constitute the top tier in public warehousing in our country, have not extended their network of warehouses to the rural parts. It is almost impossible to distribute effectively in the interior outlets in the absence of adequate storage facilities. Due to lack of adequate and scientific storage facilities in rural areas, stocks are being maintained in towns only.

4. Problem of Availability of Appropriate Media. It has been estimated that all organised media in the country put together can reach' only 30 per cent of the rural population of India. The print media covers only 18 per cent of the rural population. The radio network, in theory, covers 90 per cent. But actual listnership is much less. TV is popular, and is an ideal medium for communicating with the rural masses. But, it is not available in all interior parts of the country. It is estimated that TV covers 20 per cent of the rural population. But, the actual viewership is meagre. The cinema, relatively, is available more as a medium of rural communication. But, these opportunities are very low in rural areas.

5., Problem of Village Structure. The village structure itself causes many problems. Most of the villages are small and scattered. It is estimated that 60 per cent of the villages are in the population group of below 1,000. The scattered nature of the villages increases distribution costs, and their small size affects economic viability of establishing distribution points.

6. Problem of Finance (credit/finance). In rural markets, distribution is also handicapped due to lack of adequate banking and credit facilities. The rural outlets require banking support to enable remittances, to get replenishment of stocks, to facilitate credit transactions in general, and to obtain credit support from the bank. Retailers are unable to carry optimum stocks in the absence of adequate credit facilities. Because of this problem they are not able to offer credit to the consumers. All these problems lead to low marketing activities in rural areas. It is estimated that there is one bank for every 50 villages, showing the poor banking facilities in rural areas.

7. Underdeveloped people and Underdeveloped Market. The agricultural technology has tried to develop the people and market in rural areas. Unfortunately, the impact of the technology is not felt uniformly through out the country while that are pockets—some districts in Punjab, Haryana or Western Uttar Pradesh—where a rural consumer is somewhat comparable to his urban counterpart, there are large areas and groups of people who have remained beyond the technological breakthrough. Even today about 75 districts in the country are drought prone and no new technology worth the name has percolated to increase the standard of living of these people. In addition, the farmer with small agriculture land holdings have also been unable to take advantage of the new technology. The member of people below poverty line has not decreased in any appreciable manner. Thus, the rural markets by and large, are characterised by underdeveloped people and consequently underdeveloped market. A vast majority of the rural people are tradition bound, fatalistic and believe in age old customs, traditions, habits, taboos and practices.

8. Problems of Many Languages and Dialects. The available media for communication is not of practical utility due to different languages and dialects vary widely from state to state, region to region and probably from district to district. The message have to be delivered in local languages and dialects. Even though the number of recognised languages are only 16, the number of dialects is estimated to be abound 850.

9. Low Per Capita Incomes. Even though about 33 to 35 per cent of Gross Domestic Product is generated in rural areas, it is shared by 74 percent of the population. Hence, the per capita income is low, compared to urban areas. This apart, the distribution of income is highly skewed, since the land holding pattern, presents a lightly heterogeneous scene. Given the low per capita income and population spread in villages, what will be the off-take of any product by rural consumers, say from a village shop? What should be the inventory levels to be maintained by a rural shopkeeper and how long will it take for a rural shopkeeper to liquidate his stocks? If a company opts to distribute the product upto village shop level what should be the frequency of distribution? These aspects require very careful consideration while evolving distribution strategies for rural markets.

10. Market Organisation and Staff. The size of the market organization and staff is very important to have an effective control. Comparatively, catering to rural market will involve large marketing organization and staff. How many manufacturers and marketing men can afford such huge investments in terms of personnel and also keep an effective control on it, needs examination.

11. Logistics, Storage, Handling and Transport. The widespread nature and varying size of villages, organizing a distribution set-up poses a number of questions. Are there good storage facilities available in rural areas? Already it has been seen that the transport facility in general is poor in rural areas. A lending company, which distributes its consumable products in rural areas has used bullock carts and camel backs for physical transportation of goods to inaccessible areas. How to motivate a rural person to open a shop in the village? Whether he will have the requisite capital for the same? What will be the off-take from the shop in a day or in a week? How many times will one be able to turnover the capital invested? Thus willingness to enter the rural market alone is not sufficient, but identification of potential shopkeepers, offering them credit, assuring periodic surplus and motivating them also become very essential. This will obviously have an adverse impact on the distribution costs and whether a company can afford much costs should be examined.

12. Product Positioning. In a highly heterogeneous market, product positioning becomes very difficult. Otherwise the product range should be very wide. A typical example is that of cigarette companies which have numerous branch to suit the different income segments of both rural and urban population. A large product range will give rise to distribution problems. For a product, like tractors the positioning becomes fairly easy since it is meant for progressive farmers with good irrigation facilities and having at least 20-25 acres of land. Here again the example of a consumable product like tea is interesting. Even the very large tea companies like Brooke Bond or Lipton have tea packets priced from 25 paise onwards so that all segments of population are taken care of. So this might warrant designing new products or redesigning the existing ones to suit the rural wants, habits and needs, based on purchasing power.

13. Hierarchy of Markets. As seen earlier, the rural consumers have identified market places for different items of their requirements so there cannot be a uniform distribution pattern for all products. It has been seen that 90 per cent of the farmers visited the nearest town, where an agriculture produce assembling market is situated at least once a quarter for either selling the produce or for purchase of their requirement. Thus depending upon the rchase habits of rural people, the distribution network for different commodities has to be different.

14. Seasonal Demand. The distribution of any product in the rural areas, either agriculture inputs, consumables or durables should necessarily follow a seasonal pattern. Since 75 percent of rural income is generated through agriculture operation; which is seasonal, the demand pattern is also seasonal. A typical example of this is fertilizers. The demand for fertilizer is always high during the start of Kahrif and Rabi seasons. This is the time at which the rural people have substantial cash inflows. Hence, the distribution should be fairly intensive during peak crop harvesting and marketing seasons. This arrangement would result in adequate sales realisations. Thus the distribution system has to gear itself to the seasonal pattern of demand. In addition, festival seasons like Sankaranthi or Pongal in southern regions as opposed to Baisaki or Deepawali in north are also demand seasons. So the distribution for rural areas should be more and frequent during harvest and festival seasons, as opposed to a fairly uniform demand pattern in urban areas. It should be recognised that rural market is a higway heterogeneous market, widely spread with seasonal demand and poor transportation and communication facilities, both in terms of physical movement of products and also in communicating with the target audience.

15. Low Level of Literacy. The literacy rate is low in rural areas as compared to urban areas. This again leads to the problem of communication or promotion expenses. The dependence should be more on electronic media, cinema, radio and television while the access to cinema and radio appears to be fairly easy and common, it is not so in the case of television. In addition, television advertising is very expensive. The problems in operating company onward media vans have already been discussed. Today, there are professional rural promotion organisations like. 'video express' and 'video on wheels' who specialise in mobile rural advertising companies like HMT, Karnataka/soaps and Detergents Ltd., have already taken to such rural promotion vans. Recently Colgate-Palmolive have also commissioned their vans in collaboration with their distributors. The promotion of the product alongwith distribution is also being resorted to by many.

The problems referred above can be classified under the following heads for easy understanding:

(a) Consumer motivation and buying habits;

(b) Location and degree of concentration of demand;

(c) Dealer availability, attitude and motivation;

(d) Mass communication media;

(e) Logistics, storage, transport arid handling; and

(f) Marketing organisation and staff.

Any strategy for rural marketing should take the above problems into account, so that the investments made are easily recovered.

SUGGESTIONS FOR IMPROVING RURAL MARKETING

The producers, in India became the scapegoats of the merchants and agents, middlemen and moneylenders, the farmers can get good price for agricultural products so that their raw materials reach in industries without wasting time and disorder in production schedule. The present system of marketing mechanism is to be reshuffled. That is why so many remedies are suggested.

The Royal commission on Agriculture and Central Banking Enquiry Committee studied the situations and screened the following remedies:

1. Recommendation of Regulated Markets.
2, Co-operative Marketing.
3. Govermnent Intetrventions.
4. Establishment of Directorate of Marketing Inspectors.
5. Market Research and Commodity Surveys.
6. Provision of Grading and standardisation.
7. Market extension.
8. Statutory Regulation of Markets and Market Practices.
9. Marketing Intelligence cell.
10. Training of Market Personnel.
11. Marketing committee.
12. Marketing Improvement and Development cell.
13. Product development.
14. Distribution management.
15. Marketing communication.

1. Recommendations of Regulated Markets. Regulated market is a wholesale,market where dealing or buying and selling are regulated or controlled by the State Government through a 'Market Committee', which consists of representatives of producers, traders, agents, local bodies, co-operative societies and Government. It is a market where the activities are to take place under set rules and regulations and the malpractices like incorrect weighment, unnecessary deductions are curbed. Moreover, the regulated markets provide for settlement of disputes, if any, amongst the sellers and buyers.

Regulated market works under a business code of conduct framed by the 'Market Committee' to be followed by producers and traders. Producer is, interested in getting higher prices for his produce. On the contrary, traders are prepared to buy more only at a low price. This may result in misunderstandings or disputes. To bring about compromise or to settle the matter, the regulated market works well and tries to protect the interests of both parties but, particularly, the interests of farmers who are ill organised. Existence of fair competition is quite essential for the healthy growth of markets so, that the fair prices can be determined. It is possible when purchases and sales are regulated by a statutory body. This is a 'fair deal' in marketing. The produce at an acceptable and fair price, so that the farmer is not hit hard he facilities offair dealings are provided in the regulated markets.

The establishment of regulated markets is not intended at creating an alternative marketing system. The basic objective has been to create conditions; or efficient performance of the private trade, through facilitating free and informal competition. In regulated markets, the farmer is able to sell his marketed surplus in the presence of several buyers through open and competitive bidding. The legislation for the establishment of regulated markets does not make it compulsory for the farmer to sell his produce in the regulated market yard. Instead, voluntary action on the part of the farmers to take advantage of such a market is assumed.

2. Co-operative Marketing. The establishment of cooperative marketing societies as another step which has been taken to overcome the problems arising out of the present system of marketing agricultural produce. The objectives of economic development and social justice can be furthered by channelising rural produce through co-operative institutions. Co-operative marketing is the co-operative venture or an association designed to perform one or more marketing functions, relating to the agricultural produce of its members. In a broad sense, co-operative marketing implies both buying and selling of rural produce. To be more appropriate, co-operative marketing confines itself with the selling functions related with marketing of produce, such as, acting as selling agent, supply of market information, standardization, storage, assembling, processing, packing etc. Private agencies dominate the Indian foodgrains trade. Producers complain of the marketing system because they get lower. prices, due mainly to high marketing charges and the prevalence of malpractices. The efforts of the government to improve the marketing system of rural commodities have been only partially successful in creating healthy conditions for scientific and efficient marketing. Moreover, the progress of regulated markets is not uniform in all areas. The need for strengthening co-operative organisation has therefore, been recognised for the marketing of the produce of producers and for making inputs available for them at the right price and time., The co-operative institutions are expected to function as competitors of the private traders in the market. These organisations pool the produce of the small producers having a, small surplus to market and improve their bargaining power.

A co-operative sales association is a voluntary business organisation established by its member patrons to market farm products collectively for their direct benefit. It is governed by democratic principles, and savings are apportioned to the members on the basis of their patronage. The members are the owners, operators and contributors of the commodities and are the direct beneficiaries of the savings that accrue to the society. No intermediary stands to profit or loss at the expense of the other members. Co-operative marketing organisations are associations of producers for the collective marketing of their produce and for securing for the members the advantages that result from large-scale business which an individual cultivator cannot secure because of his small marketable surplus.

3. Government Intervention. In the interest of public welfare, the government intervenes is the marketing system. The extent of intervention depends on the objectives of the government and the extent of defects and malpractices prevailing in the system. Government intervention may be direct or indirect; and it may take anyone or a combination of the following forms:

(a) The framing of rules and regulations for the protection of the interest of some sections of the population. These may relate to the grant of monopolies, restriction on the activities of traders, licensing and market regulation.

(b) Promotional activities such as storage and warehousing, transportation and communication facilities; credit facility, grading and standardization, and encouragement of co-operative marketing.

(c) Influencing supply and demand by import, export, internal procurement and distribution.

(d) Administration of prices at different levels of marketing guaranteeing minimum support prices to producers, providing commodities at fair prices to consumers, and fixing the rates of commission charged by commission agents.

In India, the government has intervened in the marketing system in various ways at different points of time. The sectlons which follow deal with the description of the government's efforts to improve the marketing techniques of rural commodities.

4. Establishment of Directorate of Marketing and Inspection. On the recommendation of the Royal Commission on Agriculture, 1928, and the Central Banking Enquiry Committee, 1931, the Central Marketing Department was established in India in

1935. The office of the Agriculture Marketing Advisor to the Government of India was established in Delhi on January 1, 1935. The aim was to build up a body of knowledge of the marketing of agricultural commodities and suggest measures for the promotion of an orderly and efficient marketing system for farm products. At the same time, similar departments were set up in the erstwhile provinces and princely states. On the recommendations of the Patel Committee, the Inspection Directorate of the Ministry of Food was merged with the Central Marketing Department, and was renamed as the Directorate of Marketing and Inspection. The responsibility for the compilation of statistics and for the dissemination of market news by the Central Department was shifted to the Directorate. This Directorate of Marketing and Inspection functions as an attached office of the Ministry of Agriculture or Rural Development, Government of India, with its head office at Fandabad (Haryana) and a branch head office at Nagpur (Maharashtra). It is headed by the Agricultural Marketing Adviser (AMA), who is assisted by a Joint AMA, Deputy AMAs, Directors of Laboratories and other technical staff. The directorate has established five regional offices the headquarters at New Delhi, Kolkata, Mumbai, Guntur and Chennai. All the regional offices are headed by Senior Marketing Officers.

The Directorate of Marketing and Inspection is assigned the task of implementing the Rural Produce (Grading and Marketing) Act 1937; Cold Storage Order, 1980 and Meat Food Products Order, 1973. Besides these, the Directorate of Marketing and Inspection is actively associated in rendering assistance, guidance and advice to the State Marketing Departments in regard to the framing of legislation and subsequent implementation of rural produce markets Acts for bringing about regulation of rural produce markets. The Directorate of Marketing and Inspection undertakes programmes of market research and surveys, training of market personnel, extension and publicity. Between the Head Office, Faridabad and Branch Head Office, Nagpur, the sharing of responsibility in respect of these functions is as follows. The Head Office at Faridabad looks after *(i)* administration of the Agricultural Produce (Grading and Marking) Act, 1937, rules and other related matters; *(ii)* administration of Meat

Food Products Order, 1973; *(iii)* administration of Cold Storage Order, *(iv)* market regulation, development and extension; and *(v)* market planning and design. The Branch Office at Nagpur is responsible for *(i)* market research and planning; *(ii)* training programmes in Rural marketing; *(iii)* livestock marketing cell; and *(iv)* Market Planning and Design Centre (MPDC).

5. Market Research and Commodity Surveys. Market research surveys and investigations were the first basic functions entrusted to the Directorate at its inception in 1935. The programme was designed to conduct in depth study of the marketing system so as to help planned development thereof. The directorate has conducted surveys and brought out a number of commodities survey reports covering 150 rural, livestock and forest products. The reports include a survey of the prevailing system of marketing of each commodity in the country, the costs of marketing and the defects in the marketing system. This information facilitated the attention of all concerned on the defects. In addition to commodity surveys, the Directorate has conducted surveys and brought out reports on the specific functions and institutions concerned with agricultural marketing, such as cold storage, regulation of markets and co-operative marketing.

6. Provision of Grading and Standardisation. To secure for farmers the prices which are commensurate with quality grading is essential. To promote the production and marketing of quality goods and maintain uniformity, the Agricultural Produce (Grading and Marking) Act was passed by the government in 1937. The products graded under this Act are marked with the AGMARK label. The important functions of this cell are:

(a) To draw up grade specifications far various agricultural commodities far internal consumption as well as far exports;

(b) To test the working of these grades;

(c) To supervise the grading work; and

(d) To exercise effective quality control.

The Directorate of Marketing and Inspection has formmulated grade specifications far 142 rural products. By the end of March 1990, sixty-three rural commodities were graded before sale in 1040, grading units functioning in different States and Union Territories. The total estimated value of the commodities graded at the producer's level at these centres was Rs. 2103.63 crore in 1989-1990.

7. Statutory Regulation of Markets and Market Practice. The regulation of markets is a State subject, the Directorate renders guidance and advice to all the State Governments in framing market legislation and its enforcement. To bring about uniformity in the marketing practices over space, the government has set up regulated markets under the Agricultural Produce. The Act provides for the sale of rural produce by open auction in the presence of an official of the Market Committee, the payment of the value of the produce by the buyer immediately after the purchase without any deductions for muddat, the use of standard weights and measures, the sale of clean and graded produce, and the deduction of only the authorised market charges from the value of the produce. Upto March 1990, 6217 markets were regulated in the country.

8. Market Extension. The main function of this cell is to apprise the producers, traders and consumers of the various voluntary and regulatory measures brought into farce for the improvement of the marketing system. This work of the extension cell is carried of through various publicity media, such as documentary films, cinema slides, exhibitions and distribution of literature.

9. Market Intelligence Cell. Producers, traders and the other market functionaries involved in the marketing of rural produce are provided with information on prices (daily, weekly, fortnightly) and on market arrivals, and on the estimated supply of and demand for rural products for different markets in the district, the State and the country. The collection of information and its dissemination through various media are the respo.nsibility of the technical staff posted by the Directorate of Marketing and Inspection. Daily prices of important rural commodities far the important markets in the area broadcast by all the regional stations of the All India Radio. Television has also been pressed into service for this purpose. Newspapers disseminate information on prices. Stocks and arrivals are compiled by the State and Central Government.

10. Training of Market Personnel. The Directorate of Marketing and inspection imparts training to different marketing personnel so that they may effectively carry out the various development activities associated with the marketing of Rural products. The training provided by the Directorate includes:

(i) **Diploma Course in Rural Marketing.** This course was first organised in 1956-57 specially to train the senior personnel of the marketing organisations in different states. The duration of this course is 11 months and is offered at Nagpur.

(ii) **Training Course for Grading Supervisors.** The course was started in 1957 and is designed to equip personnel to administer the regulated markets efficiently. The course is of four months duration, and is offered at Hyderabad and Lucknow.

(iii) **Training Course for Grading Supervisors.** This training is imparted to the supervisory Staff of commercial grading centres. This course was started in 1963 and is of three months' duration and is offered at Nagpur.

(iv) **Training Course of Graders and Assesors.** This training was started in 1972, is of three months' duration, and enables the trainees to became good grader. The course is being offered at Chennai and Lucknow.

(v) **Training Course in Marketing of Livestock and Livestock Products.** This training was started in 1955 and is given to the officers of the Animal Husbandry and Veterinary Departments of the States for a period of six months to train them in the marketing of livestock and livestock products.

(vi) Training in Grading of Special Commodities. This training is given to persons engaged in grading of special rural crops, such as tobacco (six months training), cotton (four months), jute (three months) and animal casings (four weeks).

(vii) Other Training. The Directo rate also conducts training courses for chemists to train them in the analysis of ghee, vegetables, oils, butter, spices and honey. In addition to these, in service training course for the officers of the Directorate of Marketing and Inspection has also been started in 1978.

11. Market Committee. Another step which is taken by the Government to improve the system of rural marketing is the establishment of marketing committee system. It is a three tier system named as primary marketing societies, central marketing committee and at the State level State Marketing Board. These are the decentralised markets which are controlled, awned and regulated by the State Marketing Board. The necessity of a central organisation to supervise and provide guidance to market committees was realised with the establishment of a network of market committees. Agricultural Produce Market Acts were modified to make the provisions for the establishment of State Agricultural Marketing Boards, which were established in 16 States and 2 Union Territories *viz.* Rajasthan, Punjab, Haryana, Uttar Pradesh, Madhya Pradesh, Karnataka, Assam, Gujarat, Himachal Pradesh, Andhra Pradesh, West Bengal, Maharashtra, Orissa, Tamil Nadu, Bihar, Delhi and Chandigarh. There is a variation in the organisation, functions and composition of the Board from State to State. Rajasthan is a solitary example, where an Economist has been included amongst the members of the Board. The chairmanship of the Board also differs from State the State.

In Rajasthan, the Rajasthan Agricultural Produce Markets Act, 1961 was amended in 1973 to provide for the establishment of an apex body of market committees at the State level. Accordingly the Rajasthan State Agricultural Marketing Board was established on

17th June 1974, with its headquarters at Jaipur. The Board is an executive-cum-advisory body, and is concerned with bringing about improvements in the regulation scheme. It also supervises the functioning of regulated markets and advises market committees and the State Government on related matters.

12. Marketing Improvement and Development Cell. The main functions of this cell are:

(a) To estimate the internal and external demand for different rural commodities and to render advice to Central and State Government on the fixation of prices;

(b) To regulate forward trading in rural commodities; and

(c) To advise the government in building up buffer stocks and on the disposal of surplus stocks;

(d) To formulate strategies for co-operative sales and purchase societies.

13. Product Development Cell. This normally includes new product development, product innovations, marketing innovation, product life cycle, product mix and product diversification. But in the context of rural marketing it mainly means either new product development or modification of existing product to suit rural areas.

Following points must be kept in view when performing this operation:

(a) Product must be simple in design, simple to understand, operate, maintained repair if need be.

(b) Functional aspect matter than sophisticated looks.

(c) Packaging should be simple, should make the product easy to use and should be economical. If the package can lead to economy in use it will be better still.

(d) Price should be well within the economic competence of the rural consumer.

(e) The brand name should suit rural background.

Considerations of the above points will help the marketing man to meet the requirements cf villagers and thereby increase sales.

14. Distribution Management. Following are some of the channels that may be exploited to service rural markets. *(a)* Ration shops *(b)* Retailers dealing in agricultural inputs *(c)* Semi-wholesalers in mandi-towns *(d)* Retailers in a village may be given some incentive to bring it from the wholesaler in a nearby town. *(c)* National consumer co-operative society in the towns through their Apex body. *(f)* State consumer, cooperatives societies. *(g)* Individual consumer cooperative society.

The better type of transport is road, or rail-cum-road agency or company owned delivery vans.

15. Marketing Communication. The following are the aid of communication:

(a) Advertising *(b)* Radio *(c)* T.V. where possible *(d)* Painted walls *(d)* Stalls in Rural Fairs *(e)* Hoardings *(f)* Vernacular newspapers where they are popular (2) Personal selling. *(a)* Salesman with vans from village to village. Vans may be fitted with projecting equipment or music system to collect people. Salesmen can then talk about his product and do spot selling. Wherever possible on the basis of these sales a local dealer may be motivated to keep stock. *(b)* Demonstration teams at trade fairs *(c)* Spot selling by offering Premia *(d)* Distributors Salesman.

The Rural Marketing system is improving day by day as a result of the efforts made by the government, the producers, middlemen and other independence agencies. From the last one decade, the government is giving much importance to the upliftment of rural industries and rural development. In the Union budget of the government of India 1994-95 a special provision has been made to develop the rural marketing scene. Cooperative marketing, regulated markets, marketing committees are also helping and contributing a lot towards the attainment of rural marketing objectives and goals.

❐

9

Customer—Retailer Relationship

After having examined the shopping behaviour and buying practices of rural consumers, now in this section, an attempt is made to analyse the customer-retailer relationships in terms of customer satisfaction. Retailers should be deeply interested in maintaining harmonious relationships with their customers, which is to a longer extent, is determined by the level of customer satisfaction. Customer satisfaction is vital for the long run survival and growth of retailers. Retailers' job does not end with selling of the goods but continue into post-purchase period. They should be sensitive to the feelings of their Consumers. They should have fundamental understanding of the problems, reactions and level of satisfaction of customers with regard to retailing practices, goods, services, etc. This is going to create a more congenial atmosphere and relationships between the retailer and its customer. Trust and confidence are crucial for building good customer-retailer relationships.

The customer's satisfaction is a function of the closeness between the customer's expectations with regard to retailers' products and services and the performance they actually receive. In brief the customer satisfaction (S) is the function of (f) expectations (E) and perceived performance (P); (S = f (E, P)) If the product, prices, quality and other important services of retailers are matched with expectation, the consumers will be satisfied, if it exceeds, they will be highly satisfied. In other words when there is a gap between consumer's expectation and performance, it will lead to customer dissatisfaction. The larger the gap, the greater the customer dissatisfaction. Dissatisfied customers may resort to abandon the product and the store.

In this section, as attempt is made to investigate into the levels of satisfaction with regard to products, prices, quality of goods and important customer services provided by rural retailers, in order to find out reasons and suggest measures for strengthening good relations between rural customer and rural retailer. The level of awareness among rural consumers with regard to various consumer protection laws and their reactions to retailers practices are also examined. This analysis not only provides a good measure of performance evaluation but some insights into the extent to which the rural retailers had really become customer-oriented.

Level of Satisfaction Regarding the Availability of Merchandise Assortment

Regarding the availability of merchandise assortments in the local retail stores, the sample consumers were asked to reveal their level of satisfaction on a five-point scale as 'highly satisfied', 'satisfied', 'neither satisfied nor un-satisfied', 'dissatisfied' and 'highly dissatisfied'. Their responses are given in Table 1.

An analysis of responses to the availability of merchandise assortment in rural retail stores, on the whole reveals that a majority (59.67%) of respondents felt from 'dissatisfied' to 'highly dissatisfied', while 24.12% were 'satisfied'. About 16% of respondents stated that they were 'neither satisfied nor 'dissatisfied'. Important reason for the high level of dissatisfaction among the respondents was that the depth of the product was less. Rural retailers were carrying wide variety of goods of different products, but within each product line the depth was very insignificant by and large, two to three products in each line. As a result or this, rural consumers were forced to purchase only the available goods. Choice of selecting goods of their interest was not much with the rural consumers like this urban counterparts. Consumers also complained that the local retailers were maintaining, to a larger extent, goods of local and duplicate brands on which there was a maximum margin when compared to national brands.

Table 1.

Level of Satisfaction of Rural Consumers regarding the Availability of Merchandise Assortment in Rural Retail Stores

Degree of Satisfaction	Respondents I_1 No.	%	I_2 No.	%	I_3 No.	%	Total No.	%
Highly satisfied	—	—	—	—	—	—	—	—
Satisfied	37	30.58	15	24.19	3	6.67	55	24.14
Neither satisfied nor dissatisfied	20	16.53	14	22.58	3	6.67	37	16.22
Dissatisfied	36	29.75	20	32.26	20	44.14	76	33.33
Highly dissatisfied	28	23.14	13	20.97	19	42.22	60	26.31
Total	121	100.00	62	100.00	45	100.00	228	100.00

Source: Questionnaire data.

However, a significant number of lower (30%) and middle income (24%) respondents expressed satisfaction with the available merchandise assortments, particularly in case of groceries only. Because essential goods were available in local stores. With regard to other product lines, they were dissatisfied with the product mix of local stores as they were not available, and, as a result of which they were to go to towns for purchasing them. Respondents of big villages, where comparatively big stores offering wide variety of goods were existing, expressed satisfaction.

Level of Satisfaction with Regard to Quality of Goods

Regarding the quality of consumer goods available in rural retail stores, the respondents were asked to give their responses on a five-point scale as 'very good', 'good' 'neither good nor bad', 'bad' and 'very bad'. Their responses are presented in Table 2. Which reveal that, on the wbole, tbe proportion of respondents who perceived the quality of consumer goods from 'bad' to 'very bad' was high at 44.73 % while 32% of the respondents perceived tbe quality of goods as good'. A significant proportion of respondents forming 23.25% reported as 'neither good nor bad'. This was mainly due to their ignorance and indifference towards the quality. The data further explains, the varying perceptions of respondents belonging to different income groups with regard to the quality. In case of lower income respondents, more than 1/3 expressed as 'good' and about another 1/3 were indifferent between good and bad. Just more than 1/3 of respondents reported the quaiyty from 'bad' to 'very bad'. More or less the perception of middle income respondents resembled with the perception of lower income group. Contrary to this, a great majority (73.33%) of bigher income respondents rated the quality of goods from 'bad' to 'very bad', while 22.22%, perceived as 'good'. A negligible proportion (14.45%) of respondents of this group expressed as 'neither good nor bad'. This was one of the important reasons for purcbasing goods in towns by higher income respondents. A majority of lower and middle income respondents rated either as 'good' or 'bad' expressed ignorance about the quality. There was no other alternative for them to purchase their goods. They were neither able

Table 2.

Level of Satisfaction of Rural Consumers regarding the Quality of Goods of Rural Retail Stores

Response	*Respondents*							
	I_1		I_2		I_3		*Total*	
	No.	*%*	*No.*	*%*	*No.*	*%*	*No.*	*%*
Very good	—	—	—	—	—	—	—	—
Good	41	33.88	22	35.48	10	22.22	73	32.02
Neither good nor bad	36	29.75	15	24.19	2	4.45	53	23.25
Bad	24	19.83	13	20.97	18	40.00	55	24.12
Very bad	20	16.53	12	19.35	15	33.33	47	20.61
Total	121	100.00	62	100.00	45	100.00	228	100.00

Source: Questionnaire data.

to purchase goods required for a month, at a time, from a big village/ town nor can afford to go to towns everyday. Most of the agricultural labourers purchased their groceries on daily basis. But those felt 'bad' and 'very bad' about the quality of goods were narrating their experiences of purchasing adulterated and poor quality goods inspite of paying higher prices. They reported adulteration in case of edible oils, coconut oil, chillies, turmeric powders, kerosene, rice etc. They were apprehensive of getting low quality, duplicate brand goods particularly in case of soaps, powders, creams etc., which were resembling to a larger extent, the national brands in colour, lable, size etc., but at the prices of national brand items or slightly lower one.

It was found by the researcher during the field study, that in the retail outlets of small villages, almost all the popular national brand products particularly soaps, creams having closely imitating duplicate brands. These duplicate brand items were similar in colour, content, size. wrapper, etc., but with wider price variations when compared to national brands. The brand names, though different for educated consumer were almost identical to rural masses. The following is the list of a few duplicate brands available in rural stores for the following popular national brand packaged items:

National Brand	—	*Duplicate/Imitating brand items*
Rin	—	Run, Rudrama, Rank, Ralak, Prim, Ruthra, Risa
Nirma	—	Verma, Insat, Hit
Lifebuoy	—	Shakti, Lucky
Rexona	—	Rajani, Ranjani
Pond's toilet powder	—	Polar, Plato
Ashoka	—	Shimla, Channel
Eta	—	Cta
Fair & Lovely	—	Friend & Lovely, Cute & Lovely
Vicco Turmeric	—	She—Turmeric

Such imitating brands are also found in other product lines such as Kazals, Tilakam, Shampoos, etc. However, retalers contested this by stating that because of low purchasing power, rural masses cannot afford to purchase national brand products, and prefer only these duplicate brands. There were complaints of shrinkage and fading of colours in case of clothes. Few rural consumers also revealed that inspite of ISI mark on garments like banians, those were not durable. There were also complaints of selling duplicate stainless steel items which were broken after using them for about one month. It is interesting to note that most of these complaints came from lower and middle income respondents who purchased these goods from local outlets.

Lower and middle income respondents also expressed that it was because of their ignorance and illiteracy, the rural retailers were supplying poor quality goods and charging higher prices, They also felt that at the same time, influential rich farmers and educated consumers were supplied with good quality goods at reasonable prices for fear of being exposed to their unfair practices.

Rural Consumer's Reaction Regarding the Prices of Goods Charged by Rural Retailers

In order to examine the consumer reactions to the prices charged by rural retailers on consumer goods, the rural consumers were requested to rate their responses on a three point scale as 'very high', 'high', and 'reasonable'. The responses of sample rural consumers are analysed and presented in Table 3. It is evident from the Table that, on the whole, more than 64% of respondents rated the prices charged by rural retailers on consumer goods from 'high' to 'very high'. About 26% of them reported that the prices were 'reasonable',—A sizeable portion of respondents (9%) expressed their ignorance about whether they were 'high' or 'reasonable', However, there were differences in the perception of respondents of different income levels with regard to the prices charged by the retailers. Among the lower income respondents, more than 74% rated the prices from 'high' to 'very high', while only 10% of them

Table 3

Prices Charged by Rural Retailers

Response	*Type of Respondents* I_1 *No.*	*%*	I_2 *No.*	*%*	I_3 *No.*	*%*	*Total No.*	*%*
Very high	60	49.59	21	33.87	4	8.89	85	37.28
High	33	27.27	16	25.81	13	28.89	62	27.19
Reasonable	12	9.92	20	32.26	28	62.22	60	26.32
Cheap	—	—	—	—	—	—	—	—
Don't know	16	15.70	5	8.06	—	—	21	9.21
Total	121	100.00	62	100.00	45	100.00	228	100.00

Source: Questionnaire data.

reported the prices as 'reasonable'. A significant proportion of this group expressed ignorance about the prices, Among the middle income respondents too, a majority (59,68%) reported the prices from 'high' to 'very high'. But a significant proportion of 32.26% reported the prices as 'reasonable' contrary to the responses of these groups a majority (62%) of higher income respondents expressed that the prices charged as 'reasonable', It was also observed during the field study that lower income groups were apprehensive of the attitude of the rural retailers to charge higher prices for them and reasonable prices to higher income group. This attitude of retailers was contradictory to their assertion of charging uniform prices to all the consumers. The lower and middle income respondents felt that local merchants were afraid of charging higher prices to rich farmers and employees as they question the rationality of higher prices. A few lower income respondents were citing examples of the differences in prices charged by local Rhops and shops of big villages and towns on to prove their charge.

Retailers Services and Customer Satisfaction

Prompt, efficient and courteous performance of customer services is one of the most effective tool in attracting customers and holding their patronage. Therefore, it is now proposed to evaluate the services provided by the rural retailers from the point of view of rural customers. To measure the level of satisfaction of rural consumers, they were asked to indicate, the services of rural retailers, on a five-point scale, with ratings 'highly satisfied', 'satisfied', 'neither satisfied nor unsatisfied', 'dissatisfied' and 'highly dissatisfied'. The important services of rural retailers which were identified for the purpose of the study included: *(1)* credit extension, *(2)* merchandise return, *(3)* weighing and measurement practices, *(4)* redressal of customer complaints, *(5)* retailers' behaviour, and *(6)* working hours.

For the purpose of quantification of the responses, weights have been assigned as +2, +1, 0, -1, and -2, for the responses of 'highly satisfied', 'satisfied', 'neither satisfied nor unsatisfied', 'dissatisfied' and 'highly dissatisfied respectively. Final scores for each service is calculated by multiplying the number of responses by the weights of corresponding responses. The resultant weighted scores of these services provided by rural retailers are shown in Table 4.

Table 4.

Rural Consumer Satisfaction with Regard to Rural Retailer Services and Practices

Services	Aggregate scores I_1 Scores	Rank	I_2 Scores	Rank	I_3 Scores	Rank
Credit extension	—147	6	—4	2	—3	5
Merchandise return	—62	2	—11	3	—1	3
Weighing and measuring	—82	4	—17	5	—4	4
Redressal of customers complaints	—73	3	—12	4	—2	2
Retailers' behaviour and courtesy	—94	5	—26	6	—5	6
Working hours	+166	1	+28	1	+12	1
Total scores	—292	—42	—3			
Ideal scores*	1452	744	540			
Least scores**	—1452	—744	—540			
No. of respondents	121	62	45			

* Ideal scores are calculated by multiplying the number of respondents in each category with +2 and the product with total number of services in question.

$$I_1 = 121 \times 2 \times 6 = 1452$$

$$I_2 = 62 \times 2 \times 6 = 744$$

$$I_3 = 45 \text{ X } 2 \times 6 = 540$$

** Least scores are calculated by multiplying the number of respondents in each category with —2 and the product with number of services in question.

$$I_1 = 121 \times -2 \text{ x } 6 = -1452$$

$$I_2 = 62 \times -2 \text{ x } 6 = -744$$

$$I_3 = 45 \times -2 \times 6 = -540$$

Source: Questionnaire data.

A close examination of the rankings reveals that, on the whole, the rural consumers were not satisfied with the services provided by rural retailers. Comparatively, dissatisfaction is high among lower income respondents, (–292) and low among higher income respondents (–3). It was moderate (–42) in case of middle income respondents. The performance of all the services in case of all the categories of respondents is far away from their ideal scores of 1452, 744, and 540 for lower, middle, and higher income respondents respectively. Only with regard to working hours of rural retail outlets the responses were positive among all the categories of respondents.

The data further explains that there are wider variations with regard to the levels of satisfaction or dissatisfaction among different categories of respondents. Among the lower income respondents highest dissatisfaction is found in case of credit extension (–147) followed by retailers' behaviour and courtesy (–94), weighing and measuring practices (–82). Highest dissatisfaction among middle income respondents is found in case of retailers behaviour and courtesy followed by weighing and measuring practices (–17), redressal of complaints (–12).

Interestingly, credit extension which received highest dissatisfaction by lower income respondents, received lowest dissatisfaction (–4) among middle income respondents. Among the higher income respondents too, retailers' behaviour and courtesy received highest dissatisfaction (–5). This is followed by weighing and measuring practices (–4), and credit extension (–3). Among all the types of respondents, lower dissatisfaction is found towards merchandise returns.

Thus, there is general distrust among the rural customers with regard to the behaviour, courtesy, practices and services of rural retailers. Further, this is more so in case of lower and middle income respondents, when compared to higher income respondents. To a larger extent, higher income respondents were indifferent with regard to rural retailers practices, as they were not purchasing the goods in villages. Lower and middle income respondents narrated their experiences to illustrate non-cooperative and high handed behaviour of rural retailers particularly of Kirana stores. There were instances of being warned by the retailers that the customers should not come to their shop next time, whenever they ask. about unfair trade practices like charging high prices, under weighment etc. On the occasions of non-payment of dues. and merchandise returns, being abused by the retailer was a very common thing for rural consumers. It was also revealed that rural retailers never provide any information with regard to prices etc. There were instances of charging interest on outstanding dues, besides charging higher prices on credit purchases. As admitted by lower income respondents, it is their low purchasing power, illiteracy and ignorance which were exposing them to this type of treatment by retailers. For their dissatisfaction, with regard to weighing and measurement practices, rural consumers revealed that, intentional underweighing by retailers, was a most common practice. Weighing method adopted by them varied from person to person depending upon their socio-economic status. The use of traditional measures particularly for weighing the agricultural commodities sold by consumers to the retailers was on a wider scale. Hipher income respondents revealed that because of the poor services and narrow product lines of small quantities, they generally purchase most of their consumer goods in towns.

In the ultimate analysis, it can be observed that, on the whole, rural consumers are not happy, with the services of rural retailers. Further, it is the lower and middle income rural consumers who are exposed more to various unfair trade practices by rural retailers. Rural consumers themselves admitted that, it is their low purchasing power, illiteracy and ignorance, which make them more susceptible to these practices. On the other hand, higher income respondents are not susceptible to these practices and discourteous behaviour of retailers to the extent to which lower and middle income consumers are exposed. Because, they purchase most of their consumer goods in towns. Busides, retailers are afraid of incurring displeasure of higher income consumers. This was due to higher purchasing power, more awareness with regard to brands, quality price etc., among this group of consumers.

However, in reply to these complaints of rural consumers, retailers gave their own version of the problems with rural consumers. Rural retailers were apprehensive about the unusual delays in collecting dues, sometimes extending upto 6 months or 1 year. The customer after availing the credit facility, generally do not turn up again to the shop, until he pleases to clear off the existing debt. Whenever, they find cash with them, consumers go to other shops for purchases. With regard to merchandise return, by the rural consumers, retailers revealed that, it has been their habit to return goods. Most of the lower income consumers send their children for purchasing goods and later their parents insist on returning them in the shop on one pretext or the other. Though rural consumers admitted about delays in paying their dues due to seasonal nature of their incomes and lower purchasing power, they revealed about charging higher prices and collecting interest for compensating these delays. They did not agree with, other complaints. On the whole, the rural consumers expressed a negative opinion of retailers with regard to their goods, services and practices. There has been a feeling among rural consumers that the retailers were in a position to ensure their profits by passing on their inefficiencies to consumers by way of increased prices and other unfair practices rather than attempting to operate more efficiently.

It was rightly observed that there is a general distrust on the retailer and his 'gimmics' and the continuous price rise in the economy is adding to this distrust. Consumer dissatisfaction finds expression at retail outlets and reduction sales, consumer promotions, sale of deceptive goods, etc., are all considered as tools for exploitation of consumers. Therefore, haggling or comparative shopping after affirmation at a number of outlets are considered necessary by rural consumers for effective buying.

The existing situation calls for a change in the attitude of retailers from traditional 'caveat emptor' methods of selling to modern, 'vendee emptor' methods, for improved efficiency and good customer-retailer relationships. But, old fashions, discorteous and non-cooperative methods, practices and services of retailers and insensitivity to the consumer problems and feelings calls for a change in the retail management methods. This can be done by improving things like provision of credit, emphasis of courteous behaviour and other customer services etc. In view of the importance attached to credit facility, working capital management becomes an important aspect of retail management. But as recovery is a serious problem in rural areas due to seasonal nature of purchasing power of consumer alternate availability of credit should be ensured to the retailers by the banks, through the provision of adequate working capital. The imperative role of retailers will be to strengthen goodwill among the rural consumers.

There is a need to establish a system of sound redressal of consumer complaints which ensures that dissatisfied customer receives proper attention. Complaints, generally, arise because of faulty merchandise, higher prices, resentment with credit collection methods etc. Therefore, the retailer must offer satisfactory services. When consumers approach them with legitimate complaint. Habitual complainers should be tackled in a tactful way. In order to reduce the possibilities of complaining situation, it is better, if the retailers return the defective merchandise to the suppliers and also improve the internal operations by actively attending to their complaints. Proper disclosure of the terms of credit will also help in creating goodwill between retailers and consumers. Systematic review of work, regular appraisal of the nature of the consumers experiences with the store, its products, services and practices can be beneficial to both the parties.

Retailers should solicit customers suggestions for improvement in products and services. The rural retailers should take up all the steps with regard to merchandise assortment, prices, quality and customer services, in order to create a trust and goodwill in the minds of consumer. They should also take steps which will make shopping more pleasant on the part of the eonsumers who are far from satisfied now with the treatment they receive now from the rural retailers.

Rural Consumers and Consumerism

Various problems facing the consumer and their dissatisfaction with traders and producers with regard to their practices led to consumerism. It is a movement which seeks to protect and augment the rights of the consumer in relation to marketing people-producers, middlemen, etc. It aims at educating consumer and reducing the distribution costs. As it was rightly observed that marketing is not an end in itself. It is not the exclusive province of business management. Marketing must serve not only business but also the goals of society, It must act in concert with broad public interest.

In the words of Buskirk and Rothe, consumerism is the organised efforts of courses seeking redress, restitution and remedy for dissatisfaction they have accumulated in the acquisition of their standard of living. This movement should influence the attitudes of marketing people to share social responsibility and responsiveness to consumer problems on one hand, and to unitedly resist the unfair trade practices of businessmen by the consumers, on the other. The role of Government in solving the consumer problems cannot be over emphasized. It has been very responsive to consumer needs and have

Table 5.

Rural Consumers' Awareness Level of Different Government Legislation

Legislation	Fully aware		Aware to some extent		Note aware		Total	
	No.	%	No.	%	No.	%	No.	%
ISI Certificate Act. 1955	38	16.67	42	18.42	148	64.91	228	100.00
Agmark	18	7.89	28	42.28	182	79.82	228	100.00
Prevention of Food Adulteration Act	14	6.14	36	15.79	178	78.07	228	100.00
The Essential Commodities supply Act, 1955	16	7.02	32	14.04	180	18.95	228	10000
The Standard Weights and Measures Act, 1956	4	18.42	68	29.82	118	51. 75	228	100.00

Conted.

Packaged Commodities (Regulation) Order, 1975	36	15.79	39	17.12	153	67.12	228	100.00
The Display of Prices Order 1963	28	12.28	32	14.04	168	73.68	228	100.00
The Agricultural Produces (Grading & Marketing) Act, 1937	19	8.33	26	11.40	183	80.26	228	100.00
The Drugs Act of 1940 and the Drugs Control Act of 1954	6	2.63	12	5.26	210	92.12	228	100.00
The Consumer Protection Act, 1986	20	8.77	25	10.96	183	80.26	228	100.00

Source: Questionnaire data.

enacted various laws from time to time to protect the consumers' interest. In the light of these developments in the matter of consumerism, rural consumers of sample villages were asked to indicate on a three point scale as to what extent they were aware of the laws that sought to protect their interests. The responses of rural consumers about the extent of awareness of different legislation related to consumer goods are presented, in Table 5. It is evident from the responses of sample rural consumers that consumers movement had not made any dent in the rural areas. Of the 10 Acts listed, in no case, at least 50% of the respondents revealed that they were aware of these Acts, either 'fully' or to 'some extent'. A sizeable number of respondents revealed that they were, fully aware of a very few acts like the Standard Weights and Measures Act, 1956 (18.42%), ISI 1955 (16.67%). Packaged Commodities (Regulation) Order, 176 and the Display of Prices Order, 1963 (12.28%). Most of these respondents belonged to higher income group and were living in big villages. A majority of rural consumers indicated their ignorance with regard to a majority of Acts. It is due to the ignorance, illiteracy and consequent lack of knowledge of various consumer protection laws, rural consumers are exposed to unfair trade practices by the retailers. Added to this, there are number of loopholes in actual implementation of these laws and many of these laws are becoming archaic, since they could not keep pace with the prevailing marketing situation.

❒

10

Rural Trade and Challenges

TYPES OF RURAL MARKETS IN INDIA

The rural marketing structure is not uniform in all parts of the country. The type of structure prevalent in a particular State or Region depends on various factors like the state of development of agriculture, condition of transport and communication facilities, purchasing power of population, etc. In the North-Eastern region and farflung areas of the country where the 'agricultural production and levels of income are low and communication and transport facilities are not available the marketing structure comprises predominantly. Primary markets like hats and shandies which have sprung-up at convenient places to cater to the needs of the local population. At the other end are areas in North-West like Punjab and Haryana where the agriculture and other facilities are developed. The market structure comprises a larger number of organised markets. However, Rural markets of India can be broadly categorised into three types. They are:

1. Periodic Markets. Periodic markets are the important characteristic feature of the rural marketing in India. In spite of urbanisation and development of retail stores, periodic markets are also playing an important role in rural economy as well as in social life of the rural masses. The periodic marketing function is performed by two institutions, *viz.*, fairs, and weekly markets.

A fair denotes a gathering of people who assemble at regular intervals in certain fixed places—generally around shrines or other religious institutions. Although, by far the largest number of fairs have a religious background, there are some which owe their origin to purely economic considerations. A general concept regarding fair is that they are simply an occasion for the recreation of rural folk. These fairs provide an opportunity for rural people for yearly and half-yearly, some times be-bennial or once in 12 years like that of Kumbha-mela, Godavari Pushkarmas, etc. The purchase and sale of goods, etc. The important fairs draw people not only from surrounding tracts, but also from very distant places. There are about 1700 fairs organised in different parts of the country involving produce and also livestock. There are a few fairs which are attended by a few lakhs of population and there are others which are attended by a few thousands. On an average, the attendence per fair works out at about 16,000. The periodicity of fair varies from one fair in one state with that of another in other States also from one region to another within the State. The time schedule of a fair may vary between 1 day to 7 days. The various types of fairs include:

1. On the basis of Primary Purpose: *(a)* religious fair, *(b)* commercial fair, *(c)* commodity fair, *(d)* cattle fair, *(e)* exhibition fair, and *(f)* mixed fair.

2. On the basis of the periodicity: *(a)* one-day fair, *(b)* short-duration fair, and *(c)* long-duration fair.

3. On the basis of their importance or area of influence: *(a)* local fair, *(b)* regional fair, *(c)* inter-regional fair or national fairs.

Now-a-days international fairs are also organised by the Governments. Festivals of India, organised by the Government of India in important cities of several countries like U.S.A. France and Germany, etc., belong to this category. However, with the change in rural economy, the pattern of shopping in fairs has also been changed The development of permanent shops in rural areas and easy contact with towns have also changed the shopping practice of the rural people. But the importance of fairs is still the same, due to behavioural pattern of rural people who always wait for the purchase of many items. The State Governments are also helping in popularising the fairs.

Paintings, hats, shandies, bazaars are different names employed in various parts of the country to designate periodical markets held usually once or twice a week and in some cases even often. They are commonly known as weekly markets. However, there is slight distinction between these terms. For example, the term painths, is used in united province to denote a periodical market dealing more in agricultural produce than in livestock, whereas in a hat the reverse is the case.

As the goods and services of daily market or permanent shops are not available in remote rural areas, most of the villages are not connected with all-weather roads. Added to this, the state of agriculture is subsistance, peasants have to dispose their meagre surpluses on one hand and have to purchase limited manufactured goods on the other. Created out of this situation in rural areas are weekly markets, and to purchase their daily consumption goods. A periodic market is a public gathering of buyers and sellers of commodities meeting an appointed or customary location at regular intervals. Though the time varies between different regions, in most of the cases these meet once in a week.

The number of hats or weekly markets held in various parts of the country are estimated around 22,000. These markets are found in greater numbers (80%) in the eastern and north eastern regions of the country comprising Assam, Bengal, Bihar, United Provinces and Central Province. Out of the States, Hyderabad State occupies the first position with as many as 1,000 hats. Gwalier, Travancore, Mysore and Bhopal followed with 300,225, and 200 hats respectively.

Most of the weekly markets serve an area within a radius of 8 to 16 kms. In some States like Maharashtra and Tamil Nadu, these markets serve a larger area while in northeastern states these serve a smaller area. Transactions are mostly on cash basis though the barter system is still in practice.

The volume of produce traded, commodities traded, number of villages and the population served by the weekly markets differ considerably from State to State and from market to market within the same State. For example, the number of villages served varies from 27 in the case of markets in Andhra Pradesh to 277 in case of markets in Bihar. In terms of the population served, the variation is 40,000 in respect of a market in Andhra Pradesh to 1,83,000 in the case of market in Gujarat.

.However, the weekly markets at the village level are generally devoid of most of the market facilities. The consumers are subjected so many malpractices indulged in by the traders both in purchasing farms produce from the rural masses and also in selling their required consumer goods to them. In spite of this, these markets serve as an important marketing institution in rural areas. Most of the agricultural labour who get their wages once in a week visit these markets and purchase their consumption goods.

2. Mobile Traders. There is another important agency known as mobile traders to fulfill the limited needs like vegetables, fruits, clothes, utensils, cosmetics, spices, toiletries etc. of rural consumers. The practice of mobile trading is not a new one, but even in ancient India this phenomenon was common. The mobile traders are those merchants who move from one place to another, from one house to another in order to sell those commodities which are often required by rural masses. As it is rightly observed by Stine, important reason for the existence of mobile trader is that "when the maximum range is smaller than the threshold requirement of the firm, the firm either ceases to function or else it becomes mobile. Even in those villages where there are permanent shops and weekly markets, there is a phase for mobile traders because of behavioural pattern of rural masses. Mobile traders move from one village to another on foot or bicycle or buses, bullock carts, etc. They visit the villages once or twice in a week. Sometimes, they visit those villages which are on the way of weekly markets in return direction after attending these weekly markets.

While moving from one house to another within the village they loudly announce the name of the commodity which they sell such as chadar. (bed sheet), pandlu (fruits), gajulu (Bangles), palu, perugu (milk and curd), etc. There will be too such haggling in price fixation. The payment is made either in cash or in kind in the form of foodgrains. Sometimes these traders extend credit upto periods harvests.

Mobile traders move in groups or 3 to 5 persons carrying different types or similar types of articles. They move only in those parts of the village, they have decided at the time of the entry. Female mobile traders are also found significantly dealing in cosmetics, utensils, toiletries, plastic goods, spices, etc. During harvesting season, the frequency of visits by mobile traders is more. Most of these traders belong to certain castes like poosala in Andhra Pradesh. These mobile traders are an integral part of the rural marketing system.

3. Permanent Retail Shops. Permanent retail shops are developed as the population of villages increased, their incomes improved, the demand for goods and that too on daily basis increased. The traditional fairs, weekly markets or peddlers were not able to meet the situation and this led to the emergence and growth of permanent shops. Permanent shops were set up as a result of the demand of the rural inhabitants primarily of the same village. The number of shops, their various forms largely depends upon the size of the population of the village, their incomes, purchasing power, their preferences, etc.

In the Indian context, the most sophisticated types of retail outlets comparable to that of western countries, which are discussed in the first chapter, are found in metropolitan cities, while in rural areas (with population less than 10,000), only the traditional independent general stores or small-scale retailing are prevailing.

The various aspects and dimensions such as importance, role, economic significance, types based different classification, their emergence were discussed at length in the second chapter.

In rural areas, only traditional methods of distribution, *i.e.*, wholesaler and retailers are working as usual. The modern methods of distribution, such as chain stores, super markets and franchise shops are not existing in rural areas because of small size of villages and lower income of rural folk.

RURAL CONSUMER

As the rural consumer is an important and integral part of rural markets, now an attempt is made to discuss the types and peculiar characteristics of rural consumers in India.

Consumer behaviour basically means how a consumer reacts to marketing strategies and appeals relating to different products. This is essential to have an inside look into his feelings on different aspects of product like quality, price, different services offered by the retailer etc.

Types of Rural Consumers

Major occupation of the households of consumers can be taken as basis for classifying rural consumers. Because, there is an intricate combination of caste-class-occupation to represent different consumers with different socio-economic groups. Further, the occupation is related to both class and caste classification of population particularly in rural areas. Based on landholdings and occupations, rural consumers can broadly be classified into six categories.

(1) Land owners, which includes feudal 'tribute gatherers' like Zamindars, rich money-lenders and traders who acquired large tracts of land and companies or persons who own large plantations, *(2)* Rich Farmers, owning more than 10 acres of land and who belong to the dominant caste of the area, *(3)* Small and Marginal Peasants, owning land upto 5 acres and 2.5 acres respectively, *(4)* Tenant-farmers, operating on rented lands belonging to the large landholders and working on small uneconomic land-holdings, *(5)* Agricultural labourers, who work on the lands of landlords and rich farmers, *(6)* Artisans, such as weavers, potters, basket-making, smiths, toddy tappers, etc.

A close look at these groups will provide a clear picture of the life styles and needs of each of these categories.

(1) The Landlords. There are former Zamindars or Deshmukhs who do not have real roots in rural areas. They are composed mainly of absentee land lords who have large properties in cities and towns. Their children are educated in urban centres or even sent abroad. Their life-style is nearer to the urban upper class.

(2) Rich Farmers. They are the rich cultivators belonging to the dominant caste in the region like Reddies in Telangan a and Rayalaseema regions and Kammas and Kapus of coastal region of Andhra Pradesh. They live in villages and have strong roots in rural India. They are wielders of power and influence ranging far above the rural population in terms of social, economic and educational status. This class of farmers alongwith the proprietors of land have adopted mechanisation in agriculture. With increasing property they aspire for better living conditions and a greater interaction with urban centres.

(3) Others. This category includes small, marginal farmers, tenant-farmers, agricultural labourers, artisans and others. They constitute 62 % of the population with a per capita monthly expenditure of Rs. 55 and below and are extremely poor and live most often below subsistence level. Their needs for consumer products are bare essentials like food and clothing.

Characteristics of Rural Consumers

Important characteristics of the rural consumer denoting his peculiar behaviour include the following:

1. A rural codsumer is living in an environment of his own.
2. Majority of the rural consumers are not in a position to understand the implications of trade and price policies followed by traders or Government.
3. They have low purchasing power.
4. Most of the rural consumers are least bothered about quality or standard.

5. Rural consumers are mostly disorganised and do not create enough pressure on traders or government to bother for their interests.

6. They have very low level of literacy.

7. They are ignorant of their rights as customers.

8. The goods offered by retailers should fit into living system of rural people. Though the product is good, if its proper utilisatian is not there in rural areas, consumers may not accept.

9. Rural consumers have lesser reading habits Personal selling cannot reach everyone. Display in village markets will give wide exposure to the products.

10. If the prices are outside the buying capacity of rural consumers, goods will be discarded. Therefore only those goods which suit the price ranges of rural consumers are to be offered.

11. Sense of security while buying a product is expected at a greater scale by rural consumers.

12. Studies also revealed that rural consumers mostly does haggling over each purchase. This is because of want of price uniformity and unpopularity of 'Agmarking' and 'ISI marking'. Consequently, personal inspection becomes a habit.

13. Rigid social and religious customs, climatic considerations, dual ownership due to prevalence of joint family system, also influences the buying habits of the rural population.

14. Seasonal buying is also one of the important habits of the rural consumers. Because, important festivals like Sankranthi, Diwali, Holi, etc., coincide the crop seasons, *viz.*, Kharif & Rabi. Marriages are also performed after barvesting.

Problems of Rural Retail Markets

Rural retail markets as an integral part of the Indian consumer market, suffer from the similar problems of national market which are already discussed. However, certain problems which are typical to rural markets are discussed below.

While the large/vast untapped rural market looks extremely attractive, superficially, the marketing organisations must take into account the problems and constraints that exist in serving them.

1. Widely Scattered Villages. Geographically, distribution of Indian consumer market comprising 84.5 crores population is very peculiar. Against population living in 2,921 urban locations, the rural sector with 75% of the population is widely spread in more than five lakh villages. Further, low density of population and inaccessibility makes the problem not only difficult, but also uneconomical.

2. Distribution. It is often difficult to start distribution in the rural areas as it is done in urban areas by appointing stockists and leaving it to them to the redistribution of retailers. In the first place, locating a stockist is difficult. Secondly, there are few regular transport services. For these reasons, distribution has to be begun by physically carrying the stocks from village to village and selling them to retailers. However, this involves high distribution costs.

3. Lack of Transportation Facilities. Indequate transport facilities are one of the prime obstacles in the improvement of rural markets. By the end of 1984 only 30% of the total number of villages were connected by roads, while 70% (4.16 lakhs) of villages were not connected by any road. About 1.69 lakhs of villages were connected by all-weather roads and 92,800 had fair weather roads. The share of villages not connected by all-weather roads was highest 97% in Orissa, followed by Uttar Pradesh (91%) and Rajasthan (82%). Due to this, the retailers are put to so many difficulties in procuring goods from neighbouring towns.

4. Lack of Bank and Credit Facilities. Hardly any bank is found operating its activities in villages with population less than

2,000. There are about 5 lakh villages of this category in the country. Due to lack of credit and banking facilities, the rural retailers are experiencing several problems not only in financing their business operations, but also in making paymellts to the suppliers. For want of redit facilities, retailers are unable to carry enough stocks of credit different commodities.

5. Regional Differences. Demand for products varies for people living in different areas with different climatic conditions, occupations, level of literacy, outlook towards life and exposure to modern sophisticated things. The income differences between the wealthy few and common masses also create differences in the demand. The degree and effect of the Green Revolution on generating additional incomes varies widely in different states and different regions in the same state.

6. Inadequate Communication Facilities. On communication front, there are two problems. On one hand, modern communication facilities like post office, telegraph office, telephone, etc, are not only inadequate, but non-existing in majority villages. On the other hand, the low levels of literacy in rural areas (29.6%) posing practically an unsurmountable problem of communication. On account of this, many mass-media which is utilised and successful in urban areas for creating a primary demand cannot be effectively used in rural areas. Because of low reading habits of newspapers or magazines, advertisements in newspapers are not a reliable means. Modern communication media like radios and TVs are not within the reach of most of the rural consumers. However a survey conducted by HLL revealed that over 70% of the population listens to the radio and about 65% go to movies in Andhra Pradesh. But this is true only in villages of developed regions like Coastal area and a few villages of higher population strata in other regions.

7. Negligence of Consumer Research. Research of markets in general and consumers in particular and witbin that rural consumers is a neglected aspect of the economy. But, before attempts are made either to produce or to market goods in rural areas, it is to be remembered that, the purchasing habits and attitudes of the rural consumers should be studied carefully. But, this has been completely negbected. Current research efforts in several areas suggest that in future years, the rural consumer will be the focal point of much of our marketing and distribution plans.

Special Characteristics of Indian Rural Market

Indian rural market has the following special characteristics.

(1) The low density of population and widely scattered villages make the problem of serving them difficult and even uneconomical. For instance, there are about 79% of the villages with a population less than 1,000.

(2) Lack of transport and communication facilities making the costs of delivery of goods to these widely scattered villages twice as much as serving the urban market. It is estimated that only 45% of the villages are accessible by roads.

(3) Most of the villages do not have infrastructural facilities like warehousing, storage, banking, etc., which are essential for the deyelopment of markets.

(4) Most of the agricultural labourers purchase a part of their necessities on daily basis from shops, peddlers or shandies through barter system of exchange.

(5) The competition for consumer goods in rural areas is little. Consequently, traders and producers are under the impression that there is no need to strive for better marketing efficiency.

(6) Absence of marketing information is the main stumbling block either in understanding the existing dimensions, structure and operations of rural markets or suggesting for improved alternatives, and

(7) Most of the services like carpentry, blacksmiths, washing, pottery, etc , are rendered by village artisans in exchange of foodgrains at the time of harvests.

Regarding rural consumers, it is widely noticed that they walk over several miles to purraase their basic necessities like rice, salt, kerosene, oils, cloths, etc., on account of absence of transport facilities. Studies conducted by HLL also revealed that about 90% of the farmers visit the nearest town at least once a month to sell their produce and purchase consumer goods. Their marketing habits, practices, and buying behaviour are so primitive that they are unable to realise a fair value for the goods they purchase. The following are the features of rural consumers.

(1) Rural consumers provide a wide rane of contradictions and paradoxies which are baffling the most urban-borne marketing people.

(2) It is difficult to motivate the rural consumers to change their lifestyles. They strongly believe that the best was in the past and that old is gold.

(3) Purchasing levels of rural consumers vary on seasonal basis. During harvests and festival seasons, purchases increase abnormally.

(4) There is a general distrust of the markets and therefore, they consider bargaining and comparative shopping as necessary techniques for buying.

A Wind of Change

Despite the above general characteristics of rural retail market environment, it could also be seen that the wind of change is blowing appreciably from three angles—firstly, on account of changing rural scene towards development in different spheres. Secondly, changes in the market conditions resulted on account of transformation of sellers' market into buyers' market consequent to increased production and increased competition and stagnated urban markets, and lastly, changing government policy towards liberalisation of economy. These are likely to bring about a change in the marketing activities of rural population. Hence, the present study assumes topical interest. Rural society is being transformed into a modern, forward looking economy. Thanks to the Green Revolution, spread of education, mass communication and transportation, increased interaction with urban people, increased banking facilities, rural electrification, etc., the rural scene has been undergoing a seachange. There is a big change in the attitudes and outlook of rural masses towards modern technology and its application in agricultural sector. They are no longer averse to improving their farming techniques. The Green Revolution in India has brought far-reaching marketing implications, The green revolution in agricultural sector has resulted in higher per capita agricultural productivity which ultimately led to the generation of substantial additional incomes to the rural population. In many parts of the country, the use of better seeds, fertilizers, pesticides by the farmers resulted in higher agricultural productivity. Production of foodgrains achieved an impressive growth reaching in recent years, a new plateau of 130 to 140 million tonnes. Nearly 38% of the rice was contributed by Andhra Pradesh to the total production in the country.

The recent advent of regional rural banks in the villages and their policy of giving credit to farmers and other rural artisans, not only enabled them to get out of the clutches of money-lenders, but also to put larger resources in their productive efforts and avocations resulting a higher level of earnings.

Railways and roads linking the rural areas to urban centres are given priority in plans and necessary steps have been taken to connect feeder markets and towns to surrounding rural areas.

The increase in rural income, in recent years, has been as much as about Rs. 2,000 crores annually. A large increase in incomes of rural people, apart from other factors, was due to the Green (food grains), White (milk) and Grey (egg & poultry) revolutions. It is estimated in 1986 that there are around 14 million rural households with income over Rs. 1500 p.m. There has been enormous flow of funds into rural sector on account of Government promoted development schemes like Jawahar Rojgar Yojana, IRDP, etc. Statutory increase in the minimum wages of agricultural labour also raised the incomes of rural folk.

With their primary food needs better met today, the rural middle class has sizeable residual purchasing power to take care of their consumerist desires. As such the rural marketing in India is likely to experience unexpected trends. According to a trend analysis attempted by the ORG, the rural market for packaged consumer products has nearly trebled between 1984 and 1989 *i.e.*, it increased from Rs. 733 crores to Rs. 2083 crores. Their growth rate shot-up from 17% in 1987 to 41% in 1989. Significantly, there has been a marked change in the rural expenditure pattern with the ratio between food and nonfood items going down from 71:21 in 1976 to nearly 60:30 in 1989.

A survey of the media scene in rural India conducted by the ORG reveals that in terms of percentage of the adult population readership is 9%, T.V. viewership is 31%, radio listernship 32% for primary channel and 24% for Vividh Bharathi, Video viewership is 36%. However, there were glaring zonal and regionl variations in the above.

Owing to modern technologies and innovations there is a large-scale production leading to stiff competition among the producers of consumer goods in India. During periods of shortages, whatever, that was produced was to be sold reflecting the symptoms of sellers' market. But due ito increased production, on one hand, and saturation in urban markets on the other, changed the situation. Now, there is a shift from sellers' market to buyers' market as admitted by the leaders of business and industry.

Manufacturers finding the urban markets for certain products reaching saturation levels. Again to quote, Mr. Jalan, "industrial units afflicted by recession, accumulating unsold stocks and declining profitability were only paying the penalty for prolonged indifference to the neglect of marketing". In the light of this situation, many markets are reaching out to the rural hinterland where the demand is still on the upswing. A new cadre of entrepreneurs has sprung up which sees the rural market as its starting base instead of as a spill-over from the urban area. There are instances of flourishing manufacturers like HLL who have ability and foresight to build-up an extensive rural base for their products.

There are significant shifts in government policy towards liberalisation of the economy. The recently announced liberalisation on several fronts of the economy such as abolition of licensing policy to major industries, reduction in excise duties, liberalisation of industrial policy to invite foreign investment are certainly going to have long-run impact on the future marketing with the increased production of consumer goods and further, strengthening the buyer's market.

In the light of the above, there is no other go than to reaching the rural retail market by the manufacturers as early as possible. Thus, rural retail market assumes greater importance, day-by-day.

Importance of Rural Retail Markets

The Indian retail market has a deep rural character with a total rural population of 50.2 crores representing about 80% of the total population. This population is widely scattered among 5.76 lakh villages. Of these villages, 3.18 lakhs have a population over 5,000. In terms of population, Indian rural market is almost twice as large as the entire market of tne U.S.A. or the erstwhile U.S.S.R. Rural retail markets offer a very promising future for the marketing of consumer goods. The future market for any consumer goods manufacturers in the country is in the rural areas. In the words of J.R.D. Tata, if only 10% of rural society becomes regular buyers of industrial products, the consumer goods industry will have 5 crores of new customers added to its present market. Rural areas have a very large market potential as worked out by the Thompson Rural Market Index of 1972. Uttar Pradesh with its largest geographical area and also rural base has got the largest rural market potential of 15.46% followed by Madhya Pradesh and Maharashtra with 9.43% and 9.26% respectively. Andhra Pradesh occupies fourth position with. 8.49% rural market potential of which Telangana region constitutes a major proportion.

The marketing environment governing the rural markets has been undergoing vast changes in the last few decades. It was observed that rural market in India started showing its potential from 1960s and the '90s are going to see the full blossoming of the rural market of India. Rural prosperity and the discretionary income with the rural consumers is directly tied up with agriculture prosperity. Due to improved irriation facilities and methods of cultivation, incomes of rural people increased considerably, in recent years. It is clear from the fact that half of the total bank deposits are now coming from the rural parts of the country in the form of small saving. However, there are wider variations in the incomes of rural consumers.

There has been a significant growth in the size of rural demand for non-food items. The size of rural demand for these goods rose from Rs. 5,000 crores in 1970-71 to Rs. 13,500 crores in 1979-80 to Rs. 18,000 crores in 1987-88 by recording an annual growth rate of 2.5 %.63 For example certain durable items like radios, tape-recorders which were considered as prestige symbols by few rich farmers in rural areas, twenty years back, are now found in a majority rural houses. Rural masses who were using earthern pots and vessels have shifted to aluminium, brass and stainless steel utensils. Bicycles are found almost in every house. In clothing also there is a remarkable change, among rural consumers, in recent years. Rural consumers have moved from local hand-made fabrics to polyester or blended fabrics, and ready-made garments. Thus, the composition of the rural demand is changing significantly. The percentage of rural households using new products is increasing day-by-day. It was reported that toiletries are used by 25% of rural households, cosmetics by 12%, readymade garments by 19% baby care products by 12%, packaged foodstuffs by 25% and modern consumer durables by 29% during 1986-87.

The ORG survey reveals that in 1989 rural India accounted for over 50% of the sales of popular toilet soaps, 26% of premium toilet soaps 59% of bar soaps and cakes of washing soaps, 45.5% of detergents, 21% of all the tooth paste and 24.5% of tooth powder sold in the country. This trend is not con. fined only non-durables, but it is evident for durable goods also. For the same period, over 60% of motor-cycle sales claimed by rural market. In case of traditional domestic utensils its share was as much as 80%. The share of rural areas in all India market for all consumer non-durables rose from 28% to 37%.

The composition of the rural market in 1989, according to the ORG included: washing materials 37%, toileteries 30%, food/beverages 14.5%, cosmetics 3.5%. over the counter products 3.5%, and miscellaneous 11.5%.

However, as Professor Gopala Swamy of the Indian Institute of Management, Bangalore felt that the products for rural areas will have to be redesigned to suit rural incomes, habits, tastes and preferences. Because of the extra transport and inventory costs involved, the motivational package for rural dealers and stockists noods to be different than for urban outlets.

WEAKNESSES OF INDIAN RURAL RETAIL TRADE

In spite of the obvious importance of retail trade as an economic institution and the deliverer of standard of living there have been apprehensions about the functioning of retail trade outlets that it is unproductive and costly intermediary. The structure of retail trade in India is not skewed properly between urban and rural areas. Retail outlets are concentrated in different parts of towns thereby causing inconvenience to rural consumers. The retail practices adopted by Indian retailers particularly in rural areas are traditional with primitive methods. Telangana region of Andhra Pradesh—the study area, is one of the backward regions of the country representing almost all the characteristics of average rural India. The environment and imperfections under which rural retail trade is working in rural India are eqally applicable to Telangana region. Therefore, now, an attempt is made to probe into the weaknesses of rural retail trade. Mainly, the rural retail trade in India is suffering from the following weaknesses.

(1) Uneven Distribution of Retail Outlets. According to 1971 census, there were about 33.25 lakh private retail outlets in the country. It is estimated that there were 42 families served per retail outlet in rural areas while there were 14 households per outlet in urban areas. Thus, retail outlets in the country are skewed in favour of urban areas. At the all India level, on an average, there were 6 retail establishments per 1,000 population against 9 in U.K., 14 in Japan and 17 in Italy. A majority of outlets in India are of small size when compared to Western countries.

The NSS Survey of Household Trade 1976, revealed that there were 40.50 lakh trading households which directly or indirectly serve the needs of the consumers. Of this, 37.1 lath households were in retail business and remaining households were either in wholesale or commission agency and brokerage. Of the total 37.6 lakh retail outlets in the country, 25 lakh, constituting 6.4%, in rural areas while there were 12.5 lakhs in urban areas. The survey revealed that the average turnover per shop was Rs. 250 p.m. in rural areas, whereas it was four times more at Rs. 1098 in urban areas. Of the total 25 lakh rural retail households as much as 17.6 lakh constituting 67% were engaged in trading of food stuff, while it was 55% in urban parts of the retail households.

(2) Structure of Retail Outlets in Andhra Pradesh. According to a survey conducted by Bureau of Economics and Statistics, Government of Andhra Pradesh on 'Distributive Trade' in 1975- 76, there were about 90,549 registered retail outlets and 13,962 wholesale establishments in the State of Andhra Pradesh providing employment to 4.47 lakh persons. The total value of gross sales of various commodities traded by retail during the year amounted to Rs. 654.26 crores. The capital employed in these outlets was to the tune of Rs. 660.50 crores. By way of sales tax, this sector contributed to the tune of Rs. 33.32 crores to the State's exchequer.

Distribution of retail outlets in the State among different regions or between urban and rural segments revealed that they are unevenly distributed and skewed in favour of urban areas. Of the total trading establishments of 1,04,511 (retail and wholesale put together) 69,111 (66%) were in urban areas when compared to 35,400 (34%) only in rural areas. The number of shops for 1,000 population in rural areas is worked out to be approximately against 5 outlets for 1,000 population in urban areas. Distribution of retail outlets among three regions of the State revealed that Coastal area acccounted for a little over 61.26% of the total registered retail outlets in the State. The Telangana excluding Hyderabad accounted only for 26.17% of registered retail outlets followed by the Rayalaseema with only 12.57%.

(3) Unfair Trade Practices. There is a widespread feeling in many duarters that the consnmer in India is greatly exploited and has to be beware of marketing sharks. It was observed by Pranlal Bhogilal that Indian consumer gets a raw deal in various dubious ways like underweighment, manipulation of scales, adulteration etc. It is reported that one out of every five drugs in the Indian market including the imported ones, is spurious. The Indian consumer, according to an official survey is cheated of about Rs. 1600 crores in a year through defective weights and measures alone. It is purplexing to note that all these unfair trade practices have been indulged in spite of the estimated cost of Rs. 1500 crores a year for implementing various consumer protection laws. However, it was also observed that marketing men are not sure of intensity of criticism levelled against them and their practices, because no research has ever been conducted on what the consumer in India actually thinks about these institutions and their practices.

(4) Traditional Management of Retail Outlets. It is widely accepted that Indian retail trade lags far behind that of Western countries in many respects. It is more so in rural India when compared to the urban parts of the country. Prof. Gabriel of Kiel University has rightly observed that each nation creates a system of distribution that comes closest to its specific needs. The needs, however, are closely related to the general prosperity of the nation and thus, the most of the innovations in the distribution have largely been dependent upon the levels of standard of living of the people". It is interesting to observe that we have modern super-markets chain stores, departmental stores who have adopted the sophisticated techniques in planning and budgeting of their operations in urban areas, while the age-old traditional retail outlets with primitive methods and practices are found in the rural areas of the country. For want of education and training among the rural retailers, they are not receptive to the new methods, techniques and concepts of management and its functional areas like marketing, finance, accounting etc. The services to be provided by the retailer by way of information to the consumer with regard to the products and other related aspects is non-existent. Out-moded layout of shops, primitive method of collection of cash from the customers and a chain of artificial barriers between the product and the consumer etc., are the other examples of poor and traditional management of rural retail stores. In fact, the survival and growth of retailing depends upon meeting the genuine needs of customers by using innovative practices, tools, and techniques in relation to decor and layout, salesmanship, credit policy, assortment etc.

(5) Retailing—A Shaky Wheel. Retailing is a very shaky wheel in the distributive system. It is susceptible to various controllable and uncontrollable factors of the economy. Retailer has to confront many difficulties to establish his foothold in the market and build an image of his store. It has been said, not simply in jest, that there is no single retailer who does not sell his shirt once or twice during the course of his business career. The factors which made the retailing a shaky wheel include, unsuitability of site and location, lack of experience, lack of capital, fierce competition, inability to foresee and undertake risk etc.

(6) Rural Consumers and Their Perceptions. As the country is vast, geographically, the consumers of India are not only scattered over a vast territory but they are marked by diversity in religion, language, customs, traditions, life style, economic status, etc. While describing the majority Indian rural consumers, Marquis and Douglas opined that Indians have a philosophic outlook of life which tends to make them less interested in materialistic things. Their thinking in this respect is similar to that in Europe in the middle ages. Consequently majority of Indian consumers are not in a position to understand correctly, the implications of trade policies and practices adopred by the traders. Indian consumer possess the following characteristic: *(a)* low literacy, *(b)* ignorant of his right as consumer, *(c)* low purchasing power, *(d)* less mobile, *(e)* least bothered about quality of standard, and *(f)* lack of cooperative spirit.

However, a study conducted in an urban environment with regard to consumer's perception of marketing has thrown some light on the problems of consumers. The survey revealed that as many as 78% of the respondents believed that most of the shortages were artificially created due to hoarding. About 85% of the respondents felt that the market was full of spurious products. Over 60% of respondents considered prices at departmental stores very high.

Apart from these, retail trade in India, particularly, in rural areas has been suffering from several other deficiencies like lack of road and communication facilities, lack of banking facilities, and lack of marketing information, etc.

Thus uneven distribution of retail outlets, all-organised and ill-managed retail trade practices, on one hand, and the peculiar rural environment and buying behaviour of rural consumers, on the other, causing a further increase in distribution costs, inconvenience, and poor customer-trader relations.

The present study is, therefore, relevant to the present day problem of controlling prices and unfair trade practices to increase the purchasing power of rural masses, on one hand, and the necessity of offering suggestions for shifting from traditional and primitive practices to new and innovative methods for efficient and effective management of retail outlets and ultimately paving the way for good trader-consumer relations on the other. Because, the success of retail trade depends upon maximising the consumer satisfaction in terms of reasonable prices, reduced cost, convenient shopping, ensuring maximum value for the money spent by the consumer on one hand, and increased gross margin and return on investment to the owners by adopting new and innovative trade practices, on the other.

Further, to give the existing structure of scramble merchandising a look of an efficient, streamlined and well-knit and integrated distribution system of consumer goods is not only in the interests of the consumers alone but also that of the retailer, manufacturer, government and the community as a whole. This entails a clear understanding of the existing structure, practices and performance of rural retail trade, on one hand, and the rural consumer shopping behaviour and their reactions to retailing practices etc., on the other.

The present study is one in that direction. As it was rightly observed by Leon V, Hirsch, that basic to any attempt at improving the efficiency of marketing in underdeveloped or developing economies, is an understanding of just how the present system operates.

Need for the Study

The research conducted in developed countries in the field of distribution, to a large extent, studied the problems from the manufacturer's perspective, The analysis was geared to the identification of solutions to the difficulties faced by the producer with regard to the distribution of his goods. The intermediaries' situation was viewed through a frame-work of manufacturer's goals and needs. It is important to realise that many problems are peculiar to channel members *i.e.*, retailers and wholesalers. Channel members are not merely functionaries of manufacturers. They pursue their own goals. Their view point on the same situation is often very different, Research into this subject opens up important new areas of study and valuable dimensions on traditional problems. In a country like India, keeping in view the vast rural markets, retailer plays an important role. "Middlemen like retailer is not a hired link in a chain forged by a manufacturer, but rather an independent market". Further, the study of independent channel member can effectively utilise the knowledge and techniques of contemporary marketing, Traditionally, the study of the problems of retailers has been confined largely to locational analysis, inventory and warehousing policies and problems. But, the growing importance and rapidly changing situation of retailers demand that far more research be conducted into the distributive process from the perspective of channel members. Peter Drucker also observed that "distribution channels deserve a good deal of attention and study, much more than they usually receive". Productivity Team Report on Retailing indicated, "not that retailing is the most significant sector of distribution, but also that a deep study would be more rewarding in this field".

Apart from the various aspects of retailing, like structure, practices and performance, etc., the buyer behaviour, attitudes and satisfaction are also of critical importance. As it was rightly observed, that for any research project to be comprehensive, particularly, the one which is carried at the retailer's level, it should also be extended to find out consumers's approach and attitude towards retailers and their goods and services. In other words, a clear picture of the market, particularly at the level of retailer, cannot be obtained without reference to the consumer. If a business enterprise is to achieve good relations with the customers, who are the ultimate users of the product, two things are necessary: *(a)* the business enterprise must get to understand its customers, and *(b)* the business enterprise must get its customers to understand it.

CHALLENGES OF RURAL MARKETING

There are a number of factors, areas or activities which are responsible for the fast and continuous growth of the Rural Market. Some of these are as:

1. Green Revolution. The thrust on agriculture during the successive Five Year plans has helped improvement in agricultural productivity. Adoption of new agronomic practices, selective mechanisation, multiple cropping to include non-food crops and development of commercial activities like dairying have resulted in substantial increase in the disposable incomes of rural consumers. Over 75 per cent of villages in India have been electrified. This has facilitated a shift from dependence on rain to irrigation. Cultivators have gone for high-risk, high-return cash/non-food crops. In the process, the seasonality of income receipts has been reduced and there disposable incomes have increased.

2. Improved Transport and Communication. Over 40 per cent of villages today are connected by all-weather roads. Increase of road coverage has increased conununication links; in turn. this has led to increased market access for companies going the rural way. Road networking, oosides enhancing the mobility of rural consumers, has increased their exposure to products and services. This also has an impact on better price realisation.

3. Rising Expectations Revolution. The rural folk consciously or unconsciously are adopting modern ways of living, and this has led to a rise in the aspiration level. One can notice the among the rural people being influenced by the marketing environment. The expectations revolution has brought about a powerful change in the environmental dynamics. It has kindled their hopes, and strengthened their motivation to work, earn and consume.

4. Varied Sources of Income. As a part of planned economic development, the government has been making concerted efforts towards rural development. Plan after plan, it has been committing large outlays to sectors like agriculture, animal husbandry, irrigation, flood control and khadi and village industries. Various schemes like Jawahar Rozgar Yojana, Prime Minister's Rozgar Yojana, IRDP, etc., are being implemented in rural areas.

Statutory increase in the minimum wages of agricultural labourers has also raised the incomes of the rural folk.

Thrust on minor and medium projects and village forestry collectively have helped create new job opportunities, increasing the purchasing power of rural people.

The share of rural purchases in selected products such as bicycles, razor blades, books and stationery, and cinema shows varies from 55 to 80 per cent. The Indian rural market has grown in size, range and sophistication. Even the rural market for packaged consumer products has grown nearly threefold, from Rs. 733 crore in 1984 to Rs. 2,083 crore in 1989. The electrification of 60 per cent of the villages has further enhanced the upsurge in demand. The modernisation of agriculture has enlarged the rural market for agricultural inputs. Tlms, the rural market of India offers big opportunities and attractions to marketers. However, rural marketing is confronted with some challenges and they are given below:

(a) Widely Scattered Villages. The distribution of the Indian consumer market, comprising a population of 84.5 crore is very peculiar. The rural sector, covering 75 per cent of the population, is widely spread in more than five lakh villages. Low density of population and inaccessibility make the problem of marketing not only difficult but also uneconomical.

(b) Proper Segmentation Difficult. Demand for products varies for people living in different areas with different climatic conditions, occupations, their level of literacy, their outlook towards life, and their exposure to modern sophisticated goods and services. The income differences between the wealthy few and the common masses also create differences in the demand, customs, beliefs, etc. All these make proper segmentation difficult.

(c) Low Occurrence of Retail Outlets. This is another important constraint in effective marketing by urban producers in rural areas. It is estimated that 42 families were served per retail outlet in rural areas, while in urban areas 14 households were served per outlet (1971 Census). The position now could well be the same.

(d) Problem of Marketing Communication. The low level of literacy in rural areas poses a practically unsurmountable problem of communication. On account of this, many mass-media, which are utili sed and are successful in urban areas for creating a primary demand, cannot be effectively used in rural areas.

(e) Inadequate Bank and Credit Facilities. A large majority of the villages, especially those with 2,000 population or less do not enjoy banking facilities. Whatever RRBs are operating under the various nationalised commercial banks might be quantitatively satisfactory, but service-wise, their performance is not up to expectations. In the process, the rural retailers experience several problems not only in financing their business operations, but also in making payments to the suppliers. For want of credit facilities, retailers are unable to carry enough stocks with them.

(f) Transport Still Erratic. Though road transport facilities are improving, they are yet not adequate. As pointed out earlier, only 40 per cent of the total number of villages were connected by all-weather roads, while 60 per cent of the villages were connected by only fair-weather roads, or had no roads. About 1.69 lakh villages were connected by all-weather roads, and 92,800 had fair-weather roads. Due to all these, retailers are put to many difficulties in procuring goods from the neighbouring towns.

(g) Towards Effective Rural Marketing. Some Strategies. Rural literacy is expected to improve consequent upon the launching of the Total Literacy Campaigns (TLCs), and adult education programmes. Improvement in agricultural prosperity has been responsible for an increase in rural incomes and consequent increase in rural spending. We have seen earlier that the rural share in many products is more, compared to the urban share. The rural market still remains untapped. A few strategies for tapping it in an effective manner are.

(h) Storage and Warehousing. Rural outlets in many parts of India find it difficult to get suitable godowns. No public warehousing agencies exist in rural India. The Central Warehousing Corporation (CWC) and the state Warehousing Corporations (SWCs) do not extend their network of warehouses to the rural parts. They go only upto the nodal points or major market centres. It is not possible to service the interior outlets effectively with the existing network of CWC/SWC warehouses.

(i) Promotional Strategy. Television has an all-India exposure level of 27 per cent rural households. The exposure levels vary across the states between 15 and 38 per cent. Press exposure levels are less than 15 per cent Radio reaches relatively more people and its penetration level has grown significantly.

Keeping these and the regional variations in language, literacy, per capital income, and living. standards in mind, the communication strategy that can be followed is that of turning the content and pattern of the advertising to the regional requirement, instead of a national release. During the postharvest period, farmers become cash rich, and are in the right frame of mind to go in for buying new products. Local promotion activities should be given due emphasis which *inter alia* may include:

* Wall paintings and posters,
* Publicity vans induce brand trial.
* Stalls, hoardings and audio-visual publicity at local fairs.
* Mobile retailing-cum-merchandising units to operate in individual villages.
* Promotion sales supported by merchandising at baat markets.

One author has observed that in rural areas, it is often not the promotion of a brand that is crucial, but creating awareness about the product class. In such a situation, syndicated advertising can bring down the market development expenditure. Under this strategy, a few companies with similar product lines collaborate collectively in creating awareness of their products and in gaining consumer preference for those products

Distribution Strategy. Syndicated distribution is a viable alternative: Under this arrangement, two or more companies, in non-competing product categories, could share, for example, facilities of a distribution van with crew enabling dispersal of costs. The tie-up could be at the national level, or a lot closer to the end consumer at the district level, where most redistribution stockists represent two or three companies. The district level operation could creat synergies of coordination with a single stock-lifting point.

Barefoot approach to distribution: Companies could develop and utilise a barefoot approach, and train local talent to operate as barefoot salesmen. Fluency in the local dialect, and familiarity with the people in the area of operation, would be among the factors enhancing the efficacy of this approach. A barefoot salesman, operating on a retainer-cum-commission basis, could cook orders from retailers in villages within a limited radius of his village. Companies and non-government organisations could join hands for mutual benefit. With NGOs undertaking distribution, companies realise benefits accruing from the NGOs infrastructure and grassroots level networking.

PHYSICAL DISTRIBUTION STRATEGY

Everybody is aware of the problems of warehousing and storage in the rural marketing context. The Central Warehousing Corporation and the State Warehousing Corporations go only upto the nodal points or, at best, major market centres. It is not possible to service the interior outlets efficiently with the existing warehouses. Depending on the existing warehousing facilities, the public ones and their own, is neither adequate nor cost-effective from a commercial point of view. The rural market is operating almost without any institutionalised warehousing. Hence, State Rural Warehousing Corporations should at least be established, with a good network of warehouses in the interior. Co-operatives should also come forward to create such warehousing facilities. A combination of different modes of transport has to be adopted for facilitating efficient physical distribution. The system for serving the rural market will have to be largely built around rail-cum-trucks for the primary long distance movement, trucks for the primary long distance movement, trucks for medium/short distance movement, and delivery vans and bullock carts for local haulage. The bullock cart has a specific role in rural distribution. Bullock carts are cheaper, they are available in plenty, and they are ideal for the rural roads.

In a nutshell, the Indian rural market has grown in recent years in size, range and sophistication. This offers a big opportunity to Indian, marketers. The rural market, however, still remain untapped, in the following areas:

(a) as scattered location of villages,

(b) low occurrence of retail ontlets,

(c) problems of marketing communications,

(d) erratic transport, etc. The major strategies are to be confined to promotion and distribution. These areas have to be improved to meet the challenges. Syndicated advertising, promotion according to regional variation, suitable local promotional activities, syndicated distribution barefoot approach to distribution, improvement in rural transport and warehousing and storage are some of the needed interventions.

ROLE OF RISK IN RURAL MARKETING

Risk plays a vivid role in the profitability and successful functioning of rural marketing or any marketing system. There are number of theories of profits like uncertainty, contingencies theory, risk bearing theory, M.P. theory. The theory which is acceptable to most of the economist is the risk bearing theory: Hardy has defined Risk as uncertainty which may give you ample of benefits or it may ruin badly. At one place, he points out that no risk no profit, more risk more profits. He has defined the risk theory as, "Profit is the reward of uncertainty and Risk Bearing". Risk is inherent in all marketing transactions. There is the risk of the destruction of the produce by fire, rodents or other elements, quality deterioration, price fall, change in tastes, habits or fashion, and the risk of placing the commodity in the wrong hands or area. There is a time lag between the production and consumption of arm products. The longer the time lag, the greater the risk. The risk associated with marketing cannot be dispensed with for this risk contributes to profit. Someone has to bear the risk in the marketing process. But most of the risk is taken by market middlemen, for they have the capacity to bear it. Whenever risks are greater and varied, the margin taken by the risk bearers is higher, and *vice versa*. One who holds the commodity in the process is the bearer of the risk, because of which he may be better off or worse off.

Types of Risk

1. Physical Risk. This includes a loss in the quantity and quality of the product during the marketing process. It may be due to fire, flood, earthquake, rodents, insects, pests, fungus, excessive moisture or temperature, careless handling and unscientific storage, improper packing, looting or arson. These together account for a large part of the loss of the produce at the individual as well as at the macro level. Such losses are a loss to society, too, and must be averted to the extent possible.

2. Price Risk. The prices of rural products fluctuate not only from year to year, but during the year from month to month, day to day and even on the same day. The changes inprices may be upward or downward. Price variation cannot be ruled out, for the factors affecting the demand for, and the supply of, rural products are continually changing. A price fall may cause a loss to the trader or farmer who stocks the produce. Sometimes, the risks are so great that they may result in a total failure of the business, and the person who owns it may become bankrupt.

3. Institutional Risks. These risks include the risks arising out of a change in the government's budget policy, in tariffs and tax laws, in the movement restrictions, statutory price controls and the imposition of levies.

Minimization of Risks. The agencies engaged in marketing activities worry about the risks associated at every stage; and they continually try to minimize the effects of these risks. A risk cannot be eliminated because it also carries profit. The agencies which do not take risks hardly earn profit. The risk management by the adoption of some of the measures listed below may minimize the risks.

(a) Reduction in Physical Loss. The physical loss of a product (quantity and quality both) may be reduced by the adoption of the following measures:

(i) Use of fire-proof materials in the storage structures to prevent accidents due to fire;

(ii) Use of improved storage structures and giving necessary pre-storage treatment to the product to prevent losses in quality and quantity arising out of excessive moisture, temperature, attacks by insects and pests, fungus and rodents;

(iii) Use of better and quicker transportation methods and proper handling during transit; and

(iv) Use of proper packaging material.

(b) Transfer of Physical Losses to Insurance Companies. The burden of physical risk may be minimized by shifting it is insurance companies. There are specialised professional agencies to bear such risks. They collect some premium and provide full compensation to the party in case of loss due to the reasons for which the products are insured. In this way, the company insures a number of farmers against losses.

(c) Minimisation of Price Risk. The risk associated with the variation in prices may be minimized by the adoption of the following measures:

(i) Fixation of minimum and maximum prices of commodities by the government and allowing movements in prices only within the defined range;

(ii) Making arrangements for the dissemination of accurate and scientific price information to all sections of society over space and time: This should include information on market demand, average under a particular crop, estimates of market supply and of the import and export of commodities.

(iii) An effective system of advertising may reduce price uncertainty and create a favourable atmosphere for the commodity;

(iv) Operation of speculation and heading. The price risk associated with the commodities for which the facility of forward trading is available may be transferred to professional speculators through the operation of hedging. A detailed exposition of speculation and hedging follows.

Speculation and Hedging. Speculation and hedging are important ways of minimizing price risk in business. In the former, risk is taken by the person specialising in the business without much consideration of business trends, while in the second a calculated risk is taken.

1. Speculation. The fundamental idea underlying speculation is the purchase or sale of a commodity at the present price with the object of sale or purchase at some future date at a favourable price. The speculator is normally concerned with profit-making from price movements. He purchases when prices are low. He is, therefore, not a normal or regular trader. The difference in the prices prevailing at two times constitutes his profit. Speculator may lose in this process. The essentials of a speculator are:

(i) He enters the trade at current prices;

(ii) The transactions of speculators are completed on some future date;

(iii) The speculators enter the trade with the sole object of making profit from price movements. Sometimes, they indulge in hoarding as well;

(iv) Except in a few cases, the physical delivery of produce is neither taken nor given only the difference in the prices is paid or taken;

(v) Speculators are not regular buyers and sellers in the market. They do not conduct any regular business apart from speculative business.

Based on the legalities involved, speculation is of two types:

(a) Speculation Proper. Speculation proper refers to speculation on the part of a person who makes it his profession. Such professional speculators devote their whole time and energy to the collection of information about the future course of price movements. The decisions of the speculator are not hunch decisions. They are intelligent forecasts based on predicted trends. This type of speculation in beneficial for the economy as a whole and is usually accepted by society.

(b) Illegitimate. Speculation. This is a gamble in business. The speculators adopt such manipulative practices as create conditions of artificial scarcity in the. market and lead to a rise in prices. The main

aim of the speculatoris to earn a big profit. This type of speculation is not based on any rationale, through it influences the prices of products. Such speculation is prohibited by the government in the best interests of economy.

2. Economic Benefits of Speculation. Speculation dampens price fluctuations. Speculators buy at current prices in anticipation of a rise in prices in the future which results in pushing up the current prices. This encourages production and discourages consumption. Other speculators, who sell in the present period in the expectation of a fall in future prices, bring about a fall in the current prices, which encourages consumption and discourages production. The sum total of the effects of these speculative activities results in dampening price fluctuations.

(i) The price differentials in different markets are bridged to some extent.

(ii) Speculation helps in the adjustment of the supply of and demand for commodities at normal prices.

3. Related Terms.

(i) Spot/Cash Transactions. A transaction in which payment is made on the spot or within a prescribed short period, and delivery is taken on the same day or within a specific period are known as spot or cash transactions. Three things are essential in cash transactions:

(a) The purchaser has to take the delivery of the produce immediately after sale;

(b) The seller has to deliver the goods immediately; and

(c) Payment for the produce has to be made immediately.

(ii) Future Transactions. This is a transaction in which prices of commodities are settled in cash but the commodities are delivered on some future date as agreed. Generally, in future transactions, the loss or profit is paid or received on the expiry of the time instead of the physical handing over of the commodity. In futures transactions.

two groups of persons are involved, *i.e.* the bulls and the bears. Persons who expect that prices will go up in future are bulls; but those who expect that prices will go down in future are bears. The futures transactions take place as a result of action on the part of these two groups of persons.

(iii) Contract. A contract is a promise to deliver or accept delivery of specific grade of a commodity at a specified time in future.

4. Hedging. Hedging is a trading technique of transferring the price risk. It protects traders from extreme falls in prices. Hedging has been defined as follows:

Shephered, "Hedging is executing opposite sales or purchases in the future market to offset the purchases or sales of physical products made in the cash market.

Hoffman, "Hedging is the practice of buying or selling futures to offset an equal and opposite position in the cash market and thus avail the risk of uncertain changes in prices. Hedging refers to the purchase or sale of a commodity in a futures market accompanied by a sale or a purchase in the cash market. In this approach, each sale is entered into with an equivalent purchase of the commodity. It is assumed that prices in the two markets move exactly parallel, and that the losses arising in one market are offset by profit in another market. Hedging is based on two assumptions:

(a) The future and cash commodity prices move up and down together, *i.e.*, the basis of price changes remains unchanged.

(b) The mechanics of hedging includes the making of simultaneous transactions, but of opposite nature, in the futures and cash markets.

*5. **Benefits of Hedging.***

(i) It protects the hedger from sustaining loss and enables him to earn his normal trade profit;

(ii) Hedging enables him to keep the trade margins at a lower level because there is no risk;

(iii) Hedging facilitates the financing of inventories of stored commodities to the maximum possible extent.

Hedging is employed by many traders to protect themselves against losses due to market price fluctuations by executing cash purchases and sales practically simultaneously with future transactions in the opposite side. It is the performance of mainly the two contracts of an opposite, though corresponding, nature at the same time, one in the spot market where the physical commodity is handled, and the other in the future market, where the commodity exchange takes place.

DIFFERENCE BETWEEN SPECULATION AND HEDGING

The basic differences between speculation and hedging are:

Speculation	*Hedging*
1. Purchases and sales in the cash as well as in futures markets are made with the objective of making profit.	The purchases and sales in the cash and futures markets are made to protect oneself against excessive price fluctuations.
2. The activities of buying and selling are not necessarily opposed to each other.	The activities of buyers and sellers are always opposed to each other.
3. It is not necessary that the two types of transactions should be of equal quantity.	It is obligatory to buy and sell the goods in equal quantities in the two markets.
4. Under speculation, the speculator purchases goods and sells them when prices rise as per his expectations.	The commodities are not stored by traders. Only the difference in the price is given or taken on the due date.

FUTURE (FORWARD) TRADING

Meaning of future trading. Futures trading is a device for protection against the price fluctuations which normally arise in the course of the marketing of commodities. Stockists, processors or manufacturers utilise the futures contracts to transfer the price risk faced by them. Futures trading includes both hedging and speculation. But since hedging is its raison d'etre, it is also known as hedge-trading. Futures markets are, therefore, known as "hedge" markets. Widely divergent views exists on the effects of futures trading. A few are convinced that commodity futures trading tends to stabilise prices and reduce price variations. Others not only disagree with this view but vigorously allege that, more often than not, futures trading aggravates the price trends and increases both the magnitude and frequency of price variations. A third group denies that futures trading has any influence, either favourable or adverse, on commodity prices.

Futures trading in various group of commodities was established about the end of 19th century. In cotton, futures trading was started in Bombay. The Europeans took a hand in founding the Bombay Cotton Traders Association in 1875 for the regulation of cotton trade, which was the first step in the evolution of an organised futures market. The futures markets were established for oil seeds at Bombay in 1900, for wheat at Hapur in 1913, for raw jute and jute goods at Calcutta in 1912, and for bullion at Bombay in 1920. Subsequently, similar markets for these commodities were established at other places also. To provide against unhealthy speculation, forward trading in rural commodities was regulated under the Forward Contracts (Regulation) Act, 1952. The Act was enacted with a view to regulating forward contracts, prohibiting options in goods and dealing with certain other related matters. This job has been assigned to the Forward Market Commission, which was established in September 1953 .The government has relegated or banned forward trading in several commodities in order to check unhealthy speculation. The Act has been amended from time to time to plug the loopholes. The Forward Markets Review Committee, set up by the Government of

India under the chairmanship of Prof. M.L. Dantwala, recognised the need for futures trading even in conditions of short supply, and upheld the view that speculations in futures markets should be recognised as necessary factor for their proper working.

COMMODITIES FOR FUTURE TRADING

The commodities permissible under futures trading must satisfy the following conditions:

(i) Commodities should be in plentiful supply. If a commodity is in short supply, a few traders may corner the whole supply and charge any price they like to the buyers.

(ii) The commodity must have a minimum degree of perishability *i.e.*, it must be storable for futures delivery.

(iii) The commodity should be homogeneous and capable of being graded so that its future deliveries may be made with problems regarding quality.

(iv) The supply of the commodity should not be controlled by a few large firms. It should be available with a large number of suppliers.

(v) The price of the commodity should be liable to fluctuations over a wide range.

(vi) The commodity should have a large demand from a number of independent consumers so that a single buyer may not be in a position to impose his terms for his purchase.

SERVICE RENDERED BY A FORWARD MARKET

The forward market renders the following services to the economic system:

(i) It enables the merchants, stockists and processors to protect themselves against the risk of adverse fluctuations in the prices of the commodity. It reduces price fluctuations so that the margin of profit may be small;

(ii) The highly competitive character of the market smoothens out price fluctuations and ensures an even flow of goods from the purchaser to the consumer, avoiding gluts in the peak season and shortages in the slack seasons;

(iii) It facilitates large purchases and sales of the commodity at short notice in advance of delivery and in the absence of production;

(iv) It brings about a co-ordination of the current and future expectations by a continual revaluation of stocks of goods in the light of the changing supply and demand conditions; and

(v) It brings about an integration of the price structure of commodities at different points of time in the same way as transportation and communications bring about an integration of prices in different parts of the market.

DANGERS OF FORWARD MARKET

The dangers arising out of the forward market are:

(i) The forward market opens out the way for a large number of persons with insufficient means, inadequate experience and information to enter into commitments which may be beyond their means. In such conditions, market gets demoralised.

(ii) It enables unscrupulous speculations, with little interest in the actual supply of, and demand for, a particular commodity, to corner the supplies and organise bear raids and bull raids on the market in the hope of marketing easy money for themselves. This results in violent fluctuations in prices.

COMMODITY EXCHANGE

Commodity exchange is an organised market that functions under established rules and regulations, a market meant for the purchase and sale of commodities. It is the market setup by an association of dealer under definite rules and bye-laws. It provides a market place, where the members meet at fixed time regularly to transact the business as per the rules laid down by exchange. It determines membership to be extended to willing and competent parties, settles disputes between the members by arbitration, if any; fixes the grades of commodities handled and disseminates market information.

1. Prof. Pyle J.F. defines, "Commodity exchanges are specialised organised markets which provide a place where their members buy and sell commodities or contract for future delivery under established rules and regulations."

2. Prof. Converse, Huegy and Mitfchell, "An organisation of dealers in certain commodities which provides market place where the members meet at definite times and transact business under the rules laid down by the organisation."

Objects and Functions of Commodity Exchange

Before one goes to study the objects and functions, it is better to know the difference between commodity and produce exchange even though both the phrases are interchanged conveniently. "Produce exchange" deals in only those commodities which are used as raw materials as rural goods and certain minerals and forest products such as cotton, jute, tea, oilseeds, minerals like lead, copper and other non-ferrous metals, and forest products like logs, honey, lac, etc. On the other hand "commodity exchange" deals in rural goods, manufactured products, like jute and butter, sugar, hides and skins, oilproducts. Such produce or commodity exchanges have the following functions to perform and objects to attain. These have been beautifully described by Prof. H.E. Erdmand.

1. Providing a Market Place. A commodity exchange provides a convenient place where members can meet, at fixed hours and transact business in a commodity or commodities, according to certain established rules and regulations and such a facility is of extreme importance that helps in getting together of interested parties to settle their dealing intents, thereby safeguard their interest.

2. Collection and Dissemination of Market Information. The member buyers and sellers of commodity exchanges enter into deals for settlement in future after making an assessment of the trends of prices and prospects of rise or fall in prices of a commodity. Therefore, all information pertaining to potential supply, transportation, current consumption and demand of commodities is collected by the exchanges and is made available to the public. These relevant statistical data and information are published in daily papers that give a picture about total volume of business done, prices prevailing in all exchanges; this publication will enable the parties to guess and conclude the contracts when they can make contracts with confidence and certainty.

3. Price Registration. Commodity exchanges serve to bring about an interplay of the forces of demand and supply which determine definite market values for different commodities. The dealers on commodity exchanges are in close contact with those in other exchanging country. It is quite possible as commodity exchanges are connected by means of communication like telephone, telegraph, cable radio sets. On the basis of information gathered, they determine the prices at which they are expected to settle the transaction or hammer it out. Thus "Price making" process is done.

4. Grading of Commodities. Grading of commodity is the must, which acts as the breath of commodity exchanges. Future contracts can be entered and settled only by means of grades. If no grading is there, price fixation goes difficult and it is almost impossible, to fix satisfactory prices. Grading of goods avoids sales by inspection or simple. It increases the mutual trust and brief amongst the parties. That is why, grading results in entering into purchase and sale deals quickly and without confusion by mere description. Rules of grading are established by the committee of commodity exchanges.

5. Settlement of Disputes. In fact, certain disputes are bound to arise out of transactions in the exchanges in respect of price, quality, weighment, quantity of goods. These are settled through compulsory arbitration procedure under the established rules and regulations of exchange. Thus, exchanges bring about quick, cheaper and amicable settlement in case of disputes and avoid unwanted and undesirable litigation. With a view to maintain the ethical conduct of business by their members, exchanges have established their own codes that are strictly enforced as and when an occasion arises. Thus, an exchange provides a machinery for the arbitrary of trade disputes.

6. Regulation of Trading. Commodity exchanges are the institutions of price insurance where the business community wants to reduce the risks by shifting to the shoulders of others and wants to make profit by reading future with certain amount of accuracy. These practices are hedging or speculation. However, if these facilities of speculation are left to the sweet will and discretion of parties, it may take the form of gambling. Certain rules and regulations are designed as the code of conduct not to prejudice or aggrieve the parties of business. Different methods are laid down which are enforced and defaulters are fined hevily or dealt with all the seriousness. In this way, such regulation harnesses the insurance efficiency.

NATURE OF GOODS HANDLED

An analytical and meaningful observation of commodities traded on commodity exchanges namely cotton, wheat, coffee, rubber, silk, tea, coco etc. On the contrary, steel, brass, coal, petroleum, eggs, flesh etc., can't be traded. There are certain, basic reasons as to why there is this sort of differentiation. Perhaps, the main reason is the nature of products. Commodities cannot lend themselves to be included in the list of dealing. The commodities or products that fulfil the following conditions, will be allowed to trade in on exchange.

1. Homogeneous Products. The commodities must represent homogeneity in appearance, quantity, size, shape, price etc. Homogeneity implies uniformity of characteristics both tangible and intangible. Commodity is said to be homogeneous when the customers or dealers do not have chances of choice. Each unit is a perfect substitute for another. Even if the persons observing are different, the commodity is one and the same thing, to tell those who want to distinguish between the products. If the products are heterogeneous, future contracts can be entered into with much difficulty. For future trading homogeneity is the backbone.

2. Adaptable to Grading and Standardisation. It is well known fact that rural commodities are natural products. It may be wheat or cotton, one finds change in colour, weight, size or shape of unit. For future trading, quality is the most important factor which is the major determination of prices, "grade" is the very base of contract. Therefore, commodities must be capable of being graded, according to certain standards that are predetermined. Each party is to be certain and assured about quality before it enters into an agreement.

3. Free Flow of Goods. The supply of commodities must not only be large but must be natural and free. Of course, 'free flow' does not imply automatic transfer of commodities. Merchants and agencies will have to extend their services to move the goods from the point of supply to the point of demand. Absence of artificial control either by government or by trading conditions. In certain cases monopolies are established which may be social or governmental trading. Thus, supply of diamonds, is in the hands of a single company, namely, De Rogers Ltd., I.N.C. of Canada, have control over the supply of copper, etc. Even the regulation of price must not exist by the Government.

4. Wider Price Fluctuation. The demand and supply forces are to decide the prices, as price is the direct product of interactions of the demand and supply. Commodity exchange is an institution that is designed to shift or reduce the risks or marketing. Some are interested in making profits out of price fluctuations. Price insurance will have more value when price fluctuation danger is there. More uncertain the nature of demand and supply, more it is lucrative to the professional risk bearers like speculations, and hedge contractors. If prices remain stable and unchanged, these persons plans are to kiss to dust, and no charm in it.

5. Durability of the Products. The very name "future trading" connotes that the delivery of goods is to be given at some future date from the date of the contract. That is why, the dealer either expects the goods at future date in order to enjoy to benefit of price change. For this desired commodity must last a longer period of time, normally more than a year. To speak in terms of economics, those products that are capable of "performing time utility function" will be accepted for trading on the commodity exchanges.

6. Able to Command Wider Demand and Supply. The extent of the market for the commodities depends on demand and supply position of the commodities. Some commodities enjoy local demand and supply. Whereas some are having international demand and supply position; still some are having national continuous working of produce exchange is conditioned by the large volume of trading. Any commodity that enjoys national or international market prestige, will be able to attract large volume of trade.

To conclude, the commodity that fulfils the above conditions will be accepted as a commodity; rather a commodity which can be scientifically graded and the price of which is subject to relatively wide and frequent, fluctuations is admirably adapted to futures trading.

Economic Importance

Commodity exchange occupy a pivotal place in the economic system of the nation. It is a delicate piece of economic forces to play their role and exert their influence. It has been rightly pointed out as "commodity exchanges are the barometers of economic climate that changes often." The significant role of commodity exchanges is revealed very clearly by the services that they render to the commodity or business in particular and society in general. The services are :

1. Provide Ready and Continuous Market Information. The exchange process is of two ways. The consumers, may be industrialists or merchants, depend on the type market which is regularly functioning. Even the suppliers may be producers of merchants, will depend on the requirements of consumers. Clap will sound only when two hands come together. As ready market is there both the producers and consumers will be able to force their requirements and budget for future course of action. Forecasting is one of the major functions of successful managements of business.

2. Strengthens the Financing Ability. The commodities that are handled by commodity exchanges are generally enjoying a high degree of liquidity as they can be easily transferred with the help of negotiable warehouse receipts. As commodities dealt in on exchanges are highly standardised and graded according to nationwide or worldwide standards, bankers will come forward to advance loans against such commodities with least amount of hesitation. This helps the producer and traders to get liberal credit in the markets particularly from the bankers. On account of such financial aid that is readily obtained against such commodities and resultant avoidance of advertisements effects of price fluctuations, the parties are expected to operate on exchange with real zeal and success although there is narrow margin of profit. Narrow margin is advisable as it leads to increased turnover ultimately reflecting in larger total profits.

3. Fair Trading Practices. Economic forces of demand and supply are made to operate under the framework of certain rules and regulations. Code of conduct, guarantees the business ethics and soil responsibility on the part of business community. Many times, in the name of hedging and speculation, some business parties may spread some rumours or they may enter into fictitious transactions with the aim of manipulating the price in their favour. Such possible activities are well outside the scope of rules and regulations. However, strict, disciplined and enforcement of rules and regulations will ensure business sanctity, where interests of the parties are promoted and safeguarded.

4. Risk Transfer or Shifting. A commodity exchange is an institution that comes to the aid of traders/merchants, exporters or importers by eliminating the risks attached or clothed with trade, commerce and industry. These risks are so evenly distributed by the mechanism of exchanges as to create a surprise even to a layman to see as to how risks are assumed and absorbed within a small span of time. Producers as well as traders are protected against adverse effects or price fluctuations through the process of hedging which is a reliable device or price insurance. Again, speculation is another way out, that helps to shift risks to the shoulders of others and at the same time profit can be earned. Such risk spreading or shifting is aided by market information that is supplied during the working hours by expert, experienced and with thorough knowledge, the informatron, on which decisions can be safely based.

5. Moderating the Wider Price Change. The price changes that are there in different commodity exchanges over a period of time, are moderated by equalising the demand and supply positions. Thus, a likely supply at more quantity will lead to fall in price, in such a situation, hedging people will adjust both the sides. Thus, by balancing both the extremes, their efforts are reduced. This leads to stabilisation of market prices, change range may be minute. The shocking fluctuations that obstruct can be avoided. It is with the help of commodity exchanges that rural products worth crores of rupees produced in one corner sold to another by arbitrage. Such price stabilisation is the essence to keep the industrialists happy on the one hand aud to protect the interest of the prospects on the other.

To conclude, commodity exchange is a delicate machinery that reads the economic climate on the dial of effective functioning of exchanges. To make it still more powerful, government is to interfere with a view to control but not to cutb the growth of such exchanges which are intricately woven in the fabric of nations.

ORGANISATIONS OF COMMODITY EXCHANGES

It is a practice throughout world to organise commodity exchanges as the bodies corporate. In India, commodity exchanges have been established mainly for transacting "future" dealings, through we fined spot' dealings on some exchanges. These exchanges are being organised as registered companies under the Indian Companies Act. The produce exchanges in India can be classed into two categories: *(a)* Profit-sharing exchanges have been established and they are found in interior parts of the country. The example of this type of exchange is the India Exchange Limited, Amritsar. Non-Profit Sharing Exchanges, on the other hand, are those which are registered as guarantee companies. They are situated at central places, leading ports and industrial centres. The outstanding examples of this type are the East India Cotton Association and the Marwari Chamber of Commerce, both of which are located at Bombay. The peculiarity of the non-profit exchanges is that they have the privilege of greater stability and influence over the profit sharing exchanges. Besides these two types of exchanges, there are several unregistered exchanges working in different parts of India, which have been established mainly with the sole objective of satisfying the speculative urge or instinct.

Management. Management of exchanges in done similar to that of the joint stock companies. Usually, the majority of the commodity exchanges vest the powers of management to Board of Directors or the Managing Committee. The composition of Board or Committee varies from exchange. There are number of Committees and Sub-Committees which assist the Board. These Committees are Survey Committee, Clearing House Committee, Rates Committee, Arbitration of Dispute Committee, etc.

Transactions on Commodity Exchanges. The transactions that are traded on the commodity exchanges are of two types *viz.*, cash contracts and futures contracts. Thus depending upon the nature of transactions dealt in the exchanges may be classified either as cash or futures market. Generally, a commodity exchange is primarily a market for futures contracts.

Membership of Commodity Exchange. Anybody can become member of the commodity exchange purchasing a share and paying the prescribed fees of the association. Nobody, other than the members are allowed to transact business on the exchange. The members of the exchange may be classified as: *(1)* Jobbers, who enter into transactions and deal on their own and *(2)* Brokers, who act as the agents of others to transact business. Brokers may transact business either on behalf of other members or on behalf of non-members also. They may sell goods on behalf of producers, wholesalers, or importers and buy on behalf of exporters, manufacturers, speculators or hedgers.

Cash Contracts. Cash contracts are those which involves the payment of the price, delivery of the goods immediately or within a short period of time. Normally the delivery of goods or payment against is to be made within eight days. Cash contracts are also styled as physical contracts as the actual delivery of goods is to take place in such transactions. Again, the cash contracts are divided into two categories: *(i)* Spot contracts or transactions, and *(ii)* Forward contracts or transactions. Spot transactions are those which are entered into by dealers, where the delivery of the goods and payment take place immediately on the spot. On the other hand, Forward Contracts imply that there must be postponement either of payment or of delivery of the goods to be made within a very short period time. The cash contracts *i.e.*, both spot and forward contracts are not transacted essentially on the exchange. They may take place outside the premises of the commodity exchange and usually, they are entered into outside the exchanges.

❐

11

Development of Agriculture in Economy

Indian economy is predominantly an agricultural economy, therefore India's economic progress is not possible without its agricultural development. Prior to 1951, Indian agriculture was underdeveloped, backward and subsistence agriculture. Indian agriculture was static or its growth rate was zero. In 1951 food crops were sown over an area of 973 lakh hectares and the total production of foodgrains was 550 lakh tonnes. Growth rate of foodgrains was just 1.4 per cent. However, after 48 years of planning, *i.e.*, in 1998, the area under food crops increased to 1,245 lakh hectares or there was an increase of 27%. The production of foodgrains rose to 1924 lakh tonnes, or there was an increase of 320 per cent. It is, therefore, evident that increase in the production of foodgrains has not been due to increase in the area under food crops but its growth has been mainly due to increase in the productivity of food crops. Pattern of Indian agriculture has been on the lines of developing and commercial agriculture. In short, during the period of planning substantial development and transformation of Indian agriculture could become possible.

Need for Agricultural Development in India. Before undertaking a detailed study of the development of Indian agriculture subsequent to 1951 period, it would be relevant to have a brief examination of the need for agricultural development.

According to Eighth Plan, "Given the structure of Indian economy the growth in the national income has largely been determined by the trend in agricultural production. The reason is that agriculture is the largest component of GDP and has overall impact on other sectors *via* input linkages, employment and incomes."

Need for agricultural development in India is evident from the following facts:

1. Contribution to National Income. Roughly 29% of national income in India originates from agriculture, forests and other primary activities. During the period of plans, the contribution of agriculture to national income on different years has been ranging between 59% and 29% in 1950-51 contribution of agricultural sector to the national income was 59% which in 1997-98 cam, down to 28.7%. Contribution of agricultural sector to the national income of India is considerable as compared to the contribution of other sectors like, industry, trade etc., but, now, it has been declining gradually. In the rich countries of the world, agriculture is sufficiently developed but its Contribution to the national income is very little. In America and England, agriculture contributes only 2% of the national income. In underdeveloped countries like Egypt, the share of agriculture in the national income is about 19% and in Argentina it is 15%. In India, 29% contribution of agriculture to national income is, on the rne hand, indicative of the importance of agricultural sector but, on the other, it also symbolises the backwardness of the country.

2. Supply of Wage Goods. Main objective of agricultural sector is to supply wage goods. Those goods which are consumed by the masses of the country to satisfy their necessaries of life, are called wage goods. These include agricultural products like wheat, rice, pulses, maize, bajra, oilseeds, etc. In India, agriculture sector provides food to about 97 crore of people and fodder to 36 crore of cattle. Between 1951 and 1998, population of the country has more than doubled and the production of foodgrains has increased three-fold. Per capita daily availability of cereals and pulses was 430 grams in 1956 which rose to 484 grams in 1999.

3. Agriculture and Employment. Agriculture is the main source of employment in India. It is the main occupation of India. According to 1901 census 60% of the population was engaged in agriculture as against 64% in the year 1998. Dependence of nearly 2/3rd of the popuhltion on agriculture speaks of the one hand of the significance of this sector to the Indian economy on the other, it underlines the backwardness of the country. It is so because the productivity of labour is low in agriculture. Of the total working population, 3% in Britain, 4% in USA and 8% in Australia, is engaged in agriculture. Proportion of population depending on agriculture has been declining in other countries of the world. For instance, in USA in 1810 about 75% of population was dependent on agriculture, presently, it is 4%. On the contrary, in India, the proportion of population depending on agriculture has been rising. In 1901, just 60% of the population, was engaged-in agriculture but now it has increased to 64% of the population.

4. Agriculture and Industry. In an underdeveloped country like India, in the initial stage of economic development, agriculture has an important contribution to the growth of industrial sector, in a variety of ways, *viz. (i)* As a result of industrial development income of the people rises and so also rises their demand for cereals, hence development of agriculture is very essential. *(ii)* When productivity in agriculture increases, demand for labour in agricultural sector falls. The labour so released from agriculture will be absorbed in industrial sector. *(iii)* Industries get raw materials like cotton, jute, sugarcane, oilseeds, rubber, cereals etc. from agricultural sector. *(iv)* Income of the people rises under the impact of agricultural development. They would demand more goods produced by the industrial sector. As a result, market for industrial products would expand. *(iv)* Many cottage and smallscale industries like handloom, oil extracting, rope-making etc. depend on agriculture for their raw materials.

5. Agriculture and Foreign Trade. Agriculture is of great importance to India's foreign trade. *(a)* In the total export trade of India, contribution of agricultural products like tea, coffee, oil-cakes tobacco spices, jute etc. has been very large. In 1997-98 of the total exports about 18 per cent constituted of agricultural products. *(b)* In the imports of the country, foodgrains, edible oils, fertilizers, agricultural, implements, etc., play an important role. With fall in the production of foodgrains and oil seeds in the country, their imports increase very much. As a result of it, country,s balance of trade becomes unfavourable. If agriculture develops in the country, the shortage of foreign exchange will not be felt. Dependence of the country on foreign assistance would go down. Foreign currency earned as a result of export of agricultural products will be utilized for the import of machines, means of transport, raw materials etc. needed for the economic development of the country.

6. Transport. Agricultural production in India is characterized by regional disparities. In some States like Punjab, Haryana, U.P., Andhra Pradesh, etc. production of foodgrains has increased very much under the impact of green revolution. These states have not only become self-sufficient in the matter of foodgrains but other states also import foodgrains etc. from them. As a result, means of transport like trucks, railways, etc. have been earning good revenue by carrying agriculture products from surplus states to deficit states.

7. Internal Trade. 90% of the Indian population, spend more than 60% of their income on food, tea, sugar and milk etc. Thus, agriculture plays an important role in the internal trade of the country. Food-trade provides employment to a large number of people and also generates good deal of tax revenue for the government. Demand for agricultural products is estimated to rise by about 5% per annum.

8. Capital Formation. Large part of Indian capital is invested in agriculture. From the point of view of fixed capital assets, farmlands occupy the highest place. Capital worth millions of rupees is lying invested in the form of means of irrigation, cattle, agricultural implements, tractors and other kinds of agricultural machines, warehouses, etc. Prof. Nurkse is of the opinion that disguised unemployment in Indian agriculture is also a potential source of capital formation. In India, about 25% of the farmers suffer from disguised unemployment. If these persons are engaged in construction projects like construction of roads and other economic activities, for a couple of hours daily, as volunteers, then capital worth millions of rupees can be formed every year. Prof. Lewis is of the view that the surplus labour of the agricultural sector can be employed in urban industries at less than the prevailing rate of wages. Saving thus effected on account of low wages may be invested in industries. Agricultural sector has also, a significant contribution to the formation of human capital. It is from the agricultural sector that workers get food and other wage goods which add to their efficiency.

9. Source of Saving. After Green Revolution, agriculture may constitute an important source of saving. So far, Green Revolution has benefited rich farmers only. They have grown richer. The additional income earned by them can be saved and invested. Saving potentials are very large in agricultural sector. If the same are properly utilized, they can prove very helpful ili the economic development of the country.

10. Basis of Economic Development. Indian agriculture serves as a basis of the economic development of the country. It is so because firstly, development of agricultural sector provides capital to other sectors for their economic development. Secondly, agriculture requires relatively less capital and less foreign exchange for its development. Thus, by making use of the available resources agriculture can be developed. Agricultural development will help the development of industries, transport, foreign trade. etc. Second and Third five-year plans were unsuccessful mainly because of the low priority given to agriculture. That is why in the subsequent plans development of agriculture has been given due importance.

11. Social and Political Importance. Development of agriculture has its social and political significance. India is mainly a contry of villages. As a result of agricultural development, economic, social and political life of the villages will improve. They will take more interest in national programmes and development problems. Such type of public cooperation is very essential for all round progress of the country. Roughly, three-fourth of the total electorates live in villages. As such, different political parties make all, out efforts for their improvement through the development of agriculture.

The above account makes it sufficiently clear that there is a need for agricultural development in India. Agricultural development has a significant role to play in finding solution to come of the main problems of the modern times and to accelerate the rate of economic development. No wonder ever since the beginning of plans in 1951, great stress has been laid on the development of agriculture.

Characteristics of Agricultural Development in India

Since 1951, the main characteristics of agricultural development in India have been as follows:

1. Increase in Area Under Cultivation
2. Increase in Agricultural Productivity
3. Increase in Agricultural Production.

1. Increase in Area Under Cultivation and Growth Rate of Area. Study of increase in are.a under cultivation in India and growth rate of area, is made in two parts as follows: *(1)* Pre-Green Revolution Period (1951-65) and *(2)* Post Green Revolution Period (1965-97). Changes in area under cultivation and its growth rate between 1951-1965 and between 1965-1998 are shown in the following table.

Growth in Area of Principal Crops Since 1951

	Lakh Hectares			*% Change*	
Crops	*1950-51*	*1951-65*	*1997-98*	*1951-65*	*1997-98*
1. Food Crops	973	1,180	1,240	1.47	0.1
Rice	308	360	434	1.37	0.5
Wheat	98	130	267	1.7	2.2
Coarse Grains	390	440	321	0.9	–1.1
Pulses	200	240	238	1.2	–0.3
2. Non-food Crops	230	330	410	2.5	0.7
Oil-seeds	107	150	262	2.6	0.3
Sugarcane	17	26	40	2.5	0.4
Cotton	59	84	89	3.3	-1.5
All Crops	1,220	1,510	1,770	1.6	0.3

(Source: Economic Survey. 1999)

It is clear from the above account that prior to Green Revolution Period (1951-65) there was sufficient increase in the area under cultivation. More land was brought under cultivation and fallow land was made cultivable by extending irrigation facilities. During this period, area growth rate under all crops was 1.6 per cent. Area growth rate under food crops was 1.4 per cent and under non-food crops 2.5 per cent. As against it, in the post Green Revolution Period (1965-1997) there was an increase of 0.3 per cent in area under crops. Area under food crops increased by 0.1 per cent and that under non-food crops by 0.7 per cent. During this period, area under rice crop increased by 0.5 per cent only while that under wheat increased by 2.2 per cent. It was mainly because of the increasing use of high yielding variety of seeds of wheat.

2. Increase in Agricultural Productivity. In the post 1951 period, productivity of agriculture has increased very much. Agricultural Productivity refers to production per hectare. Increase in agricultural productivity is shown in the following Table No.1.

Table: Progress of per Hectare Productivity

(Kilograms Per Hectare)

Crops	*1951*	*1998*
Rice	668	1,895
Wheat	663	2,470
Cotton	88	213
Sugarcane	3,342	70,000
Jute	1,043	1,960
Maize	704	1,721

(Source: Economic Survey 1999)

Above table shows that per hectare production of wheat which was about 663 kilograms in 1951 rose to 2,470 kilograms in 1998. Similarly per hectare production of rice that was 665 kg. in 1951 rose to 1,895 kg. in 1998. However, India, is still far behind in per hectare productivity of all crops as against many other countries. There is large scope of increasing agricultural production in India by raising productivity.

Growth rate of foodgrains productivity which was 1.4 per cent in the period between 1951 and 1965 rose to 21 percent during the period between 1965-98. It was mainly due to the increased use of HYV seeds, chemical fertilizers and irrigation fertilizers. But, as against the other countries of the world, agricultural productivity in India was substantially low. It is clear from the following table.

Table per Hectare Productivity

Product	*Country*	*Kilograms*
Rice	India	1,895
	Japan	6,190
	U.S.A.	6,860
Wheat	India	2,470
	France	7,130
	U.K.	8,110
Cotton	India	213
	U.S.A.	770
	Turkistan	2,210
	Australia	1,380

(Source: Statistical Outline of India 1999)

The above table shows that even after long period of plans and Green Revolution; agricultural productivity in India is much less than other countries, although there has been considerable improvement in it in the post independence era.

3. Increase in Agricultural Production. Since 1951, during the period of plans, agricultural production has witnessed considerable rise. Agricultural production in India is mainly divided into two parts:

(A) Food Crops

(B) Non Food Crops

(A) Food Crops. Change in the production of food crops like rice, wheat, pulses, oilseeds etc. has an important effect on the economic development of the country. These are important wage goods. Their adequate supply means great relief to the poor and stability in the price-level. There is favourable effect on the standard of living of the people.

(1) Increase in Production. In the last 50 years production of cereals has increased by about four times of pulses almost doubled. Production of rice has increased 4 times and that of wheat by 10 times.

(2) Variations in the Trends of Production. There is good deal of variation in the production of food grains in India. During the first two Five Year Plans, production of foodgrains continued to rise, but in the third plan it came down. During this plan, growth rate became negative. In the three oneyear plans there was large increase in the production of foodgrains but in the Fourth Plan growth rate fell down. In the Fifth Plan, growth rate again rose. In the Sixth and Seventh Plans growth rate was as per the target. In the Eighth Plan (1992-97) growth rate of agricultural production has been about 3.5% and that of foodgrains about 3.4 per cent. But in the first year of Ninth Plan (1997-98) the rate of growth of agricultural production declined by 6 per cent. It was due to unfavourable weather conditions.

(3) Effect of Weather. Rainfall or weather plays an important role in the production of foodgrains in India. Excess or shortage of rainfall has great effect on the production of foodgrains. In 1976-77, due to scanty rainfall production of foodgrains fell by 8 per cent but in 1977-78 it increased by 14 per cent due to good rainfall. In 1979-80, production of foodgrains fell by 17 per cent but in 1980-81, it rose by 18 per cent. In the year 1982-83 it fell by 3 per cent but in 1983-84 it rose by 11 per cent to fall again by 1 per cent in 1987-88. It rose by about 2 per cent, 1.5 per cent and 3 per cent in the years 1988-89, 1989-90, and 1990-91 respectively. But in 1991-92, because of the erratic behaviour of south-western monsoon, production of foodgrains fell by 4.5 per cent. In the year 1992-93, it rose by 6.6. percent. In 1993-94, increase was 2.7 per cent and in 1994-95 it was 3.7 per cent, but in 1995-96 there was a fall of 3.4 per cent. But in 1996-97, it rose by 6.7 per cent. However due to unfavourable weather conditions in 1997-98, the growth rate declined by 6 per cent. Thus, Indian agriculture continues to be a gamble in monsoon.

(4) Regional Disparities. There an lot of regional disparities in Indian agriculture. In many states of India like Punjab, Haryana, Andhra Pradesh, Tamil Nadu, Maharashtra, production of foodgrains has been increasing more. But in states like Bihar, Orissa, etc. production of foodgrains has increased very little. Consequently, many states have surplus food stocks. Rich farmers have made a significant contribution to it. Farmer's income elasticity for foodgrains is low, so they sell large part of the production surplus in the market. Consequently, marketable surplus has gone up. On the other hand, because of large-scale storage of foodgrains their availability for conSumption has gone down.

(B) Commercial Crops. Commercial crops in India have their significance for the supply of raw materials, for exports and for domestic industries, changes in the production of these crops in the post independence era are shown in the following table.

Table. Production of Commercial Crops

Period	*Cotton (Lakh bales)*	*Jute (Lakh bales)*	*Sugarcane (Lakh tonnes)*	*Oil Seeds (Lakh tannes)*
1950-51	30	33	570	50
1960-61	56	41	1,100	68
1970-71	48	49	1,260	96
1975-76	59.5	44	1,400	106
1978-79	79.6	65	1,520	101
1983-84	64	77	1,740	129
1984-85	85	80	1.705	131

1987-88	64	68	1,967	124
1989-90	114	84	2,226	168
1990-91	98	91	2,403	184
1991-92	97	103	2,540	186
1993-94	107	84	2,297	215
1994-95	119	91	2,755	213
1995-96	151	89	2,830	224
1996-97	143	111	2,773	250
1997-98	112	111	2,763	220

(Source: Statistical Outline of India 1999)

The above table elucidates the following facts:

(1) Expansion of Production. During the period of plans, the production of commercial crops has increased considerably. Production of cotton has increased four-fold and that of jute has increased three-fold, that of sugarcane more than five-fold and of oilseeds more than four-fold.

(2) Significance to Export. These crops are of great importance to export. In 1997-98, agricultural products worth Rs. 23,690 crore were exported. In 1997-98, oil-cakes worth Rs. 3,404 crore, tobacco worth Rs. 1,058 crore. Jute manufactures worth Rs. 363 crore, tea worth Rs. 1,505 crore coffee worth Rs. 1,622 crore and rice worth Rs. 3,574 crore, were exported to other countries.

In short, production of agricultural products has been rising but there is no stability in production trend, as is evident from table below.

During the period of plans, there have been lot of changes in the productivity of agricultural products and the growth rate of the production of foodgrains.

The below table shows changes in the growth rate of production.

Trends of Percentage Change in Agricultural Production

Period	*Agricultural Production %*	*Foodgrain Production %*
1st Plan (1951-56)	4.3	5.2
2nd Plan (1956-61)	4.0	3.9
3rd Plan (1961-66)	-1.1	-2.2
Three Annual Plans (1966-69)	6.3	8.8
4th Plan (1969-74)	3.0	2.5
5th Plan (1974-79)	4.3	5.3
6th Plan (1980-85)	6.0	6.3
7th Plan (1985-90)	4.2	3.6
8th Plan (1992-97)	3.5	3.4
9th Plan (Target)	4.5	—

(Source: Statistical Outline of India 1999 and Eighth Five Year Plan and Ninth Plan)

The above table shows that there has been no consistency in agricultural production and growth rate of foodgrains. It increased upto the Second Five Year Plan but decreased in the Third Plan. It started rising again in the three one-year plans. In the Fourth Plan it declined but in Fifth, Sixth, Seventh and Eight Plan it again increased. From 1950-51 to 1997-98 growth rate of agricultural production was 2.9 per cent per annum, on average. According to Prof. V.KR. V. Rao, "To meet the minimum needs of agriculture and cereals in India, minimum growth rate of agricultural production should be 4 per cent and that offoodgrains 6 per cent per annum. But, whereas per hectare production of foodgrains like wheat; bajra, rice has increased adequately there has been no special improvement in per hectare production of powar, maize and pulses.

AGRICULTURE DEVELOPMENT DURING PLANNING PERIOD

The process of agricultural development since 1951 is covered in two phases:

(i) Technical phases, and

(ii) Institutional phases.

(i) Technical Phases (Methods). These include mainly *(1)* Multiple Cropping *(2)* Extansion of Irrigation *(3)* Manures *(4)* Use of HYV Seeds *(5)* Plant Protection *(6)* Scientific Methods of Cultivation *(7)* Mechanisation *(8)* Development of Agricultural Land *(9)* Improvement in Animal Husbandry.

(ii) Institutional Methods. These include mainly: *(1)* Land, eforms *(2)* Tenancy Reforms *(3)* Reforms in Agricultural Marketing and *(4)* Credit Facilities.

These methods can be described in detail as follows:

1. Increase in the Area Under Cultivation. Two factors are responsible for increase in the area under cultivation : *(1)* Increase in net sown area and *(2)* Multiple cropping *i.e.*, growing more than one crop in a given area in one year. During Five Year Plans efforts were made to develop agricultural sector by both these methods. During the period of plans, area under crops increased by 38 per cent. In 1950-51, the total sown area was about 13 crore hectares. It has now increased to about 17crore hectares. In order to increase the sown area, cultivable waste land has been reclaimed. Fallow land, *i.e.*, land not sown throughout the year, has been reduced. Efforts have been made to reclaim the land lying waste due to soil erosion. Nearly 3 crore hectres of land has been brought under multiple cropping.

2. Expansion of Irrigation. In order to increase the productivity of agriculture, irrigation has been expanded considerably several minor and medium irrigation projects have been launched in the country. In 1951, irrigation facilities were available to 18 per cent of land only. Now, about 36 per cent of land enjoys facilities of irrigation. Area under irrigation has increased considerably due to multipurpose irrigation projects and tubewell. Areas where irrigation is not possible, dry farming has been introduced. In 1997-98, irrigation facilities likely to cover an area of 912 lakh hectares.

3. HYV Seeds. Since 1964-65, high yielding varieties of seeds are being increasingly used in Indian agriculture. These seeds have proved to be the main means to increase agricultural production. HYV seeds have been evolved especially for wheat, bajra, rice, maize, jowar and cotton. National Seed Corporation has been set up for their increased production and proper distribution. In 1997-98 HYV seeds have been grown cover an area of 760 lakh hectares.

4. More Use of Fertilizers. In order to increase in the productivity of agriculture, increasing use of fertilizers is being made. Farmers are being educated to make use of cow-dung as manure and not as fuel. Compost manure is being made at they images. Use of chemical fertilizers has increased very much. In 1997-98, about 162 lakh tones of chemical fertilizers were used.

5. Plant Protection. Adequate measures have been taken to protect the plants against diseases and pests. 14 central plant protection centres have been established for this purpose.

6. Scientific Cultivation. Much emphasis has been laid on scientific methods of cultivation in Five Year Plans. Under it are included, selection of crops, preparation of land, crop rotation, selection of seeds, proper use of manure dry farming etc. In other words, attempts have been made to propagate the adoption of better methods of agriculture. "Intensive Agricultural Area programme" have launched for this purpose. Government of India has initiated "Integrated Rural Development Programme" for the development of agriculture. 23 Agricultural Universities have been established in the country to conduct research in respect" of scientific cultivation. Haryana Agricultural University, Hissar, Punjab Agricultural University, Ludhiana; and Himachal. Agricultural University, Palampur and Indian Council of Agricultural Research, Delhi have been doing creditable work in this respect.

7. Mechanisation. Many efforts are being made to popularize the use of agricultural tools and equipments, tractors and other mechanical tools; etc. stnall farmers get loans at cheap rate of interest from cooperative credit societies, community development blocks and commercial banks for the purchase of agricultural machines. In almost all the States agro industries corporations have been established for this purpose.

8. Improvement of Animal Husbandry. In order to improve the breed of the cattle, Key Village Schemes were introduced under five year plans. Veterinary dispensaries have been setup to treat cattle diseases. In order to develop the cattle wealth in the country 86 Intensive Cattle Development Projects have been launched. All measures for the development of the cattle will be undertaken in these projects.

9. Development of Agricultural Land. During Five Year Plans, enough measures have been taken for the development of agricultural land. Arrangements have been made to level the land to give it slope, contour bunding and to cultivate land along the contour lines, etc. and lands is under survey.

10. Land Reforms. Alongwith technical factors, institutional factors like land reforms are of equal importance to increase the productivity of agriculture. In the post independence period, government has undertaken several land reforms measures like *(i)* Abolition of Zamindari System. Tenant cultivators have either been given ownership rights or they have been made occupancy tenants. *(ii)* In order to reform the Tenancy System, laws have been enacted in almost all states. *(iii)* Ceiling on landholdings has been fixed. *(iv)* By 1998, task of consolidation of holdings had been accomplished over about 613 lakh hactares of land. *(v)* Cooperative farming has also been developed. *(vi)* With a view of improviug the lot of landless agricultural farmers, Archarya Vinoba Bhave launched Bhoodan Movement.

11. Improvement in Agricultural Marketing. Main purpose behind improvement in the marketing of agricultural produce is to get fair price to the farnlers for their produce. In this respect, efforts have been made especially on three different directions.

(i) Regulated Markets. Regulated markets are managed by the government appointed marketing committee. The aim is to protect the farmers against the exploitation of the middlemen. Metric system of weights and measures is used in these markets. In the year 1998, there were about 7,062 regulated markets functioning in the country.

(ii) Co-operative Marketing Societies. These societies were also set up with the sole objective of improving agricultural marketing. These societies sell the produce of the members at reasonable price. They also arrange grading of the produce of the members. The societies also provide warehouse and storage facilities. At present, 6,777 Primary Cooperative Marketing Societies have been functioning in the country.

(iii) Support Price. In order to provide necessary incentive to the farmers to produce more, it is necessary to protect them against fall in agricultural price. To that end support price system has been introduced. Under this system, government assures minimum price to the farmers for their produce. Government trading agencies arrange to buy at the support price the entire marketable surplus of the farmers. Price support policy is applicable to wheat, rice, cotton, grams, etc.

12. Credit Facilities. In order to provide cheap credit facilities to the farmers to enable them to develop agriculture, co-operative credit societies have been expanded. Number of Land Development Banks has been increased. At present, there are about 91,000 primary co-operative credit societies all over the country and 738 Primary Cooperative Agriculture and Rural Development Banks. After nationalization, commercial banks have also been giving agricultural loans on a liberal scale. Regional Rural Banks and Farmer Service Societies have also been established to provide credit facilities to farmers. National Bank for Agriculture and Rural Development (NABARD) was set up in 1982, as the apex agricultural finance institute. In 1997-98 different finance institutes had provided credit worth Rs. 30,976 crore to agricultural sector. In 1978, Integrated Rural Development Programme was launched. Main objective of this programme is to lift the poor class above the poverty line and to remove unemployment by making proper utilization of natural and human resources of the villages.

New Agricultural Policy for Agricultural Development. In order to have a comprehensive and uniform development of agriculture, Government on India presented in 1992 a draft of New Agricultural Policy before the Parliament. In the Chief Ministers Conference held in March 1993, some suggestions relating to this draft were given. On May 14,1993, the government presented an amended draft to the Parliament in place of the earlier one. Main features of this amended draft are: *(1)* To establish co-ordination between agricultural development and research programmes so as to meet the challenges of Indian agriculture. *(2)* To check the declining tendency of capital formation in agriculture sector. *(3)* To enhance government'investment in infrastructure necessary for agricultural and rural development. *(4)* To solve the problems of disguised unemployment, unemployment and malnutrition through diversification of agriculture and development of agro-based industries. *(5)* To augment facilities for processing, marketingand storage. *(6)* To develop gardening depending on rainfall and irrigation and to promote water conservation programme. *(7)* To strengthen co-operatives and local communities and to increase the participation of non-goverhment organisation in agricultural development programmes.

Provision for Agricultural Development in the Plans. Upder Five Year Plans an outlay of about Rs. 23,500 crore has been made in respect of agricultural development. As a result, production of foodgrains has increased three-fold. Progress made in agricultural sector in different five year plans is evident from the following account:

1. First Plan (1951-56). In tills plan period, an outlay of Rs. 290 crore was made on agricultural development. It constituted 15 per cent of the total plan outlay. Production of foodgrains increased to 693 lakh tonnes.

2. Second Plan (1956-61). In this plan, a sum of Rs. 549 crore was spent on agricultural development. It represented 12 per cent of the total plan outlay. Production of foodgrains increased to 823 lakh tonnes.

3. Third Plan (1961-66). In this plan period, a sum of Rs. 1089 crore was spent on agricultural development. It constituted 13 per cent of the total outlay, but due to variety of reasons production of foodgrains declined to 728 lakh tonnes.

4. Fourth Plan (1969-74). In this plan, an outlay of Rs. 2,320 crore was made on the development of agriculture. It represented 16 per cent of the total plan outlay. Production of foodgrains rose to 1,047 lakh tonnes.

5. Fifth, Plan (1974-78). In this plan, a sum of Rs. 4,865 crore was spent on agricultural development. It was 12 per cent of the total plan outlay. Production of foodgrains increased to 1,320 lakh tonnes.

6. Sixth Plan (1980-85). In this plan, a sum of Rs. 6,624 crore was spent on agricultural development. It was 6 per cent of the> total plan expenditure. Production of foodgrains rose to 1,465 lakh tonnes.

7. Seventh Plan (1985-90). In this plan, a sum of Rs. 12,792 crore was made on the development of agriculture. It was 5 per cent of the total plan outlay. Production of foodgrains increased to 1,760 lakh tonnes.

8. Eighth Plan (1992-97). In the Eighth Plan an outlay of Rs. 23,281 crore on agriculture and allied activities. Rs. 35.263 crore on rural development, Rs. 33,280 crore on irrigation and flood control and Rs. 6837 crore on special Area Programme was spent. It represented about 22.2 per cent of total outlay. In this Plan growth rate of agriculture was fixed at 4 per cent but actual target achieved was 3.5 per cent. The objectives of the plan were to take advantage of the base prepared in the previous years in respect of agricultural sector to continue with the activities regarding improvement in production and productivity in order to meet the, demands of the rising population, to increase the income of the farmers and to utilize the production capacity of the conntry by increasing the exports of agricultural products.

However the Eighth Plan failed to achieve its targets of agricultural development. During the Plan period growth rate of foodgrain production was 1.7 per cent as against 1.9 percent growth rate of population. Actual growth rate of agriculture was 3.5 per cent as against the plan target to 4 per cent. It was a matter of concern. In 1996-97 country had to import foodgrain. Three main causes of the fall in growth rate of agriculture are:

(i) Fall in public investment in agricultural sector. In 1970- 71, contribution of public sector towards capital formation in agricultural sector was 28.6 percent. In 1996,97 it fell to 16.2 per cent. Consequently, efficiency of the existing infrastructure and distribution system suffered a setback.

(ii) Lack of development of new variety of improved seeds of important food products.

(iii) Several restrictions have been imposed by the centre and state governments on trading, movement and storage of agricultural commodities.

Following suggestions are given to remove the above obstacles in the way of agricultural sector:

(i) Public investment in agricultural sector should be enhanced. there is immediate need for mobilization of resources for investment in agricultural sectoiby the joint efforts of the states. Rural Infrastructure Devlopment Fund may be utilized to some extent for this purpose.

(ii) Demand for fruits and vegetables has grown very much in India due to increasing urbanization and changing food pattern. Agricultural research should therefore be mainly directed towards improving the productivity of fruits and vegetable cultivation. This will help increase their supply according to demand.

(iii) Policy of liberalization should also be applied to agricultural sector, as it has been applied to industrial sector. Restrictions imposed on agricultural sector by the government should be reduced to the minimum.

(iv) Under export-import policy regarding agriculture, export of agricultural products of higher value be encouraged in exchange for import of essential agricultural commodities of lower value.

In short, there is need to enforce firmly improvements in agriculture sector. It will help increase growth rate of agriculture.

EVALUATION OF AGRICULTURE DEVELOPMENT SINCE 1951

Since 1951, main features of agricultural development during the period of planning ar as under:

Rate of Growth of Agricultural Production. Since 1951 to 1997 growth rate of agricultural production has been 3% per annum on average. Nevertheless, it is far less than other countries of the world In China it was 5.3 percent. Indonesia 4.1 per cent, Pakistan 4.4 per cent and Indiajust 3 per cent. Thus, the growth rate of agriculture prodoction in india has very much unsatisfactory. Agricultural production has been rising but the growth rate is much less than required.

Causes of Unsatisfactory Agricultural Development in India. The following three factors mainly account for unsatisfactory agricultural development in India:

1. Human Factors (2) Institutional Factors and (3) Technical Factors. Human factors relate to training, health and efficiency of the farmers and their social traditions. Institutional factors relate to those who take decision in respect of agricultural produce and those who take decision in respect of actual cultivation. Technical factors relate to the prevailing techniques of production. Indian agriculture is backward from all the three points of view, namely human, institutional and technical factors. Following are the main causes of the backwardness of Indian agriculture. In 1951, production of foodgrains was 550 lakh tonnes, In 1998 it increased to 1,924 lakh tonnes. In other words, production of foodgrains has witnessed 3.5 times increase.

2. Technological Changes. Technological changes especially HYV seeds, chemical fertilizers, irrigation, etc. are being used increasingly. But, inspite of all these, growth rate of agricultural production has not increased much. Even now, India agriculture continues to depend on rainfall and climate.

3. Expansion of Agricultural Area. Between 1951 and 1965, the agricultural area has expanded much. However, after 1965 the rate of expansion has been very low. This deficiency has been made good by increase in productivity due to technological changes.

4. Different Growth Rate of Productivity. Growth rate of productivity of different agricultural crops has been different. New agricultural technology and HYV seeds have influenced only wheat and rice. It is the productivity of wheat that has recorded the maximum increase. However, productivity of coarse grains like oilseeds, pulses, etc.. has increased very little.

5. Unstable Rate of Growth. In India growth rate of agricultural production is characterized by increasing instability. In the Third Plan, growth rate of agricultural production was negative—1.1 per cent. In other words, agricultural production was less than the Second Plan. However, due to the impact of Green Revolution, in the three one-year plans it increased to 6.3 per cent. But in the Fourth Plan, it fell to 3 per cent. In the Fifth Plan, it fell to 4.3 per cent but rose again in the Sixth Plan to 6 per cent. It again fell to 4.2 per cent in the seventh Plan. In the first (1992-93) year and second (1993-94) year of the Eighth Plan it fell by 4.1 per cent and 3.6 per cent respectively. But in 1994-95 it rose to 4.6 per cent. In 1995-96, it is likely to be negative to the extent of 0.1 per cent. But in 1996-97 it again rose to 9.3 per cent and in 1997-98 it became negative to the extent of 6 per cent. During Eighth Plan (1992-97) growth-rate of agricultural production has been about 3.5 per cent. Thus, growth rate of Indian Agriculture has been quite unstable during the period of Plans.

6. Regional Differences in Agricultural Development. Another feature of the development of Indian agriculture has been the variation in growth rate in different regions. On the one hand, growth rate of agriculture in Punjab and Haryana has been 5 per cent and on the other, it has been 1.5 per cent in M.P., 1.7 per cent in Assam and l2.0 per cent in Bihar.

7. Lack of Social Justice. From the point of view of social justice, development of Indian agriculture has been unjust. It has benefited rich farmers and big zamindars. Poor farmers have not been able to rise above the poverty line. Because of low rate of growth of agricultural production, employment opportunities could not increase. Consequently, unemployment situation in rural areas could not improve. It may also be noted that not only inequalities in the distribution of land continue to persist but the same have further aggravated as well. In the field of land reforms, the progress has been very slow and unsatisfactory. It can therefore, be concluded that development of Indian agriculture has not been satisfactory from the social point of view.

HUMAN FACTORS

Main Human factors accounting for the backwardness of agriculture are:

1. Pressure of Population on Land. In India large number of people depend on agriculture for their livelihood. In 1901, the number of those depending on agriculture was 16.30 crore, It has now risen to 58.80 crore. As a result, per capita agricultural land that stood at 0.43 hectares in 1901 has been reduced to 0.23 hectares at present. Besides, excessive pressure of population on land has given rise to the problems of sub-division and fragmentation of holdings, disguised unemployment, and fall in the saving capacity of the farmers,

2. Neglect of Human Aspect. In every plan, human aspect is of greater importance than economic aspect. During the period of plans, human aspect has not been given due importance in agricultural sector. Consequently, condition of prosperous farmers has improved a good deal but that of the small farmers, landless agricultural labourers and share-croppers has remained unchanged, Nothing has been done to render the farmers more efficient.

INSTITUTIONAL FACTORS

3. Defective Land Reforms. In each five year plan, emphasis has been laid on the significance of land reforms, but no concrete measures were taken to implement them. In the Sixth Plan government had to appoint a committee to make suggestions in respect of land reforms, In Japan, the pressure of population on land is greater than in India, yet productivity is many times more. The main reason for it is that in Japan, land reforms were implemented first and technical reforms introduced later.

4. Less Investment. Critics assert that less investment has been made in agricultural sector. Whatever investment has been made by the government, during the period of Plans, in the development of agriculture has benefited the prosperous farmers the most. However, no income-tax has been imposed on rich farmers, inspite the recommendations of Dr K.N. Raj Committee to this effect. Thus, increased agricultural production is being used more for the purpose of consumption than for investment.

5. Uncoordinated Policies. During the period of five year plans, many policies in respect of agriculture lacked co-ordination. For instance, framing of land reforms policy but not implementing it in all the states on a uniform pattern. Importance was given to improved technical methods but no steps were undertaken to set up the necessary organisation for the same. Prof. Gadgil has pertinently observed, "What may be called economic planning in the real sense of the term is found very little in India and in agriculture it is still less as against the other economic activities.

6. Low Priority. Critics of the agricultural policy of the plans are of the opinion that the planners have accorded little importance to the development of agriculture, In the First Plan, 37 per cent of the total plan outlay on public sector, was made on the development of agriculture and irrigation. In the Second and the Third Plan, the share of agriculture and irrigation came down to 21 per cent. In the Fourth Plan it was 24 per cent. In the Fifth Plan, it was just 22 per cent. In the Sixth Plan, it was 24 per cent and in the Seventh, 21 per cent. In the Eighth Plan it is 22 per cent. Thus, we conclude with the critics that little importance has been given to the agricultural sector in the plans.

TECHNICAL FACTORS

7. Inadequate Irrigation Facilities. Agriculture in India depends for water mostly on rainfall. Since rainfall is uncertain, agricultural production also becomes uncertain. That is why Indian agriculture is called "Gamble in Monsoon." Even 48 years after the initiation of Five Year Plans hardly 36 per cent of cultivable land can boast of irrigation facilities. Due to shortage of irrigation, the farmers produce just one crop in a year.

8. Defective Marketing. In India marketing system of agricultural produce is also defective. As a result of it, the farmers do not get remunerative prices of their produce. Due to underdeveloped means of transport, the farmer is forced to sell his produce to the village trader who pays him very low price. Because of shortage of storage facilities, the farmer is compelled to sell the crop soon after it is harvested, although prices of foodgrains are low at that time. Because of the unremunerative price of his crop, the farmer is hardly encouraged to produce more and better quality of crops.

9. Old Implements. Indian agriculture is still dominated by the use of old and traditional tools and implements. Even in this scientific age, we find Indian farmer clinging to the use of wooden plough, wooden leveller, sickle; etc. Tractors and other modern agricultural implements are used rarely. Productivity of land does not increase and agricultural production falls if old traditional implements are used in cultivation.

10. Inadequate Credit Facilities. Poor Indian peasants even today face lot of difficulties in getting credit facilities or loans. They do not get credit from the banks and co-operative credit societies in adequate quantity and on time. They still depend for consumption purpose loans on the local moneylender. It adversely affects agricultural productivity in many ways. The farmer has to part with a largepart of his income to the money-lender as interest. He also has to sell his product to the money-lender at low prices.

11. Inadequate HYV Seeds. Indian farmers do not make adequate use of HYV needs. The reason being that they do not understand its importance. Moreover there is not suitable arrangement for the supply of these seeds. Then, bette quality seeds are quite expensive. Poor peasants can ill afford them. Because of these factors also, per hectare production is low.

12. Old Methods of Cultivation. Methods of cultivation are also hackneyed in India. Rotation of crop is not practised properly. Due to it and other causes agriculture production is low.

13. Shortage of Manure. Manure plays an important role in .increasing the productivity of cultivation. But Indian farmers do not make use of manure in suitable quantity. Cow dung which is the cheapest source of manure is mostly used as fuel. Chemical fertilizer is expensive and is imported largely from foreign countries. Thus chemical fertilizer is not adequately available to the farmers.

All the three factors, *viz* human, institutional and technical account for the unsatisfactory development of Indian agriculture.

SUGGESTIONS FOR SATISFACTORY AGRICULTURAL DEVELOPMENT IN INDIA

Following suggestions may be given for the satisfactory development of Indian agriculture:

1. Less Pressure of Population. Pressure of population on land must be reduced if agriculture is to progress. This can be done by developing industry and trade so that surplus population on land is absorbed therein. Cottage and small-scale industries be specially set up at the village level. Efforts should be made to check the rising population in the villages.

2. Expansion of Irrigation. To lessen the dependence of Indian agriculture on rainfall, irrigation facilities be expanded. Canals be drawn from the rivers, wells, tube-wells and tanks, etc. be developed. Multipurpose projects can also help solve the problem.

3. More Availability of HYV Seeds. Farmers should have complete knowledge of HYV seeds and the same be made available in large quantity. Panchayats and cooperative societies should distribute HYV seeds. Small farmers be supplied these seeds on loan. Research should be made to explore quality seeds. Knowledge regarding better quality seeds also be gathered from abroad.

4. Manure. Farmers be trained to make green manure with cow dung, town rubbish and green leaves. Oil-cakes should also be used as manure. Superstitions among the farmers be removed through education and they should be mentally prepared to make use of bones and fish as manure. Production of chemical manures be increased in the country so that the same are made available to the farmers at low price and in large quantity.

5. Land Reforms. Agricultural development is very much conditioned by land reforms. Zamindari system should be abolished and the actual cultivators be, given the right of ownership of land. Ceiling and flooring on land holdings should be fixed. Efforts should be made to remove the evils of soil erosion and rising water-level. In India, roughly 160 lakh hectares of cultivable land is lying waste. It should be reclaimed at the earliest.

6. Finance. Farmers should get sufficient loans at low rate of interest. To achieve it, cooperative credit societies be expanded in the country. Land Development Banks be opened in large numbers. Activities of the moneylenders be put under check. More branches of the commercial banks be opened in villages. At the time of natural calamities, the government should give liberal taccavi loans to the farmers.

7. Agricultural Marketing. Marketing of agricultural produce be improved by removing its defects, so that the farmers may get remunemtive prices of their produce. More regulated markets be set up. Cooperative Marketing Societies be established in large number. Warehouses be constructed to enable the farmer to store his produce, till better prices prevail in the markets. This way his staying capacity will increase. Means of transport should also be developed.

8. Tenancy Reforms. Improvement of agriculture needs tenancy reforms. Rent of the tenants be fixed. As long as farmers pay the rent regularly, they should not be evicted from the land. They should not be subjected to any kind of begar (work without remuneration). The amount spent by the tenant on the improvement of land belonging to the landlord should be reimbursed to him in the event of the land having been resumed by the landlord.

9. Mixed Farming. Mixed farming should be popularised in India. Growing of crops, animal husbandry, growing of fruits and vegetables etc. should be done side by side. Emphasis should be laid on dairy farming. Thus, on the one hand, condition of the cattle will improve and, on the other, farmers will get more nutritive food that will make them physically strong.

10. Mechanisation. Cheap agricultural implements, suiting Indian agricultural conditions, be manufactured for improving cultivation. Proper arrangements be made for their sale and repair, information regarding agricultural tools and implements be conveyed to the farmers through exhibitions, etc. Arrangements be made to sell agricultural machines and equipments on instalment basis.

11. Scientific Cultivation. Scientific methods of cultivation be given wide publicity. Farmers must be informed of crop rotation. New and scientific methods be demonstrated to the farmers on government demonstration farms. Farmers who succeed in increasing production by applying new methods be rewarded suitably. Research should be conducted on perpetual basis, to evolve new methods to increase agricultural output. Research in respect of seed, manure and proper utilization of land can prove very much beneficial.

12. Price Stability. Green Revolution has given rise to another kind of problem. As a result of large-scale production of foodgrains the fear of fall in their prices has overtaken the farmer. The government should therefore ensure that farmers get remunerative prices of their crops. If it is not done, the farmers would not take to improved technique of agricultural production and the development of agriculture will not be stable.

13. Help to Small Farmers. To stabilize the gains of green revolution and to develop agriculture it is essential that small farmers be helped in taking advantage of HYV seeds, new technology and new implements. They should get liberal loan facilities at cheap rate of interest so that they may avail of new technology. By doing so, economic prosperity in the country will increase along with agricultural development.

14. Efficient Administration. The steps taken by the government in the direction of agricultural development are of great significance. But government plans and projects can be successfully enforced only if government employees are able and efficient. Only those employees be associated with Integrated Rural Development Programme, Co-operative Societies, and other agricultural activities, who have complete knowledge of village life and are willing to work in villages.

15. Use of New Technology. In order to increase agricultural production, new technology of agriculture should be used and propagated. Under this policy, special attention be paid to the use of intensive cultivation. Provision should be made for the large supply of HYV seeds, machines, chemical fertilizers etc.

Thus, in order remove backwardness of Indian agriculture, several measures should be taken in hand. "About 30% increase in output per hectare can be achieved through judicious use of fertilizers, 10% through good seeds and 20% by way of controlling various crop diseases." Development of agriculture has been duly emphasized in the Five Year Plans. In fact, Indian economy cannot develop without the development of agriculture.

❐

12

Agriculture Marketing in India

As per the regulation of GATT, the developed countries like, USA, Canada, which were allowing subsidy on agricultural products upto 50% are now bound not to allow more than 10% subsidy.

In India subsidy on agricultural products in the international market may be less than in the developed countries of the world. India has to design a solid strategy as would maximise its agricultural production specially of those commodities which are in greater demand in international markets, so that the export of agricultural products may increase. The export of agricultural commodities have increased sharply during the last few years. The data are as: In the year 1989-90 it was Rs. 234,50,000 thousand raised to Rs. 906,50,000 thousand showing an increase of 386.56%.

After the Green Revolution in the late sixties that the surplus in agricultural produce increase in huge quantities for sale on the markets, especially in rural areas, and it needed quick development of infrastructure for marketing of agricultural commodities to ensure that farmers would be paid remunerative prices for their produce. In an ideal market, it is necessary that the interests of all the parties, *i.e.*, traders and consumers are properly taken care of, but the farmers are still not getting remunerative prices for their produce because the marketing infrastructure in rural areas has not been able to maintain the pace of its growth along with that of production. Further, the farmers are not fully aware of modern marketing practices. Due to the lack of facilities for packaging, storage and transportation, the farmers have also to incur significant post-harvest losses.

Though it is the responsibility of the state governments to improve the agricultural marketing system in rural areas, considering its importance, the Central Government has continuously been helping the states by taking a number of measures to overcome these problems.

An ideal marketing system has been defined by Moore, Johl and Khusro as, one that maximizes the long run welfare of society. To do this, it must be physically efficient; otherwise, the same output could be produced with fewer resources; and it must be allocatively efficient; otherwise, a change in allocation could increase the total welfare where income distribution is not a consideration.

Meaning of Agricultural Marketing. Agricultural marketing involves the buying and selling of agricultural produce. This definition would have been suitable for olden days, when the economy of rural areas was self sufficient, where the farmers had no problems in marketing their produce as they used to sell their produce directly to the consumer on it cash or barter system, marketing of agricultural produce is quite different from that in olden days, as it passes through a number of hands before it ultimately reaches the consumer.

A market is a place where goods and services are bought and sold. According to the American Association, "Marketing includes all activities having to do with effecting changes in the ownership and possession of goods and services. It is that part of economics which deals with the creation of time and place and possession utilities and that phase of business activity through which human wants are satisfied by the exchange of goods and services for some valuable consideration." According to the Indian Council of Agricultural Research, Agricultural marketing involves three important functions.

(i) Assembling or concentration of goods.

(ii) Preparation for consumption (processing).

(iii) Distribution of agricultural products.

According to the National Commission on Agriculture, "Agricultural marketing is a process which starts with a decision to produce a saleable farm commodity, and it involves all aspects of market structure or system, both functional and institutional, based on technical and economic considerations and includes pre-harvest and post-harvest operations of

1. assembling,
2. grading,
3. storage,
4. transportation, and
5. distribution."

Agricultural marketing plays an important role not only in stimulating production and consumption, but also in accelerating the pace of economic development. Its dynamic functions are of primary importance in promoting economic development. For this reason, it has been described as the most important multiplier of agricultural development. India's age-old farming practices have taken a new turn in recent years. There has been a technological breakthrough evolution of high yielding variety seeds, increasing use of fertilizers, insecticides and pesticides, installation of pumping sets and tractorization. This technological breakthrough has led to a substantial increase in production on the farms, and to larger marketable and marketed surplus. An efficient marketing system is essential to maintain and accelerate the pace of increasing production through technological development, but for success in this programme, the farmers must receive remunerative prices for their produce. Otherwise, they would not be interested in increasing their production.

Structure of Agricultural Marketing. Agricultural commodities are not produced only in particular regions or areas: these are produced in almost all the areas of the country. Usually, the production is in small quantities. Some agricultural commodities are produced in one region, but sold in other regions of the country or of the world. The majority of farmers are not capable of selling their produce, because of its small quantity, in other regions of the country.

A number of middlemen are involved in taking the farm products form the place of production to the ultimate consumer. There may be several middlemen, engaged at different levels, and this increases the gap between price paid by the consumer and that received by the producer. For reducing this gap, the Punjab Agricultural Marketing Department has recently started the concept of Apni Mandi, where the producers of agricultural commodities sell their produce directly to the consumers. For this purpose, the concerned government agencies in Punjab are providing a number of facilities. In this way, the farmers are getting the benefit of having maximum remunerative prices for their produce, and the gap between the prices received by the producer and paid by the consumer has been minimised.

Classification of Markets. The various markets are as:

(i) Markets at Local Level. These markets are located in small nearby towns to which the farmers can conveniently bring their produce for sale to prospective purchasers. There are large number of farmers whose produce is in small quantities, and they are economically weak. They cannot arrange funds for taking their produce to district level markets where they can get remunerative prices. Due to their weak economic position, they cannot store their produce for some time after harvest. They are, therefore, compelled to sell their produce in the local market to middlemen who offer to purchase the produce. The middlemen collect the produce of a large number of farmers, and send them to the district or central markets.

(ii) District Level Markets. Some of the commodities are processed in the local markets, and they are directly purchased by the consumers. But, generally, most of the agricultural commodities are processed at the district level markets or large central markets. At the district level markets, huge quantities of agricultural commodities are assembled from the local markets. After processing, these are transported to the central/regional markets, or sold directly to consumer markets.

(iii) Central/Regional Markets. The huge quantity of agricultural commodities, which are assembled at local and district level markets, are transported to the central/regional markets where the facilities of processing, storage and grading are available. From here, these are transported for marketing in different parts of the country or abroad. In nature, these markets are professional; buyers of different states and countries visit these markets but not the local ones. For these buyers, the large markets, where they are convenient. Further, these commodities can also be transported to their ultimate destinations within the country or outside conveniently.

(iv) Wholesale Markets. Farm products are first of all assembled in large quantities in local or regional markets. Now, these have to reach the consumers in various parts of the country. Commission agents or middleman purchase the commodities in bulk and store them. After some time tllese goods are sold to retailers. The operating scale of these markets is smaller than that of the central markets. The wholesale markets do not play an important role in determining prices. The wholesalers are interested in only those operations which are necessary to meet the needs of their retail market clients.

(v) Sea-board Markets. As every farm producer or middlemen is not a position to enter export business, some markets have been established at seaports, where exporters purchase farm products brought from local or regional markets. They have the needed facilities of processing and packaging and arrange shipment of these products to other countries. The facilities for importing agricultural goods are also available in seaboard markets.

(vi) Retail Markets. Retail markets are those where the agricultural commodities are sold to the consumers. They include small distribution centres or shops in different areas of cities, towns and villages. The consumers can purchase what they need in small quantities from the rctail markets at any time. Generally, retail selling prices are slightly higher than the wholesale prices, because the retailer would earn some profit for the services rendered by him.

DANGERS/CHALLENGES OF AGRICULTURAL MARKETING

After independence, in 1947 more attention has been paid to agricultural research, and thus has increased the pace of modernisation ofIndian agriculture and introduction of technological innovations such as the use of high-yielding variety seeds, improved agricultural implements, and fertilizers and pesticides in the recent past, has brought about a big change in the production and productivity of Indian agriculture. This development is popularly known as the Green Revolution. It will be discussed in a separate chapter later on in this book. It has given rise to a number of problems in agricultural matketing. It is necessary that the pace, of green, revolution should be maintained, and farmers encouraged to produce more by offering fair prices for their produce. For this, an orderly marketing system is required. Such a marketing system is possible only when the problems cropping up after the green revolution are dealt with effectively. The following are some of the important problems dangers which have cropped up in the recent past due to increase in agricultural production are listed as:

(i) Means of Transport. Increase in production and marketable sutplus, the farmers and traders face a lot of problems for lack of adequate and quick means of transportation of agricultural commodities at village, district and inter-state levels. The transportation, facilities in rural areas are so poor that even big farmers having a large surplus for sale do not like to go to *mandis*. In rural areas, most of the roads are *kachcha*, and become unusable in the rainy season. Thus the means of transportation available in rural areas are inadequate and far from satisfactory. Most farmers usually transport their produce in bullock or camel carts from the place of production or village to the market. This means of transport; is costly and time consuming as the speed and carrying capacity of these carts are low. Where modern mechanised means of transport are available the cost is beyond the capacity of small farmer. Existing rail/road transportation facilities are inadequate for exporters of foodgrains. Export would decline sharply because of weak infrastructure.

The marketing Sub-committee on Agriculture, Forestry and Fisheries has pointed out that the incidence of freight varies from 2.1 to 21.7 per cent in case of wheat, 0.7 to 13.2 per cent for rice, 1.2 to 15.4 per cent for linseed, and about 6.2 per cent for potatoes. It is thus obvious that the cost of transportation is very high. This leads the farmer to dispose off his goods in his village haat or *shandi*, where he does not get a good price.

As far as inter-market and inter-state markets are concerned, mechanised transport facilities, *i.e.*, trucks and railways are available, but they need to be further strengthened by construction of more metalled roads. It is the basic requirement for an efficient transportation system, especially in rural areas, so that the small farmers may find it easier to carry their produce to mandis, where they can get remunerative prices. For an efficient marketing system, efficient and cheap means of transport are necessary.

2. Market Yards—Problems. Agricultural production has been increasing continuously, but spacious market yards are not available in rural areas as well as in urban areas. Business transactions are carried on in congested areas on the roadside. Recently some market committees in the country have constructed spacious market yards from their own resources, but a majority of committees are not in a position to have such spacious market yards due to non-availability of funds and land. For implementing market regulations strictly, a large number of market yards should be constructed in rural areas. They should have necessary modern marketing facilities. Spacious market yards are necessary for various marketing functions, namely, cleaning, grading and weighment of agricultural commodities. For this purpose, the government should come forward to provide necessary assistance for increasing the number of spacious market yards in the country.

3. Lack of Storage Facilities. There is lack of proper storage facilities in rural areas. As a result, farmers are forced to store their produce in carts, pits and *kachcha* store-houses which is unsafe. Whatever storage facilities are available in rural areas are inadequate, and they are so poor that about 10-20 per cent of the foodgrains are lost due to rats, insects, other pests and diseases. But the National Commission on Agriculture has estimated it at only 6.2 per cent.

Non-availability of scientific storage facilities, the farmers do not like to store the foodgrains; they try to sell them as early as possible to avoid damage. This situation substantially increases the supply of agricultural produce in rural markets, putting the farmers in a position where they do not get fair prices for their produce. In some areas, even mandis do not have sufficient storage capacity.

In the recent years warehouses have been constructed by the Food Corporation of India, the Central Warehousing Corporation of India, the State Warehousing Corporations, Cooperative Marketing Societies and the government. Individuals also have built up storage space. The available storage space in these warehouses is much less than required.

Hence, it is necessary that a large number of stores are constructed in rural areas by the central and state governments, market committees, cooperative societies and individuals so that the farmers may have adequate economical storage facilities in rural areas.

4. Market Intelligence. Increased marketable surplus, the importance of market intelligence has increased. The farmers sell their produce in the village and nearby primary wholesale, secondary wholesale and terminal markets. As a result of the farmers ignorance, the traders take advantage of it. They have full knowledge of the prices prevailing in the big markets and purchase the goods of the farmers at lower prices, and this reduces the profits of the farmers.

Though information is provided by the central and the state departments of Agricultural Marketing about the prevailing prices of a number of agricultural commodities through announcements on radio, TV and newspapers, the farmers are still being exploited by traders, as a majority of the farmers are illiterate. By the time information about prevailing prices reaches the farmers, the market prices would have changed. The farmers are unable to get advantage of the available market intelligence. Thus, it is urgent that a system, through which information about the expected prices according to arrivals of different agricultural commodities in the market and their demand and supply can be brought to the notice of the farmers in the rural areas is designed. In this connection, panchayats can play a very important role. The panchayats of the concerned villages should daily obtain information about the prevailing prices of different agricultural commodities, and this information should be displayed at their offices as well as in nearby local markets falling within their jurisdiction.

5. Grading and Standardisation of Agricultural Products. The introduction of a large number of varieties of various agricultural commodities such as wheat, rice and other foodgrains has increased the importance of grading. The steps taken by the governments and the facilities made available for grading and standardisation of agricultural commodities are inadequate. These arrangements are also not fully practised. As a result, the farmers as well as the consumers suffer. In the absence of proper grading and standardisation, the producer would sell his good quality produce along with produce of lower quality. The farmer would receive the same prices for his superior quality product and for his average quality product. The consumer will also suffer because he has to pay the same price for a good quality product and for a slightly lower quality product. Proper grading ensures that the farmers/producers receiving prices of their products according to the quality. Proper grading also provides consumers with a safeguard against any adulteration.

Adequate grading and standardisation facilities are not available, especially in rural areas. Hence, both the producer and the consumer are the losers and the middlemen, making attractive profits out of it are the gainers.

The state departments of agricultural marketing and other agencies of the state governments should come forward with a strategy to provide on a large scale facilities for grading and standardisation of agricultural commodities at the farm and market levels. It is essential that the product is graded at the farm level, because, it is very difficult at the market tevel, where during the peak season, the stocks of different commodities are in huge quantity. If adequate grading facilities are not made available in rural areas, the farmers would continue to be exploited and their profits would go into the pockets of commission agents/traders, making the farmers economically weaker. For removal of poverty from rural areas, it is also necessary that farmers receive prices according to the quality of their products and the major commission agents.

6. Regulated Markets. Agricultural marketing operations arc also being carried out in regulated markets. There are more than 34,000 markets in the country, but only 6,752 of them are regulated markets. Other than these, there are more than 22,000 primary rural periodic markets. The Centre has requested to the States/UTs to regulate 15,000 more markets during Eighth Five Year Plan. Every state has passed Market Regulation Acts. A large number of the markets set up under these Acts do not have even the basic infrastructural facilities such as auction platforms, metalled roads, cart parks, rest-houses, water facilities, etc. All the technical services for weighing and grading of commodities should be available in the markets. Malpractices like false weights and measurements should be eliminated. The existing rural marketing system needs elimination of the large number of intermediaries and the large deductions from the produce of the farmers made by commission agents/brokers who sell the produce on behalf of the farmers. As the regulated markets are run by marketing committees, it is their responsibility to arrange for necessary funds for making agricultural marketing efficient and effective. These committees may request the concerned state governments to provide assistance for improving the business activities of the regulated markets.

Note. It is separately discussed in a chapter in this book.

Conclusion. No one can underrate the role of agriculture in the Indian Economy as the share of GDP from agriculture is still maximum. The growth of most industries is dependent on growth of agriculture. Agricultural growth can be accelerated only if the farmers get their due share in the production of agricultural commodities. This is possible only when efficient agricultural marketing facilities are made available throughout the country. Efficient marketing will affect the overall economy of the country favourably. When the farmers receive remunerative prices for their produce, it will encourage them to make further efforts to increase production, so that income might increase further. This will create savings, and these savings of the farm sector may be used for the development of non-farm sectors. Hence, an efficient agricultural marketing system is a must. For this, the cultivator should have all the needed facilities such as for storage, transport, grading, etc. reasonable prices. On the other hand, farmers should be motivated and educated to join efficient marketing cooperative societies, where they can get a number of facilities for adopting modem technology to increase agricultural production and productivity, and through which they can sell their produce at the most remunerative prices as the farmers themselves are the organisers of these societies.

MANAGING THE MIX OF RURAL MARKETING

In our country, no doubt various Industries with huge production and diversified products have already captured a significant share in the urban markets. In a country like ours there is a continuous need to explore new markets, more specifically unexplored rural markets.

The Scope of Rural Markets. In Rural Marketing a different approach will be exercised as it has different system than urban systems. The rural marketing is vast and has high potential as it covers 75 crore people. Rural marketing is scattered over 5. 75 1akh villages, 90% of which are small whose population is below 2000. Rural Sector contributes about 50% to GNP. Rural marketing is still a neglected and unexploited area and offers great challenges and prospects to the marketers and researchers.

Not only this but it is a heterogenous market, encompassing cultural, linguistic, religious and economic diversities. It is highly dispersed and thinly populated market where more than 16 major national languages and around 650 local dialects are exercised by different areas of our country.

Rural Marketing Challenges. The following challenges have to be taken care for improving rural agriculture marketing:

(i) low income, *(ii)* poor purchasing power, *(iii)* low standard of living, *(iv)* low level of literacy *(v)* rural incomes are seasonal (harvest linked income) *(vi)* unstable incomes, based on the vagaries of the monsoon, *(vii)* traditional and orthodox in their systems, *(viii)* Rural consumers are more cautions while purchasing and their decisions are slow and delayed.

Despite the above odd situations a wealth generating process has recently emerged in rural India due to the following:

(i) Green Revolution,

(ii) Upsurge in agricultural product prices,

(iii) the government farm policy,

(iv) Tax relief,

(v) The role of leading financial bodies,

(vi) Rising aspirations and expectations of the rural masses will increase rural consumption.

Thus, a rapid change is undergoing in the pattern of rural demands. The Rural Market has potential only for marketers of agro-inputs, *e.g.*, seeds, cattle-feed, agricultural implements, fertilizers, pesticides, tractors, pumpsets, etc. There is a developing market for consumer sorts and durables, entertainment electronics, motorcycles and jeeps, POL, and educational supplies, along with demand for better food, clothing and toiletries. According to ORG (Operations Research Group) survey, the rural market for packaged consumer products has shown a 184 per cent growth during 1984-89, as against the 96 per cent growth in its urban counterpart during the same period. Washing materials and toiletries account for a major component of rural spending, with 37 per cent and 30 per cent respectively.

TAPPING THE RURAL MARKETING OR CHALLENGES AND STRATEGIES OF RURAL AGRICULTURAL MARKETING

The areas where care is needed which are associated with rural marketing pertaining to physical distribution. These include: Problem of transportation and its high costs, particularly in hilly areas and interior villages where no approach roads no warehousing, no communication, poor sales management, poor roads, poor and high distribution cost. It takes a longer time for a product, to reach break-even sales. Effective rural communication, creative salesmanship, promotion of sales and servicing, etc., should be extended to cover the highly scattered rural areas, using appropriate innovation, selection and adaptation of new approaching for taping Rural Marketing.

1. Physical Distribution in Rural Areas. It is necessary to evolve and implement a physical distribution system that is best suited to the rural environment the objective being minimisation of distribution cost, as well as, guaranteeing at least a minimum level of service. The existing pattern consists of stock points in feeder towns, and retailers at the village level. The feeder point is the key to distribution process in the rural areas.

The poorly developed distribution infrastructure is the major constraint at present. Many parts of rural India are still inaccessible through railways and roadways. The problem gets aggravated during the monsoons. All these result in longer lead time between points of production and points of consumption, larger pipeline stocks, high storage losses, high transportation, and distribution costs, and multi-tier distribution channels. "The transport system for serving the rural market will have to be largely built around rail for heavy volume and long distance movements, trucks for short hauls, and delivery vans and bullock carts for local haulage." Tractor trolleys and light commercial vehicles are also now emerging as useful means of local haulage. Firms like Hindustan Lever. Lipton, Brooke Bond, Tata, etc., use their own sales vans for interior transportation, but the cost of operating such vans is high.

2. Satellite Distribution System. Under this system, stockists are appointed by the manufacturer in feeder towns, and entrusted with the tasks of financing, warehousing and on sub-distribution of goods. Retailers, residing in and around the feeder town are also appointed, and are attached to the stockists. The turnover of retailers varies. Over a period of time, some of the retailers grow in stature and get elevated as stockists of the second generation. This process continues. "At any point of time, enough retail points always hover around a particular stockist," and its resembles a Satellite System. The main advantage of this system is that penetration in the interior rural market becomes easier as the manufacturer is not required to open direct stock points.

3. Channel Management in Rural Areas. Organisation of an effective distribution channel in the rural market is a more difficult task as compared to its urban counterpart. As the manufacturer cannot open and manage all the retail outlets necessary to form the forward links of the distribution chain right upto village point, due to its being an expensive proposition, the services of middlemen become necessary particularly in the rural context. The retailers are needed at the village level, the semi-wholesalers or authorised dealers at the block level, and the wholesalers or stockists at the feeder town level. These forward links are fed by backward links, comprising the manufacturer's own stock points and regional and branch office operations.

However, in the absence of his own forward links, the manufacturer cannot exercise much direct control over the whole distribution system. A Channel System, based on direct selling by the manufacturer to the consumers, may be very expensive and often uneconomic in the interior. Therefore, in spite of a large network of one's own retail outlets being more effective for deeper market penetration, one has to compromise between this advantage and the cost involved in organising such a network.

4. Sales Force Management. The task of developing a sales force for rural areas is significantly different. The techniques and approaches should be appropriately adapted to the needs of rural markets. The rural salesman must be competent in communicating with the rural folk in their own language and idiom. He should be willing to work in a mral area. As far as possible, a *Son of the Soil* should be appointed. He should be imparted training regarding the background of the rural market, the behaviours of rural consumers and marketing techniques.

5. Market Segmentation. A selective approach is essential for penetration in the rural market. Agricultural prosperity is not uniform in all the rural areas. Some areas have developed rapidly, while others have remained undeveloped. Markets will develop faster in areas where agricultural development is rapid. Likewise, those areas, where infrastructural facilities are already developed to generate high demand. Family needs dominate over all other needs; they are followed by farm needs, status needs, and comfort needs. This should be kept in mind while segmenting mral markets. Proximity to a feeder town/mand has a high influence on rural demand, as people living in nearby areas are more aware of various consumer goods and other products and are experiment-oriented too. Such proximate areas should be taken up first and developed. Further, the target may be the younger generation, as they are more literate and have greater exposure to changing values and life-styles.

6. Marketing Communication in Rural Areas. Mere generation of new wealth and creation of additional purchasing power are not adequate in themselves for sales growth in the rural market. Unless rural consumers are motivated and educated through mass communication to purchase more goods and new products, desired results cannot be achieved. It calls for great imagination and skill. The intrinsic characteristics of the rural market specific consumer behaviour non-availability of media, high level of illiteracy, linguistic diversity, and the traditional outlook of rural consumers are constraints in effective marketing communication. Print media have limited scope in the rural market, but telecasting presents an effective communication system.

Yet is covers only 30 per cent of the target population. Even among them, viewers of advertisements are meagre, On the other hand, the audio network covers more tban 90 per cent of the rural population. It needs appropriate planning for its greater use in marketing conununication. "Among all the media, cinema or video-vision parlour centres attract more of the rural population and form am effective communication media. It is also pointed out that earning from cinema forms a significant share in rural India," The selection of an appropriate media-mix, giving proper weightage of both farmland non-formal media, is essential for effective communication in the rural market. The formal media comprise newspapers, magazines, radio, cinema, television, etc., whereas mike announcements, processions, *harikatha*, demonstrations with audio-visual publicity vans, etc., on appropriate occasions like village fairs, constitute the non-formal media. Mobile audio-visual publicity vans and music records of folk songs are very popular in rural areas. Publicity through well decorated bullock carts and tractor-trolleys is appropriate in the interior. Participation in fairs, exhibitions and melas through demonstration vans is very effective, "The carrier should reach where the villagers congregate." "The WIMCO's findings in Maharasbtra indicate that 100 per cent of the total adult women population (sample) uses matches." A match box may be a good means of conveying messages to the rural population. spoken words of friends, relatives, gram sevak, village sarpanch and personal selling are also very useful communication devices of creating creditability."

7. Product Management in Rural Areas. The product features should be simple and cost reasonable. Rural requirements in respect of attributes like colour, fragrance size of unit, shape, etc. must be taken care of "Now the rural consumers are rapidly becoming brand conscious; therefore, brand names must be simple and easily pronounceable. Packing should be strong enough to withstand rough handling of products."

In spite of all complexities involved in rural marketing, the rural scene and environment are changing steadily in India. The significance and need of marketing research in rural areas to monitor these changes and their implications are increasing. The various challenges in rural marketing must be carefully tackled and appropriate strategies designed to tap the high potential of the under-explored rural markets. In view of the liberalisation policy of the government and its emphasis on rural development it can be concluded that in due course, with the help of advance technology, an effective and appropriate rural market communication mix and transportation network will be developed, and it will not be long before expanding industries capture the rural markets.

STRATEGY FOR AGRICULTURAL MARKETING

After the liberalisation of Indian economy the market place has become extremely competitive. Every segment market in every product category is flushed with a variety of brands from old players-who enjoyed monopoly for long, new entrants from within the country, with innovative strategies and prictices and transnational better equipped with resources of all kinds for probing, positioning and penetrating the market place. Today market economy, where customers have the access to all types of information and the opportunity to choose, only the genuine practice of this concept can ensure survival.

At present the concept of 'marketing' has replaced the 'concept of selling", which used to be the guiding principle of marketing managers, to promote their brands. The competition in the market place has forced them to rethink and frame an innovative package of marketing mix to ensure genuine customer satisfaction. This calls for choosing the target market, identified customers needs, developing wants-satisfying products and services, and eventually delivering value to the customers. For a long time companies pushing its products to the consumers without give thoughts to the consumers need and similarly no thought was given to the 'Target Matkets' and the satisfaction of the needs of customers.

As the degree of competition and the availability of multiple brands has forced the use of marketing concept in the rural areas. Therefore, it has become important for the companies who wish to operate successfully to first decide about target market and thereby to decide marketing mix. The marketing mix strategies; practices and techniques for selling products in urban areas have to be different in rural areas because of various changes in needs, family incomes, requirements of the products, spending habits and priority, uneducated people, nutrition, health etc. of people living in villages.

Determinants of Marketing Mix. The problem of deciding marketing mix is very crucial for a company as it has to redesign its marketing mix as much has not left in the urban market, which is already leading towards saturation point. Moreover, the Rural Market has not been trapped properly by majority of companies. The growth and development lies in the efficient exploitation of Rural Market which has more than 250 million consumers.

Reasons for Redesign Marketing Mix. There are following reasons to the companies to redesign its marketing mix:

1. Complex Business Environment. The changing business environment, economic liberalisation, increasing competition, rising costs, lower margins, splintered market, and high consumer choice have brought the consumer to die centre stage. The silent not very demanding rural customer, who was ignored, has now been replaced by one who is aware and choosy.

2 Increasing Rural Purchasing Power. Rural earnings are rising rapidly and personal social familial and cultural values are under transformation. Increasing personal disposable income will lead greater consumption of products both durables and non-durables making a vast potential untapped market presently not as tough as the urban, available.

3. Changing Buyer Behaviour. Younger, more knowledgeable, better informed and educated sons are replacing conservative fathers in making purchase decisions or have more influential role in decision making. This group, unlike the previous generation is more rational, less emotional and least interested in long-term association, but wants quick returns.

4. Increase in Standard of Living. In rural areas people have disregard the old philosophy of simple living and high thinking, these days they wish to have all types of comforts and for that they need all types of product to uplift their standard of living.

5. Role of Media-Satellite. Media has played a significant role in deciding the habits and attitudes of the people of India-urban and rural. The degree of change in rural are more with the increase of purchasing power, education and media popularity etc.

6. Tapping the Untouched Areas. Many products and services may find rural market totally untouched thus, the process of success will depend upon the package it offer to the virgin birds in the form of product offerings and value.

A CASE STUDY OF MCKINSEY AND CO. MARKETING CONSULTANT RAMA BIJAPURKAR

The challenging of betting oil an emerging market is to attain value is sight.

FINDINGS

1. Creation of Values. Insight into what will create sustained value for the customer—benefits, product architecture, packaging, delivery systems, and cost-beyond the options available to him, given that he has no prior understanding of what the product is all about; given that the need being targeted is being Obliquely and indirectly fulfilled by something else; given that the need may be nascent; given that what adds values to him (that is, his value system) will quickly change because of the accelerated pace of his evolution along the hiemchy of needs, and the speed with which better offers will be placed before him.

2. Value Judgement of Consumer Behaviour. Insight into how customers translate their value judgement into behaviour. That is, will not use. Or, will use but only in specific situations. Or, will use frequently but in small quantities. Or, will use instead of, or, in addition to, and so on.

3. Consideration with Regards to give Value Effective Package—Benefits. Insight into whether it is possible to design and deliver a value effective package—benefits, product architecture, packaging, delivery systems, and cost—that can create sustained value for both the customer and the company.

Conclusion. The fast changing consumer taste and preferences, it is not enough just to understand who your consumer is, but is essential to identify the drivers of his behaviour, how these are changing, his future needs and wants and the competitive offerings and to anticipate his needs even before he or the competitor does. The processing of the value of the consumer has to undertaken looking into his socio-ecoilomic, cultural and behavioural dimensions. Companies with inadequate insight in this regard are likely to lose.

There are good many companies which are exploiting the rural markets by not providing real value for the price they charge to their valued customers but due to growing competition, fall in profits in urban areas and increase impact of information technology (IT), if these are not careful for protective corrective measures, their product life cycle (P.L.C) may become short. The rural marketing is not complex because of the nature of the customers, types of product offerings, competition etc. But, it certainly is different from what conventional marketing companies have been doing to attract urban consumers. It is mainly with regard to products related with agriculture where there is tremendous scope for companies to differentiate their offer from those of their competitors, whether it is a core service such as offering advice, a peripheral service such as replying to customers about product availability, attributes, or price, or a supplementary service such as after sales maintenance of tractors, sprinklers, electric pumps and motors, etc.

Suggested Line of Action. The areas to be taken care are as:

1. Unbrand Products. Rural India is being offered a plethora of unbranded products. Mainly because of price difference and retailer push, some are able to make profits. But, the shift is in favour of branded products because they offer a strategic advantage by reducing the customers quest for a product. The buyers feel more comfortable while purchasing a branded product, although it is expensive.

2. Improved Packaging. Upgradation in packaging technology has made it possible to make available low unit—low priced packs. These can be launched and used successfully to widen penetration. It can also result in impulse purchases by the ever—increasing rural population. Packaging in smaller and attractive packs can be a unique selling proposition of a company which otherwise enjoys brand awareness and image as in case of Surf Excel.

3. Innovative Ideas. Companies which have high stake in rural markets can come out with innovative ideas to provide credit to rural people, who at present are not given any credit under the assumption of high-risk, or given with no high expectations of repayment as in the case of distribution of government loans. As in the case with self-help groups, where the repayment rates have been over 95%, commercially viable schemes can be initiated, including some for providing credit to poor women, agricultural workers, rural artisans, etc. Schemes can be worked out which are tied to a company's products to promote its image. This will improve the consumers' ability to purchase as financial barriers will be reduced.

4. Careful Thoughts to Hire Purchase and Lease Schemes. Innovative financial alternatives. Based on the assumption that there is not enough product differentiation between rival products, some companies can use hire-purchase and leasing schemes to beat the competition.

5. Thoughts to Consumerism. There are very few in the rural market who have resorted to consumerism. Marketers have two jobs: *(1)* to create demand and *(2)* to motivate them to buy their product. When rural consumers take purchase decisions, the alternatives available in front of them are not competing brands merely. Many a time, the decision first is with regard to the type of product, especially when the purchase is of a durable product.

6. Cut in the Cost of Output (High/Low Cost). The, mastermind Nirma Chemicals Ltd. The company is determined to price its detergents way below competing products in order to appeal to a huge section of customers-urban as well as rural—who could not afford detergent powder. The company slashed its costs by keeping overheads low, sourcing raw material at rock-Bottom prices, and simplifying its distribution. Although the product quality is lower than that of competitors, such value is not available to consumers at the price offered by Nirma. Very often, the consumer makes a trade-off between quality, price and the resultaut return on the spent unit. For this company, the payoff is a permanent competitive advantage on costs.

7. Interaction with Customers. Create and design interactions with customers. They should be beyond commercial transactions. This will send the signal that the company's mandate is to look after other needs also.

8. Change in the Attitude of the Employees. The attitude of each employee may be on high or low position requires to be responsive to customers. In this reference case of Mahindra and Mahindra worth quote: Its sales is Rs. 2782 crore utility vehicles and farm equipment manufacturer, regularly brings even its smallest customers, farmers to its shopfloors. Customers bring streams of new ideas which keep company in touch with the problems and their solution which further keep the company going ahead on the innovation and developing an improved version which may suit to its valued customers.

9. Educate Customers Regarding the use of Products. Educate your consumers to make optimum use of the product. A fertilizer company can teach the farmers the process an techniques to be followed to get maximum yield. Their employees can help farmers in identifying the crops to be sowed, selling the produce, getting the right price, etc. Example of Pepsi provides training to farmers to get a better potato/tomato crop.

10. Regular Meetings Regarding Product Innovation. Companies can organise regular meetings in association with local bodies such as panchayats, to discuss product, innovations, services, problems, etc. This can strengthen the brand equity. This strategy can be used for both durable and non-durable products. With the help of such meetings, a company can identify potential customers, recognise their needs, find out ways to meet their needs, identify loyal customers and reward them suitably, and thus establish strong brand equity for longer relationships.

11. Brand-Loyalty. The rural customers in not particularly brand loyal. This leaves much to be done on the part of marketers to influence his decisions. There is considerable scope for visual and auditory stimuli at the retailing point.

12. After-sales Service. In case of durables the sales is not everything but creation of a satisfaction among customers should be the company's goal, and quick after-sales service has a crucial role to play in this regard.

13. Arrangement with Intermediaries. Manage your intermediaries by making better offers. In urban India, escalating cost of real estate has made availability of shelf-space very costly. The promotional mix of established brands makes the entry of new products extremely expensive. Rural India has the answer to this problem faced by new entrants. They can manage middlemen by offering better returns than the established brands, and secure reasonable space and the retailers favour in pushing the product.

14. Keep Eye on Competitors. Monitor your competitors' activities and their products. Identify the reasons why consumers are attracted towards the competing products. A detailed SWOT analysis should be regularly conducted so as to bring about required changes in the companys offer to create differentiated value.

REASONS FOR INADEQUATE PERFORMANCE OF RURAL AGRICULTURAL MARKETING

The market is an arena for exchange of goods and services, where economic and behavioural forces interact to make buying or selling decisions. Marketing in the rural setting are public gathering where diversified activities are integrated at an approved place and at regular intervals. It can be described as an arrangement to provide social, political, economic and cultural platforms of people of different interests. Marketing in rural areas, therefore, is a complex phenomenon. However it is an important postulate of economic development of a country like India, where more than 70% population lives in villages.

The change in the economic policies of the Government, many companies have ventured into the rural markets. However, their efforts have not been properly rewarded. Here an attempt is made to study various hurdles behind such inadequate performance. Here an attempt is exercise to look into the challenges and thrust for optimum exploitation of the rural markets.

FACTORS/REASONS FOR INADEQUATE PERFORMANCE OF RURAL AGRICULTURAL MARKETING

The following are factors/reasons for inadequate performance:

(1) Poor infrastructure.

(2) Poor market planning and awareness.

(3) Product design.

(4) Price of the product.

(5) Poor means of distribution.

(6) Poor means of communication.

(7) Consumer behaviour.

(8) Cultural factors.

(9) Demographic factors.

(10) Purchasing decision.

(11) Buying motives.

1. Poor Infrastructure. The infrastructure broadly includes, roads, transport facilities, electricity, telecommunications, etc. However, these basic facilities are missing in most of the rural areas of India. The roads are not there, and if they exist, their condition is poor. Still, there are many parts in central and north-east India, which are totally untouched by the development in the outside world. Many areas are simply inaccessible. In such a scenario, the rural marketing concept appears unpromising.

2. Product Design. A product which is selling well in urban markets, may not necessarily be a success in rural markets, the reason being the difference in the utility value of the product. For example, consumer goods which are becoming more or less a necessity in urban areas as a result of changing life-style may still be categorised as luxuries in rural areas.

3. Poor Market Planning Awareness. Rural markets are different from urban markets. Unlike urban markets, they are unplanned in nature. Till your years back, rural markets were simply not cared about companies which have been household names for decades in urban areas, were not even heard of in the rural markets. But, with the increase in competition in urban areas, emphasis on rural areas has emerged. However, the executives in the companies do not understand the consumer psychology in rural markets, and it makes the planning process all the more complex. Lack of awareness and understanding of consumer behaviour in rural markets, creates problems in formulating strategies and plans for these.

4. Price of the Product. 'Price' is a tool with which companies can compete with one another. It is a sensitive index, while considering the product. Price plays an important role in urban as well as rural markets, but, it is more crucial in rural areas because the income is low. Moreover, price has to justify itself. The consumer must feel satisfied and benefited after paying the price for a particular product. Thus, price remains the point of contention.

5. **Poor Means of Communication.** With the given level of literacy and awareness of rural population, communication constitutes a major hurdle in exploiting rural markets. Various factors, like language, religion, superstitions, rigidity, etc. make communication in rural markets more difficult The messages used in urban areas for communication purposes, if used into rural markets, may lead to negative marketing. Thus, due consideration needs to be given while communicating with rural masses.

6. **Consumer Behaviour.** In addition to physical constraints, various other factors exercise power influence over consumer behaviour, these are known as "attitudinal factors".

The specific environment in which rural masses reside decides the attitudinal bent of mind of rural consumers. Consequently, the rural markets flourish or collapse, mainly on account of how the rural consumers feel about a particular product.

7. **Poor Means of Distribution.** Nobody ever thought of developing the channels of distribution in rural areas till the focus of the executives shifted from urban to rural areas. Only those companies which were directly related with agricultural activities, *e.g.* insecticides, fertilizers, seeds etc., contacted the rural markets. The consumer goods companies had not focussed their activities in the rural areas. Thus, adequate channels of distribution do not exist, and this restricts the exploitation of the rural markets to the full.

8. **Cultural Factors.** Culture affects the behaviour of individuals. The consumers in the rural areas are much under the influence of traditional cultural values. The culture at present is more or less the same as it was some 50 years back. Consequently, their buying decisions are the result of the culture they hail from that is Hindu culture, which restricts meat-eating habits. As a result, the fast food culture has remained restricted to urban areas.

9. **Demographic Factors.** The various demographic factors like age, sex, education, income, etc., also account for consumer

response. This is true for both urban and rural consumers. In rural areas, the educational level is very low in a majority of the rural areas. The income level also is very low. The main occupation continues to be agriculture, and the level of advancement in agriculture is also low. This results in lesser output, and consequently low income, resulting in low purchasing power.

Moreover, the rural population is heterogeneous in nature. It consists of either younger or elderly people. The people in the age group 18-40 migrate to nearby towns or cities in search of livelihood. Besides, women outnumber men in rural areas because male members move out of their places.

10. Buying Motives. Marketers have been using buying motives to handle the consumers. 'Buying Motive' provides the psychological justification for the acceptance of a product. This tool has proved a success with urban consumers, but its application to rural markets needs to be studied. It is necessary for the marketer first to identify the psychological characteristics which can act as the buying motives. Luxury is a buying motive which has been widely exploited by marketers in urban markets, but it may not prove that effective in the case of rural consumers, because of a different style of living.

11. Purchasing Design. One of the important factors affecting consumers behaviour in rural markets is the right to take the purchase decisions. In most rural families, it is the head of the family who decides what to buy and when to buy. Consequently, his purchase decisions are influenced by his own personality traits, rather than the aptitude and perception of the actual consumers of these goods. Thus, while venturing into rural markets, this fact needs probing.

SUGGESTIONS FOR RURAL MARKETING DEVELOPMENT

The above explanation of the rural marketing background, clearly shows that it needs careful planning at Macro level for the development of rural marketers. The Government and other public agencies can play an important, role in the execution of the various developmental programmes.

Suggestions at Micro Level. The main recommendations in this respect areas:

The strategies will have to be designed keeping an eyeview on *(a)* pricing of product, *(b)* means of distribution, *(c)* product design, and *(d)* communication. These will improve the organisational performance in the market.

Marketing Planning. Rural marketing needs adequate marketing planning with regard to design of product, utility of product. Price incentives in the rural areas be given due care. Hindustan Lever has following this technique successfully in rural areas.

Improving Channels of Distribution. Marketers need to be more effective by importing skill and training to the wholesalers and retailers so that these are able to perform their jobs efficiently and effectively. Some progress has been made by Hindustan Lever Ltd. in terms of the introduction of the concept of satellite marketing in rural areas, wherein a wholesaler is appointed in rural area, he further appoints sub-wholesalers in the interior, and these sub-wholesalers contact the local markets. This way, a link is formed between the company and the rural markets.

Communication Strategies. The messages being communicated are influenced by western culture, to which the roml consumer is alien. The messages to the rural markets, should be such that they are acceptable in them. The images appearing in the advertisements should be identifiable by the consumers. In order to improve communication, the media mix should also be taken care of. The media mix applicable to urban markets is not appropriate for the products marketed in rural markets, *e.g.* newspapers are not sufficient to cover the total rural population. Advertisements on national channels and regional channels of television and radio, bill-boards, theatres, etc. would provide a good means of communication. Finally comes the language in which the message is to be conveyed. Besides Hindi, the national language, and English, regional languages should be used more often.

Consumer Behaviour. With regard to handling the aittitudinal problem, the consumer behaviour in rural markets should be understood. However, in order to do this, the marketing personnel should have thorough knowledge of the concept and techniques of studying behaviour. In this context, special training and development programmes should be conducted by the organisations with the main focus on developing analytical and behavioural skills. Concepts like Transactional Analysis, Cultural Analysis, and inputs on Attitudinal Surveys should form the major contents of such training programmes. With the development of such skins in the marketing personnel, the task of formulating appropriate strategies to venture successfully into rural markets would be facilitated.

❑

13

Classification of Agricultural Products

AGRICULTURAL PRODUCTS

Agricultural products refer to the products arising out of cultivation, namely various crops, vegetables and fruits etc. In a broader sense, agricultural goods arise out of cultivation, dairy farming, poultry farming, pig farming etc. Thus eggs, butter cheese fluid milk, meat etc. are also the agricultural products.

Classification of Agricultural Goods/Products

These agricultural products are classed into two categories viz., *(1)* Industrial Goods (2) Consumer Goods.

(1) Industrial Goods. Are those used for further Industrial processing, *e.g.*, tobacco, fibre crops like cotton and jute; eggs, and butter used, in bakeries, vegetables an fruits canned and pickled, wheat and gram used by flour mills to grind them.

(2) Consumer. Agricultural goods are meant for direct use, like all food-grains, dairy products, poultly products, vegetables and fruits.

Some of the agricultural goods become both consumer goods and Industrial goods, depending upon the use to which these are put *e.g.*, case of fruits especially, if these are consumed directly by the consumers, these become consumer goods, and if the same fruits are used in canning factory, these become industrial goods. Another best example can be cited is that of groundnut. These are used for home consumption, it becomes consumer goods and if used for the production of oil, it becomes industrial goods.

Characteristics of Agricultural Products

The characteristics of agricultural goods are divided into two categories.

I. "Production" Characteristics. The production characteristics are as:

1. **Small Scale Production.** The production of agricultural goods is carried on a very small scale as compared to the production of manufactured goods the techniques and principles of large scale production are not applied to a greater extent. This is particularly true in case of developing countries, like India; and where 75 per cent of total supply comes from small scale producers even in sophisticated countries like U.S.A. Japan, etc. In India, such small production is mainly due to the small size of farms or land holdings.

   There is no economy in transaction. As a result, the farmers are unable to influence the market price by individual actions. Therefore, these have to depend upon the middlemen or co-operative societies in the marketing of their goods.

2. **Scattered and Specialized Production.** Scattered production of agricultural goods is a universal truth. The natural conditions like quality of the soil and climate make agricultural production scattered and specialised. Moreover, every piece of land and every type of climate does not suit the production of all agricultural goods. The fertility of Land varies, from place to place and particular climate and contents of soil, and rainfall go to determine the crops to be grown. Different areas are suitable for growing different crops, *e.g.* sugar cane is mainly grown in Uttar Pradesh, Karnataka, Maharashtra in India, while Jawa and Cuba, are other world producers of sugar cane. As a result of this

peculiar characteristic of agricultural production, the process of concentration in assuming greater significance in marketing.

3. **Seasonal Production.** Production of agricultural goods is seasonal. They are not grown throughout the year. They grow only during certain months of the year, depending upon the rainfall and climatic conditions. But the demand for them is spread throughout the year, *e.g.*, paddy, cotton, Jowar. etc, are harvested from December to March, but the demand is continuous. Therefore, the goods move from the producing countries to the consumption centres. Because of this, there usually occur.; a 'peak load' in their sale, and hence, on storage, transportation and financing. These services tend to increase the cost of marketing relatively.

II. "Product" Characteristics. These are further classified as:

1. **Variation in Quality.** The quality and quantity vary from area to area, time to time, depending on the changes in climate, fertility of the soil, rainfall, art of cultivation etc. It is beyond the control of producers to assure the quality and quantity. Number of natural calamities comes in the way of agricultural production. Flood, forest, drought, hail, storms, animal and plant diseases, insects, are some of the natural threats which affect agricultural production. Because of these variation, these are effects even on the storage and transport facilities. Sometimes, when bumper crops are yielded, there is more demand for storage and transport facilities and the reverse is the case when there is no or less yield. Then it is rather difficult to adjust the supply and demand and stabilisation can not be attained. Thus, there is a 'chance variation' in crops.

2. **Bulky and Perishable Products.** Agricultural goods are bulky in nature. The intrinstic value is quite low as compared

to their bulk appearance and size. This makes transportation and warehousing, costly. Majority of the agricultural goods are perishable. That is, they cannot fast long. Fruits, vegetables, milk, eggs, flowers etc., are prone to perishability of high order. Therefore, they need recent improvements in refrigeration and transportation. The food grains like wheat, jowar, rice and cotton, tobacco, which are to be stored for a considerable period of time without deterioration. do require proper storage facilities. This, again increases the cost of marketing.

3. **Inelastic Demand.** Inelastic demand is a special feature of the agricultural goods. Inelasticity refers to unchanged demand. That is, whether the price rise or fall, the demand for agricultural goods, remains more or less the same; there is no change in demand. If a product is in short supply its price rises automatically. If the supply increases, the price falls. That is why, agricultural goods always face the problem of price stabilisation. Often, the Government has to take necessary steps for this purpose.

RECENT TRENDS IN THE MARKETING OF FARM PRODUCTS

There have been developments, even in the field of agriculture, as there are developments in research and technology, these days. The age-old traditional methods, or marketing agricultural goods have been left off, and new ones have made their beginning. These recent trends, can be studied under two distinct heads.

1. Decentralisation of marketing

2. Development of Contract farming.

1. Decentralisation of Marketing. First of all, the agricultural goods used to move through the channel of local market, central, jobbing market or secondary market and ultimately to either consumers or industrial users. But now, this trend has changed and decentralisation has poked its nose even in this field of marketing. This means that there is a marked change in the distribution channel; and marketing of agricultural goods is decentralised. This decentralisation its due mainly to the following factors.

(a) **Development of Modern Facilities of Transportation.** Development of modern facilities of transportation have helped to cover the wide area, for the collection of agricultural goods. This is true, especially, in case of agricultural raw materials like sugarcane, which is collected by the manufacturers directly, from the farms of producers and some consumer goods like fruits, vegetables etc.

(b) **The Modern Communication System.** The modern communication system makes it possible to collect information about prices and supplies in the market and thus, reduces the reliance on the middlemen, in the central market.

(c) **Standardisation Grading.** Standardization and grading, speak of the quality of the products and hence, the buyers do not feel like observing and inspecting the goods.

(d) **The Improved Warehousing Facilities and Cold Storage Arrangements.** The improved warehousing facilities and cold storage arrangements have succeeded in reducing the deterioration of quality of the products.

(e) **The Tendency of Eliminating the Middlemen.** The tendency of eliminating the middlemen has reached its peak, when we look at the, establishments of certain large scale retail organisations, like departmental stores, super markets, chain stores etc.,

(f) **Rise and Development of Co-operative Marketing Societies.** Last, but not the least, the rise and development of co-operative marketing societies and regulated, markets have ensured the dencentralisation process.

2. Development of Contract Farming. Contract farming, has assisted the decentralisation process. Further, Contract farming is nothing but entering into an argument by the processors and manufacturers with farmers to grow and supply the crops or raw materials fortheir factories, well in advance of the harvest season. The best example is that of sugarcane industry. Contract farming assures the adequate supplies to the manufacturers and marketers. The co-operative marketing societies and such, other large scale retailers and manufacturers, practise contracts farming and thus eliminate the local market and central market.

CHANNEL OF DISTRIBUTION FOR AGRICULTURAL GOODS

The outstanding characteristics of farming and farm products have a greater and deeper bearing on the channels of distribution. The study of channels used would be most clear if one tries to study, different types of market that play a constructive role in performing the functions of marketing *via* the process of centralisation, equalisation and dispersion. Because of the above reason there has been developed of certain whole markets which played, are playing and will continue to play an indispensable role in the marketing of agricultural goods. These wholesale markets are classed into four classes as : *(i)* Local Market *(ii)* Central Market *(iii)* Jobbing Market *(iv)* Secondary Market.

LOCAL MARKET

What is it? The 'Local' Market or 'Local Assembly' market, or 'growers' market or primary' market is found in the close vicinity of agricultural areas. It is a market wherein producers *i.e.*, the farmers on the one hand, consumers and intermediaries on the other deal for the purchase and sale of farm products. Normally, quite a large number of wholesalers and co-operative societies operate in these markets. Their main purpose is to collect or assemble the agricultural goods in larger quantities which are to be transported later on to the central markets.

Characteristics. Following are the characteristics.

1. Absence of Qualified Buying. The purchase and sales are not based on the quality. The agencies in the local market do not care for quality as is the case in other markets. It is use, the practice is to collect small lot of scattered production and sell without grading. Since, there is dearth or lack of specialised staff and grading facilities and inability to cover the cost of grading, no attention is paid to quality.

2. Careless Handling of Goods. Agricultural goods require a lot of caution while handling them in the marketing process,. *e.g.*, fruits and vegetables may require good storage, cotton and food grains need goods packing, storage etc. perishable products like milk, eggs, may require cold storage. Rough handling may spoil the goods. Therefore, careful handling of the goods is necessary, which is not found in the local markets.

3. Lack of Specialised Services. As compared to the terminal markets the specialised services such as grading and standardisation, storage weighing etc. are present by their absence. The main reason being, the agencies dealing in this line are two men with little capital and with no specialised knowledge. As a result, the volume of business handled by these markets is quite small.

4. Imperfect Market. A market is considered as perfect, when there is a possibility of free-flow of goods from one area to another, free-flow of market information via transportation and communication system. It also calls for the existence of large number of buyers and sellers that leads to better competition. However, due to absence of the tenents of perfect competition, we may say that there is prevalence of monopolistic market *i.e.*, the market is less sensitive to the price changes.

Functions. The functipns are as:

1. Assembly of Products. The primary function of this market is to assemble the farm products at a single or a few points, so that, they can be transported economically from one point to other markets. The agencies operating in this market, collect the production in small lot from individual producers.

2. Providing Convenient Place. The local markets act as a convenient place for producers as well as buyers. Thus, it helps the producers and relives them of approaching the central markets and saving their time and money is also attained.

3. Provision of Facilities. Very few primary markets provide facilities of storing, packing etc. But however, these are not found in all the local markets.

4. Immediate Cash Release. In many cases the farmers have no patience to wait for the better prices. They want immediate cash which is being provided by dealers in the local market. Otherwise, the farmers are to go to the wholesale central markets and wait for the money. Thus, their immediate cash requirements are availed of by dealers in local markets.

Agencies in Local Markets

The following middlemen usually operate in local markets.

1. Local Resident Buyers. Local resident buyers are the persons with a fixed place of business in the local market. Their activities are limited to a single local market. Local resident buyers, are of three types *viz.*, stores, elevator companies and processing firms.

Retail stores purchase mainly for selling in the local market for consumers. They are the grocery stores that buy grains, fruits, vegetables, eggs etc. from the producers, and sell to the local consumers. 'Elevator' companies refer to the merchants whose main business is to buy and sell again. They buy from farmers in the region and sell to the wholesalers in the central market. They do undertake some marketing functions such as warehousing, grading and weighing etc.

"Processing, firm are established either in the local market, or nearer to the local market, to take advantage of the assembled raw materials, like fruits, vegetables, grains etc, *e.g.* flour mills, canning factories, meat packers etc.

2. Travelling Buyers. Travelling buyers go from one local market to another, for assembling the agricultural produce from the farmers. They establish their collection office at prominent places. They move from place to place in varying seasons. Thus they may buy the produce from growers directly or from the local resident buyers.

3. Auction Companies. These are the private firm acting on behalf of both the buyers and sellers. These auctions are in practice especially in case of fruits, tobacco, livestock and tea etc. They provide the services of storing and exhibiting the produce to be auctioned. The goods are sold to the highest bidder.

4. Co-operatives. Co-operative societies have also been playing a vivid and noteworthy role as the assembling units in the local market. They are discussed in detail, later.

The merits of auction lie in the large quantity of sales at the shortest possible period. The demerits are expensive selling and danger of price fluctuations.

CENTRAL MARKET

In the process of concentration, central market is the last link. These central markets are also termed as "terminal markets" where agricultural buyers are concentrated in larger volume from local markets. They are the last link in the process of concentration and first link in the process of dispersion. It is the confluence of the three processes of marketing *viz.*, concentration, dispersion and equalisation. The central markets are located in big, thickly populated cities like Mumbai, Bangalore, Chennai, Kolkata, Delhi, etc.

The growth of urbanisation, increasing demands of consumers for quality and quantity, scattered but specialised nature of agricultural production have led to the development of these markets.

Characteristics. The following are the charcteristics.

1. Competitive Price Fixation. Because of the free flow of Goods, information and existence of large number of buyers and sellers, the competitive price can be determined.

2. Handling of Large Volume of Business. The large number of facilities available in the central markets make it possible to handle to large volume of business. The fucilities as grading, transportation, information, packing, weighing, loading etc, are provided in the central markets which aid in boosting up the volume of trading.

3. Specialised Services. Since it is the confluence of the three-tier processes of concentration, dispersion and equalisation, it is but natural to have all the specialised markets. These markets are established in big cities where there is no dearth of specialised services as, quick and economical, transportation, scientific storage, specialized staff for grading and standardisation, banking etc.

Functions. The following functions can be deduced from the above discussion:

1. Assembling of Goods;
2. Release of the produce of secondary markets;
3. Financing and risk-bearing;
4. Warehousing and grading; and
5. Facilities for future trading.

AGENTS IN THE CENTRAL MARKETS

The functions of the central market are carried out by different types of middlemen with an assistance of the facilitating agencies.

1. Wholesale Receivers. They purchase goods on a large-scale either from farmers, direct or from the local market and assume themselves the title to goods.

2. Agent Middlemen. Commission agent, brokers, auctioneers etc. also operate in the central market. They get certain rate of commission on the business transacted by them. This is true especially in case of fresh fruits and vegetables, grains, livestock etc. He makes all the arrangements with regard to storage, grading etc., before they are sold. Then he searches out a buyer who pays the best price and sells the shipment for this he charges certain commission and deducts all his freight charges and expenses of Marketing etc. and settles his account with the dealer in the local market.

3. Public Elevators and Warehouses. These agencies survey certain services such as grading and standardisation storage etc., to these dealers in the central market and take advantage of centralised products, *i.e.* raw materials.

4. Commodity Exchanges. Commodity exchange is the heart of central market. It is an independent organisation of dealers in certain commodities. It does not make purchase and sales on its own. It provides a place where the goods can be brought and sold economically and without any discrepancies. The activities are being carried out under certain set rules and regulations and under the supervision of the authorities of the exchange.

5. Large Scale Processors. The firm operating on a large scale, and having their own plants of processing, scanning fruits and flour mills etc. do buy the commodities in the central market and take advantage of centralised products *i.e.* raw materials.

JOBBING MARKETS

Jobbing markets mainly acts as a link between the central market and retailers. Agricultural consumer goods are being brought and sold in the jobbing market. The persons operating are known as jobbers. These jobbers are the wholesaler operating in secondary dispersion market. The usual products sold are fresh fruits, vegetables, poultry and dairy products. These jobbers are intermediaries who buy from central market, in large quantities and sell in smaller lots to the retailers.

Characteristics. Following are the characteristics:

1. Dealing in Agricultural Consumer Goods. Jobbers are specialised in selling and assembling of agricultural consumer goods like fruits, vegetable, grains etc.

2. Minor Role in Price Fixation. These markets are acting as connecting link between central market and retailers. Hence, the function is more of dispersion than of equalisation. So the jobbing market has a little or no role to play in determining prices.

3. Providing Facilities to Retailers. These markets perform all such functions that smoothen the process of meeting immediate requirements of retailers such as packing, granting credit, financial aids, warehousing etc.

SECONDARY MARKETS

These are also termed as subterminal markets that act as connecting link between the individual buyers and the central market. Secondary markets are in no way different from the jobbing markets except that the former ones deal in agricultural raw material while the latter in the agricultural consumer goods. They supply raw materials to locate mills factories and processing firms. The agricultural raw materials in which they deal are wheat, cotton, jute, tobacco, fruits, groundnuts, coffee seed etc.

Thus, they specialise in the supply of raw material and provide the facilities of warehousing grading and sometimes financing also. The middlemen that operate in the secondary markets are the wholesalers.

CHANNELS FOR CONSUMER GOODS

The discussion of different markets was made with the objective of better understanding of the channels of distribution. The channels of distribution can be better appreciated if studied by bifurcating into two parts.

A Channels for agricultural consumer goods, and

B. Channels for agricultural raw materials.

A. Channels of Distribution for Agricultural Consumer Goods. From the discussion we had so far, it is clear that the channel of distribution for agricultural goods is more lengthy than that of the manufactured consumer goods. Normally they move from the producer to the resident buyers, cooperatives and auction companies in the local market to the wholesale receivers, and agent middlemen in the central market to the jobbers in the jobbing market and then to the retailers and consumers. However, the channels through which the agricultural consumer goods move are:

(i) Producer→Wholesalers→Retailers→Consumers

(ii) Producer→Retailers→Consumers

(iii) Producer→Consumers.

(i) Producer→Wholesalers→Retailers→Consumers. As we have observed earlier, the agricultural goods move generally through this channel. Majority of the goods are sold *via* this channel. In this channel, the products move from farmer to one of the wholesalers dealings in the local market, central market and jobbing market. Thus it is relieved by jobbers, from jobbers to retailers, who in turn sell to consumers. Sometimes the agent middlemen may also be employed. This again, adds to further cost of marketing. This is a common channel for the fresh fruits and vegetables.

(ii) Producer→Retailers→Consumers. Some agricultural consumer goods such as fruits, eggs, milk, butter and vegetables are being sold directly to retailers in jobbing market. Thus, the producers by pass the wholesalers in the central and local markets. The retailers directly enter the local market and buy from the farmers or producers and sell them to the consumers.

Certain merits accrue to the producers by selling through this channel; they are in a position to get higher price for their produce, The small producers can perform the function of grading and standardisation. But it is very difficult and cumbersome to assume such functions if the produce is large. It is possible to deal with large retailers like chain stores.

Similarly, the retailers also enjoy the advantages of sure supply, fresh stock, lower prices. At the same time, they are to face the problem of collecting the supplies from different producers located at great distance. Moreover, the retailer himself has to assume certain marketing functions like storage, grading and standardisation. Thus, this channel of distribution is not a practical possibility as the producers are widely scattered and as they produce in smaller quantity.

(iii) Producer→Consumers. Some agricultural consumer goods are also directly sold by the producers to consumers by eliminating both the wholesalers and retailers. A very small portion of the agricultural goods are sold through this channel. The products such as eggs, butter, milk, fruits, vegetables are being sold directly to the consumers, Following methods are used to sell directly.

1. **House to House Selling.** The products like milk, eggs are sold in this way. Hence delivery of the products is give. Again, the selling of fruits and vegetables by hawkers is an instance of house to house selling.

2. **Road Side Selling.** The farmers sell their products like fruits vegetables by the side of the road, where their farm is located. Here, the consumers came to the farm and make purchases. This is exactly opposite of house to house selling.

3. **Retail Public Market.** Retail Public Markets are the open markets where the buyers and sellers meet. The farmers carry the goods to the particular market places and sell the consumers who visit them with the purpose. In India, we call them as 'bazars' or 'hats'. In western countries, they are commonly called as 'farmers market' or 'farmers retail market'.

4. **Selling through Post.** In advanced countries, this method is followed. But this is of little importance for selling agricultural consumers goods, where there is no direct touch between the consumers and producers, contracts are being made by means of post. It is a very difficult way of selling, involves

heavy cost of packing, the problem of collection and keeping of accounts.

From the point of view of agricultural producers to get higher prices for their produce they may prefer to sell directly to the consumers. This is a practical and worthwhile proposition, if the farmers are in close proximity to the thickly populated areas. However, very negligible portion of the agricultural consumer goods are sold in this fashion. Therefore, they decide to sell directly either through the wholesalers or through the retailers. About 90 per cent of total agricultural produce moves through these two channels. On the other extreme, consumers are also not interested in buying directly as they believe and rely more on middlemen than on the producers. So all these factors make it almost impossible to sell directly to consumers except a few dairy and poultry products.

(B) Channels of Distribution for Agricultural Raw Materials. The agricultural raw materials pass through different channels as the consumer goods do. The only difference between the two is that there are no retailers in the picture, in the channel of raw materials. The raw materials such as jute, cotton, tobacco, sugarcane, groundnut, etc. are marketed through anyone or more of the following channels.

1. Producer → Local → Market → Central → Market → Secondary → Market → Industrial users.

2. Producer → Central Market → Secondary Market → Industrial users.

3. Producer → Secondary Market → Industrial users

4. Producer → Industrial users directly.

The bulk of the raw materials are sold through the middlemen in local market, central market or secondary market. However direct selling is an exception.

❐

14

Institutions and Organisations in Agriculture Marketing

Regional Rural Banks (RRBs) are the youngest members of the family of rural credit institutions set up in India. They have been set up specially to meet the credit requirements of the weaker sections of the rural society, whose problems came into sharp focus after the State Governments enacted legislation in the mid-seventies, for discharging the debts from the non-institutional sources, of marginal farmers and scaling down the debts of the small farmers etc. The legislation was enacted to response to the guidelines issued by the Central Government to implement one of the points of the Twenty Point Economic Programme, *viz.*, to liquidate rural indebtedness and pass legislation for a moratorium on recovery of debts from landless labourers, small farmers and rural artisans. Such legislation, it was apprehended, would create a vacuum in meeting both the production and consumption credit requirements of the weaker sections, as the traditional sources of credit were expected to dry up. It was in the context of these conditions that the Government of India thought it necessary to establish 'rural banks as subsidiaries of the public sector banks to cater to the credit needs of the rural people.'

Narasimhan Committee, "is an institution which combines the local feel and familiarity with rural problems which the co-operatives possess and the degree of business organisation, ability to mobilise deposits, access to central money markets and modernised outlook which the commercial banks have."

In sum the RRBs were set up as institutions which would help fill regional and functional credit gaps, help to develop the activities of the weaker sections have a local feel and familiarity with local problems and the better capacity to mobilise deposits and access to central money markets and modern outlook.

Co-operative Societies

Until 1968, it was the official policy to develop the co-operative system as the sole agency for meeting the agricultural and rural credit requirements. However, co-operatives had only 3.1 % share in 1951 which increased to 15.5% in 1961-62 and in 1968-69, the share of co-operatives was estimated to be 33%. Dr. B.P. Tyagi in his book writes that though many expert committees and economists have pointed out several defects in the working and organisation of co-operative credit. yet co-operative credit society has been considered the passing of the Co-operative Society Act, 1904 to the publication of the report of the All-India Rural Credit Review Committee in 1969, brought out the weaknesses of them existing institutions *viz.*, co-operative and commercial banks and recommended multi-agency approach. Other reports *viz.*, Report of the Committee on Rural Banks, New Delhi (1975), and Report of the Committee on Integration of Co-operative Credit Institutions, Bombay (1976) and revised the working of co-operative and bank.

Major weaknesses of the Co-operatives have been summarised below:

1. Co-operative credit societies have been successful in some area, but not so successful in some other areas, and have miserably failed in some other areas.
2. Larger credit was disbursed to the same members that major portion of loans went to larger cultivators and small cultivators did not get adequate credit. There were cases of credit transactions to rich farmers borrowing was on small farmers.
3. The benefit of credit did not go to non-cultivators and they depended on non-institutional credit agencies.

4. Most of the societies were financially and managerially weak and suffered from inadequate business and heavy overdues and had faulty and inefficient management.

Ravi Kishor pany wrote in his book three groups of weakness of co-operative society: *(i)* inadequate supply credit, *(ii)* improper distribution of credit, and *(iii)* regional variation.

Commercial Banks

The role of the commercial banks in rural/agricultural credit was negligible till the nationalisation of banks took place in 1969. In 1951-52, commercial banks finance to agriculture came to be 0.9 per cent, it was 2.2 per cent in March 1968. All-India Rural Credit Survey Committee, 1954 had concluded that there was no alternative to the co-operative from organisation. In 1965, the Informal Group on Institutional Arrangement for Agricultural Credit emphatically stressed that one cannot look to the commercial banks for providing a satisfactory system of supplementary and transitional basis for any large scheme for the cultivating population in Indian conditions, following finance by the commercial banks:

1. Urban-oriented historical origin of the commercial banks in India under the British rule with the limited objectives of catering to the need of trade, commerce and industry.

2. Absence of banks' enterprising attitude to finance agriculture, their unsuitable loan policy and procedures made the cultivators reluctant to borrow from the banks.

3. The risky nature of agricultural financing because of wide variations in income and the absence of suitable security, except land, which is subjected to various legal and other procedural complications.

4. The huge demand for bank credit of non-agricultural sector.

5. Ill-trained and inexperienced banking staff to deal with agricultural financing.

6. The poor recovery performance in co-operative credit structure.

Genesis of Regional Rural Banks (RRBs)

The setting of the RRBs in India during the year 1975, with an avowed object of financing the credit requirements exclusively of the poorer sections in countryside, represents a novel experiment of the India banking laboratory. The foundation of the institutional credit structure in rural India was laid with the organisation of co-operative credit societies at the beginning of this century.

The credit of the agricultural sector, however, increased rapidly over the years and the co-operative credit structure, which was unevenly developed in different parts of the country could not keep pace with the growing demand for institutional credit. Commercial banks were, therefore, induced into the field of agricultural credit under the policy of 'social control' over the banks in 1968 and the subsequent nationalization of 14 major commercial banks in 1969 carried the process further.

Rural branches of commercial banks expanded very sharply in the period following nationalisation. But these branches rarely went beyond district or sub-divisional towns. The failure of modern banking to penetrate rural India remained a persistent problem. There were many initial uncertainties about the right lines of development. It was in such conditions that Banking Commission (1972) recommended the establishment of a chain of 'Rural Banks' in addition to rural branches of commercial banks.

Such rural banks, in view of the Commission, could come into existence in three ways:

1. Conversion of primary co-operative societies into institutions offering full banking facilities;

2. Establishing subsidiaries of commercial banks; and

3. Establishing a special type of rural banks sponsored by commercial banks and supported by local participation.

In a large country with complex regional difference, no single type would offer a complete solution and the commission, therefore, recommended a multi-pronged programme of banking development for rural area, comprising co-operative societies, rural branches of commercial banks and sponsored rural banks. The case for the last of the three stood firmly on the realisation that co-operative credit would not succeed everywhere and that expansion of branches of commercial banks in the rural areas would not go for enough.

It took the government three years to decide that a scheme of special rural banks would be necessary, but once the decision was taken, things moved quickly.

The Narsimham study group was appointed on July 1, 1975 by the Government of India. The group bad been asked to examine in depth the setting up of new rural banks as subsidiaries of public sector banks to cater to the credit needs of the rural people.

"In an unusually quick report which the group submitted on July 30, 1975, it observed". In a country of the size and regional diversity as ours, no single pattern, be it commercial banks or co-operative credit can be expected to meet all the emerging requirements in all areas. A degree of adoptation and improvization is called for and the range of institutional alternative widened. It is in this context that we have come to the conclusion that, a new type of institution is necessary. The group could not be quite sure about the optimum size of the operations, coverage etc., and hence, it favoured a cautious approach by recommending the setting up of five rural banks as pilot institutions in selected areas.

Some feeble and multi-opposition notwithstanding the government accepted to recommendation of the group. An ordinance was promulgated on September 26, 1975, which was subsequently replaced by RRBs Act of 1976. According to this Act, the RRBs were to be set up with a view to developing the rural economy by providing for the purpose of development of agriculture, trade, commerce, industry and other activities in the rural areas, credit and other facilities, particularly to the small and marginal farmers, agricultural labourers, artisans and small entrepreneurs and for matter connected therewith and incidental thereto.

The first five RRBs were established on October 2, 1975. By the end of 1976,40 RRBs had been set up. In 1978, the government set up a Review Committee on RRBs headed by Prof. M. L. Dantwala. The Committee considered that the performance of the RRBs was good and that the financial results of the working of some of these banks showed that RRBs had the potential and capability to attain financial viability and become a profit-making institution in about 3 to 4 years. The Committee recommended that steps should be taken to initiate the process of making the RRB an integral part of the rural credit structure. The Reserve Bank of India (RBI) also made a study on viability of RRBs in 1980, and concluded that on an average, a RRB would require about 6 years time and a network of 70 branches to become viable. These studies gave the necessary impetus to the process of establishing and expanding RRBs all over country.

During the period of nearly 19 years, the total number of RRBs operating allover India has reached 196, covered 392 districts in 23 States with 15,400 branches.

Definition of Rural Banks

Rural banks make a new development in the rural credit system tailored to the needs of the rural people. "A rural bank may be said as primary banking institution set up to serve a compact group of villages generally working as a co-operative or as a subsidiary bank of a commercial bank functioning or set up in a rural area for the purpose of providing banking and credit facilities in that area."

The main purpose of the rural bank is to provide banking and credit facilities to the rural people. The RRBs have been conceived as:

(a) an answer to meet the diverse and heterogeneous needs of rural people with different socio-economic and agro-geographical conditions.

(b) diverted to specific economic and occupational groups, *i.e.*, the small and marginal farmers, agriculture labour, artisans, etc.; and

(c) to be catalytic agent to develop the rural economy by providing not only credit, but other facilities. They are supposed to be a nucleus of rural development programme in view of their relatively low cost structure, local ethos and professional management. They are government owned regionally based and rurally oriented banks to supplement the existing institutional credit agencies and not to support them in order to fill up the regional and functional gaps in the rural credit institutional system.

Objectives of RRBs

The RRBs Act has made various provisions regarding the incorporation, regulation and working of the RRBs. According to this Act, the RRBs are to be set up mainly "with a view to developing the rural economy by providing, for the purpose of development of agriculture, trade, commerce, industry and other productive activities in the rural areas, credit and other facilities, particularly to the small and marginal farmers, agriculture labourers, artisans and small entrepreneurs, and for matter connected therewith and incidental thereto."

Thus the main objective of setting up of the RRBs is to help or assist the potential rural development of agriculture and economy of the area through providing credit and other facilities to the needful people to the rural area well in time and on reasonable terms, so that they may start some viable production activity. The RRBs had been conceived as an institution and a catalytic agent for ensuring the development of rural economy by providing not only credit, but also other required facilities as an answer to meet, the diverse and heterogeneous needs of the rural folk with different socio-economic and agro-geographical conditions.

In order to achieve the aforesaid main objectives, the following operational objectives have been conceived:

1. To provide a specialized agency which would concentrate its efforts entirely on the extension of credit facilities to small farmers and other small borrowers in the rural area at a relatively very low cost.

2. To provide employment to the rural educated youth who are properly oriented to look after the needs of the rural community. This type of arrangement alone can ensure a low costprofile envisaged for these rural banks and also achieve a reasonable level of productivity through relatively more motivated rural youth. These banks will provide job opportunities also by financing subsidiary occupations, reviving rural vocations and life.

3. To gradually replace the usurous moneylender in one very significant objective of channelling credit through the RRBs and to reduce the dependence on village moneylenders.

4. Bridging the credit gaps in rural areas.

5. To remove the curse of poverty in rural areas. The percentage of population below the poverty line in the rural areas is 51. The RRBs are meant to provide finance to this extremely vulnerable section of the rural society to mitigate poverty through generation to surplus income and through better planned productive activities.

6. To mobilise rural savings. The Objective of rural banking policy is mainly to evolve an institutional arrangement to mobilise the saving of the people even in small amounts and thus to inclucate in them the habit of thrift and to replace the moneylender. It is conceived that the RRBs would, in view of their special character and composition, fulfil the aforesaid objective.

7. To improve standard of living. The RRBs were considered to be a suitable institution to provide needed credit at their door-step on reasonable terms and conditions so that the

weaker sections of people in rural areas could raise their total productivity and through it their standard of living.

8. To create a centre for an overall economic and social change. It is hoped that the RRBs would find their role more rewarding by integrating and co-ordinating their credit activity with the need for economic and social rural development.

Functions of RRBs

The main function of the RRBs is to provide credit and banking facility to the rural people. It also provides some non-banking facilities to the rural population such as constructing and maintaining godowns on their own, supplying agricultural inputs and acquiring of agricultural and other equipments for leasing it out, providing assistance in the marketing of agricultural and other products.

RRBs' functions may be listed as follows:

1. To mobilise local savings by means of the various types of deposits.
2. To provide short-term and medium-term credit for agriculture and other purposes to rural producers and long-term loans to agriculturists as agent of the land development bank.
3. To implement programmes of the supervised credit tailored to the needs of individual farms.
4. To provide various ancilliary banking services to local people such as remittance of funds, acceptance of insurance premium, safe deposit lockers etc.
5. To set up and maintain godown.
6. To undertake supply of inputs and agricultural and retail equipment to farmers as agent and in appropriate cases equipment leasing.

7. To provide assistance in the marking of agricultural and other products through marketing organisation.
8. Generally help in the overall development of the villages in its area.

RRBs and Co-operative Banks

RRBs have been established with an aim to supplement the resources of co-operative banks, but not to compete with them. However, RRBs do not enjoy facilities like automatic registration of lands and buildings, exemption from stamp duty, realisation of debts through arrears of land revenue etc., which a co-operative bank enjoy.

Difference between RRBs and Commercial Banks

The RRBs are basically scheduled commercial banks, but are different from the existing commercial banks in the following respects:

1. Status. All the RRBs are scheduled banks. Scheduled status is given to them automatically, whereas for commercial banks in order to get this status, the banks should satisfy the norms, *viz.*, *(i)* paid-up capital should not be less than Rs. 5 lakhs, and *(ii)* affairs of the bank should be conducted properly to the satisfaction of the RBI and in accordance with its norms.

2. Act Applicable. All the RRBs are governed by the RRBs Act 1976, and the NABARD Act/RBI Act, whereas the commercial banks are governed by the Banking Regulation Act, 1949, and the RBI Act, 1934.

3. Ratio Requirements. The RRBs are required to maintain 3 per cent of the total demand and time liabilities as a cash reserve ratio (CRR), whereas the same of the commercial bank is 9 to 10 per cent of the increase in deposits over 11.1 per cent in 1983. The Statutory liquidity Ratio (SLR) requirements too differ for both the banks. While the RRBs are required to have 25 per cent as SLR, the same for the conunercial banks is 37 per cent. This means that the RRBs have more loanable fund than the commercial banks.

4. Area of Operation. The area of operation in the case of an RRB is restricted to specified area comprising one or more districts in a State. The RRB s are considered as the most suitable institutions to take banking closer to the rural household. Preference is given to them in the issue of licenses for opening of branches in rural area. The main objective of the RRBs branch expansion programme is to open bank offices in unbanked areas of the villages for rural development. For this areas chosen are relatively backward or tribal areas or the areas where the coverage of commercial banks or co-operatives is poor, but which have a real potential for development breakthrough with the flow of credit. In the case of commercial banks, though thrust is given for expansion of banking in unbanked areas, yet they are also opened in semi-urban and urban places. commercial banks desirous of opening branches in rural areas should seek "no objection" consent from the RRB opening in that area.

5. Functions. Though there is no restriction on the RRBs to undertake any type of banking business, yet they have been asked to provide rural finance particularly to small farmers, marginal farmers, agricultural labourers and rural artisans, small entrepreneurs and persons of small means engaged in trade and other productive activities in the area of their operation. It means that the beneficiaries of the loans and advances of the RRBs have been pre-determined.

6. Loans and Advances. All the loans and advances granted by the RRBs fall under priority sectors, *viz.*, agriculture, small industries, small business and self-employed persons, while the commercial banks are required to advance 33 1/3 per cent of the total loans and advances to the priority sector and this was required upto 40 per cent by 1985.

7. Lending Rates. Lending rates of the RRBs are not higher than the prevailing lending rates of the co-operative societies in the concerned State. The lending rates of commercial banks are comparatively higher than the rates of the co-operatives in certain areas.

Lending under the Differential Rate of Interest (DRI) scheme at 4 per cent to weaker sections of society is not obligatory for them, while for commercial banks, it is necessary to lend 1 percent of the total outstanding advances under the DRI scheme.

8. Staffing. The RRBs follow a simple staffing pattern in comparison with the commercial banks. By recruiting people from the area of operation of the RRBs local feel and familiarity touch towards rural clientele is ensured. The problem of rural clientele are well-understood by the RRB staff in view of their rural orientation. The commercial banks recruit their staff on an all-India basis and their employees lack rural orientation.

9. Salary. The RRBs are expected to work at a low cost so that the salary structure is lower than that of commercial banks employees and at par with the employees of the State Government concerned. The salary structure of the employees of the RRBs is prescribed by the Central Government in accordance with the salary structure of the employees of the State Government and local authorities of comparable level and status in the area of their operation. In the case of the commercial banks, the salaries and allowances are decided as per the bipartite settlement.

10. Taxation. With regard to payment of corporate tax an interest earning, and other earnings, the RRBs are exempted from such liability. It is not so in the case of commercial banks.

11. Inspection and Guarantee Scheme. Statutory inspection of RRBs as per the Banking Regulation Act is undertaken by the NABARD and in the case of commercial banks the same is performed by the RBI. The fee for getting guarantee from Deposit Insurance and Credit Guarantee Corporation of India (DICGCI) on all eligible advances is at 0.25 per cent per annum. This concession is available for 5 years from 1979 or the date of entering into the agreement. No such concession is available to commercial banks. For commercial banks the advances guarantee fee is recoverable as follows:

Upto Rs. 25,000	0.50 per cent p.a., and
Above Rs. 25,000	0.75 per cent p.a.

12. Refinance. Refinance facilities are available to the RRBs on easy terms from the NABARD, sponsoring banks and the IDBI. Even short-term loans are also refinanced. But there is no scheme where short-term loans provided by commercial banks are refinanced.

The RRBs would be provided refinance at 2 per cent below the bank rate, while in the case of commercial banks it is provided at the bank rate, *i.e.*, at 10 per cent per annum at present. The RRBs have also, like the commercial banks, been made eligible for accommodation against a more declaration of the eligible loans and advances by them pending the scrutiny of the applications by the RRBs for regular limits.

Each RRB has been sanctioned an ad-hoc limit for Rs. 10 lakhs for refinance which will later on be subjected to regular conditions of the refinance scheme.

The Government of India has permited the RRBs to lend Rs. 100 for every Rs.15 of their own lendable resources, the rest being contributed by refinancing from the Government of India to the extend of Rs. 50 and from the sponsoring bank to the tune of Rs. 35. It means that the RRBs are permitted to lend Rs. 1 crore for every Rs. 15 lakhs of their own deposits.

RRBs and NABARD

National Bank has the responsibility to lay down policies for RRBs to over see their operations, provide refinance facilities and attend to problem faced by them. The National Bank has undertaken work relating, to the establishment of RRBs, administration of refinance scheme, formulation of appropriate operational policies, monitoring their performance, and keeping liaison with the RBI in regard to branch expansion and the statutory inspection of RRBs.

STATE AGRICULTURAL MARKETING BOARDS

The necessity of a central organisation to supervise and provide guidance to market committees as realised with the establishment of a network of market committees. Agricultural Produce Market Acts were modified to make the provisions for the establishment of State Agricultural Marketing Boards, which were established in 16 States and 2 Union Territories *viz.* Rajasthan, Punjab, Haryana, Uttar Pradesh, Madhya Pradesh, Karnataka, Assam, Gujarat, Himachal Pradesh, Andhra Pradesh, West Bengal, Maharashtra, Orissa, Tamil Nadu, Bihar, Delhi and Chandigarh. There is a variation in the organisation, functions and composition of the Board from state to state. Rajasthan is solitary example, where an economist has been included amongst the members of the Board. The chairmanship of the Board also differs from State to State. In Rajasthan, the Rajasthan Agricultural Produce Markets Act, 1961, was amended in 1973 to provide for the establishment of an apex body of market committees at the State level. Accordingly, the Rajasthan State Agricultural Marketing Board was established on 17th June, 1974, with its headquarters at Jaipur. The Board is an executive-cum-advisory scheme. It also supervises the functioning of regulated markets and advises market committees and the State Government on related matters. The Board consists of the following members.

(a) Then members elected by the chairmen of the market committees in the State from amongst themselves;

(b) Two traders elected by the trader-members of the market committees in the State of Rajasthan;

(c) Ten official members from the State representing the Secretary to the Government in the Department of Agriculture and Animal Husbandry, the Registrar, Co-operative Societies, the Director, Sheep and Wool, one Economist, the Regional Manager, Food Corporation of India, The Managing Director, State Warehousing Corporation, and one officer of the Agriculture Department;

(d) Two non-official members of the public nominated by the government.

The members, who are elected or nominated, hold office for a period of three years. The Chairman of the Board is appointed by the government from amongst its members, and is the chief controlling and supervising officer of the Board. There is a fund called the Market Development Fund, which is administered by the Board. All the receipts of the Board (contributions received from market committees, loans, grants etc.) are created and all the expenditure (on improvements and on the regulation of rural markets in the State, giving aid to financially weak market committee, paying salary and allowances to its employees, meeting legal expenses and the construction cost of the office and various infrastructures), incurred by the Board is debited to the Market Development Fund. The main functions of the Board, are:

(i) To carry out the training of officers and staff, create facilities for grading and standardisation, construct market roads and approach roads to the markets, construct market yard and sub-yards, establish and maintain the Board office and others as specified;

(ii) To frame bye-laws, help in the functioning on market committees, and supervise their operations;

(iii) The administrative structure of the Board consists of the following wings, each entrusted with a particular function:

(i) Administrative Wing; *(ii)* Accounts Wing; *(iii)* Technical (Engineering) Cell; *(iv)* Town Planning (Architect) Wing; *(v)* Supervisory Wing.

(iv) To tender advice to the government on the functioning of market committee and on improvements in rural marketing as and when referred to.

COUNCIL OF STATE AGRICULTURAL MARKETING BOARDS (COSAMB)

The COSAMB, an apex body of the State Marketing Boards was established in February, 1988. The need for such a body was felt to coordinate the activities of State Marketing Boards, specially those connected with credit mobilisation, central assistance for market development and some common problems. The COSAMB has made a great headway in achieving the objectives for which it was incorporated. Under one umbrella of COSAMB, the State Agricultural Marketing Boards have augmented their activities in achieving the objectives. The COSAMB has been established with a view to:

(i) setting up a common forum of national stature to build a think tank and to share the know-how and experience in the cause of strong and efficient rural marketing in the country;

(ii) providing assistance to the member states and to credit institutions to fix norms for arranging credit from the bank and mobilising central assistance for development;

(iii) undertaking and assisting professional, technical, management and infrastructural consultancy services in the working of rural marketing;

(iv) seeking representation of COSAMB in various committees of the central and state governments;

(v) assisting and advising the Central Government and the State Governments or members in setting up training centres;

(vi) setting up a common organisation to hold seminars, workshops; exhibitions and to educate and inspire various functionaries in achieving a sound system of rural marketing;

(vii) creating a national non-political autonomous body to pursue policies and issues at the national level;

(viii) setting common libraries and build a stock of literature; and

(ix) establishing contacts with other institutions and organisations in the country and abroad for the latest developments in the field of rural marketing and to build a data bank.

THE NATIONAL AGRICULTURAL CO-OPERATIVE MARKETING FEDERATION (NAFED)

At the national level, the National Agricultural Co-operative Marketing Federation (NAFED) was established in October 1958. The State Level Marketing Federations and the National Co-operative Development Corporation are its members. The head office of NAFED is at Delhi, and its branch offices are located at Bombay, Calcutta and Madras. NAFED's area of operation extends to the whole country. It has established branches in all the major port towns and capital cities in the country.

OBJECTIVES OF NAFED

The main objectives of NAFED are:

(a) To co-ordinate and promote the marketing and trading activities of its affiliated co-operative institutions;

(b) To act as an agent of the government for the purchase, sale, storage and distribution of rural products and inputs;

(c) To make arrangements for the supply of the rural, inputs required by member institutions; and

(d) To promote inter-State and international trade in rural and other commodities.

FUNCTIONS OF NAFED

(a) Foreign Trade. Export and Import of Agricultural Commodities:

Exports. Exports of rural commodities through the cooperative marketing system developed on a large scale after the establishment of NAFED, NAFED exports rural commodities, particularly onions (canalised), potatoes, ginger, garlic, nigerseed, seasame seed, gum, deoiled cake of groundnut, soya bean and cottonseed, fresh and processed fruits and vegetables; spices-black pepper, cardamom, turmeric, cuminseed, coriander seed; cereals-rice, barley, bajra, jowar, and ragi and jute bags to various countries including Sri

Lanka, England, Mauritius, Australia, Belgium, Canada, Fiji, Hongkong, Japa , Malaysia, the USA and number of African, West Asian and Gulf Countures.

Imports. NAFED arranged for the imports of pulses, fresh fruits, dry fruits nutmeg (jaiphal), mace (javitri), wetdates and chicory seed and inputs particularly fertilisers and machinery as and when asked to do so by the Government.

(b) Price Support Operations. NAFED is being appointed as the agency of the government to undertake support price purchases of commodities like groundnut since 1976-77, soyabean and mustard seed since 1977-78, gram, tur, moong and urad since 1978-79 and bajra, jowar, maize, barley, toria and sunflower seed since 1985-86. Government of India have designated NAFED as the nodal agency for implementing the price support policy for oilseeds and coarse grains during Seventh Five Year Plan period (1985-90), NAFED has standing instructions to intervene in the market when ruling market price falls below the minimum support levels for oilseeds and pulse crops.

(c) Internal Trade. NAFED is engaged in inter-state trade in rural commodities, particularly foodgrains, pulses, oilseeds, cotton, jute, spices, fruits, vegetables and eggs with a view to assuring better prices to the producers. The objectives of internal trade operations are both the market support to producers and maintaining steady supply of commodities to consumers at reasonable prices. NAFED purchases rural commodities through the co-operatives, public sector organisations and state agencies.

(d) Developing Cooperative Marketing of Tribal Produce. A separate cell to develop the marketing of produce of the tribal areas (minor forest products) having economic value has been set up with the assistance of NAFED. NAFED arranges market intelligence, established better system for auction of tribal produce and develops markets for other commodities like chilgoza, gum, karya etc.

(d) Setting of Scientific Storage System. NAFED has set up a cold storage alongwith an ice factory and a warehouse in Delhi.

NAFED has also made pioneering effort in finding ways of developing modern storages. It has set up an onion warehousing complex at Nagapattanam.

(f) Promotional Activities. NAFED maintains expert staff which conducts market studies, collects data and circulates the results among the members. Other promotional activities of NAFED are intensive development of selected marketing societies as pilot centres for cooperative marketing of rural produce in each state; improvement in market intelligence services for cooperative marketing societies; conduct of market surveys; training of market personnel; promotion of market regulations and development of infrastructures.

(g) Processing of Fruits and Vegetables. NAFED has set up a multicommodity fruit and vegetables processing unit at Delhi and at Vellore (Tamil Nadu). The basic purpose is to develop the processing industry in cooperative sector in a major way so as to make fruits and vegetable marketing and processing to the advantage of the producers.

❐

15

Nature and Scope of Co-operative Marketing

A co-operative sales association is a voluntary business organisation established by its member patrons to market farm products collectively for their direct benefit. It is governed by democratic principles and savings are apportioned to the members on the basis of their patronage. The members are the owners, operators and contributors of the commodities and are the direct beneficiaries of the savings that accrue to the society. No intermediary stands to profit or loss at the expenses of the other members. Co-operative marketing organisations are association of producers for the collective marketing of their produce and of securing for the members the advantages that result from large-scale business which an individual cultivator cannot secure because of his small marketable surplus. In a co-operative marketing society, the control of the organisation is in the hands of the producers and each member has one vote irrespective of the number of shares purchased by him. The profit earned by the society is distributed among the members on the basis of the quantity of the produce marketed by him. In other words, co-operative marketing societies are established for the purpose of collectively marketing the products of the member producers. It emphasises the concept of commercialisation. Its, economic motives and character distinguish it from other associations. These societies resemble private business organisation in the method of their operations; but they differ from the capitalistic system chiefly in their motives and organisations.

History of the Co-operative Marketing. The Royal Commission of Agriculture (1928) stressed the need for group marketing instead of individual marketing. The Central Banking Enquiry Committee (1931) also underlined the need for organised marketing. The XI Conference of Registrars of Cooperative Societies (1934) emphasised the importance of Cooperative marketing. In 1945, the Cooperative Planning Committee recommended that at least 25 per cent of the marketable surplus should be channellised through Cooperative Societies within the next 10 years by forming one society for a group of 200 villages. The All India Rural Credit Survey Committee (1954) brought to light the dismal performance of the existing marketing cooperatives. In a sample of 75 districts surveyed, there was no cooperative marketing society in 63 districts. In remaining districts only around one per cent of the total sale of rural produce was done through the societies. The committee suggested the establishment of primary cooperative marketing societies and linking of credit with marketing. The First Five Year Plan (1951-56) laid stress on the establishment of rural marketing and processing cooperative societies. In 1958, the National Agricultural Cooperative Marketing Federation (NAFED) was established as the apex body of cooperative marketing. In 1963, the National Cooperative Development Corporation (NDC) was set up for promoting programmes relating to processing storage and marketing of rural produce through cooperative markets.

The Mirdha Committee (1965) recommended that the membership of Agriculture marketing societies should be restricted to the agriculturists and traders should not be allowed to join agricultural marketing societies. The Dantwala Committee (1966) stressed the need for cooperation and integration among the various cooperative organisations after reviewing the pattern of cooperative marketing, distribution of inputs to producers and supply of consumer products. Based on the survey of the co-operative marketing societies in 1968, the Reserve Bank of India recognised that effective linking of credit with marketing was necessary. The All India Rural Credit Review Committee, 1969 also recommended the strengthening of cooperative marketing, with a view to helping the government agencies in the execution of price support programmes and thus fulfilling the interests of the producers.

On the basis of the commodities dealt in by them, the cooperative marketing societies may be grouped into the following types:

(i) Multi-commodity Co-operative Marketing Societies. They market a large number of commodities produced by the members, such as foodgrains, oilseeds and cotton.

(ii) Single Commodity Co-operative Marketing Societies. They deal in the marketing of only one rural commodity. They get sufficient business from the farmers producing that single commodity. The examples are Sugarcane Co-operative Marketing Society and the Cotton Co-operative Marketing Society.

(iii) Multi-purpose, Multi-commodity Co-operative Marketing Societies. These societies market a large number of commodities and perform such other functions as providing credit to members, arranging for the supply of the inputs required by them, and meeting their requirements of essential domestic consumptions goods.

STRUCTURE OF COOPERATIVE MARKETING

The co-operative marketing presents a pyramid structure. At the primary level, Primary Marketing Societies are operated at the intermediate level Central Cooperative Marketing Societies are functioning and at the top level State Marketing Societies are working. The co-operative marketing societies have both two and three-tier structure. In the states of Assam, Bihar, Kerala, Madhya Pradesh, Karnataka, Orissa, Rajasthan and West Bengal, there is a two-tier pattern with primary marketing societies at the taluka level and state marketing federation as apex body at the state level. In other states, there is three-tier system with district marketing society in the middle. At the national level, NAFED serves as the apex institution. The pattern of the three-tier structure has been discussed in the paragraphs that follow:

1. Primary Co-operative. At the base level there are primary cooperative marketing societies. These societies market the produce of the producer members in that area. They may be single commodity or multicommodity societies depending upon the production of the rural products in the area. Primary marketing co-operatives are those which are operating in the small and limited area, may be either a taluka or a block. The members are the producers engaged in production of rural produce. These co-operatives will either buying from members or acting as agents for the grower producers to sell, on behalf of them. They sell the members' produce directly to consumers or industrial users. They make advances of loans to the members on the security of their produce. They also provide for manures, fertilisers, equipment etc.

2. Central or District Level Co-operative Societies. After the primary co-operative societies operating at block level, there are cooperative marketing societies covering a larger area or a district. These district level co-operative societies are called federations or marketing unions. These are engaged in the task of buying selling and extending credit facilities to primary cooperative societies. Their main job is to market the produce brought for sale by the primary co-operative marketing societies of the area. These are located in the secondary wholesale markets and generally offer a better price for the produce. The primary cooperative marketing societies are members of these unions in addition to the individual producer members. In the two-tier structure, the state societies perform the functions of district level societies by opening branches throughout the district.

3. State Marketing Societies. At the State level there are apex body that is State Co-operative marketing societies which serve the state as a whole. Their members both the primary co-operative societies and the Central Cooperative Union of the State. They are above the level of central co-operative marketing societies which is grown as a provincial society. The basic function of these is to co-ordinate the activities of the affiliated societies and conduct such activities as inter-State trade, export-import, procurement, distribution of inputs and essential consumer goods, dissemination of market information and rendering expert advice on the marketing of rural produce. They undertake the task of granting credit that facilitates needy and deserving co-operatives, whether primary or central.

Further, membership is extended to individuals of repute. These societies are to act as the lenders of last resort. In addition, the State Marketing Co-operative Society is expected to co-ordinate the activities of different societies at the primary level and bring about, overall sound development of co-operative structure. It is at commanding height to watch the activities of primary and central co-operatives.

In fine, we conclude, that unfortunately, the pyramid structure is neither well knit nor well developed because all co-operatives are not co-operating with one another. This is the sorry state of affairs, as there prevails 'step mother policy' in business relations which is acting as the strong impediment for the success of co-operative societies. At present, the co-operative marketing is having 30 state level co-operative societies, 180 District level societies and 2900 primary co-operative societies and 3490 Special Commodities Societies.

FUNCTIONS OF CO-OPERATIVE MARKETING

The main functions of co-operative marketing societies are:

1. To arrange for the export of the produce of the members so that they may get better returns.
2. To make arrangements for the transport of the produce of the members from the villages to the market on collective basis and bring about a reduction in the cost of transportation;
3. To market the produce of the members of the society at fair prices;
4. To arrange for the supply of the inputs required by the producers, such as improved seeds, fertilisers, insecticides and pesticides.
5. To safeguard the members from excessive marketing costs and malpractices;
6. To make credit facilities available to the members against the security of the produce brought for sale;

7. To provide the facilities of grading and market information which may help them to get a good price for their produce;
8. To act as an agent of the government for the procurement of foodgrains and for the implementation of the price support policy.
9. To introduce the system of pooling so as to acquire a better bargaining power than the individual members having a small quantity of produce for marketing purposes;
10. To make arrangements for the scientific storage of the members produce;

CO-OPERATIVE MARKETING SOCIETIES

Co-operative marketing is the co-operative venture or an association designed to perform one or more marketing functions, relating to the rural produce of its members. In a broad sense, co-operative marketing implies both buying and selling of rural produce. To be more appropriate, co-operative marketing confines itself with the selling functions related with marketing of produce, such as, acting as selling agent, supply of market information, standardisation, storage, assembling, processing, packing etc. There is only one main objective of co-operative marketing and that is, to maximize the income of members of the extent possible and feasible. To fulfil this objective, co-operative marketing has provided two sets of factors *viz.* to get higher prices for the produce of its members and to cover the cost of marketing. These can be achieved with the development of orderly marketing, better selling methods, improving the quality of the produce through standardisation and grading, eliminating the trade abuses and improved bargaining position of member-sellers; costs can be reduced by adopting improved methods of marketing.

NEED OR OBJECTIVES OF CO-OPERATIVE MARKETING

1. To Eliminate Malpractices. Different malpractices prevailing in the system of Rural marketing, and such as arbitrary deductions from the price manipulation of weights and measures, collusion between brokers and the business buyers, are of special mention. These malpractices were regarded as nothing less than scientific theft by Royal Commission. The impact of these was further aggravation by critical financial position where producers are indebted to traders or money-lenders. In such a situation, co-operative marketing can help the producers to reduce, if not to eradicate malpractices to a greater extent.

2. To Establish Appropriate Reward for the Efforts. There exists a large army of middlemen participating, with deep interest in collection, storage, financing insuring grading, scale and transportation of rural produce. One must appreciate their services that are vital victorious marketing. However, their charges for such services are not proportionate and hence not appropriate. In some case, such charges are not only prohibitive but exorbitation. As a result poor producers do not get their due share in the price paid by the ultimate users. Co-operative marketing, if efficiently and honestly organised, will be able to reduce the 'price spread' between the producer and the consumers, thereby giving fair return to the producers, without affecting the interests of the consumers.

3. Concomitant of Integrated Programme. Co-operative marketing has developed as concomitant of large scale expansion of co-operative credit. Co-operative marketing societies will be acting as the agents to collect or to recover the loans advanced by co-operative credit societies. Therefore, the successful working of credit co-operatives, depends largely, on the development of marketing societies. That is, only co-operative marketing societies constitute a vital feature for integrated programme of co-operative development, envisaged in this country. .

4. To Stabilise the Agricultural Price. If the market mechanism is completely left to the sweet will and caprice of the private intermediaries, one can hardly expect price stabilisation, which is essential ingredient of a balanced economic development. So longers private sector dominates; "profit motive" will have upper hand, where normal market conditions deviate from healthy practices to the unwanted practices of speculation; hoarding will be resorted to, resulting in price manipulation and reflection of undesirable price fluctuations.

Outstanding Features of Co-operative Marketing Societies. The marketing co-operatives have certain special features of their own, which distinguish them from other concerns engaged in the marketing of the rural produce. These co-operative marketing societies are formed, with a view to assist their members to maximise their income. Following are the outstanding features of co-operative marketlng societies.

1. Membership. (i) Ordinary Members. Individual farmers, co-operative farming societies and service societies of the area may become the ordinary members of the co-operative marketing society. They have the right to participate the deliberations of the society, share in the profits and participate in the decision making process.

(ii) Nominal Members. Traders with whom the society establishes dealings are enrolled as nominal members. Nominal members do not have the right to participate in decision making and share in the profits.

2. Sources of Finance. In 1966, the Dantwala estimated a capital base of Rs. 2.00 lakhs for a co-operative marketing society. At 1991 prices, it should be at least Rs. 14,000 lakhs. The following are the major sources of finance of a co-operative marketing society.

(i) **Share Capital.** Farmer-members and the State Government subscribe to the share capital of co-operative marketing societies. Members may purchase as many shares as they like. They are encouraged to invest sufficiently in the share capital. They are also persuaded to invest their dividend and bonus in the shares of co-operative marketing societies.

(ii) **Loans.** Co-operative marketing societies may raise their finance by way of loans from the Central and State Co-operative Banks and from commercial banks by pledging and hypothecation and also by clean credit to the extent of 50 per cent of onward capital.

(iii) Subsidy. The co-operative marketing societies get a subsidy from the government for the purchase of grading machines and transport vehicles to meet their initial heavy expenditure. They also get a subsidy for a part of the cost of the managerial staff for a period of 3 years to make them viable.

3. Service Motto. The co-operative societies are formed, mainly for the purpose of providing and extending various services, to the members and not to earn maximum profits. The service facilities, like providing seeds, manures and fertiliser, grading and standardization, selling the members' produce at prices that are favourable. Therefore the co-operative marketing societies are organised for the purpose of providing services and not for making profits, solely.

4. One Man One Vote. Irrespective of the shares held by the members of the co-operative societies, each member has a right to vote as a single unit of a 'single'vote so one man one vote is the principle of co-operative marketing societies. This is based on the democratic principles and freedom. Nobody is to become the thumb rule of few people as is in the case of joint stock companies where the right to vote given to the members in proportionate to the number of shares held by them. It is free from the practices of discrimination among the members of the co-operative marketing societies.

5. Open Membership. In co-operative marketing societies to become a member is open for all. Any person can become a member of the society provided he is a producer of the rural product. Any time he can enter or exit the membership as per his desires and convenience. Moreover, the procedure to become a member is very simple, free from the complications and formalities.

6. Reasonable Reward to Capital. The practices of tlle co-operative marketing societies are very genuine and based on the principle of equality and fraternity. The capital invested by the members and paid at the rate of 6% or the loans and advances enjoyed by the members are also charged with the same rate of interest. This is so because of the capital is degraded and hence the human race is elevated. The capital investment is not rewarded properly and the return in the form of interest is given at the rates mentioned above. This makes the profitability of the marketing societies a limited one.

7. Teaching the Principle of Co-operation. The basic principles of co-operative movements are "One for all and all for one" "self help, through mutual help". The existence of co-operative marketing societies is based on these principles. It creates the sense of co-operation, ferternitism and mutual, help. These things are helpful in better marketing, better business, better living, and better citizenship of the societies. All this education is imparted through co-operative marketing societies.

8. Self Government. The management of the co-operative societies is kept in the hands of its members. Every member is to take part in the management, functioning and proceedings of a co-operative society. He exercise these powers by using the right to vote. The government of the cooperative marketing societies is called a self government because it is of the members, for the members and by the members of the co-operative societies. This government is totally based on the principle of democracy where the government is of the people, by the people and for the people. Thus it is following the sound principles of democratic practices.

9. Distributive Justice. Unlike the principle of one man one vote, the members are distributed the share of profits in proportion with their contribution in the total network. More the contribution of the members, higher the dividends they will get and *vice-versa*. The profits of the cooperative societies are the result of the contribution made by the members. So they must be rewarded according to their contribution in total network.

Methods of Business adopted by Marketing Co-operatives. The following are the important methods of operation of Co-operative marketing:

1. Outright Purchase and Sale. Outright purchase and sale implies the actual buying of commodities by paying cash at the ruling prices in the market and then reselling to others. Here, the Marketing co-operatives buy the produce of their members, at the prices prevailing in the marketing and make them payment of cash immediately; hence the section afford all the risks of storing the goods and fluctuations of prices. The society deducts all the expenses involved in buying and selling and the specified dividend to be declared amongst the members on the basis of the amount of business done with the society or through the society. Mass marketing co-operatives handle the produce of their members by this methods. This method has the following merits:

Merits. There are advantages that are enjoyed by the producers through this method are as:

(1) Immediate requirements of cash is assured *(2)* The immediate payment made by the marketing co-operatives, helps the farmer-members, to tide over their financial difficulties and *(3)* other obligations with social and psychological stings. Therefore, the producers can sell their produce only to the society and thus secure better prices because of co-operatives; moreover there is no cheating as it is their own organisations *(4)* Co-operatives are following the usual practices prevalent in the market and therefore, the producters are conversant with them.

Demerits. As per the opinions of experts, this method has three defects too. *(a)* The co-operatives have to take for granted the risks along with the purchase; that is to say, the market risk of price fluctuation is to be shouldered by the society itself, which sometimes proves to be costlier. At times, they have to assume the risk of piling up of stocks, as the demand pattern is not encouraging. *(b)* Moreover, working capital is warranted to make the purchases as immediate cash is to be paid. This brings pressure on the working capital position, and more, in the off seasons *(c)* Co-operatives have to appointed skilled managerial personnel for carrying on such a business acumen will be available only at higher salaries. This increases the overall cost of management.

2. Agency Method. The relationship of members and society is that agency, wherein the society buys and sells the produce of its members as an agent. That is, it does not take title to the goods nor pays cash immediately. For performing the services of an agent, these Agencies charge certain commission; thus it collects the produce of the member-farmers and remits the amount to the members, just after the sale by subtracting some commission and other incidental charges. This method has its own advantages and disadvantages.

Merits. It has three merits. *(a)* The producers obtain the prices which the quality of their products can fetch in the open market. The marketing cooperatives, however, help the members to obtain higher prices with wider contacts working with the least developments in the markets; *(b)* As the co-operatives are acting only as the agents of the members, they are not to make the payment for the price immediately; they pay only when they sell and collect the bill from the buyers; *(c)* As they are acting as only intermediacies they are not to assume the risks which are the botheration of the farmers themselves; thus the risks associated with the price fluctuations of even stocks piling are avoided.

Demerits. The disadvantages are two, in number: *(a)* the marketing co-operatives are compelled to charge, higher rate of commission, since the cost of maintaining records and keeping of accounts and conducting actual 'business is more. *(b)* As the societies are interested only in getting commission, they may fail in obtaining higher prices for the members' produce.

3. Pooling. The third method of handling members, produce by the marketing co-operatives is pooling. Poolings is defined by Bakken and Schaars as "the commingling of products of many producers and after deducting average expenses, paying the average price received for the same, usually on the basis of established grades. From this definition, it is clear, pooling may *(a)* involve the physical mixing of the products of different members; however, in actual practice, it does not imply only the mingling of the produce but the delivery of the produce of products by the members and the sale of the same by the co-operatives separately also. Of the products, that are delivered to cooperatives, are in small lots, in that the societies may commingle the products so as to make it convenient to sell on the basis of the grades already established. On the contrary, if they are in sufficiently larger quantities, they need not be mixed and therefore may be sold distinctly.

The payment to the members, under the method is made in three distinct ways. If the product pooled by the members are sold without grading, the societies realise the sale proceeds and distribute the same amongst the members as per the quantity delivered by each member, after deducting the expenses thereto *(a)* If products are graded and pooled in a single pool, payment is made on the basis of quality of the products or on the basis of quantity; if they are put in a separate pool after grading *(c)* If the products are sold separately without mixing, the co-operative collect the sale proceeds and deduct the proportionate share in the common exp nses and pay the remaining to the individual members. This method has the following merits and demerits.

Merits. The merits accruing to the members are: *(a)* it helps in minimising the risk to loss due to fire, theft, damage etc. The pooling method, provides for the loss arising out of price fluctuation. *(b)* Orderly marketing of products is facilitated by this method. The surplus quantities are stocked and the quantity demanded in the market is released, thus encourag.ng the better prices. *(c)* On account of orderly marketing, the bargaining capacity of producers, also increases *via* co-operatives, as the pooling facilities standardization, and grading *(d)* Pooling also results in reduced cost of transportation, grading and storage, as they are in larger quantities. It assists in finding out new markets for the members' produce and expanding the operations of existing markets.

Demerits. That way, every method has its own laxities, which cannot be plugged completely. The demerits of pooling system are not very severe and therefore, we have conveniently left. It can be said that the merits outweigh, the demerits and therefore, the defects are not being given hair splitting importance.

4. Sales Policies of Marketing Co-operatives. In order that the marketing co-operatives become real success, they have to follow, design and develop sound sales policies. The aim of obtaining higher prices for members produce can be achieved by pursuing sound sales policies. The co-operatives sell the produce to the wholesalers in central markets or through the brokers or commission agents or auction companies, that are working in central markets. Majority of societies, sell directly to the manufacturers or the buyers who are desirous of purchasing in larger quantities. Such as large scale retail organisations and public institutions.

5. Members' Contract with Co-operatives. The success of marketing co-operatives lies in the regular and continuous business that it transacts. Regular supply of products can be assured by the members to the society, through the execution of a contract. In this contract, the member assures and gives guarantee of the delivery of produce to the co-operative only. Further, the contract specifies are to be paid by the members if the contract is broken.

Thus, members' contract ensures steady, regular and continuous business to the marketing co-operatives.

6. Advancement of Credit and Procurement of Foodgrains. Cooperative marketing societies advance finance to producers against their stock of foodgrains in the godowns of the societies. This increases the holding power of the producers and prevents distress sales. Generally, societies advance credit to the extent of 60 to 75 per cent of the value of the produce stored with them. The recoveries are effected from the sale proceeds of the produce of the producer. This function involves no risk to the society. Moreover, it increases the business. Co-operative marketing societies act as agents of the government in the procurement of foodgrains at the announced procurement prices.

MERITS OF CO-OPERATIVE MARKETING

Co-operative venture has its own set of merits to its credit and a few limitations on the counterpart.

Merits: 1. Development of Orderly Marketing. Development of orderly marketing implies, establishing balance between the demand and supply forces, to better the position of the farmers, which is the need of the hour. Our farmers, do sell, in villages especially at the time of harvest, that results in dumping and creation of glut in the markets, whereby, the price level swings down to the bottom, thus leaving nothing but pessimism. Cooperatives by buying or collecting produce, from farmers would be able to regulate the demand and supply position. The supply is made as per the needs and moods of the market. Thus, co-operatives will stabilize the prices over longer periods. Thus, seasonal fluctuations are avoided for safeguarding the interests of the producing units and ultimately the consumers.

2. Realisation of Higher Prices. Maximization of income to the farming class is the objective of co-operative marketing. This can be attained only when price that the farmer gets is higher. By co-operative efforts, they will get better prices for their produce, provided they sell to the co-operative societies and not to the private dealers. It is because, the price for the produce is realized by the co-operatives on behalf of the members. It is mainly due to the united effort, where bargaining capacity improves and gets stronger. Individual effort, to sell will bring him down where he is pulled down. However, co-operative attempt is the fine answer to this sort of exploitation.

3. Lower cost of Production. These marketing co-operatives are rendering valuable service to the class of producers by providing the requisites of better farming. They buy and provide better seeds, fertilizers, and implements at economical rates, as they enjoy the benefits of large scale units, operating in the market. Such benefits are not available to farmers as individuals.

4. Elimination of Trade Abuses. The malpractices which are common in private trading centres are not resorted to, because co-operatives will be rendering the service, rendered by the merchant middlemen. As it is a common approach strengthens the bargaining capacity. The 'Scientific theft' is no more there. This is another reason to increase earning to our farmers.

5. Better Selling Methods. Co-operatives, apply better methods to push the agricultural products. Even they resort to advertising, branding, to claim superiority in the market. Such efforts are beyond the reach of individuals.

6. Control of Quality and Better Grading. To make greater success, better seeds are provided, farmers are advised to produce or grow only certain breeds, which makes grading more easy and economical. Here, the farmers are better rewarded as quality results in higher prices, Since individual production is limited, he cannot resort to grading, but co-operative will make him to have his cake and eat it too.

7. Essence of Integrated Programme of Credit. The programme of credit expansion, as a part of integrated approach on the part of Government of India, is going to the greatest success, provided marketing co-operatives are married to credit co-operatives. Collection or recovery of loans granted is done easily by marketing co-operatives. If other agencies are employed, the recovery remains a dream. Hence, marketing co-operatives should be given the role to play in the collection of loans and they should become part and parcel of the overall co-operative structure.

8. Instrument of Education. Farmers can better appreciate their problems and difficulties as they are made to govern themselves. They learn as to what problems are practically faced, and how to solve them. Thus, this society becomes a training ground. They are bound to get enlightened on the importance of co-operation that is based on "one for all" and "all for one" "self help through mutual help".

LIMITATIONS AND PROBLEMS OF CO-OPERATIVES

1. Disloyalty of Members. The affection and attachment of farmers is lacking where farmers are having misunderstandings. Again they expect too much from co-operatives. They feel they are exploited indirectly.

2. Lack of Scientific Management. This is the greatest limitation, that impedes the growth of co-operative sector. The managing body does not consist of enlightened experienced people. The office bearers be polite, trained, and experienced who must know the basic principles of co-operation. If good managerial staff is required for efficient management, the society is to pay better price for the services of these people with knowledge, experience and business knack.

3. Rivalry from Private Traders. Since private sector is dominating the scene of business, co-operative child is no where, which is ill-treated. Private sector is deadly against, to be the cause of its collapse. Thus, everybody except Government, hates co-operative societies. Traders compete away the business by offering temporarily favourable terms. Since they can not afford to pay reasonable price for the efforts of other agencies like warehousing, transportation, banks manufacturers etc., they hesitate to have trade relations.

4. Defective Business Techniques. The major factors of successful business are adequate finance and better management. In these societies, cannot find providing for future contingencies and for programme of growth and expansion. Personal interference, favouritism will have upper hand where syndicate and indicate will make their headway.

MERITS OF CO-OPERATIVE MARKETING

It is observed uptil now that Indian rural producers have been suffering a great deal, on account of undeveloped, unorganised and confusing marketing system. Producers are discouraged in undertaking production of crops, because of the unsuitable marketing facilities. The uneducated, innocent and ignorant producers are duped and exhorted by the dubious merchant traders and money lenders. This issue becames more acute with the onset of "Green Revolution" in our country. To avoid these and to improve the marketing mechanism for the distribution of rural produce at higher price, and in order to provide more income to the producers, co-operative marketing is an important instrument that we have already discussed. Now let us throw light on to what extent they have been progressing and helping rural marketing in our country.

Co-operative Marketing covers almost all the important secondary and terminal markets in our country. At present there are 6900 primary marketing societies at the Mandi-level including 700 special commodity Agricultural Marketing Societies, 240 Central/District Co-operative Marketing Societies, 30 State/Apex Co-operative Marketing Federations and the National Agricultural Co-operative Marketing Federation (NAFED) and its 30 main branches.

The volume of rural produce marketed through the co-operative marketing societies increased form Rs. 53 crore in 1955-56 to Rs. 6274 crore in 1989-90. The produce marketed through these societies account for 8 to 10 per cent of the marketed surplus. The important commodities marketed by these societies are foodgrains, sugarcane, cotton, oilseeds, fruits, vegetables and plantation crops. The progress of co-operative marketing societies has varied from State to State and within each State from commodity to commodity: Maharashtra, Uttar Pradesh, Gujarat, Punjab, Karnataka, Tamil Nadu and Haryana together account for more than 80 per cent of the total rural produce marked through co-operatives in the country. The other important function performed by these societies is the marketing of rural inputs *viz.* fertilizers, improved seeds, insecticides, pesticides, rural implements and machinery. Over 70,000 retail outlets of these societies deal in these inputs. The value of rural inputs marketed by marketing societies has increased from Rs. 36 crore in 1960-61 to Rs. 2117 crore in 1989-90.

During the last 30 years (from 1960-61 to 1989-90) the number of Primary Agricultural Co-operative Marketing Societies increased from 3108 to 6908. There has also been two-fold increase in the number of co-operative sugar factories and cotton spinning and processing societies in the country. In Punjab, Maharashtra, Uttar Pradesh, Andhra Pradesh and Tamil Nadu, 75 per cent of the foodgrains are marketed by co-operative societies. In Maharashtra and Uttar Pradesh, 75 per cent of sugarcane, 75 per cent of cotton, and in Karnataka 85 per cent of plantation crops are marketed by the co-operative societies.

SUGGESTIONS FOR STRENGTHENING OF COOPERATIVE MARKETING SOCIETIES

(i) In the selection of the officials of co-operative marketing societies, weightage should be given to business experience and qualifications. After their selection, the officials should be given proper training so that they may deal efficiently with the business of the society. The efficiency should be rewarded, wherever possible.

(ii) There is a need for bringing about a proper co-ordination between credit and marketing co-operative societies to facilitate the recovery of loans advanced by credit societies, and make available sufficient finance for marketing societies.

(iii) The area of the operations of the societies should be large enough so that they may have sufficient business and become viable. Most of the societies at present are not viable because of the small volume of their business.

(iv) The societies should acquire the transport facility to bring the produce of the members from the villages to the mandi in time and at a lower cost.

(v) The public procurement and public distribution programmes should be implemented through co-operative marketing societies to increase their business turnover.

(vi) Co-operative marketing societies should develop sufficient storage facilities in the mandi as well as in the villages.

(vii) Co-operative marketing societies should diversify their activities. They should sell the produce and inputs, and engage in the construction of storage facilities.

(viii) Marketing societies, like the private traders, should provide accommodation and the drinking water facility for their members when the latter come to the mandi.

(ix) The societies should give adequate representation to the small and marginal producers in their organisational set-up.

(x) The co-operative feeling among members should be inculcated by proper education by organising seminars and by the distribution of literature.

❐

16

Fertilizers, Seeds and Plant Protection

CHEMICAL FERTILIZERS

An important factor that has contributed to the increase in agricultural production in the U.S.A. and the continent of Europe is the introduction of synthetic fertilisers. The fixation of atmospheric nitrogen as a result of scientific and engineering advances has brought about a tremendous change in the last 30 to 40 years in the relative importance of nitrogen should dependent upon chemical production. But recently criticism has been levelled against its effect. Their continuous and sole application has deleterious effects on the soil due to various causes. The classical researches of Colonel Mc Carrison and B. V. Nath in India and those of Mackeridge and Bottomley in Europe and Clarke and Roller in America, have conclusively proved that crops raised with the organic manure, are pre-eminently superior in their nutritivc value to those raised with artificial fertilizers, and seeds produced ftom the field, treated with organic manure possess greater germination power than those obtained from lands manured with artificial fertilisers. Improving the texture and water-holding capacity of the soil and providing food for the innumerable and invisible organisation inhabiting the soul are the benefits which organic manure confers on plant growth. In addition to these indirect advantanges, orgnic manures appear to give plants a better balanced nutrition and provide certain nutritive factors, which chemical fertilizers either do not supply or supply only imperfectly. The application of chemical fertiliser, should, therefore, be supplemental to bulky organic manuers like manure at cattle manure.

Types of Fertilizers

Chemical fertilizers are usually of three types, *viz.*, nitrogenous fertilizers, the phosphatic fertilizers and the potassic fertilizers.

Nitrogenous fertilizers, comprise saltpetre, nitre, ammonium sulphate, sodium, nitrate and urea etc. Nitrogen influences crop growth in many ways *e.g.*, it encourages the development of foliage; imparts a green colour to leaves; in case of cereals, it tends to produce lumpness in seeds and it tends to produce succulence or tenderness in the plant. But if used in large quantities, nitrogen may prove harmful to the crop for it may lower its quality: it may delay maturity; it may decrease resistance to disease, and it may weaken the stems and cause lodging in cereals.

Phosphatic futilizers are given to soil in the shape of phosphorus which is derived from various sources like bones and rock phosphates. When prowdered rock phosphate is applied to the soil, phosphoric acid becomes readily available. Phosphorus helps the growth of plant in many ways *e.g.*, it hastens maturity of crop;. it encourages root development; decreases the ratio of straw to grain in cereals it strengthens stems, and reduces the tendency to lodge in cereals; it increases resistance to disease and it improves the quality of crops. Phosphorus balances or off-sets the harmful effects of excessive nitrogen and even if it is applied in excessive quantities it produces no bad effect on the crop.

Potassic fertilizers are given to the soil in the form of potassium chloride and potassium sulphate. These fertilizers help the transference of food materials from one part of the plant to another; they provide the needed green colour to the leaves; they tend to increase plumpness in grains and they tend to have a balancing effect between the first two types of fertilizers. Its presence in large quantities in the soil produces no detrimental effect on the crop.

A Comparative Performance of Artificial and Organic Manures

Crops	Artificial			Organic		Organic & Mixed	
	N	P_2O_5	NP	Cakes	F.Y.M.	Green manuring	Mixed
(1) Average response for lb. of plant nutrient							
Paddy	15.4	13.0	32.0	14.4	13.2	15.9	21.8
Wheat	7.3	5.1	14.2	7.2	6.9	15.9	8.0
Sugar-cane	102.4	56.0	107.5	172.0	67.6	15.9	276.8
Cotton	6.8	0.9	10.8	4.2	6.6	15.9	6.8
Pulses	Negative	7.7	12.8	6.4	8.6	15.9	—
Oilseeds	6.9	8.8	13.3	9.5	3.0	15.9	—
(2) Percentage increase over no manure yields							
Paddy	23.2	20.4	30.0	42.3	39.9	31.5	10.3
Wheat	27.8	23.6	69.4	43.7	58.8	29.1	28.9
Sugar-cane	47.8	30.3	43.6	62.7	22.3	18.0	144.0
Cotton	27.2	19.2	54.4	39.6	41.5	15.5	98.5
Pulses	Negative	99.8	128.0	57.7	120.5	15.2	179.0
Oilseeds	49.4	19.0	44.0	47.9	39.9	—	48.1

Time of Application

The time of application of fertilizer often makes a considerable difference in its utilization by the crop. Plants absorb large quantities of nitrogen, phosphotic acid, and potash during the early stage of growth. Therefore, the fertilizers should be applied to most crops at or before sowing time. Fertilizers need not be applied to annual crops in the latter stages of their growth. A late application of nitrogen to a crop increases the nitrogen content, prolongs, the growing period and delays maturity. But crops of long duration, like sugarcane, require the application twice or thrice at suitable intervals. The phosphatic fertilizers should be applied a little before or at the time of planting the crop, as phosphorus is not leached out of the soil. Potash is applied at the time of planting and to a limited extent as a top-dressing a later stage of crop growth.

Response to Fertilizers

The response to fertilizers varies with the nature of the soil, the crop grown, and whether it is rain-fed or irrigated. Results of extensive trials conducted throughout India in cultivator's fields show that the "best response, with nitrogen fertilizer on rice was 'obtained on old alluvial soils with an increase of 859 lbs. of paddy over the control plot. In decreasing order the responses on the other soils were black soil, red soil, red gravelly soil, and on a mixture of red and black soil. The least responses with nitrogen fertilizer on paddy was obtained on coastal alluvium deltaic and saline soils, new alluvium and laterite. The increase in paddy yield over the, control plot as a result of appling 30 lbs. of N was 514 lbs of grain. The respective yield in case of bajra was 155 lbs., ragi 412 lbs., wheat 289 lbs., per acre over the control plot.

Methods Used

The methods generally used applying fertilizers are:

(i) Broadcasting during the preparation of the soil before planting.

(ii) Placing in rows either before or at the time of planting.

(iii) Side-dressing or top-dressing the crop during the growing season.

(iv) Applying liquid fertilizers.

Considerations Governing use of Fertilizers

It may be stressed that in order to secure maximum response to fertilizers the crop should be irrigated immediately following their application and at suitable intervals thereafter, because the response of the crop under unirrigated conditions is usually uncertain and relatively small.

Secondly, the maximum profit from the use of fertilizers depends on such factors as nature of the soil, kinds of crop grown climate, price of fertilizers, the market price of the produce, etc. All economic results.

Thirdly, the use of fertilizers is also subject to the Law of Diminishing Returns. This means that the rate of increase in crop Yield decreases after a certain point is reached regarding the quantity of fertilizers used, and consequently the value of the additional yield annually becomes less than the cost of the fertilizers. Usually, the smaller applications of fertilizers produce greater percentage increases of yield than larger application.

Fourthly, it should also be noted that the adequate supply of nutrients is only one of the factors that determine crop yields and that the application of fertilizers is not the sole means of making good nutrient deficiencies in soils and plants. Equal attention must be paid to the other soil and crop management practices such as good tilth, proper drainage, required soil reaction, soil conservation, good land use, suitable crop rotation, adequate bulky organic manure in the soil and satisfactory soil micro-organism activity. Each one of these plays a vital role in determining eventual production. Neglect of one of these factors leads to reduction in yield and creates the need for still heavier manuring.

Finally, manuring should not only be balanced in itself, but should also be designed to supplement the good effects of proper land use and beneficial soil management.

The demand, for fertilizers has been rapidly increasing in recent years but it has not been possible to meet it in full due to lack of internal production capacity and shortage of foreign exchange needed, for imports. Therefore, the Fertilizer Distribution Committee has emphasised on the use of fertilizers in the form of mixture with a view to promoting balanced fertilization and making the best use of supplies of nitrogen fertilizers, improved arrangements for distribution and attention to quality, and reduction in costs of distribution.

The secret of good farming is how to manure in order to raise the best crop at the lowest level of manuring. Most of the Indian soils suffer from deficiencies of nitrogen. Red, black and alluvial soils are deficient in nitrogen, phesphoric acid and humus, while laterite soils have sufficient humus and nitrogen. The deficiency of laterite soils is in potash, phosphoric acid and lime. Other three soils have sufficient potash and lime. These deficiencies can be made up by applying organic materials as well as the inorganic fertilizers.

Land is actually like a living being. It gives nourishment to crop and in return calls for nourishment. These inputs are water, manure, seed and human or cattle labour. Neither the soil conservation programmes alone, fertilizer alone, improved tillage alone can each give a small uneconomic increases on good soil but the combination commonly gives a three to sixfold increase in harvest.

Per hectare fertilizer consumption also indicates the increasing trend during, the plan period. Per hectare fertilizer consumtion was only 0.5 kg in the year 1951.52. which increased to 1.9 kg per hectare in 1960-61. A sharp increase in the use of this input too place after this period due to the introduction of new technology and it was found that the per acre fertilizer consumption was 13.6 Kgs. by the end of 1979-71. The increasing trend in fertilizer consumption was visible by the end of 1980-81 when it increased upto 32.0 Kgs. per hectare of cropped area. The recent Statistics indicates that by the end of 1984-85. the per bectare fertilizer consumption was nearly 46 kgs. The uptrend has continued in the current year even though the weather conditions during the year were not favourable.

Therefore we see that since the adoption of the New Agricultural Technology, the fertilizer consumption has been growing rapidly.

But in spite of rapid increase in the consumption of fertilizer in the country in the recent years its distribution did not fare well during the past 15 years. There is a significant variation in fertilizer consumption from region to region and from State to State. Table gives State-wise consumption table given below gives statewise consumption' of plant nutrients per unit of gross cropped area for 1980-81 and 1984-85. It is evident from the table that per hectare fertilizer consumption was 151.19 kg in 1984-85 while it was about 46 kg; per hectare for the country as a whole.

Consumption of fertilizers kg/hectare

States	*1980-81*	*1984-85*
Assam	2.71	4.01
Andhra Pradesh	46.87	75.14
Kerala	34.08	43.96
Karnataka	32.26	52.61
Tamil Nadu	75.95	99.94
Gujarat	33.37	46.28
Madhaya Pradesh	9.20	17.13
Maharastra	20.77	28.51
Rajasthan	7.79	11.11
Haryana	42.26	57.78
Uttar Pradesh	46.83	65.11
Jammu and Kashmir	21.26	29.72
Himachal Pradesh	17.12	22.92
Bihar	18.35	35.90
West Bengal	37.12	54.81

Manipur	13.71	15.66
Meghalaya	11.50	14.30
Nagaland	0.48	1.76
Tripura	5.27	8.15
Orissa	8.74	13.04
Sikkim	4.65	13.00
Punjab	111.63	151.19

There is intra-regional, intra-state and intra farming group variation in fertilizers consumption. The performance of cooperative agencies in distribution of fertilizers has not been upto expectation in many areas due to lack of marketing experience, inadequate distribution margins etc. Fertilizer distribution has in many cases been a monetary drag on the co-operative system. The credit available to farmers from a co-operative sector for purchase of fertilizer was also low about 30 per cent of the total borrowing of rural households.

With a view to minimising the regional imbalance in the fertilizer use, an intensive promotional campaign by mobilising the efforts of State Governments and fertilizer manufacturers has been launched in 100 selected districts. The campaign covers those districts which have good irrigation potential but are low in fertilizer consumption. In this campaign, preference has been given to districts having assured rainfall for developing agricultural production based on available technological package. For each district a lead manufacturer has been designated, and State Governments have been advised to ensure a higher rate of growth in collaboration with the manufacturers. Besides the Hindustan Fertilizer Corporation Limited with the assistance of the U. K. Government has initiated a special fertilizer promotion programme in 25 selected districts in the States of Orissa, West Bengal Assam, Bihar, Madhya Pradesh and Uttar Pradesh.

Improved Seeds

Of all the methods of improving agricultural technique none has brought about such progress as the improvement of plants through selection and cross breeding. These methods of improvement entail considerable expense and constant care where as the use of improved varieties of seeds only involves the agriculturist in the slight extra expense represented by the surcharge of a few rupees per capita of seed. The introduction of a better variety in an agricultural area means an immediate profit for the agriculturist. It improves the crop either in quantity or in quality while scarcely; increasing the cost of cultivation. The creation of variety with an improved yield and quality is therefore one of the simplest and most effective means of raising the general level of the country's economy. The methods of producing better varieties include the introduction of new forms selection from variations occurring in nature and from those artificially induced by hybridisation of plants and indeed all those means by which conscious improvements of plants may be accomplished, In the production of 10 to 15 per cent can be obtained from improved varieties.

Plant genetics is advanced enough to develop seeds strains almost to order. Natures slow process of mutation has been speeded up by irradiation of seeds with radio isotopes and selecting strains with the desired qualities. Indian scientists have produced strains which are not only prolific yielders but also flood-resistant drought-resistant and disease-resistant and which mature early. These are meeting the conditions of water logged areas semi-arid tracts and the requirements of the multiple cropping.

Importance of Improved Seeds

Demonstrations have revealed that the natural average yield of rice was 1.15 tonnes per hectare in 1971-72, 85 per cent of the national demonstration plots with HYV seeds gave a yield exceeding 4.5 tonnes. The figures of wheat were 1.31 tonnes per hectare on 81 per cent of the plots in 1971-72. The analysis of the yield data reported from various states indicated that as compared to traditional varieties, the yield of these varieties was significantly higher. The higher yield of paddy touched the level of 13,000 kgs. per hectare (I R 8 in Karnataka) and the average yield in different states ranged between 2,100 Kgs. and 5,500 Kgs. per hectare. In the case of hybrids, yields as high as 7,835 Kgs.. 7,500 Kgs. and 6.527 Kgs. per hectare were obtained for maize, jowar and bajra res pectively. The per hectare yields of maize ranged between 1,404 Kgs and 3,500 Kgs. in different states and those of hybrid bajra ranged between 1,300 Kgs. and 3,875 Kgs., and of jowar between I.215 Kgs. and 3,767 Kgs.

However, several administrative, organisational and institutional problems faced of the implementation of the programme of high yielding varieties were identified during the Evaluation Studies conducted by the Planning Commission and Agro-Economic Research Centres. The problems included provision of additional facilities in certain research laboratories, strengthening of soil testing facilities fuller utilization of available soil testing facilities, greater emphasis on demonstration and improvements in training progrmme better publicity, popularisation and use of treated seeds, quality control of fertilizers and pesticides and increased supply of institutional credit.

Some Improved Varieties

Quite a large number of improved varieties of food have been evolved, which have helped in boosting up the production of foodgrains. The All-India Co-ordinated Project on Improvemet of Wheat has evolved new varieties which have a high degree of resistance to all types of rust and which mature earlier that the older varieties. Research work is being carried on at 20 centres. The varieties evolved are suitable for rainfed conditions particularly in Central and western Regions of the country, comprising Punjab, Haryana. Rajasthan, M.P., U.P., North Bihar, Gujarat and Maharashtra. Most of the varieties ripen within 120 to 140 days and their yield potential varies from 20-25 quintals to as much as 70-80 quintals per hectare.

Based on field trials the following varieties of wheat have been considered suitable for rain fed as well as high fertility conditions. Larma Rajo, Sonara-64, Sharbati Sonara, Kalyan Sona. Sonalika, S-311 (Chotti Lerma), Safed Lerma, Hira (H.D-1941). Narmada-4c. Meghdoot (H 1-7483). H. S. 1097-11, Moti Pusa Lerma,U.P. 215, U.P. 310. H D-1925, H D-1982, H D-1999. H D 4502 and W. G. —

377. Some of these are of short duration, while others are late sowing varieties and are grown where irrigation is available even up to the middle of January after the harvest of sugar potato, toria, radish, carrots or turnips.

Even more heartening are some of the exotic varieties of paddy which can stand high doses of fertilizers and give yields ranning from 3500 Kgs to 7500 Kgs per hectare. So far more than 400 superior varieties have been evoloved which give 10 to 20 per cent more yield. The All-India. Co-ordinated Rice Improvement Project is involved in bringing our new varieties of dwarf and high vielding ability. Many of these varieties are of better grain qulity, early maturing and drought resistant; while others are susceptible to severe disease (bacterial leaf blight) pests, (stem borers and leaf and plant hoppers) unsuitable under water-logged conditions, coarse glutinous grain and poor consumer acceptance. Therefore, now such varieties are being raised which are devoid of these problems.

The main varieties suitable for general cultivation are I R-8 Jaya, and Vijaya. Those suitable for specific regions are Bala Cauvery, Kandi, Krishna, Padma, Pankaj, and Jagganath. The varieties for special situation are Sabarmaji, Jamuna, Ratna, and I R-20. Other six dwarf varieties for specific regions are : Hamsa Annapurna Karuna, Sarju-49 and Suma and Kusuma.

The All-India Co-ordinated Project on Pulse Crops was under-taken in 1967 with a view to evolve quick yielding varieties which can be fitted into suitable multiple cropping and relay-cropping patterns in areas with assured irrigation and also high yielding strains which are resistant to pests and diseases. The I A R I scientists have developed a new short duration (75 days) variety of green gram (*viz,* Pusa Baisabhi) for growing between rabi and kharif crops yielding over a tonne of grain per hectare.

About 7,000 varieties of chana (Bengal Gram) have been under trial at IARI. Besides, thousands ef varieties of Arhar, moong and other pulses have been screened in the regional centres at Hyderabad, Coimbatore, Jabalpur, Ludhiana, Varanasi, etc.

Under coarse grains, new varieties of maize, bajra, jowar and sorghum have been evolved under the programmes of the All-India Co-ordinated Millets Improvement Project. Six hybrids H 8—1 to H B-4 of bajra and two others have been released which take about 75 days to mature and give yields of about 4000 Kgs. per hectare. But these strains are subject to pests and diseases and hence have not been very popular. However, efforts are on way to overcome these problems. Two hybrids-CSH I and CSH 11 of Jowar have been evolved. These take about 3 to 4 months to mature and yield about 4000 to 6000 Kgs. per hectare. But these have not found much favour with the cultivators, because when they are about to mature rains deteriorate the quality of the grain; and some of these hybrids are not suitable for high rainfall areas; and they also do not meet the consumer demands.

A number of high yielding hybrids and composite varieties of maize has been evolved under the All-India Co-ordinated Maize Breeding Project, such as the Ganga 101, Ganga-3, Ganga-Safed 2, Ranjit, Deccan, Himalayan 123 and Hi Starch. These mature between 85 to 120 days and give about 45 to 75 quintals per hectare. They have been adopted in some areas like the northern plains, southern Rajasthan, Gujarat and Maharashtra, and in some parts of Deccan, but in others there has been considerable resistance from the farmers because the available varieties do not fit in well with the existing patter of rabi crops and, moreover, they are non-resistant to pests and diseases.

So far as oilseeds are concerned, high yielding and early maturing varieties have been for castor (Aruna CSH-2, Suphala), ground nut (M-13) C-148 and KG—61—120); rust-resistant varieties of linseed; and high yielding tall and dwarf hybrids of coconut. To meet the increasing requirements of edible oils in the country, large scale cultivation of soyabean is undertaken in Maharashtra, Gujarat U. P. and M. P. Sunflower is also being grown over large areas in the country particularly of the Russian variety, in Tamil Nadu, Maharashtra, Karnataka, Andhra Pradesh, Gujarat and some parts of

North India. Demonstration schemes for castor summer-irrigate groundnut and implementation of aerial ground spraying of other in seeds is also under way.

Superior strains of sugarcane have been evolved at Coimbatore, which are more vigorous aad good yielders. Co 312, Co 313, Co 419, Co 421, Co 427, Co 527, Co 453, Co 8 and Bo 11 are important varieties. But because of low rate of multiplication of seed and tardiness in the adoption has been the main problem in their popularity.

A large number of improved types of arboreum herbaceum and American varieties have been evolved under the Central Cotton. Committee such as the Kalyan, Vijaya Laxmi, Pratap, Virnar, Jarila Jayther, Garoni Uganda, K-2 K-5, N-14, C-l, C-12, F-216, F-231, R 420, Malwa 9, and Indore 1. But many new varieties have now been developed by IARI MCU - 5 (Sujata and Suvin), Gujarat Hybrid 4; Varalakshmi, PR 9. PS 10 and SS 67 are not only short of duration, but also long-staple, superior cotton with high ginning capacity. These are being raised in the command areas of Rajasthan Canal, Tungbhadra and Nagarjunsagar.

Under fodder crops pusa Giant Napir grass gives 2500 to 3000 quintals of green matter per hectare per year. It contains 25 per cent more protein and 12% more sugar than thc Napier grass, Pusa Giant Berscem gives an additional 900 to 1000 quintals of green fodder per hectare per year, and is frost-resistant.

In the field of horticulture and vegetables, improved varieties giving good performances as regards yields and freedom from diseases have been evolved. Important among the vegetables are tomato brinjal, bottle gourd, sweet potato, garden peas, field peas. cabbage, cauliflower, turnip, carrot, khol-khol, lady's finger and many others.

Among the fruits, the development of crops like nuts (almond and walnut) has been promoted in the Himalayan region. Grape ultivation has been given a fillip in the Deecan and Peninsular India with a new promising variety Anab-e-Shahi. Another variety Pusa Seedless is now being cultivated in Delhi region.

Besides, many foreign vegetable crop varieties and fruit have been released for commercial cultivation. Important a these are high-yielding tomato and garden Varieties from the U.S.A Cowpea variety from the Philippines pea varieties of water melons from the U. S. A and Japan, and a pea varieiy from U.S.A. and Japan, and a pea variety from Austrilia.

Sugarbeat is also being cultivated efficiently in Punjab, Rajas than, U. P., Haryana and in selected areas in Maharashtra.

Techniques of Obtaining High Yields

High yields are obtained from hybrid varieties through:

(a) Thick Sowing, i.e. the plant density is increased *e.g.*, the idea plant Population of maize, jowar and bajra are respectively 50,000 140,000; and 120,000 plants per hectare.

(b) Fertilizer dosages, To reap rich harvest it is necessary to apply about 100 kgs, of nitrogen, 50 kgs. of phosphorus and 30 kg. of Potash per hectare. With increased yields elements like salphur zinc and boron get depleted. Therefore, in areas of intensive cropping, these are supplied as a routine procedure.

(c) Pest and Disease Control. For producing high yields plant protection measures are needed.

(d) Proper Timing of Fertilizers and Irrigation. Where heavy doses of fertilizers are being applied, it is important that 75 per cent of the dose of N should be given at the time of sowing. Irrigation; at the time of grain development is essential.

Genetic Improvement of Crops

Genetic improvement of crops and plants are of highest importance and urgency for several reasons, such as:

(i) Large yield increases are dependent to a large extent on a suitable variety, which is capable to produce high yields, provided other associated factors are available in proper combination.

(ii) Inter-actions and responsiveness of improved varieties with fertilizers, additional moistures and other inputs are substantial.

(iii) Improved varieties are one of the most important components of strategic inputs, which farmers would like to use for attaining a higher yield.

Agricultural production can be increased further if efforts are made on putting the scientifically bred, processed and tested seed on the land. This programme will necessarily in volve efficient production of breeder, foundation and certified seeds, their processing, storage, quality control, and seed distribution and marketing.

The production of breeder seeds is determined by the moisture, sunlight, temperature patterns, susceptibility to disease and pests, drainage situation, and consumer preferences of every area. These dictate the optimality of the seed whieh can maximise yields for a particular area. The agencies for releasing breeders seed may be ICAR, agricultural universities or the private seed agencies.

Production of foundation seeds require that such seeds are inspected frequently in order to ensure a high yield with disease-free, well filled and viable seed grains. Harvesting, cleaning, bagging and fabelling have to be carried on under expert supervision. Such seeds can be produced on seed farms of large size which enjoy adequate facilities and good technical staff for their production.

Certified seeds are produced with foundation seeds for use by farmers and which are certified as fulfilling prescribed purity, germination (namely 95 per cent) and other standards. Such seeds are generally produced in progressive farmer's farms under contract.

Seed multiplication programme requires that for multiplication of seeds, irrigated and fertile areas are chosen carefully, so that quality farmers seed can be prodoced without risk of disease and pests. Secondly, irrigation with large compact areas under production, good inputs, processing, storage facilities. Finally, adequate incentive should he maintained to spur the seed farmers to produce quality seeds.

The National Commission on Agriculture in its Interim Report on seeds of high yielding varieties and hybrids of cereals has dealt with certain aspects relating to multiplication and distribution of quality seeds of cereals with a view to ensuring regular supply of quality seed in adequate quantities. It has spelt out the responsibilities of various agencies in multiplication and distribution in different stages—breed's foundation and certified seed.

With regard to breeder's seed, it has laid down that responsibility should be on the research institutions and the Indian Council of Agricultural Research. For foundation seed it has advocated that the National Seeds Corporation should be responsible for varieties of all-India importance and State Goverments should designate agency or agencies with regard to varieties of State importance.

With regard to certified seed, the Commission has advocated a multiplicity of agencies both for production and for marketing and has suggested their development by providing necessary incentives and facilities. The responsibility for assessment of the requirements of seed at various stages has been assigned to the production and marketing agencies subject to supervision, guidance and co-ordination by the State and Central Governments.

There are three large all-India Organisations for production of certified seeds, *i.e.*, the National Seeds Corporation, the Teral Development Corporation, and the States Farm Corporation of India; besides two all India associations of private seed producers, *i.e.* All-India Crop Improvement and Seed Producers Assocation and All India Seed Growers, Merchants and Nurserymen Association. State

Some governments have also their own seed corporations which manage their seed multipliction farms.

National Seeds Corrporation

This Corporation was established in 1963 mainly as an organisation to produce, stock and supply foundation seeds for hybrid particularly hybrid maize which were released by that year. The Corporation launched a major programme of seed production of certified seeds of hybrid maize, hybrid jawar. hybrid bajra and Taichung Native in December, 1965 and January, 1966.

Seven Regional units have been set up in different parts of the country to the Corportion to facilitate timely supply of parent seeds and to provide technical guidance and seed and inspection and certification of hybrid seed crops, 14 processing plants have also been set up to facilitate the processing of seeds. Each plant has a capacity of nearly 3,000 to 4,000 quintals per year. It has also popularised land levellers and planters by providing these on lease.

The Corporation has been providing besides hybrid seeds of maize, jowar, bajra, rice etc., vegetable seeds also, cuch a Pusa Sawani Bhindi. Pusa Rubby tomato, Pusa Purple, Long brinjal, Pusa Katki cauliflower new Pusa Chillies, Guntur 3 chillies, Coimbatore long Karela. Bonnervile and Perfection New line peas and Asiriva Murtunde groundnut.

The Terai Development Corporation, set up in 1869, has made appreciable progress in production of seeds particularly of paddy, maize, sorghum and soya beans.

The table given below shows the quantity of certified breeder and foundation seeds produced during 1985. It is an over all replacement rate of certified seeds at country during the Seventh Five Year Plan. There are number of on-going programme like setting up seed development of seed farms, strengthening of seed testing lovoratory and creation of additional storage capacity. The continue to receive attention during the Seventh Five Year meeting the emergent needs of seeds in different states the programmes for building up buffer stocks of seeds by National seeds Corporation and reserve stocks or seeds by the Government taken up on a larger scale.

Production of Seeds, 1985

Crops	Certified (Lakh Quintals)	Breeder Thousand Quintals	Foundation Thousand Quintals
Cereals	37.29	7.3	310.0
Puses	2.40	2.1	34.2
Oilseeds	4.71	2.1	24.3
Fibres	1.78	0.3	7.3
Potato	3.51	17.0	55.0
Others	0.28	—	0.1
Grand total	49.97	28.8	43.09

Progress of Area Under HYV

High yielding varieties of seeds are the core of our agricultural progress. They are considered as 'miracle seeds'. Within a short period the area placed under High Yielding Varieties of seeds increased considerably. In four years from 1967-68 to 1971-72 the proportion of area under HYV of seeds to the area under foodgrains trebled from about 5 percent to 15 percent. The total area under HYV seeds was about 1.89 million hectare. It sharply rose to 43.0 million hectare in 1980-81. The total area under HYV seeds became about 62.4 million hectare during 1987-88. Table given below shows the progress of tbe area under HYV seeds. 1t is estimated that 57.6 percent of the total area of Paddy crop, 83.3 percent of the total area of Bajra Crop was under HYV seeds in 1986-87. Similarly about 32 percent of the total area of Maize and Jwar crop was under HYV seeds in the year.

Area Under HYV of Seeds

(million hectare)

Crops	*1966-67*	*1968-69*	*1980-81*	*1987-88*
Paddy	0.89	2.6	18.2	25.0
Wheat	0.54	4.8	16.1	19.0
Jower	0.19	0.7	3.5	5.0
Bajra	0.06	0.7	3.6	5.0
Maize	0.21	0.4	1.6	2.0
Total	1.89	9.2	43.0	56.0

PLANT PROTECTION MEASURES

Magnitude of Losses due to plant Pests and Diseases

In India crops are damaged not only by insect pests anti diseases of crops but also by did animals and natural calamities. Various estimates have been made about the losses suffered from insects nematodes fungi, bacteria, viruses parasites, weeds, rodents and other animal like birds, snails and snugs. One estimate puts the loss at 15%. amounting to about Rs. 4500 million per annum. According to an estimate made recently by the Pesticides Association of India. on in average 18% of the crop is lost due to pest attack. In 1973-74, the provisional estimate of gross national product value of agriculture was Rs. 26,900 crores, and on the basis of 18% loss through pests, the total farm production loss worked out to Rs. 5000 crores. Though colossal the loss is avoidables.

Besides rodents also cause an enormous loss during pre and post-harvest periods when the crop is still in the field. There are about 2400 million rats in India and it has been estimated that 20 rats could consume the quantity of food sufficient for one person. On a gross estimate this means that rats are responsible for the spoilage of at least one-fifth of the grain produced. On the basis of consumption of 1 tonne of grain by rats per year the total consumption by the entire rat cotnmunity comes to about 24 m. tonnes. In terms of money, this would come to about Rs. 18,000 million, when calculated at the rate of Rs. 750 per tonne.

Besides animal pests and animals like elephant, wild boar jackals,locusts, monkeys, crows, stray cattle, porcupines, flying foxes rabbits paraquets, parrots, sparrows, and goats also damage standing crops to a large extent. Diseases of crops also are very dreadful as they bring about deterioration of quality as well as quantity of agricultural produce after harvest, in storage, transit and even at differeat stages of consumption. Plant protection measures are needed for the following reasons.

(i) Efforts to increase the yield with the application of fertilizers, adoption of other improved techniques, provision for irrigation may not bear fruit if the crops are exposed to the ravages of pests and diseases.

(ii) If plant protection measures are adopted, the entire food deficit can be made good in due course of time.

(iii) In view of the high yielding varieties programme, the plant protection has become more urgent and necessary as some of the varieties are relatively more susceptible to pests and diseases. The application of higher doses of fertilizers promotes negative growth and increases vulnerability of these for the attack of pests and diseases.

Objectives of Protection Measures

The objectives of plant protection measures are two fold. Long term objectives comprise of evolving and strengthening, extansion, quarantine, production, quality control and marketing of pesticides, equipment and air-craft in order to optimise to protection of plants, and produce and to minimise the net loss. Short term objectives are concerned with preventing of pests and diseases or fighting them with the cooperative endeavours of the farmers and scientists.

Plant protection measures, therefore, relate to protection of crops: *(a)* against seed-borne bacterial or fungal diseases through treatment of seed before sowing (fungicides); *(b)* against soil and surface insects through protective and curative spraying of pesticides (and nomaticides or soil fumigants) through biological, cultural or other means; *(c)* against weeds, through manual weeding or application of weedicides and herbicides; *(d)* against rodents and non-insect pests through mechanical and chemical means (rodenticides); *(e)* against snails and snugs by using molluscides.

Causes of Plant Diseases

Diseases in plants are mainly caused by fungi, bacteria, virus and the deficiency of essential foods. Such diseases produce wilting, stunting, drying up, and malformation of parts like roots stems, branches, flowers, leaves and fruits. Fungi attack not onty the plant during its growth but also the produce after harvest during storage and process. High humidity and warm climate help growth of fungi. They spread through air current. Bacteria and virus multiply themselves very first. Viruses are transmitted from plant to plant through minute sucking insects (called aphids), throngh nematodes in the roots and certain other insects, and they act like poison.

Diseases caused by fungi and bacteria can be to a great extent prevented by prophylactive treatment with fungicides and bactericides, virus diseases, can be controlled by use of virus-resistants, strains, avoidance and destruction of infected seeds, better insect and nematode control and other measures.

Plant Protection Measures

The plant protection measures may be broadly classified as:

(1) Chemical control, which consists in spraying and dusting the plant by chemicals and poisons or mixing these into soil to kill pests and diseases which inhabit the soil. Some of the important chemicals used for pest control are *(a)* pesticides-comprising of chlorinated hydrocarbons and Organ-Phosphorus insectides (like DDT, BHC, Aldrin, Dieldrin, Endrin, Chlordane and Fndosulfan

phosphates, etc); *(b)* fungicides (zinc Ethylene, discarborimide, copper oxychloride, Colloidal sulphur, Manganese Ethylene, Karathene, Phenyl, mercury acetate, Captan, Thiram. etc.); *(c)* Weedicides DNOC, PCP, MCPA, Ambean, Atrazine, Bromacil, Propanil, and prefix Ioxnil); (d) Rodeniicides (zinc phosphide, Calcium, and sodium cynamide, barium, carbonate, fumarin, war fin, etc.); *(e)* Nematocides (DD soil fumigant sodium, nemagon, and metham sodium); and (f) Fumigants (like EDCT, ethylene dibromide, aluminium phosphide and sodium cyanide, etc.).

(2) Mechanical Control includes eradication of the field rats mechanically, through traps, or fumigation of burrows in buildings, poisoned baits and use of rat repellants ; scaring away birds, monkeys and other animals: collection of eggs of insects and pests and burning them; and destruction of young shoot of plants and the infested parts.

(3) physical Control measures include the application of radiation, and manipulation of temperature, humidity, etc; fruit fly rot fungus can be prevented in dry fruits and vegetables through cold storage.

(4) Cultural Control includes proper rotating crops, spacing of plants, ploughing, irrigating land at appropriate time; and late sowing of crops.

The removal of all stubble after harvest of paddy, sugarcane, cholum or cotton will prevent bores resting in them and attacking the subsequent crop. Many pests feed on weed and grass when their food plants are not in the fields. Army worm, ricebug, paddy meal bug are examples of such pests. Periodical we ding of the fields would' obviously keep down the severity of attack from such pests. the depths to which the soil must be ploughed to exterminate these weed varies; the average appears to be about 10 to 11 inches, though in some areas it is as much as 15 inches. This may be done by means of tractors. Investigation should be directed into the eradication of waterhyacinth to noxious weeds which seriously interfere with the cultivation of land Portions of dead trees of plants should be removed immediately.

(5) Biological Control includes control of pests by introducing their natural enemies like parasites and predators.

The Central Government created in 1947 a Plant Protection Quarantine and Storage Organisation to help in saving crops which destroyed by insects, pests and plant diseases. The functions of this Organisation are to control the plant diseases and flying pests like locusts, to advise and organise plant protection service to provide personnel and medicines to enable the State to keep up their struggle for agricultural improvements, to prevent the import of foreign diseases and pests, to act as an inter-state exchange for information on plant diseases and to organise research on discovery of parasites and pests living on undesirable plant pests.

(6) Legislative Control includes enactment of legislation to force the farmers to adopt plant protection measures when attack is detected in a particular case.

Finally, there should be developed a strong organisational network at state, district and block levels for effective plant protection efforts. These primarily include issue of timely warning about independing epidemic of pests and diseases, demonstration of scientific use of chemicals, organising surveys of pests and diseases, continuous liaison with research and experimental stations. popularisation of prophylactic treatment and other plant protection techniques and training of farmers and keeping application equipment in working conditions.

Need of Crop Insurance

The need for protecting the farmer from natural calamities arises for the following reasons:

(i) In India mother Nature has always been moody and temperamental. She is unpredictably generous to one State and disconcertingly bad-tempered to another. This fickleness of weather conditions in different parts of the country upsets the whole agricultural economy and makes one part bountiful, while the other starves.

(ii) Besides droughts and floods, locusts, hailstorms, frosts, fires, plagues and plant diseases have always been a serious enemy to agricultural industry by destroying standing crops and thereby reducing the producers income.

(iii) Majority of the holdings are small, from which the cultivators get marginal surplus in good years and incur heavy deficits in bad ones.

(iv) Farming is more hazardous than any other form of enterprise The weather can make all the difference between success and failure. Consequently, many farmers particularly the small ones, fight shy of adopting the techniques. The fear of loss is so overwhelming that even when convinced of the gain accruing from the application of science and technology, they prefer to go along the beaten track of low productivity. Once freed from fear by crop insurance they can quicken the pace to high productivity.

The Fourth Five Year Plan observed, "Severe distress is caused to the farmers by crop failure resulting from drought, floods and other natural calamities. This risk is likely to get accentuated under conditions of large invesments in fertilizers, pesticides, improved seed and other inputs which are proposed to be used on a large scale during the Fourth Plan. One of the important means of the alleviating distress arising out from natural calamities could be the organisation of crop insurance."

The advantages of crop insurance are recognised on all hands such as:

(i) It provides protection to farmers against losses caused by crop failure and thereby ensures stability in farm income: increases their credit worthiness from the point of view of institutional credit, and relieves them from the clutches of the moneylenders.

(ii) In high-risk areas, because of crop insurance, cultivators may be induced to cultivate land which otherwise they would not have cultivated. By protecting the economic interest of the farmers against possible risk of loss, it accelerates the adoption of improved agricultural techniques.

(iii) Economic stability of the farmers improves the farming productivity. According to Dr. P.K. Ray, "Insuranee gives farmers greater confidence in venturing upon the adoption of new and improved.farming practices and in making greater investment in agriculture for improving crop yields and increasing agricultural production."

(iv) Crop losses are spread over space and time. Losses 'suffered by farmers in certain localities are borne by many scattered over wide areas. The burden of loss, therefore, does not fall upon the poor cultivators alone.

(v) It reduces to a great extent, government expenditure relief measures extended to meet the havoc caused by natural calamities.

(vi) The strengthens the position of cooperatives and other credit institutions that finance agriculture to the extent it enables the farmer members to repay their loans in years of crop failure.

(vii) The payment of premium in time encourages a habit of thrift and self help among the farmers.

Observes Dr. Ray, "The chief merits of insurance as compared to relief and concessions, are that insured farmers in cases of losses can claim indemnities as a matter of right. Second, what is of greater significance, the losses are shared wholly or partly (where the Government undertakes to pay part of losses) by the farmers themselves".

Speaking of the many advantages flowing from the crop insurance, an official of the U.S. Federal Crop Insurance Corporation said that it is fundamentally for the purpose of creating catastrophic insurance and is intended to ensure a minimum return to the farmer which enables him to stay in business in case of severe loss. The justification for the Government insurance is not alone the need of protection of the individual farmer and his continued income and buying power. This affects vitally labour, industry, trade, banking and the entire community of which the farmer is a part.

In the words of Shri S.K. Patil, "Crop insurance is the Mogna Carta of the Indian agriculturists. It will mitigate rural poverty and will change the psychology of the Indian farmer in a radical manner."

Nature of Crop Insurance

Crop insurance indemnifies loss or damage to growing crops resulting from a variety of causes such as hail or drought, frost, flood fire and disease. The farmers pay a premium and protection is given to them on the same basis as in other insurance. When the production from an insured acreage falls below the insured coverage, the farmer is entitled to an indemnity. Coverage and premium rates are settled on the basis of productivity and susceptibility to risk of the lands under cultivation in the same area. Besides an all risk crop insurance, there are three other main types of insurance to cover the risk from fire, hail and flood.

Crop Insurance in India

The idea of crop insurance in India was mooted about three decades ago, when a Sub-Committee on "Land Policy, Agriculture Labour and Insnrance," inter alia, had recommended a national scheme of cattle and crop insurance with agriculturist, the village or the district and the nation collectively contributing to its successful operation.

The first experiment in crop insurance was attempted in M.P., in 1943 in Dawas Junior with a view to provide benefits to the farmer in case of crop failures, if he had paid premium which was based on the actual land revenue assessment. The scheme was compulsory and administered by a Corporation.

In 1946, a "Crop Insurance Scheme" was proposed by Dr. Narayanswami Naidu, for Madras to help stabilize farm incomes— in respect of rice and other major cereals. He suggested that: *(i)* A crop insurance premium of one anna per acre of land under cernal crop may be collected with land revenue in all the districts except in dry areas susceptible to famine where a higher rate of premium may be charged. *(ii)* The scheme should be on a cash basis; (iii) The protection should be given thus: complete failure of crop may be compensated with the value of eight anna crop (or less may be covered up to 50 per cent of the crop,) where only less than four-anna crop has been harvested, the yield should be brought up to the level of eight anna crop."

The Co-operative Planning Committee, 1946, also recommended that "experimental scheme of crop and cattle insurance should be organised under State initiative."

Later on, the preparatory Asian Regional Conference (1947) held in Delhi recommended that "with a view to affording a large measure of income security to cultivators, governments should consider the possibility of organising crop and cattle insurance schemes, either for the country as a whole or for those parts in which it may be possible to take immediate action."

The first concrete step towards introduction of the scheme a was taken by the Government in 1948, when a special officer Shri G. S. Priolker was appointed to investigate a systematic and scientitic basis for formulating an experimental pilot scheme. Dr. Priolker in his Report, 1949, recomdended a pilot scheme covering four crops, (rice, wheat, cotton and sugarcane). Madras rice and cotton), Bombay (cotton), M.P. (cotton, wheat and rice) and U, P. (wbeat, rice and sugarcane) were suggested for experimentation. The financial responsibility of the State Governments was to the extent of paying *(a)* entire expenses of administration, *(b)* direct subsidy, and *(c)* operating deficits. Shri Prolker recommended that *(i)* the scheme should be compulsory with government in over-all charge and it should subsidise it ; *(ii)* the procedure to be adopted in determining premium and insurance coverage was to be dealt with after taking into account the average yields, soil factors, availability and type of irrigation facilities, variety of crops etc; *(iii)* The rates of premium were not to exceed 4 per cent of the average yield and were to vary according to the amount of insurance desired."

This scheme was examined by an expert committee, which suggested the introduction of the scheme at 12 centres. In 1952 the four States of Bombay, Uttar Pradesh, Tamil Nadu and Madhya Pradesh were asked whether they would be able to implement the scheme by sharing 50 per cent cost on State level organisation. While Madhya Pradesh was willing to try the scheme if the entire cost were borne by the Centre the other States were unwilling to undertake it. The scheme was later examined by the FAO Working Party on Crop and Cattle Insurance meeting at Bangkok in l956. Experts in insurance and agriculture also considered it suitable for implementation. On account of financial stringencies, however, the Government of India decided to defer the introduction of the Scheme.

Incidentally, it may be mentioned that in 1948-49, almost simultaneously with the Priolkar Scheme, Dr. B. Natarajan prepared scheme of Crop Insurance for the State. He asserted that the seheme could he distinct fiscal success, bringing to the treasury a net reveuue of Rs. 1 crore per annum. To begin with, the scheme could be distinct fiscal success, bringing to the treassury a net revenue of Rs. 1 crore per annum to begin with, the scheme was to be limited to paddy. A suitable agency for the administration of the scheme was also suggested.

The need for crop insurance is well recogoised today. A credit linked pilot crop insurance scheme was taken up by three States of West Bengal, Gujrat and Tamilnadu in 1919. By the end of the Sixth Plan period the scheme was in operation in 12 States and the scheme had benefitted 6.2 Lakb farmers covering an area of 6.9 Lakh hectares.

It has been planned to take up comprehensive crop insurance scheme during the Seventh Plan period beginning from kharif 1985. All crop loans given to the farmers by co-operative, Commercial and Regional Rural Banks would be covered by the scheme and then could be built-in crop insurance cover in all crop loans as part of service to the farmers. To start with, wheat paddy millets, pulses and oilseeds would be covered under the scheme. The rate of subsidy on premium payable by the small and marginal farmers would be 66.66 percent to shared equally by the Central State Governments. The scheme would be run with the help of Central Crop Insurance Fund which would be set up and administered by General Insurance Company and State Crop Insurance fund to be setup by the various State Governments.

New Scheme

A scheme has now been drawn which envisages compulsory insurance in areas in which it is to be introduced. The important features of this scheme are:

(i) Crops and areas are to be specified by the State Governments over which the scheme is to be implemented on a campulsory basis;

(ii) The area covered will be divided into homogeneous sub-areas and for each sub-area insurance value for each unit (crop plot) will be based on normal yield valued at the average market price of the commodity during the preceding three years;

(iii) The calamities to be oovered are draught flood hailstorm, cyclone, frost, and locust attack;

(iv) Premiums are to be fixed with due regard to probabilities of damage and will not ordinarily exceed 50 per cent of insurable value;

(v) Indemnity will be paid the yield falls below 75 per cent of the normal, due to natural calamities, in a sub-area and will be two-third's of the value of the difference between the estimated yield;

(vi) The valuation will be done with reference to coverage of price in the three succeeding years.

(vii) The maximum indemnity per acre will be half the value of the normal payable in case of total crop failure.

(viii) In order to get indemnity against the loss, the farmers will be required to give notice of damage, which will be paid on the basis of loss as assessed by officers appointed under the Scheme; and

(ix) The scheme is intended to become self-sufficient in course of time though initially administrative expenditure of the scheme would have to be met from government funds.

Future Scope and Problems

Although much scope lies for the introduction of agricultural insurance in India, yet a large number of problems stand in its way, such as:

(i) Indian agriculture is beset with uneconomic size of holdings, disincentive tenure condition, uncertain weather conditions, inadequate and costly non-institutional credit facilities; non-availability of inputs and adequate technical knowledge and experience.

(ii) Inadequacy of essential and reliable long period data on crop yields and losses, occurrence of pests and diseases upon which to base an actually sound insurance programme.

(iii) Variety of agricultural practices, which differ widely not only from crop to crop in the different regions but also for the same crop even in single region. These affect crop yields and hence construction of premium rates creates difficulty and complexity.

(iv) Limited resources at the disposal of the farmers render the levy of premium rates unrealistic.

(v) Ignorance and poverty of the farmers not only makes it difficult for them to understand the real meaning and significance of insurance but also prevents them from paying insurance premium regularly, even if it is a small margin left out of the low Income.

(vi) The dearth of sufficiently trained personnel to supervise and execute insurance claims particularly at the field level.

(vii) Complicated land tenure system, incomplet and unreliable records, and absence of proper registration of tillers render it difficult to determine the insurable interests.

Inspite of these hurdles, the necessity of crops insurance cannot be over-emphasised. The basic condition is that necessary inputs be made available to the farmers, and their economic conditions improved by improving agricultural practices. Insurance protection which spans crops failure gap, may then prove an essential part of a well rounded agricultural programme designed to provide security to the farmer. This will need that:

(i) cheap and safe insurance schemes be introduced in selected areas;

(ii) the schemes should cover all risks and losses due to natural calamities which are beyond the capacity of the individual farmers;

(iii) the premium rates should be reasonable and vary according to the nature of crop insured and other natural conditions of the area involved;

(iv) the scheme should be a compulsory one and therefore the areas should be selected with caution.

❐

17

Role of Agricultural Price Structure

Agriculture produces food stuffs and raw materials, the demand for which in the aggregateis relatively stable in the shon run, while the supply of agricultural products fluctuates widely from year to year and from one part of the year to another, on account of the varitions in yields, due to (i) seasonal and weather conditions, (ii) variations sue to supplies being-more abundant in certain months of the year, (iii) deliberate variation attempted by the producers, and (iv) variations arising out of conditions of marketing. These fluctuating supplies constitute the most important factor responsible for the wide fluctuation in agricultural prices. These fluctuation in the price of agricultural products are the greats thurdle in the way of agicultural development, for they bring ruin to many. It was this reason that agricultural countries suffered during the depression of 1929. According to Sir Roger Thomas, "next to rain, price changes have been the greatest enemy of the farmer."

Most farmers cannot ordinarily adjust, in response the changes in the price level, the quantity and quality of their output by altering the quantity and quality of the input. Unlike in industry, nature plays a very significant role in agriculture in the determination of the quantity and the quality of the output. Farming is a biological process and there is a greater time-lag between the changes in prices and adjustments in production. Moreover, farming is often a complementary enterprise so that certain products have to be included in the production schedule not because they can be produced at the lowest, unit cost but because they increase the overall profitability of the farm. Technical efficiency in farming is not, therefore, synonymous with the economic efficiency.

In the production of most farm products, the overhead costs form a relatively large proportion of the total costs than the variable costs which determine the quantity of the output. The entire cost structure agriculture; relatively rigid and moves more slowly than level of prices, especially in times of falling prices. The position is made worse by the slow turnover of agriculture. In times of falling prices, therefore, a farmer cannot save muchby reducing the quality of his production. He may actually increase his produce then and sales with an attempt to maintain his money income and per will itself tend to lower prices further. This is especially true of peasen farmers carrying on agriculture with family labour, as a way of life rather than as a business, buying only small quantities of raw materials and among whom competition is more or less perfect. Cyclic influctuations in agriculture therefore, reffect themselves not so much in the variations in the output and employment as, they do in industry as in the change in the farm products and prices. It is therefore, inadvisable to leave agricultural prices to seek their of levels and it is necessary to resort to corrective measures for arresting the fall in prices not only for securing stable price incoms to the farmers but also for securing, some stability for the entire Indian economy of which agriculture forms the very base, as about 70 per cent of the total population is still engaged in agriculture.

Price Staitilisation its Meaning

A disquieting feature of Indian agricultural economy is the uncertain trend in the movement of price of agricultural commodities. Success of agricultural development programmes has long been hindered for want, of estabilised agricultural prices. The Famine Enquiry Commission observed, Given price stability, much can be done-by linking up credit, agricultural improvements and marketing so as to supply the facilities needed for agriculture, whether water or manure or seed or machinery or organisation. Without it we are building on sand."

Price stabilization is not the same thing as holding the price line. It is a much broader concept and signifies a policy aiming at prevention of violent fluctuations in the prices on both sides. It consists of measures that the Government might take to prevent a fall or rise in prices if and when it occurs. The Government measures consist of buying all that is offered for sale at the predetermined minimum support prices in a bid to prevent undue fall in prices and selling the reserve stocks at control rates to check a rise in prices beyond what is considered a fair level.

Price stabilization is to be clearly distinguished from various forms of farm relief and legislative measures which are introduced with the idea, of raising domestic price levels. As pointed out by the Businessmen's commission of 1927 on Agriculture in U. S. A. "Real price Stabilization would affect a mitigation in price fluctuation but this would involve scaling down of the heights of prices as well as an elimination of their depths. Though this would not make an incompetent producer rich it would prevent the ruin of reasonably efficient farmers whose production is really needed and who tend to be replaced by new comers liable to suffer from the same fate. Price stabilization of agriculture would thus enter into the wider field of stabilised income and stabilised wages of not only those engaged in the field of agriculture. but also the mass of non-agricultural workers as well. It would also further raise the productivity of the soil.

The Need for Stabilization or Agricultural Prices

The importance of fixing fair prices for agricultural products cannot be over-emphasised in India for unless the producers get money for their marketable surplus, no increments' in efficiency and amount of production can successively raise the standard of living of the masses. Time and again this fact has been recognised that "when a general expansion of agricultural production is aimed at a guarantee of minimum price is an effective measure to adopt and it forms therefore, an essential part of the policy of agricultural development. This effective guarantee of a minimum price introduces not only an element of stability in agriculture but also prometes stability in other spheres of economic life. The Famine Enquiry Commission, 1945, observed that "a fair return to the cultivator is one of the foundations not only of agricultural prosperity but general prosperity also."

The Price Sub-Committee on Agricultural Prices (under Shri Krishnamachari) recognised the need of stabilization of agricultural prices on the following grounds:

(1) In order to protect the farmer from heavy losses due to vagaries of the weather and damage by insect pests and price fluctuations prices should be guaranteed with a view to securing comparative stability of agricultural incomes and prices so that a reasonable parity is established between the agricultural and industrial incomes.

(2) To safeguard the interest of the consumers, it is necessary that prices should be prevented from rising beyond a prescribed maximum. Such prices should be fixed within a range which would be fair both to the producer and the consumer and capable of being put into practice.

(3) The fair price should be such as would, leave to the producer an income sufficient to maintain him and his fataily at a reasonable standard of living. This fair price should cover the cost of production.

(4) The minimum price for a commodity should be calculated for principal producing areas the basis of Fair Average Quality (F.A.Q.) of the product. Suitable should be allowed in respect of differant grades and qualities. The minimum price of other areas should be worked out by adding to this figure the normal transport, marketing and other incidental expenses. The maximum, price should be based of the price making allowance for the normal trade differences, the storage charges and the market fluctuatious in supply and demand. The maximum price shonld not be lower than the parity price. It should be fixed at 25 per cent above the

minimum price or alternatively at the fair parity price, whichever level is higher.

(5) The fixation of minimum price would require that the Government should guarantee to purchase all supplies offered to it at that price at an adequate number of marketing centres within an easy access to cultivators in order to enforce prices at the minimum level. The State may regulate the foreign trade by means of quotas, tariffs and State trading.

(6) When prices move above the prescribed maxumum the State should provide supplies to the market by sales from its own stock at a price not exceeding in maximum. In order to prevent the prices from rising above the maximum, the State should have power to requisite stocks to regulate the distribution of supplies and to enforce the control of prices by law in an emergency.

(7) The State should have special powers to regulate acreage under individual crop in a particular area on an all India basis and to enforce adequate standards of land management.

(8) The minimum and maximum prices should be fixed up for principal food grains like wheat, bajra, jowar, as their prices are likely to influence those of other foodgrains. The principles of price policy recommended for food crops should it also apply to commercial crops and the mode of implementation would have to be modified to suit the special circumstance of each crop. For animal husbandry products the price should be regulated by the State Government on a regional basis.

When the First Five year Plan was formulated, the prices of wheat and rice were 5 to 5 1/2 times higher than the pre-war level. It was, therefore, not surprising that the plan was concerned with ensuring that the prices of foodgrains are held stable at levels within lite reach of the poorer sections of the community. The Plan described price problem as to define a level which may be consired reasonable under given circumstances, and to ensure through direct controls or through fiscal and other device that producer of foodgrains is not placed at an undue disadvantage." It further said "A policy of price stabilization must have in view certain maxima as well as certain minima. At a time when the economy is subject to inflationary pressures, the emphasis is inevitable on the maintenance of the maxima. But if the trend of prices is persistently downward, a system of controls with defined procurement prices can be used to safeguard the interest of production by preventing prices from falling unduly. Judicious purchases by Government at defined prices are thus an excellent device for stabilizing prices and for levelling out the inter-State disparities.

Subsequent Plans have reiterated this policy with only some minor changes in emphasis. The Third Five- Year Plan stated: "The producers of food grains must get reasonable return. The farmer, in other words, should be assured that the prices of food grains and other commodities that he produces will not be allowed to fall below a reasonable minimum....The farmer should have necessary incentive to make these investment, and to put in a larger effort. The policy designed to prevent sharp fluctuations in prices and to guarantee a certain minimum level is essential. In the interest of foodgrains production.....The other objective no less essential, is to safeguard the interest of the consumer, and, it is the interest of the consumer, and, particularly necessary to ensure that the prices of essential commodites such as food grains (to not rise exctessively. Government must ways be in a position to regulate effectively the course of foodgrains prices.

The Fourth Five Year Plan provided for "assurance of minimum prices for major agricultural commodities for securing a higher rate of increase in production of foodgrains and major commercial crops........So long as the general trend of prices was towards a rise, guaranteed minimum prices which were bound to be invariably lower than market prices, cannot be ruled out. This should be avoided because any appreciable fall in prices is likely to stand in the way of the farmer using costly inputs and new technology for raising farm output. The guaranteed minmum price scheme, therefore; becomes a part of the programme of providing incentives for increased production."

TRENDS IN AGRICULTURAL PRICES

The Second World War Period

Declaration of the outbreak of war gave a spurt to the rise in prices which increased from 100.03 in August 1939 to 1378 in December, 1939. Since this rise in prices was mostly speculation oriented, it began to fall touching 108.4 in August, 1940. Thereafter rise of prices became a permanent feature of the Indian economy 'touching the height of 145.6 in 1945-46. Maximum price rise was recorded in the case of agricultural commodities (127.5 in 1939-40 to 272n. in 1945-46) followed by primary commodities (124.6 and 246.6) and manufactured articles (13 1.5 to 240.0) and raw materials (118.8 and 210.1), against the base year August 9, 1939. Rising prices were atributed to : *(i)* Increase in export of consumer goods especially to British Empire countries; *(ii)* Blockade of import of food grains rice from Burma; *(iii)* Decline in production of rice due to Bengal famine: *(iv)* maldistribution of commodities due to loose implementation of rationing and price control; *(v)* hoarding and stockpiling by traders and other agencies; *(vi)* increased supply of money.

Independence and After

After the partition of the country, there developed an acute shortage of foodgrains in the country, for many of the wheat and growing tracts had fallen to the share of Pakistan. The prices therefore showed a sharp rise. During 1952 to 1955, there was, however a break and decline in these prices. An upward turn in prices started again In 1956, and continued till 1962-63. The rise was gradual and spreadover evently over the period. From 1963 to 1967 a serious rise in prices was noticed.

Agricultural Price Treucls

The rise in prices at the beginning of the planning era was in a way an after eftect of the post-world war II economic policies and measures. The price level continued to rise because of partition of the country in 1947 removal of price control devaluation of rupee In september 1949 growth of population and the Korean War in June 1950. Thus at the beginning of the First Five Year Plan in 1950-51. there was a shortage of food articles and other essential commodities and the prices were high. One of the declared objectives of the First Five Year Plan was to combat inflationary pressures in which it largely succeeded due to good monsoons.

The general price index (base: 1952-53=100) rose from 92.5 in 1955-56 to 105.3 in 1956-57, 112.9 in 1958-59 and 124.8 in 1960-61. In the case of food articles the rise was from 86.6 in 1955-56 to 1023 in 1956-57, 115.2 in 1958-59 and 120 in 1969-61. There was a spectcular rise in prices after,1962, due to the lean crop of 1962-63 and the declaration of National Emergency and reimposition of food control measures. In 1962 the support prices for rice and wheat were fixed and arrangements were also made for the purchase at support prices in case market prices tended to decline unduly. In December 1962 procurement of rise was intensified. With effect from 1963.64 crop support measures were also extended to jowar. Agriculturally 1965-66 attd 1966-67 were bad years. Prices and other controls were further tightened up.

Agricultural Prices Commission

The appointment of the Jha Committee on Foodgrains Prices on Ist August 1964 marked the beginning of a new phase in the evolution of agricultural price policy in India. The Committe was asked to render advice on the fixation of prices of rice and wheat for the 1964-65 season and also advice on terms of reference which would be suitable for an agency to provide such advice on continuous basis in respect of future seasons, the suitable. form of such agency and the kind of personnel it should have.

On the basis of the recommendations of the Committee suitable producers price for standard varieties of coarse paddy were announced for the 1964-65 season and State Governments were authorised to do the same for other foodgrains. This was done with an idea of guaranteeing a reasonable price to the farmer to act as an incentive to greater production and to provide protection against undue decline in prices.

Following the Report of Jha Committee, the Agricultural Prices Commission was set-up in 1965 to advise the Government "on the price policy of agricultural commodities particularly paddy, rice wheat, jowar, bajra, maize, gram and other pulses, sugarcane oilseeds cotton and jute with a view to evolving a balanced and integrated price structure in the perspective of the over all needs of the economy and with due regard to the intrest of the producer and the consumer."

The Commission is to keep under review studies relating to the price policy and arrangement for collection of information regarding agricultural commodities and other data: *(i)* suggest improvement in these arrangements; *(ii)* review the developing price situation, and make appropriate and timely recommendations within the framework of the overall price policy, examining wherever necessary, the prevailing methods and costs of marketing agricultural commodities in different regions; *(iii)* to suggesting measures to reduce the costs of marketiag, recommending fair price margins for different markets; *(iv)* the need to provide incentive to the producers for adopting improved technology for maximising production; *(v)* the head to ensure rational utilisation of land and other production resources and *(vi)* the likely effect of the price policy on the rest of the economy, particularly on the cost of living; level of wages, industrial cost structure etc. It is also the responsibility of the Commission to make the price policy effective in respect of different commodities. The Commission has close liaison with the other agencies connected with its work including the Steering Group on Wages, Incomes and Savings policy and Food Corporation of India.

Since may 1965 the Commission has been tendeing advice on a continuous basis on minimum and procurement prices of both, kharif and rabi cereals.

Foodgrains Enquiry Committee's Observations on Prices

The Foodgrains Enquiry Committee (with Shri Ashok Mehta as Chairman) was set up in July 1957. The Committee recommended that prices of foodgrains can be successfully cotrolled only through cotrolling of demand and supply of food grains. The idea underlying is the purchase of stocks in the harvest season and selling the same in the market at a reasonable price in the lean season is an effective way of preventing undue seasonal rise in prices. If a part of the excess production of a bumper year is carried over to meet the defict in a subsequent lean year much of the distress resulting from the price fluctaution can be avoided and a measure of needed resilience imparted to the market.

In a period of rising prices direct sales of cereals is necessary through modified ration shops and limited compulsory procuremeat by Government in surplus areas for replenishing its reserve stock. In a period of sharp deflationary trends, on the other hand, the action to be taken should include announcement of guaranteed minimum prices supported by accelerated purchases of foodgrains in the given market by the Government, subsidies sale of fertilizers to farmers and acceleration of local development works in depressed areas. The Committee favoured the formal announcemeat and effective enforcentment of minimum prices throughout the country as a necessary condition when there may be possibilities of prices falling sharply.

The Committee viewed "that buffer stock operations can be west effective instrument for the stabilization of prices of foodgrains. Whenever prices tend to fall Government should step and start prochasing at reasonable prices and sold to the State Governments for distribution through ration shops, cooperative societies or through the employer's associations. Compulsory procurement should be made for replenishing the reserve stocks and maintaining supplies to vulnerable sections of the population at reasonable prices by coidoning off certain areas and making the Food Grains Stabilization Organisation the sole buyer in these areas."

The Committee recommended the setting up of a high powered authority, known as the Price Stabilization Board, for the formulation of policy and programme for price stabilization in general. It also recommended the establishment of Food Grains Stabilization Organisation to execute that part of the policy and programme framed by the Price Stabilization Board as may relate specifically to purchase and sale operations in foodgrains.

The Committee also maintained that "until there is a social control over the wholesale trade, we shall not be in a position to bring about stabilization of foodgrains prices. Our policy should be that of progressive and Planned socialisation of the wholesale trade in foodgrains."

State Trading In Foodgrains

In the light of the recommendations of the Food Grains Enquiry Committee the scheme of State Trading in food grains was accepted by the Central Government in April 1959. The high-lights of the scheme are:

The scheme falls into two parts, *viz.*, Interim scheme of state trading in foodgrains and its ultimate pattern of co-optrative marketing of produce. The primary objective of the state trading is "to maintain price levels which are fair to the producers and consumers and to reduce to the minimum the spread between prices received by the farmer and the prices paid by the consumer throughout the season and over the agricultural cycle."

In the interim period wholesale traders are permitted to function as licensed dealers who make purchases on their behalf but pay specified minimum prices to the farmers. While the government have the right to acquire the wholesale or a portion of the stocks from the licensed traders at controlled prices, the traders are at liberty to sell the remaining stocks to the retailers at prices not exceeding the controlled prices. They are required to maintain proper accounts of their purchase and sales transactions and of their stocks and submit periodical returns to the state government.

The ultimate pattern of state trading provides the collection of farm surpluses through Co-operatives as the village level and the channelling of surpluses through marketing co-operatives and apex marketing societies for distribution through retailers and consumers so that the ultimate objective can be readily realised.

Other features of this scheme are: In the initial stages state trading was confined only to the two major cereals, rice and wheat. *(i)* To ensure that the producers get minimum prices, the government set up agency for making direct purchase of foodgrains from the producers. *(ii)* The purchase and sale operations as a whole was conducted on a "no profit-no loss' basis. *(iii)* Uniform purchase price was generally fixed for a whole State or region. *(iv)* While the state trading scheme provided for the sale of foodgrains by the wholesalers to retailers at controlled prices it did not fix retail prices. It left it to states to fix retail prices provided they were in a position to enforce them without causing any dislocation of or interruption in, supplies.

The Commission keeps under review studies relating to the price policy and arrangement for collection of information regarding agricultural policy, and other related data, suggesting improvement to these arrangements, reviewing the developing price situation and making appropriate and timely suggestions.

The Food Corporation was set up in 1965 to undertake purchase, storage, movement, transport, distribution and sale of foodgrains, procured more than 55 lakh tonnes of foodgrains out of 1969-70 crop as against 47 lakh tonnes in 1968-69. In 1970-71 kharif Season it purchased about 81 lakh tonnes. In 1973-74 the quantity purchased was about 51 lakh tonnes.

The Corporation had, a Storage capacity of 1.95 crore tonnes as on 1 September 1977. Its turnover (purchases and sales) in 1976-77 was over Rs. 4,000 crores.

Agricultural Price Policy

Agricultural price policy can play a positive role in development planning for agricultural development has to see to it that favorable conditions are created for securing an orderly increase in supply of food and raw materials to match the growing demand. At the same time it should protect the interest of the consumer in general and the vulnerable Sections of the community by effectively checking the rate of increase of foodgrain prices to ensure growth with stability. A slowly rising price level would be desirable in a Mixed Economy provided the existing income distribution was not very much uneven. In the context of mass poverty in a developing country like India, free market mechanism is not sufficient as the main determinant of resource allocation. Therefore, in a mixed economy where private sendor exists in a significant manner, the planning authority should have a clear idea as to what behaviour of price is desirable so that any deviation from the realisation of the twin objectives of growth and fair distribution of income may be corrected through the use of appropriate government policy instruments." The private investor make their decisions on profit maximising considerations; the consumer's aim is to maximise utility derived from consumption as a third dimension. It is the public investments which are primarily motivated by growth considerations and since a plan coordinates these public and private decisions, Price policy (while influencing supply and demand) is inevitable an integal part of the overall Economic Policy.

On the basis of the above considerations, certain important objectives of Price Policy could be enumerated as: *(a)* The Price Policy should attain and maintain prices stability primarily in respect of food articles, but to the extent possible ingeneral; *(b)* Aggregate demand should be made equal to aggregate supply; monetary and fiscal measures have an important role to play In this sphere; *(c)* It should provide necessary incentives to stimulate production of all essential consumer goods. *(d)* It should protect the vulnerable sections of the community, by effectively checking the rate of increase of foodgrains price (but this should not reduce the incentives to greater production in agriculture). *(e)* Price Policies should be such as to stablish some consistent relationships between agricultural prices, prices of manul facturers and the prices of various services.

Formulation of agricultural policy is complicated by the multiplicity of often conflicting functions which agricultural prices perform, including allocation of resources between agricultural and non-agricultural sectors; allocation of resources within agriculture; facilitation of higher rates of savings and investment and hence growth in the capital stock, and distribution of income among regions sectors and income groups. In one of his articles Mellor focusses his attention on agricultural price as signal to both producers and consumers for the requisite allocation of resources, and secondly as a distributor of income between the different social groups both rural and urban. Agricultural price policy is of particular importance with respect to income distribution because agriculture produces the consumer goods on which poor people spend most of their income. In comparison with developed nations, the demand for agricultural commodities in developing nations is much more responsive to change in price. The prices of agricultural products also affect capital formation in the industrial sector by their influence on distribution of income, wage rates, industrial profits and government net revenue.

The price for agricultural commodities has to be formulated on a comprehensive and continued basis. The objectives of a sound price policy are *inter alia* to maintain price stability by adjusting supplies to demand; to encourage production through providing incentive prices (since technological changes involve higher costs); it should protect the vulnerable sections of the community by effectively checking the rate of increase of foodgrain prices to ensure a proper price relation between the goods produced by the cultivator and the inputs required by him.

The First Five Year Plan described the price problem as "to define a level which may be considered reasonable under given circumstances, and to ensure through direct controls or through fiscal and other devices that the producer of foodgrains is not placed at an undue disadvantage". After the record production of cereals in 1953-54, there was a virtual end of food controls, Prices having fallen to low levels the accent of the price policy shifted from ceiling to floor. The controls of foodgrains were removed buffer stocks for wheat maintained and rice imports were stopped. Since March 1955 the prices started rising and the Foodgrains Enquiry Committee was appointed in 1957 to review the situation.

The Committee was of the view that the solution of the food prices problem lies between complete free trade and full control. Therefore, the Food grains Enquiry Committee recommended progressive and planned socialisation of the wholesale trade in foodgrains wherein the State should assume the role of a dominant trader is the economy in order to influence the demand and supply for foodgrains. This was in fact the essence of state trading in foodgrains as a major plank of agricultural price policy. The ultimate particular of state trading provides the collection of farm surpluses through co-operatives at the village level and the channelling of surpluses through marketing co-operatives and apex marketing societies for distribution through retailers and consumers so that the ultimate objective can be readily realised. The Food Corporation was set up in 1965 to under take purchase storage. movement transport distribution and sale of foodgrains.

The real break-through in price policy came in 1964 when the Government introduced the following measures on the recommendations of the Jha Committee on Foodgrains Prices:

(i) Setting up of the Agricultural Prices Commission in 1965.

(ii) Fixation of minimum support prices well in advance of the sowing season for major foodgrains.

(iii) Restrictions on inter-State movements of foodgrains.

(iv) Building up of buffer stock;

(v) Procurement of part of the marketable surplus at less than market price.

(vi) Modification and strengthening of the Poblic distribution system.

Observes A.S. Kahlon the then Chairman. Agricultural Prices Commission — that the agricultural price policy was more concerned with the stabilisation of consumer prices while ensuring minimum prices to the producers. It is now widely recognised by economists that besides institutional and technological factors the price factor also helps agricultural growth. The price support for certain crops has the-purpose to induce the farmers towards the new technology in agriculture. In early eighties, the agricultural price support policy covered 15 crops. The minimum support procurement prices for these agricultural commodities from 1976-71 to 1981-82 show a rising trend. During these years, the aim of supporting agricultural prices has been to ensure remunerative prices to farmers and to maximise procurement for public distribution and buffer stocking.

The major aim of agricultural price policy should be to correct distortions. which are socially or economically harmful and which emerge from time to time the imperfections of market mechanism. Such price regulation becomes necessary to safeguard the interests of producers as well as consumers. In the situation of a bumper harvest and the consequent sudden and sharp fall in prices the Government has to intervene through price support operations. On the other hand when in a general situation of inflation a shortfall in production results in a steep rise in prices particularly in essential commodities like food-grains the Government has to protect the consumers.

This is all the more important in a country like India in which a large proportion of the population lives below the poverty line. In such a situation a system of public distribution has to be operated to supply reasonable quantities of foodgrains at reasonable prices. particularly to the vulnerable sections of the population. Such a system of public distribution necessarily implies procurement from domestic production of sufficient quantities at reasonable prices. Observes the National Commission on Agriculture in their Interim Report on Agricultural Price Policy:

"It must be emphasised that supporting the price above the likely level of market price in times of abundant crops and procuring a portion of marketable surplus at below the market price in times of scarcity are parts of the same composite price policy. Since the farmers benefit from the enforcement of minimum support price they should also agree to the procurement system "intended to make available foodgrains to the vulnerable sections of the population at reasonable prices."

❑

18

Defects of Agricultural Marketing

We now discuss the main defects from which the marketing of agricultural produce suffers in India:

1. Lack of Organisation. The first thing that strikes the observer is the lack of any kind of collective organisalion among the produrers. The buyers of agricultural produce specially in the case of money crops, usually operation a larger scale and are organised while the producers are invariably small ryots scattered over a wide in a with no common organisation to guide them and to protect their interests, while purchasers of commercial crops on the other hand, are largescale operators on an organised basis. Under the circumstances it is common to find that the producers of agricultural products as a class are being exploited by the purchasers.

2. Forced Sales. The farmer in general sells his produce at as unfavourable place and at an unfavourable time and usually he gets very unfavourable terms.

Place, time and terms, there three factors, provide us with the close for an understanding of the existing position. Because of poverty and indebtedness, unsatisfactory nature of communication, lack of staying power and the need for finance, the produce is sold soon after the harvest when there is a glut in the market and hence the price offered is very low. There is an all round depression in prices to the price to the extent of 20% in the case of wheat and 25% in the case of linseed.

A cultivator, who has to borrow heavily for a growing crop, often mortgages it in advance so that the sale of produce, which is hardly more than a mere formality takes almost in his fields as soon as the crop is harvested. In all other cases where crop is not formally mortgaged it has to be disposed of almost immediately after harvest in order to pay off the deht to the Sahukar.

The nearest place where a farmer sells his produce is his own village. "It has, we think, been established that where the cultivator is in a position to dispose of his produce in a market, however limited its scope and badly organised its character be, he obtains a much better price for it even when he disposes of it in his own village." The effective price realised by the cultivator is further reduced by malpractices which are as a rule more common in a village than in a market.

In pre-Independent India Mr. Hussain had estimated that 60 per cent of wheat, 35 per cent of cotton and 70 per cent of oil-seeds are sold in the villages or village markets in the Punjab. For U. P. the respective figures were 80 per cent wheat, 40 per cent cotton and 75 per cent oilseeds. In Bihar, Orissa and Bengal 5 per cent of oilseeds and 90 per cent of jute was sold in villages. In U. P. 30 per cent of the wheat grown was sold in the village, in Lyallpur the percentage was 52, while in Attock district (Punjab) it was as high as 98. As for paddy, 89 per cent was sold in the villages in Bihar, 72 per cent in Bengal and 89 per cent in Tamil Nadu. In the case of cotton, the village sales amounted to 79 per cent in Sind, 81. 4 per cenl in Khandesh. 51 per cent in Central Gujrat, 80.5 per cent in the Punjab. With regard to the sale of linseed, it was estimated that the all India average of the percentage taken to the markets for sale by cultivators themselves was only 20 percent as against 40 per cent sold by landlords and 35 per cent by beoparis".

It may be noted that in the village, the produce is sold to the Sahukar bania. landlord prosperous tenants, beoporis and agents of wholesale merchants. The Rural Credit Survey Committee found that in nearly two-third of the sale transactions entered into with the traders the commodity is delivered in the village itself.

Causes of Heavy Sales in the Villages

The following are the chief causes leading to heavy sales in the villages:

(i) The most important cause for the high percentage of produce sole the village is without doubt, the indebtedness of the producer. A cultivator who had to borrow heavily for growing a crop often mortgages it in advance so that the sale of produce which is hardly more than a mere formality takes almost in his fields as soon as the crop is harvested. In other cases where the crop is not formally pledged it has to be disposed of almost immediately after harvest in order to payoff the debts the sahukars. The proportion of produce in the markets dimishes as cultivators are debt ridden or carry on subsistence farming in tiny holdings. In Attock district of the Punjab 98.6 per cent of the cultivators dispose of their surplus wheat to local banias who happen to be their *sahukar* also.

(ii) The second important factor which is responsible for the high percentage of village sales is the unsatisfactory nature of communication with the nearest market. With bad roads transport costs tend to become heavier. At times the producer has no cattle and cans of his own by which he can transport his produce to the market-place. In sugarcane growing areas the animals are either engaged in crushing cane just after the winter paddy harvest or in transporting cane to the mills, so that the supply of carts for the transport of other kinds of agricultural produce is very short. In irrigated tracts in the west of Uttar Pradesh, where cotton or fodder crops are sown just after the harvesting of the Rabi or spring crops, the grower has practically no time to go personally to the market.

(iii) The element of time is an important factor and this for double reason. The marketing possibilities of perishable commodities depend very largely on the rapidity with which they can be transported to the market-place. Communication is therefore of the utmost importance in this case. As regards non-perishable commodities the price to be realised by the cultivator depends, among other things on the time when his produce is marketed. The majority of the Indian cultivators sell their produce within a very short period, after the harvest with the result that the market is glutted and the prices -go down considerably. According to the Marketing Adviser to the Government of India there is an all-round depression in prices to the extent of 20 per cent in the case of wheat and 25 per cent in the case on linseed.

(iv) Most of the cultivators are hard-pressed for cash to meet the claims of their creditors and to pay off rent and other charges. Even when they know fully well that by holding up the crop for a few months, they would be able to secure a better net return they have usually no other alternative but to market the produce immediately in order to meet their urgent liabilities. Cases are by no means rare where a cultivator in dire need for cash, sells his wheat or rice at the peak season when prices are very low but is compelled after six months or so to buy perhaps with borrowed money foodgrains for his own consumption and even seed for cuitivation.

3. Superflous Middlemen. Majority of farmers dispose of their produce in the village itself. The result is the intervention of most middlemen between the producer and the final consumers of his produce. The agencies in the chain of marketing from the producer to the manufacturer and consumer depend-upon the nature of the crop. Paddy usually passes from village merchant to the mill or to the wholesale dealer in the assembling market and from the mill rice passes on to the wholesale dealer in the consuming market and then through one or, more retailers to the consumers. Between the wholesalers or miller in the producing end and the wholesalers at the consuming end, a host of intermediaries intervene and execute orders on the strength of samples.

In the case of groundnut, the route taken comprises the grower, the village merchant, the broker, the decorticating merchant, the exporters' agent and finally the exporter. Similarly, in the marketing of wheat the agencies that help in the collection of wheat are:

Marketing of Wheat

Those who bring their own wheat themselves to the market	Whose who collect others produce and bring it to the market
1. Growers.	1. Cultivators collecting produce of other growers.
2. Landlords.	2. Landlords collecting the produce of their tenants.
3. Cultivators.	3. Village bania.
	4. Itinerant dealers.
	5. Kachcha Arhatiya.
	6. Pukka Arhatiya.
	7. Co-operative commission shops.
	8. Wholesale merchants.
	9. Mills and their representatives.
	10. Exporters and their agents.

While in the case of potalo main channels of assembling are: *(i)* wholesalers like village merchant or trader or representatives of commission agents who buy potatoes in small lots and arrange for their despatch to that consuming centres; *(ii)* wholesalers who are engaged in retail distribution of potatoes in the consuming markets. The agencies engaged in the task of wholesale distribution of tobacco are: growers, professional curers; village merchants and money-lenders, commission agents and wholesalers, manufacturers, co-operative societies and exporters. According to Dr. Dantwala, "All those acquainted with the ready cotton trade know that in its transit from a farmer to a ship or a spinning mill not more than three or four transactions are made, The cultivator of jute disposes of his produce to a beopari who received advance from mahajan or a broker on the understanding that he gets as much as he can for the latter. The mahajan in turn sells to big buyer, a baler, or another broker by whom preliminary sorting, grading and bulking is effected. Similarly, in rice the paddy is taken over from the cultivator on threshing fioor either by the middlemen acting on behalf of the mills, by speculators or by local traders known as jungle brokers.

It will, thus, be noted that there exist as many as 10 to 12 intermediaries comprising of the village bania, itinerant merchant of *beopari, dalal, kutcha* and *pucca arhatiya*, co-operative commission agents. wholesale merchants and the retailers. They function at various stages in the process of assembling and distribution of the produce. The existence of a long chain of middlemen reduces the share of the consumer's price received by the actual cultivator. According to the findings, of the Marketing Surveys, the share of producer in a rupee paid by the consumer ranges from 52 paise in case of rice to 57 paise in case of wheat, in case of linseed it is 62 paise, in case of potato 50 paise and in case of groundnuts paise.

The wholesalers' margin in the case of different commodities at different places varies to a considerable extent *e.g.*, in rice it is 0.5 to 3.8 per cent; wheat 0.8 to 1.0 per cent; linseed 1.4 to 1.7 per cent and potato 10.4 per cent. Same is the position of the retailers. Retailer's margin varies from 3.7 to 6.4 per cent in the case of rice, 3.8 to 4.8 per cent in the case of wheat and 10.4 per cent in the case of potato. Dr. Munshi found that in marketing the produce the cultivator gets somewhere between 42.3 to 73.7 per cent of the consumer's price and from 26.3 to 57.7 per cent goes to the middlement.

However, the price-spreads are not very high when we take into accouut the fact that the producer's share in the consumers' doilar in U.S.A. comes to 68 per cent for poultry and eggs, 61 per cent for meat, 59 per cent for dairy products, 34 per cent for fats and oils and 52 recent for fruits and vegetables. But the point that deserves notice in the case of India is that the high costs (If Marketing are not due as in U. S. A. to hygienic processing; packing, storage and handling of commodities and superior servicing, but due to high freights too many points of handling and multiplicity of middlemen.

In India the incidence of freight varies from 2.1 to 21.7 per cent in the case of wheat; 0.7 to 13.2 per cent in the case of rice; 1.2 to 15.4 per cent in the case of linseed and about 6.2 per cent in the case of potato.

4. Multiplicity of Market Charges. The marketing charges payable by the producers are numerous and varied in unregulated markets and they tend to reduce considerably the return to the producer from the sale of his produce. On a sale of produce worth Rs. 100, a much as 21.5 per cent of the income of the producer goes to meet the various expenses.

In the market the cultivator has to arrange with a *kachcha arhatiya* for the sale of his produce and in the larger markets he has to employ a broker or *dalal* to get into contact with the *kachcha arhatiya*. For their services he has to pay some commission. In addition to the arhat paid to the *arhatiya* and the *dalal* a number of other charges have to be incurred. *Tulai* has to be paid for the weighing of the produce, *palledari* to cover the cost of the labourers who help in unloading the cart, preparing the produce, filling the scale-pans, holding the bag open where the produce is being measured, etc. the seller has also to submit to a deduction known as *garda* for impurities in the produce, and *dalta* for possible loss of weight and *dona* given to sweepers, watermen and even beggars. During the measurement and in almost all the markets deductions are makers from the amount due to the seller for dhamada or charity, dispensary, gaushalas, pathshalas.

5. Malpractices of Markets. In unregulated markets, malpractices tend to be common. These are:

(1) Scales and weights are manipulated against the seller. This ptactice is rendered easier by the fact that till recently there had been 110 standardised weights and measures nor was there any provision for regular inspection.

(2) There are all kinds of arbitrary deductions for religious and charitable purposes and for other objects. The burden falls entirely on the seller and he has no effective means of protest against such practice.

(3) Large quantities are taken away from the produce of the cultivator as *bang* or sample. According to the Royal Commission on Agriculture this amounted to as much as five to eight seen per cart of cotton in Khandesh.The cultivators are not paid for them even when no sale is effected.

(4) Bargains between the agent who acts for the seller and the one who negotiates on behalf of the buyers are made secretly under a cloth so that the seller remains ignorant of what actually takes place.

(5) The broker whom the cultivator employs is more likely to favour the purchaser with whom he comes into contact almost daily than the seller whom he only sees very occasionally. This tendency becomes all the mole pronounced when, as it frequently heppens the same works for both parties.

(6) When disputes arise the cultivator has no means of safeguarding his interest. The enquiries made by the Indian Central Cotton Committee showed that "greater use of the markets is not made by cultivator because of the disputes which arise after arbitrary deductions from the weight." Some of the practices obtaining in the market amount to nothing less than common theft.

That the poor agriculturists have to face great difficulties and expenses in marketing their produce can be easily brought out by the study of the following figures given by Mr. Mukerjee.

Place	*Fruit*	*Percentage of sale proceeds received by producers*	*Percentage of sale proceeds received by middlemen*
Poona	Guava	33.6	66.0
Poona	Orange	53.4	6.6
Nagpur	Mosambi	28.6	71.4
Nasic	Papaya	36.9	63.1

6. Multiplicity of Weights and Measures. Till recently there had been an absurd multiplicity of weights and measures in India.

The chaotic state of weights and measures in India has been more clearly brought out in all the reports published by the Central marketing staff. Weights made of sticks, stones and bits of old iron are even now a common feature in the markets and villages. A seer may range from 31 tolas to 102 tolas as in the Punjab, a *panseri* (which is five seers) may range from 5 to 9 seers and maunds may go up to 64 seers. as in parts of Bihar and Orissa. Even in the tola normally the weight of one rupee is not always the same.

This multiplicity of weights and measures employed in India has deplorable effects in several ways firstly, it affords greater opportunities for cheating the ignorant, cultivator unscrupulous dealers readily avail themselves of such, opportunities. Secondly it gives rise to needless complications in practice as between one market and another which is by no means conducive to the interests of trade and commerce. Thirdly, for the collection of data on price movements the relative level of prices in different regions, the volume of agricultural production, etc. lack of standard weights and measures is bound to be a great handicap and seriously affects the accuracy of statistical calculation.

The multiplicity of weights and measures makes supervision difficult and affords greater opportunities for cheating the producers, creates an element of uncertainty in trade and renders fraud on the part of retailers as easy as it is profitable.

The report of the Marketing Sub-Committee has rightly observed that, "Deliberate malpractices, ignorance and carelessness have all combined to make the consumer in India pay an unnecessarily high price for many goods of different qualities."

7. Adulteration. Adulteration is often resorted to while marketing crops; and one of the most important reasons for such deliberatt adulteration of agricultural produce is the high amount of refraction khad allowed in most markets and the non-mutual terms. In most of the wholesale markets in the producing areas a fixed deduction is made for impurities (say 5%) and the terms are non-mutual, *i.e.*, a producer offering cleaner produce which has only 1% of impurities receives the same price as the producer offering produce containing 5% impurities. Naturally when this is the case the seller whether he be the middleman or the farmer takes care to see that the produce is adulterated to the maximum limit allowed in the market.

Adulteration of Commercial Crops

Various devices of adulteration are in vogue. Such as:

Damping of cotton is done by the middleman on the contention that "the kapas comes in so very hot that if one puts one's hands into it, they would be blistered." In many places, damping is encouraged not only with a view to cause little harm to the pressing machine, but due to a mistaken notion that moderate damping makes it look glossy and increases the length of the staple. In other places unginned cotton is carried to markets on the back of buffaloes packed in strong bags and it is necassary to damp the cotton so that more can be pressed into the bags. The usual practice is not to water the cotton directly, but old gunny bags are put over it and water poured on bags. Sometimes hose pipes are also used to water the cotton directly. Recourse is also had to "false packing," by putting portions of one wet bale into the middle of a dry bale at the time of packing.

In the case of cotton, short staple in usually mixed with large staple. This admixture is done partly due to the cultivator growing and selling a mixture of different varieties of cotton by the seed mixed in the ginneries and partly because the cotton of the locality is a natural mixture.

In packing sann-hemp, small bundles of twist folded and tied fibres and tied heads which contain extraneous matter as "stick" leaf and dirt is usually resorted to.

The practice of adulterating wool with foreign matter is almost universal in the country starting in both the villages and the producers. Extraneous substance such as earth dust, sand and even sheep and cattle dung are added to increase the weights not only by the primary producers but also by village and other merehants. Cases have been recorded when sand and dust were sprinkled on the wool before rolling and bundling it. Moistening of wool before sale is not an uncommon feature.

Adulteration in Food Crops

In wheat refraction may comprise of' dirt or foreign matter including oilseeds, barley and other food and non-foodgrains: damaged and touched grains; shrivelled or immature grains; weevilled grains: and mixtures of red wheat in white. Barley and other grains are all of mixed.

Rice is also adulterated with inferior rice imported from abroad, new rice if passed off as old rice and clay balls are often mixed with rice.

The survey undertaken by the National Consumer Service of the Bharat Sewak Samaj has revealed some very curious facts. The survey says that "Dhania and zeera sold in some of the country's markets contain dried grass while curry powder in several cases has been found to be heavily adulterated with horse dung.

Tomato sauce is often only a mashed pumpkin with a small percentage of tomato. Vinegar in some cases has been found to acetic acid. Small chippings of white stone have been found in rice in some localities.

"Most of the common salt contains large quantities of white chalk, while turmeric is adulterated with lead chromate which has a deep yellow colour. In red chillies, many unscrupulous traders used lead oxide to brighten the colour and add weight"

The admixturing and adulteration in food and non-food crops has brought bad name to the country. Instances have been common when whole consignments were returned for wrong quality goods sent.

8. Inadequate Storage Facilities. In most of the villages ryots store their produce in pits or receptacles variously known as kudurus. *kallis* or *thekas*. In the up-country markets produce is stoted in *kothis* or kulthal/as (earthen cylinders) and *khattis* (pits in the ground lined with mud and straw) and in a few centres in *pakka khattis* made of concrete. But that there is a general inadequacy of good storage facilities both in rural and urban areas can hardly be denied.

The losses due to inadequate storage have been estimated to range from 1.5 per cent (Foodgrains Investigation Committee) to 2 per cent to 2.5 per cent (The Prices Sub-Committee) to 5 per cent (as estimated by Dr. Baljeet Singh). A recent estimate puts the loss at from 5 to 15 per cent by weight of the production and it is due to defective stage. This in turn is due to moisture absorption, excessive heat, insects, mites, rodents and birds. Even at 5 per cent the loss of cereals, millet, spices, oilseeds, jute, cotton, tobacco would come to over Rs. 4,000 million every year in India.

With the change of temperature, grains loose weight. When wheat is harvested, it contains some moisture which evaporates in summer and is regained during the monsoon month. Dampness raises the moisture content of the grain, thereby making it soft and therefore susceptible to insects. The damage is greater when the grain is stored in kaccha underground pits where the sub-soil water table ranges from 8 to 10 feet below the surface.

It is quite obvious that the foodgrain stocks held by co-operative societies, grain merchants and even by farmers are not kept in proper conditions. Therefore, the losses are substantially larger. In addition there are crops like jowar, pulses and maize which are incested by stored grain pests even before harvest. The insects form inside the kernel and are invisible until the threshed grains are put in storage. By the time the infection is detected, internal damage to grain becomes very great.

Losses due to rodents are also very great. The rats start damaging the gram right from the field to the time it is consumed. According to Dr. P. J. Deoras. there are approximately 2400 million rats in India. He has estimated that about 20 rats could consume the quantity of food sufficient for one person. On a gross estimate this would mean that rats are spoiling at least one fifth of the grain produced. Calculating on this basis of a tonne of grain being consumed by 100 rats per year the total consumption by the rat population of 2,400 millions would amount to about 24 m. tons. In terms of money this would come to about Rs, 18,000 million when calculated at the rate of Rs. 750 per tonne.

The nature of damage studied by. Dr. Deoras is as follows:

(i) It has been noticed that apart from damaging crops and foodgrains in storage, rats carry foodgrains to their nests in burrows. As much as 15 kg. of grain have been recovered while digging out nests from about 30 rats burrows. *(ii)* The rats damage 10 times the quantity of food material they eat. They would execrate about 86 faecal pellets in 24 hours which would get mixed up with food. grains. *(iii)* They void 1½ gallons of urine during the year, an further contaminate grain by shedding thousands of hair from their bodies.' *(iv)* In Bombay as many as 9,000 bags of foodgrains are auctioned as they are unfit for human consumption because they are damaged by rats in yards and godowns *(v)* The small mice in the paddy fields have been found to climb up to the paddy plant and eat every grain while the big field rat usually cuts the whole plant.

Besides rats "Insects, beetles and moths are prolific breeders and each couple lay anywhere between 100 to 400 eggs and their life-cycle is completed in 4 to 6 months. It bas been estimated that weevlled grain in the case of wheat varies from 1 to 2 per cent or more peas 1 to 5 per cent or more and arhar upto 2 per cent."

According to an estimate made by the Pesticides Association of India, on an -average about 18 per cent of the production of crops is lost due to past attack. In 1973-74, provisional estimate of gross national product value for agriculture was about Rs. 26,900 crores. Therefore, in terms of value the loss amounts to an alarming figure; of about Rs. 5,000 crores, canulated at the existing price level. It is estimated that the maximum loss is caused due to weeds (33 per cent.), followed by plant disease (26 per cent) and insects (20 per cent), while the storage loss could be put at 6 to Hyper cent. Rats are estimated to cause about 6 per cent loss to the standing crops.

In 1973-74, nearly 12.5 million tonnes were subjected to avoidable loss due to pests and diseases, according to the Association. For rice and wheat alone, Rs. 1,900 crores were lost, while in groundnut the loss was estimated to be Rs. 350 crores other oilseeds Rs. 90 crores, cotton Rs. 90 crores, sugarcane Rs. 284 crores, potato Rs. 30 crores, tea Rs. 77 crores, coffee Rs. 10 crores, and fruits (including in storage and transit) Rs. 200 crores.

9. Transportation Means not Well Developed

In India with her vast distances, the existing means of transport are woefully inadequate. "Communications from the field to the village and from village to the mandi are often extremely poor and defective. Bad roads, lanes and tracts connecting village with the markets not only add to the loss of transportation and aggravate the strain on bullocks and other pack animals, but also lead to the multiplication of small dealers and intermediaries. They also restrict market by hindering cheap and rapid movement of agricultural produce." In the construction of the railways in India administrative and strategic consideration, seem to have had more weight than the provision of marketing facilities to the ryot by linking up the producting areas with markets by a good system of feeder lines. The freight policy followed by the railways also has given rise to considerable dissatisfaction. Railways in India do not afford the maximum possible facilities for the quick and safe transport of perishable products such as fruits, vegetable and dairy products. This naturally restricts the markets for such produces and reduces the incentive for intensive cultivation.

The road milage position in India in relation to area or population is extremely unsatisfactory. There were only 52 miles of roads per 100 sq. miles of area as against 63 miles in Japan: 114 miles in U.S.A., 169 miles in Germany, 215 miles in U.K. and 430 miles in France per 100 'Sq. miles in 1974. Per 1 lakh of population these mileages, are 85, 2,018, 314, 382 and 1630 respectively.

There is not only mileage deficiency but there is also a lack of feeder-roads connecting villages to market towns and the nearest railway stations so that product cannot be advantageously transponed to mandies. Most of the village roads are rather tracks which cut all connections with the mandis during rains.

Due to this lack of transport facilities much loss occurs. According to the Directorate of Storage Inspection, the loss of marketable surplus of food crops in transport is about 0.5 per cent of the quantities transported.

According to the Foodgrains Investigation Committee the losses are 1/2 to 3 1/2 per cent in mail transport; 1/4 to I 1/4 per cent in road transport and 1/2 to 1 per cent in river transport.

10. Absence of Grading and Standardisation of Agricultural Produce. Absence of grading and standardising agricultural produce is another defect. The reputation of Indian agricultural producers in the world's market is low. Even the Export Promotion Committee (1949) emphasised the poor quality of Indian exports. The Royal Commission on Agriculture investigated into the position of the Indian agricultural products in the world's markets and came to the conclusion that much of the produce was marketed in an unsatisfactory condition in spite of the work of the Indian Central Committee adulteration mixing and damping, particularly the mixing of short with long stape cotton prevailed to an undersirable degree. Bad rating. bad grading and selection and excessive moisture were characteristics of much of the jute exported. The case of hemp was worse still. The position with regard to oilseeds other than groundnuts is a bit satisfactory.

There are no standard grades commonly accepted throughout India even for such important commodities as rice and wheat. In the absence of certain standard grades accepted by the whole trade as the basis for commercial transactions, attempt of individual producers-merely secures the ordinary market rate. In fact the present practice of data sales wherein heaps of both good and bad produce are sold together as one lot common in most markets, gives a premium to the inefficient producer as the good produce is made to carry along with it the poor stuff also. This practice of selling ungraded products of mixed quality has naturally reduced the reputation of Indian agricultural produce in the world markets. As pointed out by the Central Banking Enquiry Committee, the price paid by the consumer in Europe for these products is based very largely on reputation and this reacts unfavourably upon the price received by those cultivators who have improved their quality.

11. Lack of Information Regarding Price. Absence of market intelligence as to prices is another defect. The villagers have practically no contact with the outside world nor are they in touch with the trend of market prices and they mostly depend on hearsay reports received from the village bania who is not at all interested in supplying them the correct information as to prices obtaining in the wholesale market. Even in cases where information as to prices in available prices are not comparable on account of *(i)* the lack of standard grades acceptable to the whole country: *(ii)* variation in the amount of refractions allowed and the terms of standard contracts obtaining in different markets; *(iii)* inaccuracy of information supplied by various agencies concerned; *(iv)* variation in the price quotations given by local and Central Government; *(v)* the considerable variations in weights and measures used in several markets in the absence of standardisation of weight and measures.

12. Lack of Financial Facilities at Cheaper Rates. The cultivator is financed by the village Sahukar-cum-trader who is in his own turn financed by *arhatiya* and the indigenous hanker in the absence warehouse and the lack of facilities for making advances against the warehouse receipts there cannot be any system of cheap finance against security of goods. There is at present no proper link between indigenous bankers or commercial bankers and the Reserve Bank of India. The various marketing agents borrow funds at a high rate of interest. This naturally leads to a rise in the cost of marketing with the ultimate result that the share of the price received by the producer is correspondingly reduced.

❑